TWENTY YEARS AT PLAY

A New Play Centre Anthology

Edited by Jerry Wasserman

Talonbooks   •   Vancouver   •   1990

ᵧright © 1990 Talonbooks Ltd.

published with the assistance of The Canada Council

Talonbooks
201 / 1019 East Cordova
Vancouver
British Columbia   *V6A 1M8*
Canada

Typeset in Bem by Pièce de Résistance Ltée. Printed and bound in Canada by Hignell Printing Ltd.

First printing: August 1990

Canadian Cataloguing in Publication Data

Twenty Years at Play

ISBN 0-88922-275-4

1. Canadian drama (English) – 20th century.
1. Wasserman, Jerry, 1945 – II. New Play Centre
PS8315.T93 1990   C812'.5408   C90-091184-0
PR9196.6T93 1990

Contents

INTRODUCTION

Twenty Years at Play

For more than twenty years the New Play Centre has been one of the best-kept theatrical secrets in Canada. Partly because of its emphasis on new play development rather than production, partly because of its distance from the higher profile theatres and media of central Canada, the Vancouver-based organization has been relatively invisible compared to similarly mandated companies that came into being during the great flowering of alternate theatre in the early 1970s, companies like Toronto's Factory Theatre, Tarragon and Toronto Free. Like them, the New Play Centre has been instrumental in the development of English-Canadian playwriting. But unlike them, it managed to get through its first two decades without having been the subject of even a single article in a national publication.

During one brief period alone, 1980-85, plays that were developed and/or first produced by the New Play Centre won or were runners-up for a total of nine Governor General's, Chalmers and Canadian Authors Association best play awards: Ted Galay's *After Baba's Funeral* and *Sweet and Sour Pickles,* Margaret Hollingsworth's *War Babies*, Betty Lambert's *Jennie's Story*, John and Joa Lazarus's *Dreaming and Duelling*, Sheldon Rosen's *Ned and Jack*, Sherman Snukal's *Talking Dirty*, and Charles Tidler's *Straight Ahead* and *Blind Dancers*. By the time of its award, each of the plays had had a major production in Ontario, and in many cases had become publicly associated with the second producing theatre. A similar kind of identity-transference took place with Tom Walmsley's *The Working Man*, and *Something Red*, as well as Betty Lambert's *Sqrieux-de-Dieu* and *Under the Skin*. At times this erasure has also carried over into print: neither the Canadian nor American published versions of *Ned and Jack,* nor the American publication of Tom Cone's *Herringbone* makes any reference to either script's New Play Centre origins. In doing one of its jobs very well—feeding its plays into the North American theatrical mainstream for second and subsequent productions—the New Play Centre has ironically reinforced its own anonymity.

The New Play Centre arose out of the artistic and nationalistic ferment that swept Canada in the late 1960s and early 1970s, leaving in place, when it finally ebbed, most of the pieces of a fragile but dynamic new Canadian theatre.[1] Arts funding had begun flowing through the Canada Council in 1957, and a regional network of professional theatre companies and buildings had come under construction starting with the Manitoba Theatre Centre in 1958. Further impetus for the consolidation of such gains would be provided by the Centennial celebrations of 1967, which included an all-Canadian Dominion Drama Festival. An amateur theatre organization, the DDF had held regional and national competitions annually since 1932 to help develop Canadian playmaking skills. In 1967 for the first time all the plays in national competition—sixty-two of them—had to have been written by Canadians. The results were extremely encouraging, throwing into sharp relief the relative lack of Canadian plays being produced in Canada's burgeoning professional theatre, and the need to find ways of fostering Canadian playwriting.

At its 1969 meetings the Dominion Drama Festival board heard a proposal from two of its west coast governors that the organization establish an annual competition for original plays, as well

---

1. See *Modern Canadian Plays*, ed. Jerry Wasserman (Vancouver: Talonbooks, 1985), 9-19.

as regional play development centres across the country. They were University of British Columbia reference librarian Sheila Neville, a long-time participant in the amateur theatre community, and Douglas Bankson, a professor of creative writing at UBC whom Neville had recently brought into the DDF. But with the Dominion Drama Festival about to dissolve, a victim of Canadian theatre's new professionalism, Neville and Bankson decided to go ahead with their own regional play development centre. In May 1970, with a $500 grant from the Koerner Foundation, they founded the New Play Centre with a constitutional mandate "to encourage and develop dramatic writing in British Columbia."

The very same month in Toronto, Ken Gass was founding Factory Theatre Lab, which would call itself "The Home of the Canadian Playwright." The timing of these two events was no coincidence. All across Canada in the first few years of the new decade, new theatre companies were devoting themselves to giving Canadian dramatic voices a chance to be heard. In the late sixties Vancouver's major professional theatre, the Playhouse, had had great success with B.C. playwrights Eric Nicol (*Like Father, Like Fun*) and George Ryga (*The Ecstasy of Rita Joe, Grass and Wild Strawberries*). But they were exceptions to the Playhouse's predominantly British and European repertory. Neither the Arts Club, oriented to Broadway and the West End, nor UBC's semi-professional Frederic Wood Theatre produced Canadian plays. If local stages would not produce their work, how could local playwrights ever perfect their craft? And if local writers could not get any better, how could local theatres justify producing them?

Initially, the New Play Centre was primarily a script critique service. During its first year and a half, all thirty or so scripts submitted to the organization were read and evaluated by Bankson himself plus a professional director, and six were given rehearsed public readings by professional actors downtown at the Arts Club theatre or the Vancouver Art Gallery. With the hiring of Pamela Hawthorn as managing director in January 1972, the New Play Centre substantially expanded its operation. Hawthorn, trained as an actress at UBC, had just completed an MFA in directing at the Yale Drama School. Unlike Neville and Bankson, she felt it insufficient just to critique scripts and bring them to the attention of producing companies. She would continue the critique service and the readings. But as she told the *Vancouver Sun* in August 1972, "we felt that out of the readings we now had three plays at the stage where they merited production. And it was a feeling that the New Play Centre would become better known if we did some scripts. We don't really think of ourselves as a producing body but it was a kind of natural development."[2] For the next seventeen years under Hawthorn's direction, and subsequently under the administration of her successor, Paul Mears, the New Play Centre would concentrate on both new play development and production. The second item in its constitution pledges the New Play Centre "to promote, produce and present all manner of theatrical events . . . ."

The New Play Centre's first production was Sharon Pollock's first play. The full-length comedy *A Compulsory Option* opened August 14, 1972, for a week-long run at the Art Gallery, with a cast of Michael Ball, Jim McQueen and Frank Maraden. Sheila Neville was production manager, Paul Robillard designer and stage manager, and Pam Hawthorn directed. Reviews were mixed. Both the *Province*'s Ray Chatelin and the *Sun*'s Christopher Dafoe had serious reservations about the play but liked the production. The actors, Dafoe wrote, "squeeze every possible drop of interest out of the script. But there isn't that much juice to spare." Chatelin summed up both reviews with his feeling that, if the evening was "an indication of what's to come, then the [New Play Centre]

---

2. Alison Appelbe, "Reality Finally Comes to Canadian Plays," *Vancouver Sun*, 14 August 1972, p. 27.

experiment could very well be worthwhile and interesting.'''[3] The following week featured a program of one-acts by Cherie Stewart and Tom Grainger, directed by Bill Millerd and Doug Bankson's son Jon. An impressive cast list included Derek Ralston, Al Kozlik, Doris Chilcott, Robert Graham, Richard Newman, Debbie Roberts, Frank Maraden, and Barbara J. Gordon. The three plays were mounted under Equity jurisdiction with ten actors, three directors and a staff of three on a total budget of $5000.[4]

The following year saw a variety of production formats: a week's run of one-acts by George Povey, Margaret Hollingsworth and Leon Rooke in association with Playhouse 2, the Vancouver Playhouse's second stage; and "Collage 3," two programs of short plays and excerpts from work in progress including pieces by Pollock, Cone, Rosen, Lambert and Leonard Angel, plus a production of Elizabeth Gourlay's full-length costume drama, *Andrea del Sarto*. By this time the New Play Centre had instituted what would become its most important service between script critique and public reading or performance: the workshop, in which a promising script is read aloud and discussed by a professional cast and director in the presence of the playwright who gets suggestions for rewrites which can then be incorporated into subsequent workshop sessions in an ongoing developmental process. The entire operation, including workshops, readings and rehearsals, was being run out of an unheated loft above a store in Kitsilano, the countercultural heart of the city. The New Play Centre had no performance space of its own, but was drawing increased attention from writers and public alike.

In 1974 a series of developments combined to give the organization the direction it would take as a producing company through the end of its first decade. First, it found an attractive production venue in the Vancouver East Cultural Centre, a sixty-year-old former church on the city's east side which had been saved from demolition and converted into a 350 seat theatre. "The Cultch" quickly became a fixture in the city's non-mainstream cultural life, giving the company an identification which almost guaranteed it an enthusiastic young audience willing to entertain non-traditional shows. In March, in conjunction with Jon Bankson's Troupe, the New Play Centre presented at the Cultch its first full productions of plays by Tom Cone (*The Organizer*) and Sheldon Rosen (*The Box*). Both were directed by Jace van der Veen, who would remain one of the busiest New Play Centre directors until leaving for Alberta in the early eighties. The plays and their productions were greeted with critical enthusiasm, van der Veen's direction and Tom Hauff's performance in Rosen's two-hander coming in for particular praise.[5] The two American expatriate writers, Cone and Rosen, would become the mainstays of the New Play Centre stable, the company's first unofficial stars, along with Hollingsworth, Angel and Grainger. These five provided the contents of the first New Play Centre anthology, *West Coast Plays*, published in 1975,[6] and have to date accounted for twenty-five New Play Centre productions among them. Finally, the New Play Centre secured corporate funding from du Maurier's Council for the Performing Arts to produce what would become its annual spring showcase, the du Maurier Festival of Canadian Plays. The first du Maurier, presented in April-May 1974, featured pairs of one-acts by Cone,

3. Christopher Dafoe, "First Production Almost a Play," *Vancouver Sun*, 15 August 1972, p. 27; Ray Chatelin, "Experiment in Theatre Succeeds with New Play," *Vancouver Province*, 15 August 1972, p. 17.
4. Pam Hawthorn, "New Play Centre—A Retrospective," 2-page press Backgrounder, 1987.
5. Bob Allen, "Exciting Theatre Provided by 2 Original Productions," *Vancouver Province*, 15 March 1974, p. 27; Christopher Dafoe, "The Play's the Thing—With Full-Scale Production," *Vancouver Sun*, 15 March 1974, p. 35.
6. Connie Brissenden, ed., *West Coast Plays* (Vancouver: New Play Centre—Fineglow, 1975) includes Leonard Angel, *Forthcoming Wedding*; Tom Cone, *Cubistique*; Tom Grainger, *The Helper*; Margaret Hollingsworth, *Operators*; and Sheldon Rosen, *The Box*.

Grainger, Hollingsworth and Rosen. Over the next two years Tom Walmsley, John Lazarus, Dennis Foon and Sherman Snukal would have their New Play Centre debuts at the du Maurier Festival.

Those years were notable for others reasons, too. To increase its commitment to women writers—never sufficiently represented by New Play Centre productions even to this day—the company mounted the 1975 "Ms. en Scene" competition. Winning playwrights included Cam Hubert (Anne Cameron), and the all-female production team featured directors Hawthorn, Svetlana Zylin and Kathryn Shaw. Hawthorn and Shaw, along with Jane Heyman (who had directed both the Lazarus and Hollingsworth New Play Centre premieres) and later Kathleen Weiss, would be the most frequent directors of New Play Centre shows over the next decade. They had a particularly rich acting pool on which to draw during this period. Casts for the 1976 New Play Centre season included Tom Wood, Lally Cadeau, Allan Gray, Susan Wright, Brian Torpe, Michelle Fisk, Wayne Robson and Goldie Semple. Another major development of the mid–seventies was the hit show. Both Cone's *Herringbone* and Lambert's *Sqrieux-de-Dieu* followed their 1975 New Play Centre openings with tours that took them as far east as Quebec, bringing New Play Centre products rave reviews and commercial success outside Vancouver for the first time. The director of *Sqrieux-de-Dieu* was Richard Ouzounian who had his own New Play Centre hit in 1977, *British Properties*, which he rewrote as *Westmount* for its central Canadian run.

Another big hit, Rosen's *Ned and Jack*, had two Stratford Festival productions in 1978-79 following its 1977 New Play Centre premiere. The Stratford connection was effected by Urjo Kareda, former *Toronto Star* theatre critic who had become the Festival's literary manager under artistic director Robin Phillips. Committed to opening up the Festival to new Canadian work, Kareda had come west on a scouting trip and brought back with him to Stratford in 1978 not only *Ned and Jack* but also Cone's *Stargazing*, both Cone and Rosen themselves for terms as writers–in–residence, and Hawthorn to direct *Stargazing* on the Third Stage. Kathryn Shaw directed on the Third Stage in 1979, and in 1980 Cone's adaptation of Goldoni's *The Servant of Two Masters* played Stratford's Avon Theatre after a series of New Play Centre workshops.[7]

Meanwhile the pipeline of fine new plays continued to flow eastward from the New Play Centre: Walmsley's *Something Red* (1978), Ted Galay's Ukrainian-Canadian family portraits, *After Baba's Funeral* (1979) and *Sweet and Sour Pickles* (1980), Charles Tidler's jazzy *Blind Dancers* (1979)—which introduced another key New Play Centre director, Bob Baker—and later its companion piece *Straight Ahead* (1981), the Lazaruses' *Dreaming and Duelling* (1980) and Lambert's *Jennie's Story* (1981). Two of the company's biggest hits were penned by veteran playwright Eric Nicol, the sex comedy *Free at Last* (1979) and *Ma!* (1981), Nicol's tribute to legendary B.C. newspaperwoman Margaret Murray, given a legendary performance by actress Joy Coghill. The best-selling New Play Centre show of all, Sherman Snukal's *Talking Dirty*, was never actually produced by the company but went through three years of its workshops before opening in a 1981 Arts Club production that ran for over a thousand performances. Later the play would win a Chalmers Award in Toronto.

Nicol's *Free at Last* opened in November 1979, the final production of the 1970s and the first in the New Play Centre's new permanent home, the Waterfront Theatre. Designed by Pam Hawthorn's architect husband Henry, the 240-seat theatre is strategically located on Granville Island, a former industrial wasteland on the south shore of False Creek near the heart of the city. The Waterfront shares the very popular island with two of the Arts Club's theatres, the Emily

---

7. See John Pettigrew and Jamie Portman, *Stratford: The First Thirty Years* (Toronto: Macmillan, 1985), II: 141-44, 153-54, 178-80.

Carr College of Art, a busy farmers' market, and dozens of artisans' shops and restaurants. The New Play Centre shares the Waterfront, and two nearby buildings that house offices and rehearsal hall, with Carousel Theatre for young people. A third tenant, Westcoast Actors' Society, went defunct in 1982, a victim of the deep recession that hit B.C. particularly hard just as the New Play Centre was settling into its new home and somewhat more mainstream place in the local theatre community.

The years 1982-86 were difficult: audiences shrank, talent headed east. Critic Max Wyman has described how a "mass trend to conservatism forced theatre producers to retrench. Experiment and outrageousness, once the lifeblood of the Vancouver theatre scene, became the exception." At mid-decade, battered by the effects of the recession, Vancouver's theatres fell under the shadow of Expo '86 with its giant publicity machine and myriad attractions, including a festival of world theatre, which "effortlessly vacuumed up most of the available box-office bucks."[8]

The New Play Centre responded to these conditions not with any obvious kind of retrenchment; but the new work it produced seemed to suffer from a subtle loss of both quality and adventurousness. There were exceptions. Leonard Angel's gentle study of a Jewish family, *The Unveiling* (1982), remains one of Pam Hawthorn's all-time favourite New Play Centre shows. Ted Galay continued exploring Ukrainian culture in *The Grabowski Girls* (1983) and the mega-musical *Tsymbaly* (1985), the largest production ever mounted by the company and a record-breaking hit in 1986 for the Manitoba Theatre Centre. Hollingsworth's *Alli-Alli-Oh* (1983) and *War Baby* (1984), and Lambert's posthumous *Under the Skin* (1985) maintained the valuable connections between the New Play Centre and its veteran writers. But where was the new blood? The most exciting young writer under development during this period, Jesse Bodyan (*The Store Detective*, 1983), had a number of productions across the country but has yet to live up to his potential. The 1985 du Maurier Festival featured modest experiments in mixed media, three veteran playwrights teaming up with specialists in music, dance and movement. That year also saw the first new competition for women writers in a decade: five "Women's Short Takes" were given four performances, two of them at midnight. "Short Takes" was also the title of a national competition the New Play Centre held for its productions in the Canada Pavilion at Expo '86. Among the six pieces presented was Michel Tremblay's *L'Impromptu des deux "presses,"* a sketch for what would become *The Real World?*

The post-Expo, post-recession recovery that took place after 1986 forced the New Play Centre to reassess its role in Vancouver's realigned theatrical ecology. Producing companies like the Arts Club and Touchstone Theatre were becoming increasingly involved in developing their own new plays, and the Vancouver Fringe Festival, founded in 1985, had also begun feeding new work into the system. At the same time City Stage, a major producing company, had gone under. So beginning in 1987 the New Play Centre shifted its emphasis even further towards production by presenting full seasons of new plays at the Waterfront. The immediate result was the best year in a long time, three fine plays by David King (*Backyard Beguine*), Dennis Foon (*Zaydok*) and a major new discovery, Ian Weir (*The Idler*). The decade ended with some exciting combinations of the old and new: first-time playwright Alex Brown's award-winning *The Wolf Within*; Mavor Moore's Socratic *The Apology* in a staged reading; Tom Cone's return to the New Play Centre stage after more than a decade away with a controversial deconstruction of the nuclear family, *Love at Last Sight*; and David King's wonky comedy, *Harbour House*, which broke all attendance records for a New Play Centre production. The nineties began with a new version of the du Maurier called "Springrites," a festival

---

8. Max Wyman, "The Lessons of Recession and Expo: British Columbia, 1982-86," in *Canada on Stage: 1982-86* (Toronto: PACT Communications Centre, 1989), xiv.

of play readings, panels and full productions of four one-acts by first-time playwrights in the best New Play Centre tradition. One of them, Jaan Kolk's *Chew the Blade*, promises to be the company's first classic of the new decade.

In 1989, after two decades of service to the organization she co-founded, Sheila Neville gave up her position on the New Play Centre board due to illness. Doug Bankson had remained with the organization for several years as president and then chairman, but had long since given over these roles to people more adept at fundraising, and gone back to teaching playwriting full time. Pamela Hawthorn also left the New Play Centre in 1989, going to work for Telefilm Canada as Assistant Manager, Creative Affairs. In some ways this was a logical extension of one of the new directions in which she had begun to take the New Play Centre in the late eighties, instituting programs to critique and develop screenplays and TV scripts in response to the burgeoning film industry in Vancouver. Never a radical innovator, Hawthorn held the organization on a clear and steady course during her seventeen years at the helm. For some tastes she was a little too partial to the well-made, naturalistic play. But she was always willing to take a chance on the surrealism of a Tom Cone or Jesse Bodyan, to nurse into art the raw, undisciplined talents of a Tom Walmsley or the rich and painful visions of a Betty Lambert. The organization has owed its success to a lot of talented people. But as Bankson told theatre historian Denis Johnston in 1990, "The New Play Centre wouldn't have gone anywhere without Pam."

Her successor, Paul Mears, is a University of Victoria theatre graduate who had five years directing and workshop experience at the New Play Centre under Hawthorn. Early impressions indicate that his regime will not differ substantially from hers. With a 1990 budget approaching half a million dollars, Mears continues to divide the New Play Centre's resources between development and production, with perhaps a little more emphasis on the latter, and with high hopes of upgrading production quality. Asked to sum up his philosophy for the organization, Mears says what Sheila Neville or Doug Bankson or Pam Hawthorn might have said at any point in the last twenty years: "New plays by new people with new voices, new ideas."

A New Play Centre Anthology

I have intentionally subtitled this book *A*, rather than *The*, *New Play Centre Anthology*, making no claim to be definitive. In choosing plays for inclusion I have been guided by a number of criteria, most of them subjective and self-imposed. I first began attending New Play Centre shows in 1974, and acting in its workshops and productions in 1975, so I have very personal feelings about a lot of this material. My selection of plays begins in 1975, picking up essentially where *West Coast Plays* leaves off, and carries on to 1989, as close to the present as possible. To be as representative as possible I have chosen only one play per writer. The limit of eight plays has been imposed on the book by the economics of dramatic publishing. Because one of the purposes of this anthology is to place the New Play Centre in context as a source of plays that have remained "living" as part of a national and even international repertoire, I have chosen only works that have had at least a second production, and in every case a production outside British Columbia. Most of the selections have had "major" or "important" productions elsewhere; they have had some impact on audiences and critics. All have been important events within the New Play Centre itself. But ultimately these are the plays that have given me the most pleasure, moved me the most.

If more space had been available I would very much like to have included David King's *Harbour House* and Dennis Foon's *Zaydok*, Charles Tidler's *Straight Ahead* and *Blind Dancers*, and something by Richard Ouzounian, Eric Nicol, Ted Galay, Tom Grainger and Leonard Angel. For the sake of symmetry and a few other extrinsic reasons, among them the fact that she is one of my favourite living writers, Sharon Pollock's *A Compulsory Option* would have been a convenient choice. But it seems to me of interest mainly as a first play, flawed by the overwriting and stereotyping of a young writer still finding her footing. Except for Lambert and Hollingsworth, women are conspicuous by their under-representation in this volume as they are in the New Play Centre production list. This is a problem that I have examined briefly elsewhere,[9] but it remains unresolved. I can only say that none of the plays by any of the other women produced by the New Play Centre met my criteria. I could easily have added Hollingsworth's *Alli-Alli-Oh* or Lambert's *Jennie's Story* if I hadn't decided to stick with only one play per writer.

Each play I have included appears in its most current production draft, fully revised and corrected by the playwright. In many cases it is a substantially different script from the one originally produced by the New Play Centre. I have tried in my brief introduction to each play to indicate as specifically as possible the nature of the changes wherever these have occurred. The introductions are mostly concerned with the writer's biography and the play's production history. Otherwise I let the plays speak for themselves. I will say, though, that my favourite among them is *Under the Skin*.

Many thanks to all those people at the New Play Centre who have helped put this project together and given me access to scripts, archival material, and their own personal reminiscences, especially Paul Mears, Pam Hawthorn, Doug Bankson and Jane Heyman. Thanks also to the playwrights for their cooperation, and in some cases lengthy and informative chats. Thanks to Karl and Jeff and Christy at Talonbooks, to Glen Erikson for providing such generous access to his photographs, to my wife Susan and to my friend and colleague Denis Johnston. Thanks most of all to the dreamers, Sheila Neville, Doug Bankson and Pam Hawthorn, to whom this book is dedicated.

Jerry Wasserman
June 1990

9. Denis Johnston and Jerry Wasserman, "The New Play Centre: Twenty Years On," *Canadian Theatre Review*, 63 (Summer 1990), pp 28

Herringbone

Tom Cone, Skip Kennon, and Ellen Fitzhugh

Tom Cone is probably the writer most closely associated with the New Play Centre, where seven of his plays have premiered since 1974. Born in Miami in 1947, he arrived in Vancouver with a B.A. in English and Philosophy from Florida State, enrolling at Simon Fraser University where his first play, *There*, was staged in 1973. Beginning with *The Organizer* (1974), the New Play Centre produced a string of offbeat and highly imagistic plays which brought Cone to national attention: *Cubistique* (1974), *Herringbone* (1975), *Whisper to Mendelsohn* (1975), *Beautiful Tigers* (1976), and *Shotglass* (1977). In 1976 Cone was playwright–in–residence for Westcoast Actors, which mounted his musical version of *The Imaginary Invalid*, written with John Gray. His two terms in residence at the Stratford Festival led to its productions of *Stargazing* (1978) and *A Servant of Two Masters* (1980), an adaptation. In 1981 Cone went to New York to pursue the fortunes of *Herringbone*, winning the Drama League Award for his unproduced play, *The All-American Girl* (1984), before moving back to Vancouver and reconnecting with the New Play Centre on *Love at Last Sight* (1989). In addition to his work for the stage, Cone has written more than thirty radio plays for the CBC.

The original version of *Herringbone*, a one-act with only four songs, was a *tour de force* for Eric Peterson. He played George—in that version, a ten-year-old Depression-era vaudevillian trying to pass himself off as a 35-year-old midget—and thirteen other characters, accompanied by John Gray on piano. Reworked with different material by Gray and Peterson, this format would reappear a few years later in *Billy Bishop Goes to War*. Following its New Play Centre run, *Herringbone* was remounted by Vancouver's City Stage in a production starring John Hamelin and directed by Ray Michal. Its 1976-77 cross-country tour, including stops in Victoria, Calgary, Edmonton and Montreal, elicited startling reviews. *The Albertan*'s Scott Beaven wrote, "This is theatrical perfection, *A Chorus Line* for one," and Myron Galloway of the *Montreal Star* called it "one of the most original pieces for the theatre anyone is likely to see in a dozen years of theatregoing." The play was adapted for CBC-TV, and also ran briefly in New York in 1976, in an off-off-Broadway double-bill with *Cubistique*, directed by Sheldon Rosen. *Herringbone* was published along with *Cubistique* and *Beautiful Tigers* in *Three Plays by Tom Cone* (Pulp, 1976). In 1978 a new full-length version played at the Lennoxville Festival and at Seattle's Bathhouse Theater.

The current version of *Herringbone* is its third incarnation: a full-scale musical with new songs and music, and a substantially different (and even more bizarre) story. Instead of pretending to be an adult, young George is now possessed by the spirit of a dead hoofer. The scene in which George, his possessor, and a woman are all in bed together—all played by a single actor—offers boggling theatrical possibilities.

The new *Herringbone* is credited to Cone (Book), Skip Kennon (Music) and Ellen Fitzhugh (Lyrics). Kennon, longtime classical music critic for the *Hollywood Reporter*, is a veteran theatrical composer and winner of the Cole Porter Award for Theater Composition. Fitzhugh's credits include Tony and Drama Desk Award nominations for her lyrics to the Broadway musical *Grind* (1985), a collaboration with Henry Mancini on songs for MGM's *That's Dancing*, and a 1989 Emmy nomination for songwriting. Their *Herringbone* premiered at Chicago's St. Nicholas Theater in 1981, and was revised again for its 1982 New York debut at Playwrights Horizons where it starred Tony Award winner David Rounds. First published in *Plays from Playwrights Horizons* (Broadway Play Publishing, 1987), the new *Herringbone* has its Canadian premiere scheduled for the Vancouver Playhouse in spring 1991.

Herringbone was first presented by the New Play Centre at the Vancouver East Cultural Centre on April 30, 1975, with Eric Peterson as George Herringbone and John Gray as the Pianist, directed and composed by John Gray, designed by Glenn MacDonald, with costumes by Sandi Walton.

Eric Peterson and John Gray (at piano) in the New Play Centre production of *Herringbone*. Photo by Glen Erikson.

HERRINGBONE

CHARACTERS

HERRINGBONE, our narrator, assumes the following roles:

    ARTHUR

    LOUISE

    GRANDMOTHER

    GEORGE

    LAWYER

    NATHAN MOSELY

    SALES CLERK

    HOWARD

    LOU

    DOT

THUMBS DUBOIS, his pianist

SCENE

HERRINGBONE's story takes place in 1929, in Demopolis, Alabama, and Hollywood, California. Production requirements are a trunk, straight-back chair, cane, and hat. THUMBS DUBOIS is on stage throughout, at his baby grand piano.

SCORE

Herringbone is scored for piano, bass, and percussion.

MUSICAL NUMBERS

Act One

"One of Those Years": HERRINGBONE
"Not President, Please": GEORGE
"Oh, Billy: GRANDMOTHER, LOUISE, AND ARTHUR
"GOD SAID": ARTHUR

"How to Build a Man": HERRINGBONE

Finaletto:

"Little Mister Tippy Toes": GEORGE
"George": LOUISE
"The Cheap Exit": ENSEMBLE

Act Two

"What's a Body to Do?": HERRINGBONE
"The Chicken and the Frog": LOU
"Lily Pad Tango": HERRINGBONE, LOU, AND GEORGE
"A Mother": HERRINGBONE
"Lullabye": LOU, AND GEORGE

Three Waltzes:

"Tulip Print Waltz": DOT, LOU AND GEORGE
"Ten Years": LOU
"3/4 for Three": DOT, LOU, AND GEORGE

Reprise:

"One of Those Years": HERRINGBONE

ACT ONE

Music Cue: "Opening Fanfare." NOTE: If preferred, the following may be a pre-recorded announcement.

THUMBS DUBOIS: Good evening, Ladies and Gentlemen. Let's have a warm welcome for that bon vivant and raconteur, Mr. George Herringbone!

HERRINGBONE:
    DID YA EVER HAVE ONE OF THOSE YEARS . . .?
    ONE OF THOSE HEAD-SHAKIN' YEARS . . .?
    FIFTY-TWO WEEKS
    OF GIGGLES OR SHRIEKS
    AND UP-AGAIN DOWN-AGAIN CHOICES . . .
    WITH OR WITHOUT HEARIN' VOICES . . .
    A MESS OF SUCCESS,

OR AT TIMES, JUST A MESS,
TO THE LULLABY OF GRINDIN' GEARS . . .?
DID YA EVER HAVE ONE OF THOSE YEARS?

That year for me was the grand year of nineteen-hundred and twenty-nine. If I know my American history, I believe it was the year panic became respectable.

WE WERE SURE HAVIN' ONE OF
THOSE YEARS . . .
ONE OF THOSE HAND-WRINGIN' YEARS . . .
TIME AFTER TIME,
YA DIG FOR THE DIME
TO FIND ONLY LINT IN YOUR POCKET—
YA HOCK YOUR DEAR GRANDMOTHER'S
LOCKET—

YOU'RE CAUGHT IN THE FLAME,
AND YOU'RE NEVER THE SAME,
'CAUSE IT PURIFIES YA AND IT SEARS.
DID YA EVER HAVE ONE OF THOSE YEARS?

YOU HOLD OUT HOPE . . .
THERE'S ALWAYS HOPE . . .
YOU'RE HOLDIN' UP, HOLDIN' ON,
SLIP, AND YOU'RE GONE,
KEEP HOLDIN' ON—

WON'T SOMEONE COME?
YOU'RE DANGLIN' FROM
THAT SLIPP'RY EDGE . . .
BUT, WHAT THE HELL,
WHAT'S LIFE WITHOUT A WINDOW LEDGE?

MAYBE YOU'RE HAVIN' ONE OF
THOSE YEARS . . .
ONE OF THOSE TAIL-SPINNIN' YEARS . . .
YOU COME TO THIS PLACE
FOR A CHANGE IN YOUR PACE—
A COMFT'RBLE KIND OF DIVERTIN'—
ONE MAN CAN'T BE THAT DISCONCERTIN'.

YA CAUTIOUSLY CHOSE
THE SMALLEST OF SHOWS
FOR THE SWITCHIN' OF YOUR
ATMOSPHERES,
(with perverse glee)
AND THE SHOW'S ABOUT "ONE OF THOSE
YEARS"!

My orchestra . . . its leader, Thumbs Dubois, Ladies and Gentlemen! He's got a lovely string section if you let yourself go. Hear that? That's my cue to introduce our principal players. They don't know there's only one in the cast.

HERRINGBONE now calls out the names of the characters as he quotes upcoming lines from each, giving us the flavour of the "cast."

The Mother:	"How would you like to save us, George?"
The Daddy:	"Goddamnit, son, you are terrific!"
The Lady, Dot:	"How old did you say you were?"
The Chicken:	"Do you like to dance, George?"
And the Frog:	"Turn the key, George."
And Me?	"My name is George."

HERE'S THE STORY OF ONE OF THOSE YEARS,
ONE OF THOSE MAKE-OR-BREAK YEARS.
STRANGE AS IT SEEMS,
IT'S STRANGE AS IT SEEMS,
AND APT TO GET QUITE A BIT STRANGER.
STAY OUT OF THE AISLES, 'CAUSE THERE'S
DANGER.

ADVENTURE GALORE—
MAYBE LESS, MAYBE MORE,
DEPENDIN' ON WHAT WE ARE ABLE . . .
(a secret)
SOME FOLKS IN THE CAST ARE UNSTABLE.

YES, I'LL DO MY BEST,
WHILE ALL OF THE REST
MAKE FUN AND MAKE DO
AND MAKE FACES,
WHILE SINGIN' IN UNLIKELY PLACES.

SO, AS WE PROCEED,
JUST FOLLOW MY LEAD,
'CAUSE WHEN THE SMOKE OF PANIC
CLEARS,
ANOTHER WINDOW LEDGE APPEARS . . .

AND WE MUSTN'T MAKE FUN OF THOSE
WHEN WE'RE IN ONE OF THOSE
YEARS!

I was only eight years old durin' that erratic year, and my family was livin' in Demopolis, Alabama. Now, unlike the other citizens of our humble town, my parents had somethin' that they could count on . . . my mother's wealthy brother, my Uncle Billy. Ya see, he was a Cultural Attaché to the glamorous capitals of the world and he had just died . . . killed by a victim of the crash, falling on top of him from seventeen stories above.

Music Cue: "Anticipation."

Oh, I can recall the anticipation as my family was preparin' to present themselves at the readin' of my Uncle Billy's will.

Music out.

ARTHUR: (*calling*) George?! (*checking his appearance*) Are you ready for this godsend, Louise?

LOUISE: Wipe your face, Arthur. You're perspirin'.

ARTHUR: We need a godsend, Louise.

LOUISE: I know, Arthur, but there is such a thing as respect for the dead.

ARTHUR: Yeah, and there's such a thing as food for the livin'! How 'bout you, Miz Saneebly? You ready?

GRANDMOTHER: My comfort is in knowin' that the Lord will provide in His own time.

ARTHUR: Well, let's pray He's not a procrastinator. Where's that son of yours, Louise?

LOUISE: (*calling*) George! George! Where's our little hope?!

GEORGE: (*calling*) Up here, Mother!

LOUISE: (*calling*) What are you doin', Darlin'?

GEORGE: (*calling*) Practicin' my speech, Mother!

HERRINGBONE: Oh! I shoulda mentioned . . . I was havin' my anxious days, too. I was preparin' for the annual Lion's Club Speech Contest, adjudicated by Mr. Nathan Mosely, one half of that very famous vaudeville team, The Chicken and The Frog.

LOUISE: (*calling*) Oh, you take my breath away, George! (*aside to ARTHUR*) He's practicin' his speech, Arthur. He could be President someday. (*calling*) You could be President someday! Do you know that? Now, get dressed, sweetheart! We don't wanna be late for Uncle Billy's gift, do we?

GEORGE: (*calling*) No, Mother! (*rehearsing his speech as he absently dresses himself*) Being an American is so special that . . . (*he forgets; tries again*) Being an American is so special that . . . (*he forgets again; gives up in frustration*)
THERE'S SO MANY THINGS I WANNA BE—
A PRIZEFIGHTER,
A FAMOUS WRITER,
A TWIN,
AND WITH SO MANY THINGS I WANNA BE—

A RACE DRIVER,
A DEEP SEA DIVER,
INVISIBLE . . .
I'VE GOT TOO MUCH TO DO
TO BE MAMA'S PRESIDENT, TOO . . .

NOT PRESIDENT, PLEASE.
THE PRESIDENT, HE'S
IN CHARGE . . .
AND HE HAS A DESK . . .
AND HE'S LARGE.

I WOULD BE BABE RUTH OR
BUFF-LO BILL,
BUT IF SHE SAYS BE PRESIDENT . . .
I GUESS I WILL.

I DON'T WANNA DO IT.
I DON'T EVEN KNOW HOW.
DON'T MAKE ME DO IT.
NOT THAT, NOT EVER, NOT NOW.

NOT PRESIDENT, PLEASE,
'CAUSE HE NEVER SEES HIS FRIENDS,
AND HE NEVER PLAYS . . .
OR PRETENDS.
AND I'D RATHER DO WHAT I ENJOY.
BUT IF SHE MAKES ME PRESIDENT,
THEN PRESIDENTS DO ANYTHING,
SO I COULD MAKE THE PRESIDENT
SOME OTHER BOY.

Music cue: Transition to the lawyer's office.

LOUISE: (to GEORGE) I want you to sit down here quietly and practice your speech.

ARTHUR: Sit down, everyone. Well, Mr. Lawyer, we're all here . . .

HERRINGBONE: I'm sorry, I forgot to tell ya . . . the title of my upcoming speech was, "I Am an American."

ARTHUR: Well, Mr. Lawyer, this is the day we all been waitin' for.

LAWYER: I'm gettin' to it, Mr. Nookin.

LOUISE: Arthur!

LAWYER: Thank you, Mrs. Nookin.

Music Cue: "Oh, Billy."

LAWYER: "I, William Saneebly, hereby bequeath all my aspirations, all my hopes and dreams, to the three closest members of my family . . ."

Music stops abruptly for aside.

HERRINGBONE: I can tell you, all three of those relatives were anxious to receive his aspirations. From where I sat, the tension was glowin' from their necks.

Music continues under.

LAWYER: ". . . My visionary mother, Sarah Jane Winslow Saneebly . . ."

GRANDMOTHER:
   OH, BILLY . . .
   YA KNOW, I ALWAYS ADMIRED THAT BOX—
   WITH THE DOUBLE LOCKS—
   TRIMMED WITH LIZARD HIDE—
   BET THERE'S CASH INSIDE.
   HOPE IT ISN'T STOCKS,
   THE STUFF IN THE BOX, THE BOX, THE BOX,
   THE—

LAWYER: ". . . My sister, Louise Saneebly Nookin . . ."

LOUISE:
   OH, BILLY . . .
   YA SAID YA HAD YA A SILVER MINE . . .
   THAT'D BE JUST FINE.
   THAT CAN SURE BE SOLD
   SILVER'S GOOD AS GOLD.
   I CAN SEE IT SHINE—
   THAT SILVERY MINE, FOR US, FOR GEORGE,
   THE—

LAWYER: ". . . And her husband, Arthur R. Nookin . . ."

ARTHUR: (in ecstasy)
   OH, MONEY—(Correcting himself)
   I MEAN, BILLY . . .
   YOU LIVED IN STYLE,
   YOU ROLLED IN CLOVER.
   YOU MADE A PILE,
   NOW HAND IT OVER.
   SO LONG, BILLY-O . . .
   HELLO TO THE DOUGH, THE DOUGH,
   THE DOUGH,
   THE DOUGH, THE DOUGH, THE DOUGH,
   (growing louder)
   THE DOUGH, THE DOUGH, THE DOUGH—

LOUISE: Arthur!

LAWYER: "Embodied in my aspirations is a wealth no one ever dreamed I had. What I leave behind is considered in business terms 'a package deal'. It's short and sweet . . ."

GRANDMOTHER:
   IT MUST BE LOCKED IN THE BOX, THE BOX,
   THE BOX, THE—

LAWYER: ". . . and an opportunity that is so glittering . . ."

LOUISE:
   HE STRUCK IT RICH WITH THE MINE, THE
   MINE, THE MINE, THE—

LAWYER: ". . . that will bring you pleasure for the rest of your lives . . ."

ARTHUR:
   OH, BILLY-O,
   YOU WERE LOADED WITH DOUGH,
   DOUGH, DOUGH
   DOUGH, DOUGH, DOUGH—

LAWYER: (*seizing the moment*) "So, because of my great love for these three people, and considerin' the economic conditions of this country, I hereby bequeath to them, one . . . big . . . bundle . . . of advice: (*music stops*) Culture Durin' Hard Times Does Real Well. Take it or leave it."

ARTHUR: Well . . . go on, Mr. Lawyer.

LAWYER: That's it, Mr. Nookin. Everythin' was given away, 'cept . . . oh, yes . . .

ARTHUR: There'd better be an "Oh, yes" . . .

LAWYER: He leaves you his car if you so desire it.

ARTHUR: Why, that son of a—(*Music in as he grabs the paper, looks it over.*)
OH, BILLY!
WE'RE YOUR FAM'LY!
FAM'LIES GET CASH!
WHO WANTS YOUR AUTO?!
SPESH'LY A NASH!
AND, DAMN YOUR MOTTO!

OH, BOY, BILLY BOY,
JUST WAIT 'TILL I DIE, DIE, DIE—

GRANDMOTHER:
NO BOX, NO BOX, NO BOX—

LOUISE:
NO MINE, NO MINE, NO MINE—

ARTHUR: Oh, Billy . . .

LOUISE: (*apprehensively, to her son*) Oh, George . . .

HERRINGBONE: Oh, by the way, Daddy made a copy of Uncle Billy's advice, and nailed it to the bathroom door . . . eye level.

ARTHUR: Whenever you're sittin' in there, be sure to see those words. They might help you out with your . . . hard times.

HERRINGBONE: Thought maybe you might want to know that.

Music Cue: "I am an American." *Transition and underscore for the speech contest. GEORGE begins. From "the back of the room" his parents look on.*

GEORGE: I . . . am . . . an . . . American . . . by George Nookin.

ARTHUR: Boy doesn't even have his necktie on straight.

LOUISE: Patience, Arthur.

GEORGE: My first responsibility is to a bird.

ARTHUR: He'll never get through it.

LOUISE: He's just started, Arthur.

GEORGE: This bird flies and perches on limbs high above us, lookin' down on our freedom. This bird's name is Eagle.

ARTHUR: Oh, Jesus. Get your purse, Louise.

LOUISE: He's doin' very well . . . sshhh.

GEORGE: Eagle is the name given to the first Indian set free by the settlers of America. Like the Indian who was set free by the settlers of America, our forefathers, this bird is free. And, it is against the law to shoot it.

ARTHUR: You wrote this, Louise?

LOUISE: (*somewhat proudly*) I did.

GEORGE: Bein' an American is so special that . . .

His memory is gone. Panicked, he searches the crowd, spots LOUISE, who mouths the word, Sacrifice, which he gets, blurting it out and continuing.

GEORGE: Sacrifice was necessary in the past life to get its citizenship. And in this life my rewards for becomin' an American will become sacrifices for our Heavenly Father in the next.

Christ knew of the United States! For it was here that His disciples longed to be. America! The United States! Demopolis, Alabama!

Music out, signalling transition to the end of the contest.

LOUISE: (*applauding*) Congratulations, George!

GEORGE: I won!?

LOUISE: Ya did real fine and . . .

ARTHUR: Of course he did real fine. Ya did better than that, boy.

LOUISE: Let's see the presents ya got, Honey. Oh, look. A lendin' card to the mobile library.

GEORGE: And I got a book on fascism.

ARTHUR: And a twenty-five dollar Baby Bond. I'll just bank that for ya, George.

LOUISE: (*sees MOSELY*) Arthur!

ARTHUR: (*misunderstanding*) Time the boy made a contribution, Louise.

LOUISE: (*whispering*) It's Mr. Mosely, Arthur . . . Chicken Mosely, the adjudicator. (*approaching MOSELY and looking up*) Ummm . . . Mr. Mosely . . . we want to thank you for awarding first prize . . . This is ummm . . . my husband Arthur R. Nookin. I'm . . .

MOSELY: Sara Jane's daughter.

LOUISE: Why yes, Mr. Mosely. How did you . . .?

MOSELY: And this?

LOUISE: Oh, why that's . . .

MOSELY: What's your name, child?

GEORGE: George.

MOSELY: He's very good. I mean he could be very good.

ARTHUR: Damn right he's very good. Just won us a $25 Baby Bond which I do thank you for.

MOSELY: And if I may suggest that you cash in that Baby Bond and reinvest it in the boy in the form of professional actin' lessons, I believe he may have a future.

ARTHUR: In what?

LOUISE: Actin', Arthur.

ARTHUR: Are you going to swallow that, Louise?

MOSELY: Come here, George. Child stars are doin' real well on the talkies these days, Mr. Nookin. Now stand lookin' at me!

MOSELY bends, examines the boy; then suddenly is aware of something disturbing in GEORGE, and is taken aback; turns to go.

MOSELY: Ummm . . . Good night.

LOUISE: But, Mr. Mosely . . .

MOSELY: Pleased to have met you.

HERRINGBONE: What was it that Mr. Mosely saw in my eyes that day, I wonder? Funny how some flowers bloom on plants you would've never guessed. Now where were we?

Music cue: "Sleigh Bells."

HERRINGBONE: Oh yeah . . . Christmas nineteen-twenty-nine. While the three of us were stringing lima beans on the sorriest-lookin' Christmas tree you ever did see, my grandmother, who was always in the Christmas pageant, had started rehearsin' her production . . .

GRANDMOTHER: Well, I feel that activity keeps the heart alive. Even durin' the times the Lord is testin' us out.

HERRINGBONE: They referred to themselves as . . .

GRANDMOTHER: Yes. God's Actors. We kept that name 'til a member of the congregation thought we were takin' the Lord's behavior in vain. Now we refer to ourselves as The Earthly Thespians of the Lord. Yes.

ARTHUR: Ummm . . . Louise?

LOUISE: Yes, Arthur?

ARTHUR: Uhh, Louise, do you think what your mother is doin' in there is culture?

LOUISE: Well, I guess so Arthur. I mean she is a thespian isn't she?

ARTHUR: That's all I need to know. I think you should bring out your mother, Louise.

Music Cue: "More Sleigh Bells."

HERRINGBONE: Grandmother was huddled in the corner of the couch holding onto her fingers. Daddy was sittin' in the sofa chair and Mother was standing in the doorway.

ARTHUR: I believe I've got an idea.

GRANDMOTHER: Oh bless us, Lord!

ARTHUR: I believe He already has, Miz Saneebly.

Music cue.

THUMBS AND MUSICIANS: (*singing: a heavenly choir effect*) AH-AH . . .

ARTHUR: Last night I was sittin' contemplatin' the sad and sorry state of this family, when suddenly I saw the fiery finger of the Lord . . .

THUMBS AND MUSICIANS: (*singing*) AH-AH . . .

ARTHUR: And it pointed to Uncle Billy's words I'd hung up there on the bathroom door . . .

THUMBS AND MUSICIANS: (*singing*) AH-AH . . .

ARTHUR: And all at once, for the first time, I understood those words of Uncle Billy's: "Culture Durin' Hard Times Does Real Well." And I listened as the Lord spake unto me . . .
GOD SAID, "GO YE TO HOLLYWOOD."
AND I SAID, "GOD, FORGIVE ME, BUT GOD, WHY HOLLYWOOD?"
GOD SAID, "TRUST ME, I GOT A HUNCH THAT HOLLYWOOD'S THE PLACE FOR YOUR EARTHLY THESPIAN BUNCH."

I SAID, "YOU MEAN MIZ SANEEBLY?"
BUT I SAID IT FEEBLY,
SCARED LIKE I WAS, WITH GOD RIGHT THERE—
WHILE I'M ON THE TOILET.
DIDN'T WANT T' SPOIL IT,
HIM TALKIN' CULTURE.

SO, THEN, GOD SAID THAT BY ALL RIGHTS IF WE MAKE CHRISTIAN MOVIES, HE'LL GET HIS NAME IN LIGHTS.

GRANDMOTHER: If that's not the most heretical talk I ever heard!

ARTHUR: Wait'll ya get your first paycheque, signed by Cecil B. De Mille!
GOD SAID, "GO TO THE STUDIOS."
AND I SAID, "GOD, I DON'T KNOW MY WAY 'ROUND STUDIOS."
GOD SAID, "GO FIRST TO M.G.M."
HE SAID IF WE GET GUFF AT THE GATE, JUST MENTION HIM.

GOD SAID, "THOUGH YOU NEVER BEEN THERE,
NOW YOU HAVE AN 'IN' THERE.
GO YE, AND LIE BY SWIMMIN' POOLS."
I MEAN, WHAT DO WE KNOW?
HE KNOWS VALENTINO.
WE'RE TALKIN' CULTURE!

GOD SAID, "GO FORTH, FOR IT IS GOOD.
YOU TAKE YOUR TRIBE TO WANDER THE HILLS OF HOLLYWOOD."

ARTHUR: We'll make movies! We'll make money! We'll make . . . personal appearances! Right across the country by train! The Nookins, God, and Cecil B.! Stoppin' everywhere! People stampedin' the train station to see us! Callin' for us! Callin' for God! Topeka!

THUMBS AND MUSICIANS: AH-AH...

ARTHUR: Texarkana!

THUMBS AND MUSICIANS: AH-AH...

ARTHUR: Tallahassee!

THUMBS AND MUSICIANS: AH-AH...

ARTHUR:

> GOD SAID, "MOVE AMONG THE MASSES.
> GET SOME TINTED GLASSES.
> MAKE YE THESE MOVIES, THEN GO 'ROUND AUTOGRAPHIN' BIBLES.
> BIBLES YOU INSCRIBE'LL SPREAD GOD AND CULTURE!"

In the name of God, we'll step up and raise our arms to all those celestial fans!

> GOD SENDS GREETINGS FROM HOLLYWOOD! THEN BIG APPLAUSE, BECAUSE WE'RE THE 'STAWS' OF HOLLYWOOD!

ARTHUR: Lights!

THUMBS AND MUSICIANS: AH-AH...

ARTHUR: Camera!

THUMBS AND MUSICIANS: AH-AH...

ARTHUR: Action!

THUMBS AND MUSICIANS: AH-AH...

ARTHUR:

> I SWEAR TO GOD, THAT'S WHAT GOD SAID!

HERRINGBONE: As Mother was rolling Daddy's eyes into place, she whispered: "That is a wonderful idea." The shock of hearin' that from Mother seemed to break the spell.

ARTHUR: Never heard you compliment me before, Louise.

LOUISE: Never was witness to your fertile imagination before, Arthur. Don't you think that's a glorious idea, Mother?

GRANDMOTHER: Damned if I take my thespians to Hollywood.

LOUISE: (*a moment of cunning; to ARTHUR*) Oh dear. Well, since you insist on goin' to Hollywood, and Mother is unwilling, we should consider our son, George. "Child stars are doin' real well on the talkies these days."

ARTHUR: But George is no actor! George can't satisfy my dream for Hollywood. Are you crazy, woman?

GRANDMOTHER: It's you that's crazy, Arthur!

ARTHUR: Do you want to go back to your room?

GRANDMOTHER: No!

LOUISE: (*separating them*) Will you two stop it? I don't think we have a choice, Arthur. Now, the first thing I want you to do is to cash in that Baby Bond, and buy George a suit.

ARTHUR: What?

LOUISE: Then, we're going to go over and make ourselves present to Mr. Nathan Mosely . . . reinvest . . . as he so generously suggested . . .

ARTHUR: Holy Christ, Louise.

LOUISE: I'm talkin' Hollywood, Arthur.

ARTHUR: I just find it hard to understand how a retired performer who spent twenty years playin' straight chicken to a midget frog is going to elevate our son to the screen, much less the talkies.

LOUISE: Step by step.

ARTHUR: Yeah . . . well . . . there's somethin' humiliatin' in askin' your son to learn a trade for your own benefit . . . (*thinking it over*) But . . .

LOUISE: Oh, thank you, Arthur! (*a beat as she singles out GEORGE; looks at him*) How would you like to save us, George? Now, Arthur, there's a boy's store . . .

ARTHUR: No, Louise, we're goin' to the men's store. If he's gonna be a man he deserves a man's suit. C'mon, George. (*Music Cue:* "To the Men's Store.") How long will these lessons take, Louise?

LOUISE: Who's to say, Arthur?

SALESCLERK: Well, Sir, I don't think we have your son's size. This is a men's store, and just down the street—

ARTHUR: I know that! I know that! When you bring a boy to a men's store— Why . . . you think I'm bein' foolish? My boy is a man today, and deserves a man's suit.

SALESCLERK: How old are ya, Sonny?

GEORGE: Eight.

ARTHUR: Now, whatta ya got to show off his manliness?

SALESCLERK: I suppose we can make a suit for him. Somethin' simple but extra for his age . . .

HERRINGBONE:
YOU BEGIN WITH THE BODY OF A BOY, UNDRAPED,
AND YOU WORK FROM THE OUTSIDE IN.
ALL YOU NEED IS A LADDIE WHO IS STILL UNSHAPED,
WHO IS NOT AS YET STRONG-WILLED.
FROM THIS BASIC BOY, YOU BUILD
A MAN.

STAND HIM UP ON THE ALTAR OF THE VIRGIN WOOLS,
WITH THE PRIEST OF THE INSEAM LENGTH,
WHO PERFORMS LITTLE MIRACLES OF TUGS AND PULLS
FOR A FAIRLY MODEST SUM.
WATCH A BASIC BOY BECOME
A MAN.

HOW TO BUILD A MAN . . .? HOW TO BUILD A MAN . . .?

'CAUSE A MAN'S WHAT WE ALL WANNA BE, AIN'T IT?
WE ALL WANNA BE A MAN . . .
WHO CINCHES UP AND HITCHES UP AND BUCKLES THE BELT,
BUTTONS DOWN THE COLLAR,
LOCKS UP THE CUFFS,
BATTENS DOWN THE FLY AND
TIES UP THE TIE—
LOOK HOW THE TIE CLIP CLIPS!

OH, WE GOT US A MAN. WE KNOW IT'S A MAN.
IT BUCKLES, IT BUTTONS, IT ZIPS.

Music continues under.

SALESCLERK: How about a nice worsted?

ARTHUR: Whaaa?

SALESCLERK: Worsted.

ARTHUR: Don't like the sound. Give him somethin' with a more dignified name.

SALESCLERK: Herringbone?

ARTHUR: Say it again?

SALESCLERK: Herringbone.

ARTHUR: I like it. Set 'im up.

HERRINGBONE:
AS HE WAITS FOR THE MAKIN' OF HIS MAGIC SUIT,
AND THE DAY OF BECOMIN' GROWN
ALL HIS THOUGHTS TAKE A SWAGGER DOWN A DIFF'RENT ROUTE—
AS HE DREAMS, THE NEEDLE SEWS . . .
IN THE TAILOR'S HANDS, THERE GROWS . . .
A MAN.

HOW TO BUILD A MAN . . .? HOW TO BUILD
A MAN . . .?

'CAUSE A MAN'S WHAT WE ALL WANNA BE,
AIN'T IT?
WE ALL WANNA BE A MAN.
WE WANNA BE A MAN-TO-MAN KIND OF A
MAN,
CHAMPION OF WOMEN,
WINNER OF WARS,
BACON-ON-THE-TABLE
UPSTANDIN' TYPE—
GRIPPER OF MANLY GRIPS!

THEN WE GOT US A MAN. WE KNOW IT'S A
MAN.
IT BUCKLES, IT BUTTONS, IT ZIPS.

*Music continues under as HERRINGBONE
becomes GEORGE, donning his new jacket and hat
with mysterious reverence.*

HERRINGBONE:
NOW . . .
WE . . .
GOT SOMETHIN' FINE IN A MAN, AIN'T WE?
YEAH, WE GOT US ONE FINE MAN.
WE GOT US THE POTENTIAL OF
ROBERT E. LEE,
BARRYMORE AND GETTY,
WOOLWORTH AND FORD,
AUDUBON AND DARROW,
JESUS, WE GOT
GREATNESS INSIDE THIS SUIT!

YEAH, WE BUILT US A MAN.
YEAH, ANYONE CAN,
WITH ONLY A FEW LITTLE SNIPS.

HE BUCKLES. HE BUTTONS. HE ZIPS.

Music Cue: Transition to MOSELY's.

HERRINGBONE: Goin' to Mr. Mosely's
seemed like somthin' outta this world to me.
An old garden is what we saw from the road.
Strange vines circulatin' in mid–air and exotic
orchids hangin' around the front door.

Music out.

LOUISE: Don't touch Arthur!

ARTHUR: (*pulling back his hand from the
overhanging vine*) What is it, Louise?

LOUISE: Who knows? Oh, I hope we've
made the right decision!

ARTHUR: What's that Louise?

LOUISE: Fix your tie, George. Are ya ready?

GEORGE: I think so, Mother.

*LOUISE knocks. THUMBS makes the sound on
the keyboard lid. From the other side of the door,
HERRINGBONE suddenly takes on a mad smile,
holds it. Doesn't like it.*

HERRINGBONE: I gotta get this right for
ya, otherwise it won't make any sense. (*tries
smile again*) There! (*smiling as he opens the door*)

LOUISE: (*shocked*) OH! Umm . . . we're here
to see . . . umm . . .

LOU: (*making his first vocal appearance through
GEORGE*) The Chicken.

LOUISE: George! (*embarrassed at her son's out-
burst, she addresses the figure at the door*) Could you
please tell Mr. Mosely the Nookins are here?
Thank ya.

HERRINGBONE: I'm sorry. I shoulda
mentioned that Mr. Mosely had a man servant
by the name of Howard. A quiet fellow who
took to standin' and doin' but never did hear
a word ever come outta his mouth.

MOSELY: Who is it, Howard?

LOUISE: It's us, Mr. Mosely. You remember George?

MOSELY: (*not happily*) I certainly do.

LOUISE: I'm sorry about this bargin' in but
there was no way we could get in touch with
ya and . . . Mr. Mosely?

MOSELY: (*staring at GEORGE*) Do ya see
him, Howard?

LOUISE: We would like to take up your offer of some actin' lessons . . . Well, with George winnin' that speech contest and your encouragement we just felt that if there was any way of pullin' ourselves outta this Depression . . .

ARTHUR: (to LOUISE) What's he . . . lookin' at?

MOSELY: (circling GEORGE) Feet! Howard?

LOUISE: Is that possible, Mr. Mosely? See, we've cashed in George's Baby Bond and we're prepared to pay.

MOSELY: Let me just look at you, son . . .

HERRINGBONE: Whatever it was that Mr. Mosely saw in my eyes before . . . wasn't there now.

MOSELY: (to ARTHUR) Two dollars a week.

ARTHUR: Two dollars a . . .

MOSELY: It's not your money, Mr. Nookin. Get my old script, Howard. Thank you very much for bringing your son to me. I will try to do something with him.

LOUISE: Oh, bless you, Mr. Mosely!

MOSELY: Good day. (ushers ARTHUR and LOUISE out; turns to GEORGE) Stand up there! Your frame ain't for bendin'. You got a spine?

GEORGE: Yes, sir.

MOSELY: Straight is the answer! Look out over their heads and pause on a sinkin' syllable! Demand from the audience the next phrase. They'll know it if they're listenin'. Give him the script, Howard. Now read the first page to me.

GEORGE: My name is . . . Frog.

MOSELY: No, no, insert your own name when necessary.

GEORGE: My name is . . .(with uncertainty) George.

MOSELY: I don't know if the spoken word is your forte, son. Do you like to dance, George?

GEORGE shrugs.

MOSELY: Splendid. Why don't you try placing one foot out. Now the other. Excellent. Now what was that line I gave you? Surely you can remember it, son.

GEORGE: My name is George.

MOSELY: He's got a memory, Howard. Now tap the left foot on the "my" and then the right on the "name."

GEORGE: (tapping tentatively) My . . . name . . .

MOSELY: Now the left on the "is" and the right on the "George."

GEORGE: (again). . . is . . . George.

MOSELY: Now . . . can you do that all together?

GEORGE: (after a moment's preparation, tapping excellently) My . . . name . . . is . . . George! (surprised at himself)

MOSELY: Well, Howard, who said I didn't have an eye for talent?!

Music cue: "Whatever Happened to Baby George?" Transition to ARTHUR and LOUISE's bedroom as they ready themselves for the night.

LOUISE: Arthur . . . have you noticed somethin' about George, Arthur? Have you noticed somethin' . . . different?

ARTHUR: Well I . . . (*a plink at the piano and ARTHUR turns abruptly*) Hello, George.

LOUISE: Oh, excuse me, George. I didn't see you there.

GEORGE: I didn't know I was here, Mother.

A troubled LOUISE stares out. Transition to MOSELY's.

MOSELY: Howard? A working tempo.

Music Cue: "Finaletto." Music is continuous to the end of the act.

MOSELY: Now, George, with the music. (*speaking on the beats*) Left foot, toe heel; right foot, toe heel; good, George, keep it up. Toe, heel, toe, heel, that's it; very good.

GEORGE elaborates on the step.

MOSELY: What was that, George?

GEORGE: I dunno, Mr. Mosely.

MOSELY: Well, I certainly do. You are very good. My, my!

Again, GEORGE exceeds the step.

MOSELY: Wait! Howard? Did you see that step? Last time I saw that combination was . . . No. No.
    ROUND AND ROUND AND—

MOSELY: Can you spin, George? Can you dance while you—?

GEORGE does.

MOSELY: Excellent. son.
    LA DA DE DA DE DA DE DA DE . . .

GEORGE is now dancing far beyond the step.

MOSELY: Amazing, George! Where did you learn this?

GEORGE: I dunno, Mr. Mosely.

MOSELY: Come, now. You've done this before.

GEORGE: No, Mr. Mosely. (*winds up with a big finish*)

Transition. LOUISE on the telephone.

LOUISE: Arthur? I saw George's teacher today. She told me that they caught him on the playfield dancin' and yellin' at himself. Now, don't you find that peculiar? Arthur? He's dancin' ten and twelve hours a day. That can't be right, Arthur! Arthur?

The phone connection is broken. Transition back to MOSELY's.

MOSELY: Our pot of gold is here, Howard. (*to GEORGE*) You been studyin' those words this week? Let's hear if you've got 'em under your belt.

GEORGE: (*as he dances*)
    LITTLE MISTER TIPPY-TOES
    HAS TO DANCE, 'CAUSE HEAVEN KNOWS
    MISTER TIPPY'S TAPPIN' TOES MAKE HIM HAPPY—
    A-TIP-TIP-A-TAPPY.

    MISTER TIPPY TIPS HIS HAT
    AS HE TAPS THAT PIT-A-PAT.
    MISTER TIPPY'S TOES ARE SNAPPY AND ZIPPY—
    A-TAP-TAP-A-TIPPY.

    ROUND AND ROUND AND ROUND—
    HEAR THAT TIN-TIN TAP-U-LA-TIN' SOUND—

    A BIT O' TITTILATIN' TALENT.
    MISTER TIPPY'S TAPS ARE TOPS
    WHEN HE PULLS OUT ALL THE STOPS.
    MISTER TIPPY-TOES IS ONE HAPPY CHAP—
    A-TIPPY-TAP-TIP-TAP-A-TIPPY-TAP-TAP.

MOSELY: (*seeing GEORGE to the door*) George, you tell your parents they are to plan on seein' an exhibition from you next time. (*calling after him*) And don't stop practicin'!

Transition to GEORGE, exhausted, tapping as he walks home.

GEORGE: No more dancin'. No more dancin'. (*He flops down to stop the tapping.*) Oooh. (*the feet continue moving*) I know you're alive. Can you fly away? No? Mamma hopes you fly away. But Daddy doesn't. Mamma knows. Mamma knows. Why won't you let me walk the way I walk? Are you there?

LOU: (*the voice seems to ripple upward from the feet*) Hello.

GEORGE: (*giggles as if he did it himself*) Will I know who you are? Are you in me?

LOU: (*same effort of the voice to rise*) Yes.

GEORGE: (*still smiling*) Why? (*smile fades as he begins to rise to his feet*) Why? Why?

Transition to the NOOKIN home.

LOUISE: George, can you stop dancin' for a minute? George, then can you listen while you're dancin?
GEORGE, YOU WANT TO PLAY SOME CRAZY EIGHTS?
GEORGE, YOU WANT TO PLAY SOME BALL?
GEORGE, BABY, DON'T YOU WANT TO PLAY AT ALL?
TELL MOTHER.

GEORGE, YOU WANT SOME HERSHEY'S CHOC'LATE MILK?
GEORGE, I MADE IT EXTRA SWEET.
GEORGE, BABY, AREN'T YOU HUNGRY— WON'T YOU EAT?
TELL MOTHER, PLEASE.

REMEMBER, YOU USED TO FISH IN THE CREEK;
WISH ON A WISH-BONE—GEORGE?

REMEMBER, YOU USED TO PRAY EVERY NIGHT;

SAY, "GOD BLESS MOTHER"—GEORGE? GEORGE?

LOOK, YOUR FRIENDS HAVE COME AND GONE AWAY.
GEORGE, THEY BROUGHT YOUR HOMEWORK, TOO.
GEORGE, BABY, SEE THE FIREFLIES; OH, GEORGE, SMELL THE JASMINE;
ALL FOR YOU—
TELL MOTHER . . . TELL MOTHER . . . WHAT TO DO . . .

Transition to the day of GEORGE's exhibition. ARTHUR is helping GEORGE into the Nash.

ARTHUR: Watch your toes gettin' in the car, George. You don't want Uncle Billy's lemon to bite ya. We'll show him! (*calling*) Come on, Louise! We can't be late for Mr. Mosely's! It's George's big day! (*back to GEORGE*) Do you need a cushion for your feet, George? (*calling*) For Christsake, Louise! You're actin' like your carin' fell out the window!

LOUISE: (*reluctant, resigned, taking her time, settling into the car seat*) Start the engine, Arthur.

Abrupt transition to GEORGE's exhibition.

GEORGE:
ROUND AND ROUND AND ROUND—
HEAR THAT TIN-TIN-TAP-U-LA-TIN' SOUND!
He struts his stuff.
LITTLE MISTER TIPPY-TOES. THAT'S ME!

ARTHUR: (*applauding*) If my eyes haven't deceived me, I'd say we had somethin' here. Goddamnit, George, you are terrific!

MOSELY: Uh, you can stop dancing now, George.

ARTHUR: Am I lookin' at a million dollars, Mr. Mosely?

LOUISE: GEORGE . . . I think he's hurt himself, Mr. Mosely.

MOSELY: He's not in pain, Mrs. Nookin, I can assure you.

GEORGE: (*out of control; the tapping is manic*) What's happening to my feet?

LOUISE: GEORGE . . . Stop him.

ARTHUR: What the hell are you doin', Louise?

LOUISE: I'm stoppin' this craziness, that's what I'm doin'.

LOU: Hi, Chicken.

Everything comes to a standstill.

MOSELY: What was that, George?

LOU: I said, "Hi, Chicken." (*LOU realizes GEORGE's body is frozen in place, and doesn't like it.*) Who taught you this pause, George?

GEORGE: Huh?

LOU: Was it Chicken?

GEORGE: What?

LOU: We're not takin' pauses, George. We're not gonna work that way.

A wrenching into body movements; a grotesque strut.

LOU:
LITTLE MISTER TIPPY-TOES—
IS IT FROG, HERE? HEAVEN KNOWS.
IS IT FROG WHO'S HERE? IS FROG LIVE AND KICKIN'?
A-CHICK-CHICK-A-CHICKEN.

LOUISE: GEORGE . . . Let's get outta here! There's somethin' wrong!

GEORGE lunges for MOSELY, who tries to push him away.

MOSELY: Stop him, goddamnit. Get him away from me.

ARTHUR: What are you doin', George?

LOU: This is it, Chicken. I'd wave goodbye if I were you.

GEORGE: (*a helpless cry as his body goes for MOSELY's throat*) Mamma!

LOUISE: George's hands are around his neck, Arthur!

The chase is becoming hysterical.

ARTHUR: Take your hands off Mr. Mosely, George, for Christsake!

MOSELY: Help me! Help me! Howard! Howard! (*choking*)

LOU: Say goodbye, Chicken. (*Strangles MOSELY animatedly and to the music's pace, then hurls him to the floor.*)

LOUISE: (*falling to her knees beside MOSELY's body*) GEORGE . . . Get someone, Arthur! Get someone!
GEORGE, OH, GEORGE, WHAT HAVE YOU DONE?

Oh, please, Mr. Mosely! Please wake up! (*her head at MOSELY's heart*) I don't feel anything, Arthur!

LOU dances grotesquely and sings "hah-hah-hah" as ugly syllables to the notes of the music.

LOU:
FAN-TAS-TIC.

LOUISE: Shut your mouth, George! Do you realize what you have done?

LOU: Done nothin', Madam.

LOUISE: Are you crazy, George?

LOU: My name is Lou, Louise.

LOUISE: What?

LOU: Lou . . . the Frog.

LOUISE: George?

LOU: (*looking at MOSELY's body*) Poor Chicken. What a cheap exit.

A final froglike physicalization is played directly to the audience by LOU as the music and the first act end.

ACT TWO

THUMBS DUBOIS seats himself at the piano and plays. HERRINGBONE enters. Aware of the place the body had fallen dead in the first act, he sings the following with an air of serious distress.

HERRINGBONE:
WHAT'S A BODY TO DO WITH A BODY?
A BODY OF, SAY, A HUNDRED EIGHTY POUND—?
IT WON'T LOOK RIGHT ON THE KNICKNACK SHELF,
AND AS IT BECOMES LESS AND LESS LIKE ITSELF,
A BODY ISN'T ANYBODY ANYBODY WANTS TO HAVE AROUND.

WHAT'S A BODY TO DO WITH A BODY?
TO DO WITH WHAT'S LEFT OF SOMEONE SOMEONE KILLS—?
IT CAN'T BE STUCK IN THE BREAKFAST NOOK,
SINCE ANYTHING NEW JUST CONFUSES THE COOK.
DISPENSIN' WITH A BODY IS A CHALLENGE TO YOUR DECORATIN' SKILLS!

WHERE TO LIE IT?
YOU TRY IT HERE, YOU TRY IT THERE,
YOU BEND IT AND TUCK IT AND TWIST IT IN SEV'RAL ARTFUL SHAPES.

WHERE TO DROP IT?
OR PROP IT UP, OR CROP IT DOWN,
OR PICK UP THE COLOUR IN THE DRAPES—
OR THE CARPET—
OR THE DAVENPORT . . .

THAT OLD DILEMMA,
WHAT'S A BODY TO DO WITH A BODY
THAT'S NOT TOO ARRESTING AND WILL SOMEHOW BLEND?
WHEN SOMEONE IS—HOW TO PUT IT—DEAD,

WHEREVER HE IS, THERE THE EYE WILL BE LED,
UPSETTING THE BALANCE AND THE NEAREST OF KIN.
OH, WHAT'S A BODY TO DO
WITH SOMEBODY YOU ALREADY DID DO IN?

Now . . . poor Mr. Mosely was dead . . . and poor me for looking like the one who did it. Howard, who had tears comin' outta himself, was frantically scribbling a note. And then of course there was Lou . . .

LOU: Aren't I marvelous?

HERRINGBONE: Poor Mother was hysterical.

LOUISE: What are we gonna do? Arthur, we've got to call the police! Will you stop dancing for a second, George!?

LOU: I told you, it's *Lou*, Louise.

ARTHUR: George?

LOU: Hello, Arthur.

ARTHUR: What the hell has happened here?

LOU: Here? I rushed him. He fell over. No. He rushed me and then he fell over. God knows why he died. I certainly don't. It was a cheap exit and I'll be sure to tell him when I see him. RIGHT, CHICKEN? (*gives a swift kick to the side of the body*)

LOUISE: We've got to take him down to the state hospital, Arthur.

LOU: Then the whole town will be smellin' something, Louise.

LOUISE: Arthur, our son . . .

LOU: Could be gold to ya.

ARTHUR: (*pause*) Gold?

LOU: Now listen, I know this may be difficult for you to comprehend, but ever since the annual Lion's Club Speech Contest, I've been watchin' over your wonderful family. And a wonderful family you are. I could detect the gravitation of the Chicken to George as soon as I heard that incredible speech. Give me the first line again, George.

GEORGE: Umm, my first responsibility is to a bird.

LOU: Brilliant. Who wrote that?

GEORGE: Mother did.

LOU: There's a vocation somewhere inside of you, Louise, that has yet to be tapped.

GEORGE: Mamma's a good writer.

LOU: And you, my boy, are going to make both your parents very proud. "*Christ knew of the United States.*" Who ever had such insight?

HERRINGBONE: And insight is, of course, what Lou had.

LOU: You need money? No need to swallow so hard, Arthur. I can sympathize. We can help you.

LOUISE: Will you call the hospital, Arthur?

LOU: The hospital, I tell ya, won't do ya no good. But the palaces of America may. The beauty of them halls is callin' for my appearance. Callin' for your son. And it won't take long. I promise ya. A few weeks on the road and money in your purse and a smile on the audience's faces and the lift I needed and never got. But boy was I close. Please? Can we make an arrangement? They'll never know I was there. Your son will be a smash and pockets will bulge and Demopolis will seem a bit different on your return. And of course, I do all this in just six weeks. I guarantee it. Is it a deal? (*extends his hand*)

ARTHUR: (*slowly recoils in horror*) This is not happening to me! It's *you*, Louise! (*moving toward her*)

LOUISE: What are you doing, Arthur?

ARTHUR: Child stars, Louise? Remember? Child stars?

LOU: Get ahold of yourself, Arthur.

ARTHUR: (*turns to LOU/GEORGE*) And you . . . you . . .

GEORGE: (*as ARTHUR shakes him*) Daddy!

ARTHUR: (*crying; realizing it's GEORGE*) Oh, my God.

GEORGE: Daddy?

LOU: (*recovering; straightens clothing*) Just a second, George. It's OK, Arthur. (*hands become clasped*) I know you didn't mean it. Now you can talk to him, George. And undo your hands. It's your body. But it isn't me. (*hands unclasp*) Thank ya.

GEORGE: I'm you?

LOU: You're me.

GEORGE: Daddy?

ARTHUR: Oh, my God.

LOUISE: (*beside herself*) What are we gonna do?

LOU: Leave Demopolis.

LOUISE: Leave Demopolis?

LOU: I'd say you have no choice. 'Bye, Chicken.

HERRINGBONE: We packed it up in Uncle Billy's sedan and headed west for Birmingham. (*music cue: then suddenly remembering*) Ahhhh,

Howard. Well, we left him with the body. With headlines across America reading: "DEAF MUTE MURDERS EMPLOYER. CLAIMS IN NOTE: KILLED BY A FROG."

Music cue and transition to the family seated side by side in the front seat of the car.

LOU: (*looking up first to ARTHUR, then LOUISE*) Now that we're on our way I thought I should explain myself to ya. I was born in Miami, Florida, to a pair of unfortunates who dumped me into the Everglades. I was raised amongst the Seminole Indians. Not a heritage one would normally associate with the burlesque, but it did give me a certain perspective. Public performin' was a daily occurrence on the reservation. It was there that I first learned to appreciate dancin'! It was at one of those pow-wows I was scouted by a tall man lookin' for a short partner. From then on it was the Chicken and the Frog.

LOUISE: Oh, Darling . . . and you think you're the midget?

LOU: Well, I was! By the time of my death I was 36 inches high and 37 years old. I was the best midget hoofer in the business. The lights were comin' my way. Which is why my career was cut short by . . . the Chicken!

LOUISE: Mr. Mosely seemed like such a nice man.

LOU: (*taking stage, though ostensibly still in the car*) Nice man, my ass!
CHICKEN ALWAYS PICKIN' ON FROGGIE, SAYIN', "JUMP FROG!
DO THAT! DO THAT! DO THAT!
FLIP FLOP! HIGH IN THE AIR!
LOW TO THE GROUND! CRAWL AROUND! CRAWL AROUND!"

"NO, NO, NO," SAYS FROGGIE, BEGGIN'.
"NO, NO MORE," SAYS FROGGIE, BEGGIN'.
"PLEASE . . . PLEASE."

THAT'S HOW FROGGIE WENT A-COURTIN'—
TOADYIN' A LOT. HE BOWED. SCRAPED.
AND THE CHICKEN SAID, "DO IT! DO IT!"

THAT'S HOW FROGGIE WENT A'COURTIN'.
FROGGIE WENT A'COURTIN'.

CHICKEN KEEP A-PICKIN' ON FROGGIE, SAYIN', "LEAP FROG!
SKY HIGH! SKY HIGH! SKY HIGH!
RAZZLE! DAZZLE! KEEP IT UP!
FLIP FLOP! HIGH IN THE AIR!
CLOSE TO THE EDGE! TO THE EDGE! TO THE EDGE!"

"HEY, WOW-EE," SAYS BABY FROGGIE.
"LOOK AT ME," SAYS TRUSTING FROGGIE.
"WHEE! WHEE!"

THAT'S HOW FROGGIE WENT A FLYIN'—
FROGGIE IN THE AIR. HE FLEW. WOW.
AND THE MUSIC PLAYED LOUDER. LOUDER.
THAT'S HOW FROGGIE WENT A'COURTIN'.
FROGGIE WENT A'COURTIN'.

Now LOU assumes a parody of the M.C. who used to introduce them.

And now . . . in their spectacular, final moments on our stage . . . The Chicken and the Frog!
AND THE LITTLE BITTY BODY ALWAYS LANDS
SAFE, SAFE IN THE CHICKEN'S HANDS.

(*LOU, as himself, the night of the incident*) Chicken! Chicken! (*as MOSELY, that night*) Told ya about steppin' on my lines, Frog!

(*as M.C. parody*)
HERE COMES LITTLE BITTY BODY BUT WHERE WAS
THE CHICKEN'S HANDS—THE CHICKEN'S CLAWS!?

(*as himself, that night*) Chicken! Chicken! (*as MOSELY, that night*) Say goodbye, Frog.
"OH, OH, GOD!" SHOUTS FROGGIE SLIPPIN'—
"GOD, OH GOD!" SCREAMS FROGGIE SLIDIN'—
"HELP! HELP!"
THAT'S HOW FROGGIE WENT A FALLIN'.
FROGGIE WENT A-THUD. KA-BOOM. SPLAT.
AND THE MUSIC PLAYED FASTER. FASTER. FASTER.
THAT'S HOW FROGGIE WENT A-COURTIN'
FROGGIE WENT A-COURTIN'
DISASTER!

Transition back to the reality of the family in the car. GEORGE yawns.

LOU: Oh, are we tired, George?

GEORGE: Just a little.

LOUISE: Are you all right, Son?

GEORGE: I'm just tired, Mamma.

LOU: Boy's got good timing. Now why don't we pull into that boarding house— the one next to the lounge with the piano on the roof? Separate rooms would be delightful. *(climbs out of the car)*

LOUISE: Don't forget, Arthur . . . that's your son talking to you.

LOU: Before we go to bed, George, I think a little confidence building is necessary here. Let's take a peek into that lounge.

LOUISE: What have we got ourselves into?

LOU: A little relief and financial independence. *(He throws open "swinging doors" and greets the crowd inside the lounge.)* Hiya, folks! The Frog Shuffle! *(Music cue: he dances, then sotto:)* Pass the hat, Arthur, pass the hat!

Transition to hall outside their rooms. ARTHUR has counted the money in the hat.

ARTHUR: Fifty dollars, Louise! Thank ya, Son. Thank ya.

LOU: Uh-uh, Arthur. Thank me! Say good-night, George.

GEORGE: 'Night.

Music cue and transition to ARTHUR and LOUISE's room.

LOUISE: Arthur! This horror has gone too far! We're going to the hospital tonight!

ARTHUR: But, Louise . . . we just made ourselves fifty dollars!

LOUISE: *(pause)* You disgust me.

ARTHUR: You're talking about our bread and butter, Louise.

LOUISE: I am still the mother of . . .*(begins to choke)* whatever George is . . . and I will do whatever it takes to get him back to his rightful self.

ARTHUR: Over my dead body!

LOUISE: Don't tempt me, Arthur.

ARTHUR: All right, all right.

LOUISE: Now, you tell Mr. Lou to get Geor . . . now you tell George to get Mr. Lou . . . You tell Mr. Lou this nonsense is over! We're taking George to the hospital in ten minutes!

HERRINGBONE: *(in transit to the other room)* Poor Daddy. He was caught between the carrot and the stick. A salivatin' humiliation if you'll pardon the expression.

ARTHUR: *(knocking)* George? *(door opens)* Hi, George.

GEORGE: Hi, Daddy.

ARTHUR: Sit down, George. Hi, Mr. Lou.

LOU: Hello, Arthur! Great to be alive, eh?!

ARTHUR: Look, I uhh, first I wanna thank you for . . . well . . . never seen so much money made so quickly.

LOU: Our pleasure. Right, George?

GEORGE: You're welcome, Daddy.

ARTHUR: But . . . um . . .

LOU: What's the matter, Arthur? You don't know how to divide it? Is that it? Let's call it fifty-fifty. There are very few sensitive managers these days, Arthur. We appreciate your concern.

ARTHUR: Manager . . . me?

LOU: You're the boss around here, aren't you?

ARTHUR: Well that's what I want to talk to you about.

LOU: And if I may speak for both of us . . . don't let a motherly emotion get in your way.

ARTHUR: Yeah, but . . .

LOU: Ponder the basics, Arthur. You need to eat, right?

ARTHUR: Right.

LOU: And I don't see you pickin' tomatoes, do you?

ARTHUR: No. No.

LOU: And you'd like to get the newspapers out of your shoes, right?

ARTHUR: Of course.

LOU: And how many times do you dream of basking in the glory of Hollywood?

ARTHUR: (too quickly) Every night!

LOU: Well then?

ARTHUR: We're leavin' in ten minutes. (returns to LOUISE) All set, Louise.

LOUISE: Oh thank God. I'll just call the hospital.

ARTHUR: Put the phone down, Louise. Look, I'm the boss and we are leavin' for Hollywood. I told you the Lord was with us.

LOUISE: You fool!

ARTHUR: We'll show you just how foolish I am, Louise.

Music Cue: "The Lily Pad Tango."

LOU: Keep your eyes straight ahead, George.

GEORGE: But I don't know where I'm going.

LOU: (knowingly) I do.

Dance begins.

HERRINGBONE: It's called "The Lily Pad Tango."

Spots of coloured lights appear on the floor.

HERRINGBONE: Clever, eh? (continues to dance until he reaches first spot) This pad is Atlanta, Georgia. The Hot Peaches Club. More rococo than anything else. And we were slidin' out the exit door of this temple with a giggle in Daddy's nerves, money in his pocket, and Mother nervously dabbing her lips with her handkerchief as if she was wipin' away a stifled cry. (more of the dance) We weren't bad. But we weren't ready.

LOU: We're gonna make a turn here, George.

GEORGE: (breathless) I'm ready, Mr. Lou.

HERRINGBONE: (turning dazzlingly into the next spot of light) We were finally ready! But we were in Dubuque . . .

LOU: Point your toes, George.

GEORGE: Where?

LOU: Out there. Hollywood!

Elaborate extravaganza dance section to end of number.

HERRINGBONE: This is the heart of Hollywood. A kidney-shaped pool outside a tourist court off The Strip. I was in an inner tube. Kickin' and splashin' away!

GEORGE: *(doing so)* Red Rover, Red Rover, Let George come over!

LOU: For Christsakes, George!

GEORGE: Don't ya love it, Mr. Lou?

HERRINGBONE: And there was Daddy, dog paddlin' his way over to me with a grin that was needin' a favour.

ARTHUR: *(water up to his mouth)* Slow down there, George.

HERRINGBONE: *(steps out of this pantomime and directly asks the audience)* Do I look like I'm swimmin'? Not an easy thing to do, ya know. *(steps back in)*

ARTHUR: *(dog-paddling in place)* I've been thinkin' how well we've been doing over the past six weeks and I was wonderin' if we should prepare for the future.

LOU: *(in the inner tube)* You want to continue?

ARTHUR: Well, I don't see why not.

LOU: Excellent.

ARTHUR: I don't want to get caught short-changed again and I wondered if you'd do a favour for your Mamma and I, and sign a will?

LOU: *(taken aback)* A will? Jesus Christ. *(starts to go under water)* Help! Help!

LOUISE: *(reaching desperately for him from the edge of the pool)* Put him up here, Arthur. I've got a towel for ya, Honey. Now . . . how does that feel? *(toweling down GEORGE)*

LOU: *(loving it)* Oh . . . oh . . .

LOUISE: George?!

GEORGE: Too hard, Mother.

LOUISE: I'd like to speak with Mr. Lou for a moment, George.

LOU: Just a little down. Oh. Yes. Right there.

LOUISE: *(her propriety assaulted, she stops)* Mr. Lou, now that we've reached Hollywood, I figure that it's time for you to go. According to our agreement? The end of the six weeks? The end of our arrangement?

LOU: Go?

LOUISE: Like you said.

LOU: Well, I don't know about that, Louise.

LOUISE: *(grabbing him)* Well, I do!

GEORGE: Mother?

LOUISE: Quiet, George. *(to LOU)* You promised!

LOU: *(shouting so ARTHUR can hear)* Arthur said we could continue!

LOUISE: *(shaking him)* I'm telling you it's over!

GEORGE: You're squeezing my arm, Mother.

LOUISE: You've got to leave now!

GEORGE: You're hurtin' me, Mother.

LOUISE: I won't take no for an answer.

GEORGE: Mother! Please!

LOUISE slaps him; is shocked with herself. Long transition as HERRINGBONE steps away from the scene, regards it, leaves it behind emotionally, and begins this down-and-dirty paean to motherhood.

HERRINGBONE:

YOU GOT YOUR MAMAS AND YOU GOT YOUR MOTHERS AND
NEVER THE TWAIN SHALL MEET.
A MAMA IS A TRAFFIC-STOPPIN' FLOOZIE WHO'S A
HUSBAND-HOPPIN' TEASE . . .
AND A MOTHER, WELL, A MOTHER . . . IS LOUISE.

NOW WHEN A MAMA CALLS HER BABY "BABY," HE
COULD BE HER DADDY, TOO.
WHEN MAMA DOES HER LULLABYIN' SHE DON'T WANT NO
BABY CRYIN', PLEASE . . .
BUT A MOTHER, WELL, A MOTHER . . . IS LOUISE.

NOTHIN' IN THIS WORLD IS GOOD ENOUGH
FOR THE PERSON LOUISE LOVES BEST.
THERE'S OVALTINE IN THE PANTRY
AND UNGUENTINE IN THE MEDICINE CHEST.

SO IF A MAMA TALKS ABOUT HER MOTHER, SHE
MAY WIPE A TEAR AWAY,
AND TELL YA THAT THERE'S NOT ANOTHER SWEET EMBRACE TO
MATCH HER MOTHER'S SQUEEZE . . .
IF THAT MAMA HAD A MOTHER . . . LIKE LOUISE.

DID YA WEAR YOUR SWEATER SO YOU WOULDN'T FREEZE?
DID YA EAT YOUR CARROTS AND YOUR PEAS?
AND DID YOU LEARN YOUR *ABC'S*?
AND SCRUB YOUR DIRTY ELBOWS AND YOUR SCUFFED-UP KNEES?
OH, YOU'RE LUCKY, BROTHER . . .
YOU HAD A MOTHER LIKE LOU—LOU—LOU—
LOUISE . . . LOUISE . . . LOUISE.

Poor Mother. That night she patiently waited 'til Daddy fell asleep . . . then pulled the top sheet of the bed gently over his head . . . and pinned the sheet to the border of the mattress with 96 pins at three-quarter inch spaces. Momma never discarded her taste for the meticulous even when she was sufferin' under desperation.

SHE LEFT HIM SLEEPIN' THEN SHE STARTED CREEPIN' TO
WHERE HER DEAR BABY LAY.
HER MOTHER'S MIND BEGAN TO PLAY WITH THOUGHTS OF HOW
THEY'D STEAL AWAY WITH EASE . . .
GEORGE AND MOTHER; GEORGE FOREVER WITH LOUISE . . .

IF I HAD MY DRUTHERS,
WE'D ALL HAVE MOTHERS
LIKE LOU—LOU—LOU—
LOUISE!

She opened our bedroom door and unfortunately we were gone. We made an escape.

Music Cue: "Running to the La Rochelle." *LOU/GEORGE again dons the herringbone jacket.*

LOU: Marriages require a name change, George. I believe ours should be Herringbone. (*aware of the upcoming pun*) It'll suit the act much better. (*a giggle*)

HERRINGBONE: The anxiety of Mamma chasin' us and Daddy chasin' Mamma was ridin' very high. But not as high as Lou's desire to keep performing. A desire I was trying to keep up with.

GEORGE: Mr. Lou?

LOU: What is it, George?

GEORGE: Will you always be with me, Mr. Lou?

LOU: Not now, George.

Transition to the La Rochelle Hotel. Suggestion: LOU knocks on the piano and appears on the other side as the desk clerk, DOT.

DOT: (*looking down*) And where are we running to tonight?

LOU: To the 14th floor and I prefer taking the elevator if you don't mind. It's the 06. The 1406. Corner room facing the music.

DOT: Well, we've been here before have we?

LOU: Certainly have. A romantic evenin' with you, Dot. Ten years back.

DOT: What?!

LOU: Think, madam.

HERRINGBONE: Now consider how odd this moment was.

DOT: No! It couldn't be!

LOU: It certainly is. I'll be here for a minimum of one night. I'd prefer the bill on leaving. I can get my own bag. Thank you.

DOT: May I ask how old you are?

LOU: Thirty-seven. (*pause*) We're gonna have to have her up for a drink, George.

DOT: I get off at midnight.

Music Cue: "The Elevator." Transition to outside room 1406.

HERRINGBONE: Lou's hideaway. That's what this was. A place to soak our feet from the swellin' of dancin' ten-a-day. By the time we reached the fourteenth floor of the La Rochelle . . . which seemed like the longest period of time I had to think to myself . . . the shock of my parents' absence was beginning to claw.

LOU: Now, turn the key, George.

HERRINGBONE: Just then I wanted to say "No" very badly.

LOU: To the right, George. Good. (*looks around the room*) Ahhh. Still brown. Let's take these clothes off, George. That bed looks like an oasis to me.

GEORGE: Mr. Lou?

LOU: Who ironed these sheets? Let's pull the cover up, George.

GEORGE: This is me.

LOU: You're very perceptive, George.

GEORGE: Me!

LOU: You're makin' me repeat, George!

GEORGE: I need more than me!

LOU: You have it, George!

GEORGE: I don't!

LOU: I said you have it!

GEORGE: I don't.

LOU: Goddamnit!

GEORGE: I feel very lonesome, Mr. Lou.

LOU: Well . . . we're feeling the same there, George. Now, look, if the management comes in they won't have any idea what to think if you're cryin' and—

GEORGE: I don't have any idea what to think, Mr. Lou!

LOU: But I do, George. Hey . . . take a deep breath. (*He does.*) That's right . . . It's been a long tour. Now, now . . . breathe in. (*a worried pause while GEORGE holds his breath*) Now breathe out, George! (*He does.*) What the hell do you think you're doin? You scared me there. Now . . . let's close our eyes. I want you to see something. (*GEORGE closes his eyes.*) Oh, yes. What do you see?

GEORGE: Herringbone.

LOU: And who's wearing the herringbone, George?

GEORGE: Me.

LOU: No, George. Look again.

GEORGE: Is it you, Mr. Lou?

LOU: Very good, George. (*settling in for the night*) Now let's go to sleep, George. (*sings, with rather a jaunty attitude for a lullaby*)
LOOK-IT OUT THE WINDOW.
LOOK OUT AT THE NIGHT.
NO MORE LOOKIN' BACK
AT ALL THAT'S OUTTA SIGHT.

THE SUN HAS SAID, "GOOD EVENIN'."
TOMORROW IT WILL SAY,
"LOOK-IT WHO JUST GOT HIMSELF
A BRAND NEW DAY."

A disturbed wrestling of wills, with GEORGE momentarily winning.

GEORGE:
LOOK-IT WHO'S AWAKE, NOW.
LOOK WHOSE EYES ARE BRIGHT,
FIGHTIN', FIGHTIN' SLEEP
WITH ALL HIS BABY MIGHT . . .

LOU: I'd really like to get some sleep, George.

GEORGE:
BUT SLEEP IS NOT FOREVER,
AND WHEN IT GOES AWAY—

LOU: Oh, for Christsake, George!

GEORGE:
LOOK-IT WHO IS GONNA HAVE
A BRAND NEW DAY.

By the end of the song, GEORGE has begun to cry. There's a knock at the door.

LOU: Jesus Christ!

Another knock.

GEORGE: Mamma?

LOU: She's long gone, George. (*A knock in code. LOU recognizes it. Leaps for the door.*) It's for me! I'll get it!

Music Cue: "Introducing Dot."
HERRINGBONE: (*ushering DOT in*) Dot! Dot was the type who took to tulip prints. She, unfortunately, was sandwiched between the matronly job of a desk clerk and the fantasies of a sweetheart romance.

DOT: (*as they all settle self-consciously on the edge of the bed*) You look so young. I don't know if I believe you. Where's your family! Gone? Are they?

GEORGE: *Yes!!*

DOT: Was that you?

LOU: What? Umm . . . yes . . . yes, it was me.

DOT: Do that again.

LOU: I uhh . . .

DOT: Oh, come on.

LOU: I can't, I can't.

DOT: Where did you say you were from?

GEORGE: Demopolis, Alabama!

DOT: It fits! Now you speak like you look!

LOU: But that really isn't my voice.

DOT: It is! It is!

LOU: No . . . look, you're wrong!

DOT: I am?

As they sit, GEORGE's feet start dancing.

DOT: What are you doing?

LOU: What?

DOT: You're dancing!

LOU: I am? (*looking at feet*)

DOT: Could you teach me a dance step?

LOU: Oh! Well . . . sure.

DOT: (*rising*) Why don't we begin with something slow . . . and simple . . . like a . . .

LOU: Like a . . .

DOT: Like a . . . waltz. Now, let's put our drinks down.

Music Cue: "The Tulip Print Waltz."

DOT: Oh, now that isn't too bad is it? (*realizing she can lift him*) You're very light on your feet.

GEORGE: (*whispering*) Mamma?

DOT: Isn't that sweet?

LOU: (*whispering*) Keep it up, George.

DOT: Are you payin' attention? Oh! That's a lovely turn.

GEORGE: I need to sleep.

DOT: Well, why didn't you say anything?

LOU: Oh, uh— (*twirls DOT*)

DOT: Oh, oh, my head is spinning. (*pause*) Do you mind if I look away?

LOU: What?

DOT: It's just that when I hear you . . . I . . . believe you . . . but if I look at you I feel I may be committin' a sin. You're so youthful. It scares me.

LOU: Oh, well, then look away.

DOT: Oh, you're such a gentleman.

LOU: (*still dancing*)
TEN YEARS, COUNT 'EM, TEN YEARS.
I HAVE BEEN WITHOUT THE WHEREWITHAL
TO BE WITH ALL THE WOMEN I COULDA
BEEN WITH,
IF I WOULDA BEEN HERE . . .
OR EVEN BEEN.

TEN YEARS, JESUS, TEN YEARS,
SINCE A WOMAN HAD ME DANCIN' CLOSE
AND
BURIED UP AGAINST WHAT I'M UP AGAINST
NOW.
OH, SO MANY WOMEN
I COULDA GONE WITH—
GONE—GONE—GONE.

GONE IS THE GANGLY GIGGLY ONE,
AND THE ROUND AND WIGGLY ONE—
AND ME HELPLESS, POWERLESS, AHHH . . .

GONE IS THE ONE WHO SWEARS,
WITH THE CROOKED SEAMS.
AND THE ONE WHO SWEATS.
AND THE ONE WHO SCREAMS.
LORD, ALL OF 'EM GONE.

TEN YEARS, TEN INSANE YEARS,
I'VE BEEN SENSIN' WOMEN CLOSE ENOUGH
TO SNAG 'EM WITH MY HAND IF I JUST HAD
A HAND.
AND NOW I CAN DO IT. YEAH, I CAN DO IT,
AND THIS WHOLE BODY
IS GONNA GET ONE!

LOU: Look . . . umm, Dot?

DOT: Yes, ummm, Lou.

GEORGE: Let's go to bed!

LOU: Goddamn you!

DOT: Now I don't think it's necessary to—

Stops waltzing. Music continues under.

LOU: I'm sorry. I'm sorry, Dot.

DOT: You're so . . . complex. May I have my hand back, now?

LOU: I'll give your hand back if you give me a kiss.

DOT: Doesn't seem very fair to me. A kiss?

GEORGE breathes heavily.

DOT: Will you give me the voice?

LOU: Yeah.

GEORGE breathes heavily.

DOT: Just a little bit of the voice.

LOU: C'mon George.

GEORGE: (*breathing heavily, then crying out*) Dot!!

DOT: Oh, very good! (*kisses him*)

GEORGE: (*reeling*)
MAMMA NEVER KISSED LIKE—
OH, OH,
WHAT IS HAPPENING?
WE KISSED HER, MISTER LOU,
LET'S GO, NOW—

I DON'T WANNA KISS LIKE—
OH, OH
LET'S GET OUTTA HERE—
DON'T KISS HER, MISTER LOU,
LET'S GO—
LET GO OF HER—
LET'S GO—
LET GO OF ME—
MISTER LOU, NO!
MISTER LOU, OOOOH!

They collapse onto the bed. The following is a series of twists and turns.

LOU:
YOU'RE SUCH A ROUND AND WIGGLY ONE...

DOT: Oh, Lou—Lou—talk about your angel skin and your baby-fine hair, and that voice, that sweet—

GEORGE:
ROUND AND ROUND AND ROUND—

DOT: Oh! That's it! That sweet voice!
GEORGE: My name is—

LOU: No!

GEORGE: Started out in vaudeville. Been on the stage—

LOU:
TEN YEARS. I SAID TEN YEARS, JESUS, TEN—

GEORGE:
TIN-TIN-TIN-TIN-TIN-TIN-TIN-TIN-TIN-TIN-TIN-TAP-U-LATIN' SOUND.

LOU: Not now! Goddamnit! Not now!

DOT: Why, Lou, it's *you* who was so anxious.

LOU: Don't listen to me. Don't look at me. Just . . . just . . . feel!
IT'S ME—HELPLESS—POWERLESS—
AH—AH . . .

DOT: Oh, but you are powerful, Lou. So very, very . . . oh my.

A few ad-libbed "Lou-Dot" moans of pleasure.

GEORGE:
DON'T MAKE ME DO IT.

LOU:
PLEASE, PLEASE, PLEASE, IT'S FROGGIE BEGGIN'.
PLEASE, PLEASE, PLEASE, IT'S FROGGIE BEGGIN'.

DOT: You don't have to beg, Lou, I'm yours!

GEORGE:
DON'T MAKE ME DO IT!

DOT: Whatever am I to think of all this, Lou?

LOU: Hold on, Dot. Hold on!
FASTER . . . FASTER . . . FASTER—

GEORGE: (*desperate*) This is me! On the stage! Red Rover, Red Rover, Let George come over! I am an American. Can ya catch me, Daddy? Mamma? This is me! Gonna be a smash! Catch me!

NOT THAT, NOT EVER, NOT—

LOU:

NOW I CAN DO IT. YEAH, I CAN DO IT.

GEORGE:

I DON'T WANNA DO IT. I DON'T WANNA DO IT.

LOU:

I'M GONNA DO IT. AND THIS WHOLE BODY IS MI-I-INE!

GEORGE: (*an unearthly call for his mother*) Maaa-Maaa!

Over music, GEORGE mouths the scream "Maaa-Maaa," and closes his eyes. Blackout. After a moment in black, lights up.

HERRINGBONE: Well . . . I certainly did give her my voice. Unfortunately, that was all I could give Dot. (*breaking the mood; to THUMBS*) Something to celebrate the morning, Mr. Dubois.

Music Cue: "A Little Morning Music."

HERRINGBONE: The ménage is now a duet.

LOU: (*as GEORGE is vigorously brushing his teeth*) You've got to stop, George! Whatta ya tryin' to do . . . bleed your gums?

GEORGE: I know what I'm doin', Mr. Lou.

LOU: I wish that could have been said of your behavior last night. I don't know what you're preparin' for . . . but we got to talk.

GEORGE: (*combing his hair*) About what, Mr. Lou?

LOU: Well, we could start with "man-to-man," but that isn't the case, is it?

GEORGE: Do ya like the part on this side, Mr. Lou?

LOU: Oh, we're looking at a mirror, George. It's hard to say.

GEORGE: But I'm lookin' at myself, Mr. Lou.

LOU: God, how am I goin' to face that woman when we go downstairs?

GEORGE: Could you tell me whether . . . the right side of the tie goes over the left or the left over the right, Mr. Lou?

LOU: Now, if I apologize to her . . . you won't open your mouth this time will ya, George?

GEORGE: The left over the right?

LOU: The right over the left, goddamnit!

GEORGE: (*attending to his tie with dignity*) Thank you. Was Dot mad, Mr. Lou? She left in such a hurry.

LOU: Let's say we were crushed under the weight of embarrassment.

GEORGE: She took my clothes off. No one's ever done that before but Mamma. She was very careful of the buttons like Mamma. I liked her hands . . . but . . . well, except . . .

LOU: I'd like to remove ourselves from the mirror, George.

GEORGE: I can't yet, Mr. Lou. I have to wash my hands.

LOU: You've already washed them, George.

GEORGE: I have?

LOU: Take your hands out of the sink, George. I said take them out!

GEORGE: But the water feels so good, Mr. Lou.

LOU: I never knew you to be married to hygiene, George. Whatta ya want, an apology? . . . I'm sorry. I tell you, I am sorry. All right? What exactly is going on here?

GEORGE: I like the coat Daddy picked out for me. Don't you, Mr. Lou?

LOU: I don't wanna put this on now, George!

GEORGE: I do. Doesn't it feel good, Mr. Lou?

LOU: *No!*

GEORGE: It will. (*goes for the window*)

LOU: Stop! What we don't need is air here. What the hell are ya doin'? Take your leg outta the window, George!

GEORGE is starting out—heaving—perched on the window sill.

LOU: For Christsake! Don't do this! (*loud whisper*) How would you like to save us, George?

GEORGE: Wha . . . ?

LOU: (*trying to fast-talk his way out*) Well, one fall was enough, don't you think? First the orchestra pit and now you offer me fourteen floors off the La Rochelle. I'm sure not to get a third chance unless it's something exciting like a diving horse. (*starts to giggle to himself*)

GEORGE: (*now giggling as GEORGE*) You're so funny, Mr. Lou . . . but . . . (*begins a lunge*)

LOU: No "buts," George, it's a lousy word! Get rid of it! It's the heartbreak of any language.

(*GEORGE tries again to lunge.*) George . . . George . . . I need you, George.

GEORGE: Look at the people waving, Mr. Lou.

LOU: I'll give you anything you want! Just name it! Name it!

GEORGE: I'd like for you to go away, Mr. Lou.

LOU: Oh, George! That's impossible! It's the only thing I can't give ya!

GEORGE: But you can do anything, Mr. Lou.

LOU: Not that! Come on, George, there must be something? Isn't your life worth anything? Think of all the years you got ahead of ya. Think of all the years I never had! I'm sorry. I didn't mean to say that. (*growing increasingly hysterical and racing through thoughts*) I know this is your body. I mean your life. I mean, what the hell am I gonna do, George? Please? I'll behave! I'll do anything you want. You'll see. Just give me a chance—I know—I know—I never gave *you* a chance. I know it's unfair. But think of the possibilities, George. Few kids ever had a career like you! I know! I'll only come out whenever we're onstage . . . or . . . or . . . whenever you think it's necessary to speak to me, you know, like one of those moments when you wanna talk to yourself— George? Are you there? Speak to me. Please? Oh, my God!

GEORGE: I hear you, Mr. Lou.

LOU: Oh, George, isn't there something I could say? I want you to live so badly! I know you think it's for me, but it isn't. I swear it! I don't wanna kill you, kid. I don't wanna be responsible. I'll be your valet. I'll be your tutor. I'll be your friend. I'll be your mother. I'll be your father. You won't believe me. I'm very good at every one of these things. God! I can't stand it! (*throws his hands over his eyes*) Don't kill yourself!

GEORGE: Mr. Lou?

LOU: (*crying*) Ooooh, God, George. I'm sorry, kid. I'm so sorry.

GEORGE: I know, Mr. Lou.

LOU: I didn't mean to take your body. I just wanted to kill the person who killed me, and I wanna make sure it never happens again. I swear it.

GEORGE: Mr. Lou?

LOU: (*crying*) Can you believe me, George?

GEORGE: First I wanna lift my head, Mr. Lou.

LOU: What — (*lifts his head, his eyes still squeezed shut*)

GEORGE: And now I want to open up my eyes.

LOU: (*breaking down*) Oh God, George, I'm so afraid!

GEORGE: (*eyes wide open*) I'm not.

HERRINGBONE: (*as though still on the ledge*)
WELL, IT IS SURELY ONE OF THOSE YEARS . . .
ONE OF THOSE HEART-STOPPIN' YEARS . . .
WHEN DESPERATE NEED
IS TAKIN' THE LEAD,
A LEAP TO YOUR DEATH IS EFFECTIVE . . .
BUT TENDS TO BE OVER-CORRECTIVE.

WITH GUTS AND WITH LUCK,
A BARGAIN IS STRUCK,

AND SEALED WITH INTERMINGLIN' TEARS . . .
AND YA HOPE IT MIGHT LAST A FEW YEARS.

With a victorious leap, breaking the "reality" of the window ledge.

WELL, HERE WE ARE!
SOMEHOW, WE ARE!
A LITTLE GEORGE IN THE EYES,
LOU IN THE FEET,
KEEPIN' THE BEAT
TO GEORGE'S SONG.
AND GEORGE'S HEART
IS FILLED WITH HEARTS—
THE INTER-BLENDIN' OF A LIFE OF COUNTERPARTS.

LOOKIN' BACK UPON ONE OF THOSE YEARS,
ONE IS ENOUGH OF THOSE YEARS.
MAKIN' IT THROUGH
IS PLENTY TO DO.
MY HAT'S OFF TO YOU IF YOU'RE IN ONE . . .
OR HOT TO GO OUT AND BEGIN ONE.

Indicating THUMBS and MUSICIANS.

MY THANKS TO MY CREW,
AND SPESH'LY TO YOU,
FOR THE LENDIN' OF YOUR EYES AND EARS,
NOW MY STORY IS DONE, OF THOSE
TIMES WE CALL ONE OF THOSE
YEARS!

Music finishes. HERRINGBONE exits; or blackout.

Music Cue: "Bows."

The Mother! (*bows as LOUISE*)
The Daddy! (*bows as ARTHUR*)
The Lady, Dot! (*bows as DOT*)
The Chicken! (*bows as MOSELY*)
The Frog! (*bows as LOU*)
And George! (*Bows as YOUNG GEORGE; then, finally, as HERRINGBONE*)

Lights out.

NED AND JACK

SHELDON ROSEN

In the original published version of *Ned and Jack*, Sheldon Rosen dedicates the play "To Pam Hawthorn, who planted the first seed, and to Tom Cone because the play could have been called Tom and Sheldon." During the mid-seventies these three were certainly the dominant figures at the New Play Centre. Cone and Rosen had ten productions between them from 1974-77, three directed by artistic director Hawthorn. (Another six were directed by NPC associate director Jace van der Veen.) From 1977-80, all three were working at Stratford, giving the New Play Centre a national profile for the first time.

Rosen was born in New York City in 1943 and educated at the Universities of Rochester (B.A., Psychology) and Syracuse (M.A., Telecommunications). In 1970 he moved to Toronto where his first plays, *Love Mouse* and *Meyer's Room* (1971), were presented in a double-bill at the Royal Alex. The next year Tarragon produced his full-length comedy *The Wonderful World of William Bends Who Is Not Quite Himself Today*, and *The Stag King*, an adaptation from Carlo Gozzi. Rosen came to Vancouver in 1973. In conjunction with the New Play Centre he shifted his focus to psychological drama: *The Box* (1974), *Frugal Repast* (1974), *Like Father, Like Son* (1975 — later retitled *The Grand Hysteric*), and *Ned and Jack* (1977). Other major plays include *Souvenirs* (1984), first staged in New York and later in a Shaw Festival/Factory Theatre co-production, and *The Duck Sisters* (Theatre Plus, 1990). Rosen has taught playwriting for many years at the New Play Centre and at New York's New Dramatists. In 1989 he was playwright-in-residence at San Jose State University.

Ned and Jack was the first full-length play to be commissioned by the New Play Centre. Initially attracted to the story of fellow New York playwright Edward Sheldon because of his name (Rosen's first names are Sheldon Edward), Rosen came to focus on the effects of Sheldon's degenerative disease and his extraordinary friendship with actor John Barrymore. (Barrymore once said that his epitaph should read, "This Goddamned Son of a Bitch Knew Ned Sheldon.") Rosen worked on the script while playwright-in-residence at the National Arts Centre, 1976-77. After its highly lauded New Play Centre debut, both play and author went to the Stratford Festival for two seasons, Rosen as writer-in-residence and *Ned and Jack* in an unprecedented two separate productions, on the Third Stage (1978) and the Avon Stage (1979). *In Stratford: The First Thirty Years*, Jamie Portman describes it as "a script overflowing with dramatic tension and rich, evocative language." Both Vancouver's Arts Club and Calgary's ATP produced *Ned and Jack* in 1980, the year it won the Canadian Authors' Association Award for published drama.

The current version of the play is based on the New York productions of 1981, both directed by Colleen Dewhurst, first at the Hudson Guild Theater, then on Broadway at the Little Theater where it suffered the fate of so many Canadian exports, closing after a single performance. The fatal *New York Times* review complained that what had been a "spirited and touching" little show in the off-Broadway confines of the Hudson Guild had become inflated and calcified in the move to Broadway. The relationship between Sheldon and John Barrymore in this script is basically unchanged from the original (published by Playwrights Canada, 1979), but the character of Ethyl Barrymore was added at Dewhurst's suggestion. This version has since had another ten productions across the United States.

Ned and Jack was first presented by the New Play Centre at the Vancouver East Cultural Centre on November 11, 1977, with Tom Wood as Ned, Jan Muszynski as Jack, and Guy Bannerman as Danny. Pamela Hawthorn directed, with set design by Richard Cook, lighting by Marsha Sibthorpe and costumes by Christina McQuarrie.

Tom Wood as Ned, and Jan Muszynski as Jack in the New Play Centre production of *Ned and Jack*. Photo by Glen Erikson.

NED AND JACK

CHARACTERS

NED, thirty-six-year-old American playwright Edward Sheldon.

JACK, forty-year-old American actor John Barrymore.

ETHEL, Jack's sister, the actress Ethel Barrymore, 43.

DANNY, a rough-hewn gentleman's gentleman in the employ of Edward Sheldon. He's in his late thirties.

SCENE

New York. November 16, 1922. Edward Sheldon's penthouse apartment overlooking 83rd Street and Central Park.

AUTHOR'S NOTE

Ned and Jack is a play about a fictional event that relates to history the way that a milkshake relates to all the ingredients that have been tossed into the blender to produce it. Edward Sheldon and John and Ethel Barrymore were real people; Danny was not. The strong relationship of Ned and Jack is fact; the evening described in the play is fiction. Dates have been changed and events juggled but I am hopeful that the integrity of the characters has not been jarred.

Edward Sheldon was a major American playwright from 1906 to the late 1920s. At the peak of his popularity, he was struck down by a crippling viral arthritis for which there was no treatment. Permanently immobilized, he removed himself from the public eye and drifted into obscurity. He was John Barrymore's friend and spiritual mentor, the person most responsible for Barrymore's transformation from a light comedian into the foremost male actor of his time.

ACT ONE

In the dark, a buzzer buzzes. A recording of "Beale Street Blues" by W. C. Handy begins to play on the victrola. The buzzer sounds again.

The lights come up on the living room of NED SHELDON's elegant penthouse apartment overlooking Central Park in New York. It is nearly two in the morning. NED is not expecting any visitors and is dressed accordingly. Casual and for comfort. Scattered about him are several books, some opened, some unopened, and an old manuscript of "The Lonely Heart" to which he has recently returned. He is restless and unable to sleep, but also unable to concentrate on any of the distractions available. He is standing at the French doors, gazing out at the view and then focusing on the cigarette he is smoking. Inhaling and then exhaling slowly and watching the smoke drift off. He then writes a note with considerable difficulty telling himself that it might be an interesting piece of stage business. He does it one more time but impatiently puts out the cigarette before the smoke has had a chance to drift off.

DANNY enters from the hall.

DANNY: Willy says it was Miss Barrymore downstairs. She wants to come up.

NED: Downstairs? I only wanted her to telephone.

DANNY: (*closes curtains and begins to tidy the room*) Let me tell her you're asleep. It's past one-thirty already.

NED: (*crossing to bar for his pills*) No, it's all right. She just wants to tell me how Jack's *Hamlet* went tonight. I can't imagine it would take her longer than one drink to do it. She'll be going to the opening night party at Arthur's.

DANNY: Are you all right?

NED: How many times are you going to ask me?

DANNY: You were taking another pill.

NED: (*going back to his work on the manuscript*) I'm all right. Just leave the chicken and have Willy bring Miss Barrymore up. Tell him to take the long way so we can get ready.

DANNY: (*picking up books and newspapers*) I just want to go on record as saying I think you're being unreasonable overtaxing yourself like this. (*crosses to bar and begins to tidy*)

NED: It may be one of the last times I can enjoy the luxury of overtaxing myself. Leave the wine. Miss Barrymore will be my last guest for a while, Danny. Now go on.

DANNY corks but leaves the wine. He picks at the food on the cart as he exits. NED starts to shrug off his cardigan. DANNY re-enters, wearing a white serving jacket and carrying NED's dinner jacket and bow tie.

DANNY: She's on her way.

NED: (*as DANNY dresses him*) None of your little hints to Miss Barrymore about my condition. I don't want anything to get back to Jack. This is not the night to burden him. I'll tell them all when I'm ready. (*noticing the jacket*) I would have preferred the blue one . . .

DANNY: There's a spot on the sleeve.

NED: That was three days ago. Why is it still in the closet?

DANNY: (*tying NED's bow tie*) It was waiting for some dirty brothers and sisters to make the trip to the cleaners worthwhile.

NED: Tomorrow I want you to take it for a little walk. I don't feel like wearing cranberry.

DANNY: I could have brought the frog green.

NED: It's a very fashionable green.

DANNY: Blue looks more like you're on your way to bed. Cranberry makes you look like you want to stay up all night.

NED: You should write for *Vogue* magazine.

DANNY: I have enough to do here.

The door chimes ring. DANNY crosses to cover Charlie's cage.

NED: Charlie's waiting to hear the news, too. (*DANNY leaves the cage uncovered. NED checks himself in the mirror, notices that his tie is somewhat askew.*) Oh, Danny . . . (*DANNY starts back to adjust the tie.*) Just go on. (*NED fixes his tie.*) Just go to bed. I'm all right.

DANNY exits. We hear his voice and ETHEL's from offstage.

DANNY: (*off*) Good evening, Miss Barrymore. May I take your coat?

ETHEL: (*off*) No, thank you, Danny. I'll keep my coat.

ETHEL sweeps into the room.

NED: Ethel, I just wanted you to phone . . .

ETHEL: Yes, I know, I know, but it was absolutely impossible with all the madness backstage. (*NED and ETHEL kiss.*) Even the rules of women and children first were abandoned there. Oh, the wine and the elevator ride have just merged. (*peering at the disk on the victrola*) Oh, how *au courant*. Not that I have ever enjoyed the telephone, my dear. It's like speaking through a keyhole. And at those rare moments when one actually has wonderful news . . . (*crosses to piano to discard her gloves and purse*) I mean, you do live on the way to Arthur's, darling, so I would hardly call this a major inconvenience. It's the little digressions that make life so interesting. (*stopping by the birdcage*) Good evening, Charles. (*to NED*) I had to climb on top of the cab, though, to see if your lights were still on. Like a beacon. I, myself, hate thoughtless intrusions. It's warm in here, isn't it? (*She takes off the chinchilla, strikes a pose.*)

NED: Well, you look wonderful. Certainly more exotic than any dream I could be having at this hour.

ETHEL: Oh, darling, thank you. I just need Charlie bird perched on my shoulder to complete the picture.

NED: A real knockout, baby.

ETHEL: My favourite kind of review. (*drapes the wrap over the back of the chaise*)

NED: With that dress and your delayed entrance at Arthur's party, you will again steal the evening.

ETHEL: What could make it a real entrance would be to arrive on your arm. Now that would be dramatic. Why don't you come along? Everyone is certainly dying to see you. You're becoming such a man of mystery up here.

NED: The Count of Monte Cristo. You know I'd love to.

ETHEL: Then you should.

NED: Not tonight.

ETHEL: You look wonderful. That must mean you're feeling better.

NED: From the moment you entered the room.

ETHEL: If only my former husband had learned to say things like that.

NED: (*referring to the cluttered chaise*) Just clear that away.

ETHEL: I've had enough sitting already this evening.

NED: Well, I've been sitting here for nearly six hours waiting to hear of Jack Barrymore's alleged performance of *Hamlet*. Now tell me.

ETHEL: That dear, ramshackle baby brother of mine was greeted like a conquering monarch at the end.

NED: Thank God. (*crosses to bar for wine bottle and wineglass*)

ETHEL: They wouldn't let him off the stage. Eighteen calls. And roses flying from everywhere. A bit like the Crucifixion with all those thorns whizzing through the air.

NED: We'll have a toast even if the old buzzard himself isn't here to enjoy it. (*handing her the bottle*) You don't mind, do you?

ETHEL: Not at all. I'm a self-sufficient woman.

NED: (*as ETHEL extracts the cork*) I've been told this is the last bottle of Grand Montrachet on the East Coast. It's tragic how Prohibition has emptied my cupboard.

ETHEL: I was going to bring Hamlet along, but right in the middle of everything, he disappeared. We were supposed to go to Arthur's together. (*pours for them*)

NED: Thank you.

ETHEL: He tiptoed out with some little girl. The bastard was always inconsiderate. (*They sit.*) His thought processes are always scattered all over the place. You can see it in the way he eats corn on the cob.

NED: Corn on the cob?

ETHEL: He never eats in straight lines like everyone else. It's always a bite here and a bite there.

NED: But he does finish it, doesn't he?

ETHEL: If he does, it's not until he's driven us all mad in the meantime. He was particularly charming tonight. Practically skewered anyone who tried to compliment him. You know that look of his.

NED: You don't mind if I leap in and toast the man before you convict and sentence him. Send him up the river.

ETHEL: I hope he'll remember a paddle this time.

NED: Well, then, I'd like to propose a toast to John Sidney Blythe Barrymore . . .

ETHEL: No. To the man who almost single-handedly dragged John Sidney Blythe Barrymore kicking and screaming into greatness. He'd still be little more than a stage clown if it weren't for your interest. Everyone in the theatre should be blessed with such support. This night is as much yours as it is his. Our beloved Ned. (*She drinks to him.*)

NED: (*quite touched by the toast*) Dearly beloved, we are gathered . . . (*Seeing the look on ETHEL's face, he raises his glass, changing his tone.*) To this moment together. (*They drink.*) How much of the performance did you see tonight?

ETHEL: The second half. My whole company agreed to race double-time through *Rose Bernd* tonight, so that they could all catch at least part of Jack's performance. I'm sure double-time improved our play. I'd been lucky enough to have seen all of *Hamlet* yesterday afternoon. Jack arranged a special dress for me. He, of course, didn't show up until the very last moment, looking like he always does when he wanders in off the street—like a Bowery bum. Didn't even have time to change out of his street clothes, so he did the whole thing in civilian dress. One minute he was this derelict; the next, he was Hamlet. From that very first moment I was his. It was like watching some dangerous animal move closer and closer. I

wanted it to last forever. But of course, the lights did eventually come up and there I was again sitting in a chair in an old theatre. The world of the imagination that is so absolutely perfect and right for me faded away and I had returned to this one, the day-to-day one, and I didn't want to be here. I suppose I don't have to explain that to you, do I?

NED: No.

ETHEL: It's all so perverse. Jack, with all his gifts, absolutely despises the stage. He'd rather go off and make those silly films. And I, who have never, ever come close to being Hamlet, well, the theatre feels like home to me. No matter how many wigs and costumes, I am always "Ethel Barrymore."

NED: Ah, but what a thing that is to be.

ETHEL: The very words of Henry Irving when I was a very much younger "Ethel Barrymore."

NED: Well, it's true. You play leading ladies because you are a leading lady, and I'm afraid you're going to have to live with that.

ETHEL: Well, I pray to God that the gentlemen of the press are fully aware of what they witnessed this evening.

NED: I can't imagine Corbin wouldn't be aware.

ETHEL: I watched Woolcott the entire time I was there. If he denies he was enraptured, I shall personally twist his tongue.

NED: Alex is such a sucker for all of you I'd be shocked if he gave a bad notice.

ETHEL: I almost forgot. I have a present for you.

NED: Oh, good.

ETHEL: (*gives him the "company shot" from the piano*) I refuse to be the only one in your rogues' gallery of leading ladies who isn't represented by a full headshot. Mine is the only company shot in the bunch.

NED: (*looking at it*) Ethel, it's not a company shot.

ETHEL: Look now small it is.

NED: That doesn't make it a company shot. There's only one other actor in it with you.

ETHEL: Look at all that scenery, for God's sake. I look like a chimpanzee emerging from a dense jungle.

NED: It's dramatic.

ETHEL: Well, I have something better. (*rummages through her wrap, removing a rolled 8 x 10 picture*) A new shot from *Rose Bernd*. The photos are the only thing in the production worth remembering.

NED: How much longer will it run?

ETHEL: We're going to take it off to do *Romeo and Juliet*.

NED: But Jane Cowl is doing a Juliet.

ETHEL: Is that for certain?

NED: As far as I know it is.

ETHEL: I'm sure once mine is announced, she'll do the right thing.

NED: It seems pretty definite.

ETHEL: When is hers scheduled?

NED: I'm not sure. I don't think they've gone into rehearsal yet.

ETHEL: I'll have to get Arthur rolling. (*gives him the new photo*)

NED: Well, there are certainly no distractions in this . . .

ETHEL: You don't think it's a terrible idea, do you?

NED: Juliet?

ETHEL: Mmmm.

NED: If you want to play one of Shakespeare's women, why not Lady Macbeth? There's a chance for you to truly enlighten us with your understanding.

ETHEL: It's not that unusual for an older woman to play Juliet. All the great ones have done it. That's the joy of Shakespeare.

NED: I don't know if it's the *joy* of Shakespeare and I'm sure you'll be brilliant, but it seems a waste to have two Juliets running neck and neck in the same season. Jane isn't ready yet for Lady M and you are.

ETHEL: That's twice now you've implied I'm too old.

NED: That's not what I've been saying . . . But you are right about this picture. It is a good one.

ETHEL: (*seeing him examining the edges of the picture*) Those are just tiny pinholes; don't worry about them. I took it down from Jack's dressing room. I'll bring him another.

NED: I'll have to have it framed.

ETHEL: (*examining photo wall*) Where shall we hang it? What about next to Mrs. Fiske? If you didn't have all these pictures of Doris Keane, there'd be plenty of room for me. You're not going to stick me in some corner, are you? (*NED laughs. ETHEL speaks to Charlie.*) Three photos of Doris and that extraordinary part in *Romance*. And here I thought all men after a marriage engagement has been broken undergo this dramatic ritual of tossing all the

reminders into the nearest sea. *You* turn around
and write Doris by far the best part of her life.
Or anybody's life. And I, who have been loyal
from day one, get only an adaptation. And
where are you going to house all your future
leading ladies?

NED: In my heart. Trust me, Ethel. No matter where I put your picture, it will immediately
command centre stage.

ETHEL: You're so full of it at times. You
think Juliet should be played by an adolescent?
For accuracy.

NED: It's not so much accuracy. I mean, it
doesn't have to be an adolescent, but Juliet is
a part that acts as a signpost along the path of
one's career, and you and your abilities have
passed beyond that signpost years ago.

ETHEL: But what about the nature of illusion and spirit, the challenge of forcing an
audience to forget who I am and what I am and
make them believe I am this child? Don't you
think that's a worthwhile challenge?

NED: Yes, but once you achieve that, what
do you do for the rest of the play?

ETHEL: I think you're wrong this time.

NED: I've been wrong many times. And I
will be delighted to be once again wrong.

ETHEL: But you don't think you are this
time, do you?

NED: I'm reacting as much to the notion of
two simultaneous Juliets as I am to anything
else. I don't like that kind of competition.

ETHEL: You think Miss Cowl will fare
better?

NED: I have never been a bookmaker, and
if I were, this is not a horse race I would bet on.

ETHEL: (*rises*) Twenty-five dollars says that

I get the better notices. (*pause*) You have to be
careful with your silences, Ned. We all get very
intimidated by what you don't say. (*pours more
wine for herself*)

NED: Would you mind putting Charlie bird
to bed? I don't want him to be cranky in the
morning.

ETHEL: Dreams of beauty, dreams of
wealth, Charlie. (*covers cage*)

NED: Thank you.

*ETHEL crosses to piano, seats herself on the bench,
and softly begins to play the barcarole from Offen-
bach's* The Tales of Hoffman.

NED: Was Jack very upset that Michael
didn't come back from Paris for tonight?

ETHEL: (*stops playing and turns to NED*) Now
there is a woman who has earned every letter
of the name "Michael Strange." "Michael
Strange, the Writer." I think that name is the
only thing she ever truly invented. Everything
else was plagiarized. Certainly in *Clair de Lune*.
I shall never forgive Jack for pulling me practically out of my sickbed to appear in the Mrs.
John Barrymore version of Victor Hugo. And
she had the gall to accuse me of not knowing
her lines. The few that were actually hers were
written in tongues. It was you that he hated
not being there.

NED: He didn't think I deserted him, did he?

ETHEL: Of course not.

NED: I feel like everyone is staring when I
go out in public.

ETHEL: You're just being overly sensitive.

*NED holds out his hand to her. She rises from the
bench and takes it.*

NED: Oh, those eyes of yours. The most
expressive eyes of any creature on God's earth.

You really must promise me that you'll save at least one space for me on your dance card.

ETHEL: You probably know all the latest steps better than I.

NED: That's only because you were born to waltz. Anything else would be too . . . transient for you.

ETHEL: Well, soon we'll both be back on the dance floor and you can personally teach me all the new steps. It's so odd how these things come and go. It's times like this you should be seeing your friends the most, not the least. The Barrymores do make house calls.

NED: You would make a wonderful Florence Nightingale, you know. Someday someone is going to write a play about the woman and you'd be perfect.

ETHEL: Who better than you to do it? I know you were only kidding, but basically it's a great idea. Picture all those wonderful battle scenes! It could be quite extravagant. And heroic. And romantic. There's hardly anything of that scope on the stage today. You're the champ when it comes to grandness and romance. (*starts to pace*) She's engaged to be married. (*a noise is heard outside*) Her fiancé has to go off to the war. She wants to marry before he goes; he doesn't feel it would be fair to her. She volunteers as well. (*more noise*) Fate reunites them on the battlefield where he dies in her arms. She decides to devote herself to nursing. (*more noise*) Can you imagine what a curtain that would make? (*noise increases*) What *is* that?

NED: There is something out there, isn't there? (*rises*)

ETHEL: No, don't get up. I'll look.

NED: It's good for my circulation.

ETHEL opens the curtains and balcony doors in time to reveal BARRYMORE easing himself over the railing. He is still wearing his Hamlet costume, but over it he has an old overcoat and is wearing a beaten fedora as well. He is carrying a sword upon which is impaled the review from the New York Times.

JACK: Ah, Ethel dear, there you are.

ETHEL: Looking high and low, were you?

Once NED fully takes in JACK's appearance, he gives in to total laughter.

JACK: That's how I thought I looked tonight. You're the first one to respond correctly. I wanted you to see first-hand what you had missed. Took me days in front of a full-length mirror from every angle known to man including Nijinsky's "Faun" before I could accept the notion of appearing in public like this. One of my thighs is a little undernourished. My God, it's not that funny.

NED: Another Barrymore setting the fashion of the day. I couldn't imagine what was crawling up my balcony. It's the toast of Broadway.

ETHEL: A little burnt around the edges. Rather thoughtless of me to go on ahead without telling you where I was going.

JACK: Forgiven. With all the crush backstage, it was necessary I get some air, and that's probably when I missed you.

ETHEL: Probably. That little apprentice seemed to run out of breath around the same time.

JACK: Which one was that?

ETHEL: Ernestine.

JACK: Emily, not Ernestine.

ETHEL: Well, you have to admit she was terribly earnest, darling. I think it's wonderful the way you make the theatre seem so democratic. You're always so willing to devote yourself to the young in our business.

JACK: Her opinions of the show are just as valid as anyone else's.

ETHEL: She must have an exquisite sense of detail. It's been at least two hours.

NED: There is an easier way into the apartment.

JACK: Sister dear, consider yourself relieved of duty for the rest of the evening. I reached the age of consent all too many years ago.

ETHEL: Yes, but has Ernestine?

JACK: (to NED) I was so thrilled to see your light still on that I just flew towards it like a moth to flame. Halfway up, though, I forgot where the hell I was going.

NED: Up.

ETHEL: Yes, at least you remembered up.

JACK: Do you think that's an unusual direction for me?

ETHEL: Why can't you use the front door, like other people?

JACK: It was locked.

NED: Wasn't there a doorman on?

ETHEL: There was when I arrived.

JACK: I'm sure Jesus Christ Almighty was still here when you arrived all those centuries before me. Even St. Peter will be off duty by the time I finally get up there.

NED: There is a doorman on twenty-four hours.

JACK: He began digging a moat as soon as he saw me. I know, Ethel, he took your arm and escorted you up all fourteen floors.

NED: Did you ask him to buzz me?

JACK: Several times. It was like negotiating with a cigar store Indian. (flourishes sword with the notice)

NED: And is this Corbin of the Times impaled there?

JACK: You mean this? This bastardized off-spring of a tree? This is my obituary notice.

ETHEL: That can't be true.

NED: Let me see. (takes review off the sword)

ETHEL: Read it aloud.

JACK: Do you have a bottle I can play with?

NED: Find a glass. And then be quiet.

JACK: Is this all you have?

ETHEL: Will you let him read?

NED: This isn't a speakeasy.

JACK: My throat is turning to dust.

NED: (propelling JACK toward the bar) I can't read and direct traffic at the same time. (reads to himself for a moment)

JACK: Must I sink to the indignity of reading aloud my own review?

NED: "The atmosphere of historic happening surrounded John Barrymore's appearance last night as the Prince of Denmark; it was unmistakable as it was indefinable."

JACK: (lifting cage cover and speaking to Charlie) Do you think there is someone other than Solomon who could explain what that means?

ETHEL: Sounds like a hit and run accident.

JACK: I'm sorry I asked.

NED: Are we going to do this with every line?

ETHEL: We'll be good.

NED: (*as JACK paces*) "It sprang from the quality and the intensity of the applause, from the hushed murmurs that swept the audience at the most unexpected moments . . ."

JACK: I kept pulling my pants down. (*leaves his sword leaning against the bar*)

NED: ". . . from the silent crowds that all evening long swarmed about the theatre entrance. It was nowhere—and everywhere. In all likelihood, we have a new and lasting *Hamlet*." This is spectacular. (*puts review on desk*) I want to keep this. This is quite an obituary notice.

ETHEL: That was a wonderful notice and you know it.

JACK: The only thing you can do in the presence of a eulogy such as this is drop dead.

NED: That's an old line, Jack.

ETHEL: You deserved every word of it. You were breathtaking.

JACK: Really?

ETHEL: Really. It was more than a job well done. It was a privilege to witness it.

JACK: Now, Ethel, you know you're only allowed to make me weep on the stage.

ETHEL: Just reporting the facts.

JACK: Well, then if ever there were an occasion that called for a drink, this is it! And what have we here? (*removing three bottles from his coat pockets*) Mumms, Mumms, and Mumms. The three sisters.

NED: My God.

JACK: A more reliable figure than that. My bootlegger. It was quite a tearful reunion after all these months. (*doffing his coat*)

NED: I don't know how you get away with it, Jack.

JACK: I have dipsomanic immunity. (*tosses his coat and hat onto piano*)

NED: What a climb it must have been with all that extra weight.

JACK: (*opening first champagne bottle*) Sport, carrying around good champagne on my back is nothing. It's being beast of burden to another man's character on stage for four hours that violates the threshold of absurdity.

ETHEL: Rumour has it that you've been a jackass with your own character a good deal longer.

JACK: Now there's the Ethel I know and love.

NED distributes champagne glasses.

ETHEL: Are you going to take all night with this, Jack?

JACK: This is the way it's supposed to be done. Without noise and without loss of a single drop. The monks of Tibet do it this way. See, it's coming. Quiet as a mouse. Actually, it's a trick I learned in the boudoir of a woman whose husband slept in the room just above us. (*cork pops quietly*) Like a baby's burp. Bring your glasses, ladies and gentlemen. Don't worry about me. I prefer the bottle. (*fills their glasses*)

NED: To a new and lasting Hamlet.

ETHEL: Yes. To my brother Hamlet.

JACK: To hell with Hamlet. To us. To an evening of wonderful intoxication. May we all scale that peak of pleasure—

NED: I am not climbing the fire escape with you.

JACK: I am proposing a toast here.

NED: The champagne will go flat by the time you finish.

JACK: I'll start over from the beginning if you don't hush up.

NED: Quiet as a mouse.

JACK: May we all scale that wonderful peak of pleasure and enlightenment that comes from the right combination of combustibles—

NED: (overlapping) The right combination of combustibles—

JACK: How the hell did you know . . .

NED: It's the same one you gave at New Year's.

JACK: Oh my God, I'm going senile.

NED: Probably "from the right combination of combustibles."

JACK: Now don't be nasty.

NED: From the right combination of combustibles

TOGETHER: At the right time and the right place

JACK: Between the right people

NED: Between the right people

JACK: Between the right people. For that is . . .

TOGETHER: Despite what the philosophers may say . . .

JACK: What life is all about.

NED: Hear, hear.

All three clink glasses.

JACK: Everywhere, everywhere.

All drink, JACK from the bottle. ETHEL drains her glass quickly.

ETHEL: (*picking up her purse and gloves*) Well, gentlemen, you have certainly gotten me in the mood for a party. I am definitely ready for Arthur's.

JACK: You're not even giving me time to catch my breath.

NED: You can catch it tomorrow.

JACK: (*to NED*) Is that what you're wearing?

ETHEL: Ned's not joining us.

NED: I would have gone to the opening if I were to go anywhere.

JACK: I was only going because I thought you were going. I came here tonight to see you.

NED: Jack, this is your opening night.

JACK: That ended at midnight. And don't tell me you're tired, because it won't work.

ETHEL: So you're not coming to your own party.

JACK: (*helping ETHEL with her wrap*) Tell Arthur I'll be there for breakfast. Pancakes and peaches. If the party isn't going to last that long it's hardly worth attending. (*ETHEL and JACK kiss.*)

ETHEL: Well, then, you two enjoy the hell out of the rest of the evening.

JACK: You heard her, Ned. We have no choice now but to enjoy ourselves.

NED: If we have to, we have to.

ETHEL: I can see myself out from here.

NED: Give my best to Arthur.

ETHEL: Of course. (*ETHEL and NED kiss.*) And you keep thinking about Florence.

JACK: (*to NED*) You going back to Italy?

NED: Nightingale.

JACK: Oh.

ETHEL: A play. For me.

JACK: Aha. Yes. All those battle scenes.

ETHEL: Any messages for Ernestine if she should wander in?

JACK: Hie thee to a nunnery.

ETHEL: Yes, I'm sure that will delight her no end. Goodnight, gentlemen.

NED: Good night.

ETHEL exits. We hear the door close, then the sound of the elevator. NED and JACK hold for a moment and then both laugh.

JACK: There under full sail goes the Queen of the Nile.

NED: Consider yourself fortunate that she's leading your navy and not the enemy's. She cares tremendously about you.

JACK: I know, I know. But it's more fun to pretend she doesn't. She makes a wonderful sparring partner. Florence Nightingale. So you've begun trying to talk her out of Juliet already.

NED: I can't believe that's Arthur's idea.

JACK: He's all for it. More champagne? Or wine? Or both? (*starts to pour both bottles into NED's glass*)

NED: Just a little more champagne should do it. (*JACK pours.*) To Juliet.

JACK: To Juliet. How are you feeling?

NED: Restless. (*He clears some books from the desk and puts them in the bookcase.*)

JACK: I was hoping you'd still be up.

NED: That's probably what caused my restlessness.

JACK: There's always Arthur's party. We could make an entrance.

NED: My Ophelia costume hasn't been returned from the cleaners yet.

JACK: We could go.

NED: No . . . (*looks once more at the review*) My God, "a new and lasting *Hamlet*." You really have gone and done it this time.

JACK: Everyone at the theatre asked about you tonight.

NED: You and your everyones. I'm sure one person mentioned me in passing.

JACK: Is this modesty night? Why wouldn't people ask about you? Just because you've become the man in the iron mask up here. Yes, those of us with an historical bent were reminiscing about you just the other day.

NED: So, tell me about it.

JACK: I thought you had the full run-down already.

NED: I want to hear it from you.

JACK: I'd say I accomplished what I set out to do. The best response was from Patrick Murphy.

NED: New York's own authority on the English language.

JACK: He came back after the performance.

NED: Didn't get out fast enough, did you?

JACK: Believe me, I tried. And of course, I couldn't resist asking him what he thought.

NED: Then you deserve whatever you got.

JACK: "It would have been perfect, Barrymore, entirely perfect, but for one thing which jarred me no end. The way you pronounced 'body'. You must correct the delivery of that word, Barrymore; then your performance will be flawless. You must under no condition allow the word *body* to come out 'buddy' . . ."

They laugh.

NED: Sounds like you were reviewed by a bicycle pump. That's not bad—you only missed by one word.

JACK: I must confess, Uncle Jack did misbehave a little bit tonight.

NED: You mispronounced "ducats" when he wasn't listening.

JACK: I couldn't resist taking my curtain call with a saxophone under my arm.

NED: You did not. You didn't, did you?

JACK: I had one in my dressing room that I'd picked up a few days ago. I liked the look of it. Make a great place to hide an extra bottle during these difficult times. Put flowers over it.

NED: But you didn't take it on stage with you.

JACK: Was that bad taste?

NED: Probably. But then, I imagine even Hamlet had his outside interests.

JACK: Exactly. "Hey, Hamlet, can you come out and play?" "No, my father says I have to stay in and practice my revenge. And now, ladies and gentlemen, I would like to play for you *My Revenge*"—four hours of it. I probably should have played it on the saxophone. Do you think Hamlet should be played as a jazz musician?

NED: Not even Othello should be played that way. And the closet scene. Did that go well?

JACK: Like a baby's burp. It felt wonderful. How often do you get to seduce your own mother in front of a crowd?

NED: Were they with you?

JACK: I think that was one of those moments of hushed murmur that swept through the audience. I'm sure there were many who felt like yelling, "Is there a doctor in the house?" . . . I was quite sexual. And Blanche went all the way with it . . . I saw my own father up there tonight. No fictitious ghosts for me this special eve.

NED: Inspiration.

JACK: Ghosts . . . "It was a lovely day in June."

NED: What?

JACK: Did you know my old man was working on a play up in that nut house out on Long Island before he died? This thick. Page after page after page of "It was a lovely day in June. It was a lovely day in June. It was a lovely day in June." (*lights a cigarette*) Probably needed some reworking. Oh, the good doctor there was very sensitive to my concern. Told me not to worry. It had been brought on by syphilis and wasn't hereditary, just contagious. Said it right in front of the old man like he was a potted plant. Potted, perhaps . . . Three years of work to create four hours of entertainment. And at the end of the evening it's gone. The greatest Indian scout in the world wouldn't find a trace of it. Not even a pile of smoking embers left behind.

NED: There's practically a forest fire gathered at Arthur's this very moment to celebrate the event. I wouldn't worry about an Indian scout. I'd worry about a five alarm call.

JACK: (*picking up champagne bottle*) And when are you going to be a witness to the deed?

NED: As soon as possible. (*takes a sip from his glass*)

JACK: Are you just going to sip all night, or are you at some point going to become a full-blooded participant?

NED: You're the goddamn sprinter. I'm a long-distance man.

JACK: (*toasting NED*) The hare and the tortoise. (*both drink*) At an early and impressionable age I was taught to drink hard and fast—not only because you got more that way, but because it made you drunk. Alcohol is not something you quietly store in your cheeks for winter. It must be allowed a full cavalry charge at your brain. (*Drinks deeply from the bottle. Ned takes another sip.*) What's the matter, don't you want to get drunk with me?

NED: Each in his own way.

JACK: Don't you realize what a great reunion this is? Me and two of my dearest friends. (*to NED*) To you, who I haven't seen in three weeks, and (*to bottle*) to you, who I haven't seen in six months.

NED: And which "to you" did you miss more? (*leans back on the chaise, jostling the cart*)

JACK: Ah, you are getting a little tipsy. (*picks up second bottle of champagne*)

NED: "A little tipsy"—I feel like I'm about to witness the only meeting between Elizabeth and Mary Queen of Scots.

JACK: That's not drunk; that's obscure. Mary Queen of Scots?

NED: Have you taken a good look at yourself in tights lately? (*JACK points the bottle he is opening at NED, but opens it quietly.*) Gesundheit. Did you actually walk through the streets like that, or did you flap and fly over?

JACK: The world wants Hamlet, not Barrymore. Let them have Hamlet . . .

NED: Queen of Scots.

JACK: I'll have you know, sport, that one of the more delightful discoveries of the evening was just what a thrilling sensation it can be to rub erotically against a woman while ensconced in tights.

NED: Well, doesn't that prove they want Barrymore more than Hamlet? Hamlet may become a memory, but Barrymore will live on.

JACK: That's not what Mum Mum told me. "Waves and actors are very much alike."— This was from the wisdom of her deathbed, so you can't contradict it.—"Waves and actors are very much alike. They come for a little time, rise to separate heights, travel with varying speed and force, and then are gone, unremembered. Our good friend Joseph Jefferson has correctly observed, 'Nothing is as dead as a dead actor.'"

NED: Well, I'm sorry to contradict Mum Mum, but the great ones are remembered.

JACK: So what? It only improves the quality of the epitaph on the tombstone.

NED: What about the "obituary notice" in the *Times*?

JACK: Stone lasts longer. He was born, he died, and he did something in between.

NED: Why are you so gifted at finding the thorn in the laurels?

JACK: It finds me. (*retrieves his sword from the bar*) What's the point of doing something as well as you can if no one you care about sees it?

NED: Patrick Murphy saw it.

JACK: (*lifting cage cover with the tip of his sword*) Charlie didn't see it. You didn't see it. (*letting cover drop*) Michael didn't see it.

NED: Is she coming back later to see it?

JACK: She doesn't want to come back. She likes it in Paris. It appeals to her bohemian nature. I don't know when I'm going to see her and the little one again.

NED: She's one of the few women who's actually stood toe-to-toe with you. I think that's good for you.

JACK: Well, she has the better knockout punch.

NED: There's always another round to go.

JACK: I don't know how many more rounds I can take. I got a wonderful letter from her the other day. "We are such a shame, you and I. It is so much easier to think of you as 'my dearest' at this distance." I've got it with me somewhere if you want to take a look at it.

NED: Not really.

JACK: There's a P.S. on it just for you.

NED: Not tonight, Jack.

JACK: All right. Signed it, "Lovingly,

Michael, with special neck huggies from your little Trepie, who is sweeter than ever." (*NED rises quietly, crosses to bar for his pills, and takes one as unobtrusively as possible.*) John L. Sullivan never set up a knockout punch so well. "I hope this message will reach you in time to bring you my best wishes ever for much, much success, and in the proper tradition of the theatre—break a leg. *Merde.*" It reached me in time. Couldn't have been better. Dear Jack, you may be a wonderful Hamlet, but as a husband and father, you are an absolute flop.

NED: Don't you think you're overreacting to what she said? It sounds sincere to me.

JACK: Sincere, my ass. I'm the one who's married to her.

NED: That you are.

JACK: Do you think I should go to Paris?

NED: Now?

JACK: Now, at the end of the run, I don't know.

NED: You have an entire company depending on you right here in New York.

JACK: She keeps asking me to come to Paris.

NED: She can't possibly mean in the middle of a run. She knows the theatre better than that.

JACK: Her universe doesn't work that way. What more dramatic tribute than for me to forsake *Hamlet* for her? (*poking at the plants with his sword*) Not quite Helen of Troy, but if she can launch one ship across the waters, her day would be complete. She uses life like we use the stage. That's what I meant about her sincerity. The streets of gay Paree. I keep imagining her carrying on from cafe to cafe, surrounded by greasy Alsatians in dark berets, cigarettes dangling from their lascivious lips and red-hot lust in their eyes. They all look like drug smugglers to me . . .

NED: She's crazy about you. You have to have a little trust.

JACK: Trust? That's exactly why I have no faith in our money, because it's got that word plastered all over it. Like my father's second wife. There's a good argument for trust. Seduced me when I was fucking fifteen years old. That's why I have such trust in them. I even go around wondering whether you and Michael have ever had a little tête-à-tête, a fling, an affair, have gone to bed together, have laughed at me behind my back . . .

NED: That is really disgusting, Jack.

JACK: Well, I can't help it. That's what goes through my head.

NED: I don't even know how you could think that of us.

JACK: I know, I know.

NED: We've had nothing even remotely resembling an affair.

JACK: (turns to face NED) Don't you find her attractive?

NED: You want it both ways, don't you?

JACK: Well, my father's wife has been an eternal inspiration to me. Why, this very evening I had my own little fling before I came here. One of Payton Westmore's little drama students.

NED: Who's Payton Westmore?

JACK: What difference does it make? I certainly didn't have it with him.

NED: No, it's a familiar name.

JACK: One of your favourite performers. Mr. Conviction. "Dinner is served, I think."

NED: Ichabod Crane?

JACK: That's it!

NED: The guppy.

JACK: The guppy.

NED: He's got that wonderful mouth. It looks like he does all his acting through a straw. (he demonstrates)

JACK: Well cast as butlers and sardines.

NED: He's teaching acting?

JACK: Some half-assed program he's drummed up.

NED: They'll all end up looking like a collection of underwater performers.

JACK: And of course, he had to bring his little group to the performance.

NED: Then at least last night they had a chance to learn from someone who knew what he was about.

JACK: I'm afraid one of them learned more than she bargained for. You should have seen her. She looked like someone's goddamn kid sister. Without the make-up, the dress-up clothes, the fancy shoes and hat, she was just a fucking child. Tomboyish even. Seeing her peacefully asleep on the other pillow once I'd finished my patented impression of a bellowing bullmoose in heat, I just wanted to kill myself. I didn't deserve to be alive . . . Have I turned your stomach? . . . Her features weren't even fully formed yet. They were in the winter of their adolescence, not quite those of a woman.

NED: Not quite those of your wife, either.

JACK: No, definitely not quite those of my wife.

NED: While you're up, could we please have the Vivaldi?

JACK: Is the mood sagging?

NED: Vivaldi goes very well with champagne.

JACK: Why do I spend half my life feeling like I'm a character in a Ned Sheldon play? Always bits of music to keep things moving. No wonder life is so difficult. There's no music playing to coax us through our moods. (poking at NED with his sword) You should market a pair of musical suspenders we could all wear to get us through the day. (Returns to the desk, slips his sword under the typewriter, and picks up the champagne bottle he has left there.)

NED: The nice thing about music, Jack, is that it doesn't give you a hangover the next morning.

JACK: But I hear music every time I open a bottle. Put this to your ear and you can hear the sounds of the vineyard from whence it cameth. The breezes dancing through the vines. The sun whispering sweet nothings into the ear of the grape. I'll match Vivaldi note for note and sip for sip. Here, listen. (puts the bottle to NED's ear)

NED: That's going to spill, Jack.

JACK: Then I shall empty it. (drinks deeply)

NED: You really are in a mood tonight, aren't you?

JACK: That's right. (NED indicates the victrola.) The music . . . (crosses to victrola)

NED: Just be careful with the record.

JACK: I could commit . . . I could perform brain surgery right now if necessary. You needn't worry about the safety of your disk. And can I entrust you with the opening of another bottle?

NED: I'm not sure my teeth are up to it.

JACK: Sorry. That was tactless.

NED: That's okay.

JACK: This thing of yours has been dragging on forever. When the hell is it going to go away so we can start doing things again? (cranks the victrola)

NED: I enjoyed it more when we were arguing about Vivaldi and bottles. (JACK puts down the needle. Music begins: "Autumn" from Vivaldi's The Four Seasons.) Thank you. (JACK bows to NED, gently dances over and picks up the third bottle of champagne from the cart.) Oh, come on, Jack! We haven't even finished this one yet.

JACK: I want fresh. Don't worry; nothing will go to waste with me here.

NED: That's what I'm afraid of.

JACK: You've sobered up awfully quickly.

NED: Well, I'm never that far gone.

JACK: Well, I for one would love to see you that far gone. That's what we should dedicate tonight to. To getting us both rip-roaring, slap-happy, fall-on-our-face drunk.

NED: I doubt whether I have the stamina for any more drinking.

JACK: You might surprise yourself.

NED: Probably all over the carpet. I don't want you getting incoherent on me.

JACK: I will not get incoherent on you or your carpet. Unfortunately, I am never incoherent. (puts bottle #3 on the piano) All right, let's leave this to the fates. Heads we open another bottle; tails we stop . . . for a while. (realizing that he's wearing tights) Do you have any coins? Hamlet has no pockets.

NED: I think we should just make a decision.

JACK: (*sweeping up the bottle and beginning to open it*) All right. We'll do it this way: If I tug on this cork and it comes out, then we are meant to drink this bottle. If I tug on this cork and it doesn't come out, then obviously we are through for the night.

NED: Be careful, Jack: that bottle is not exactly ice cold—

The bottle explodes open.

JACK: Practically a military event! (*crosses to pour*)

NED: (*covering his glass with his hand*) I'm fine, Jack.

JACK: (*pouring anyway, letting the champagne cascade over NED's hand, the cart, and the carpet*) No, you're not—It doesn't stain!

NED: (*wiping his hands*) All right, Jack, what is it?

JACK: (*pause*) What we have here, Neddo, is a simple fact of nature. You can look to any evening sky for the example. A star always burns its brightest just before it fizzles out. (*NED slowly lights a cigarette*) I've just spent three years of my life building up to this precise moment. Got myself in pretty good shape for a forty year-old fart, changed my voice and made it *très, très élégant* to do the Bard his service. Worked my goddamn ass off. And I'm not complaining, believe me. It gave my life a nice edge. And then, poof, it's all over. The whole goddamn thing is like chasing butterflies. That's why we were put on a planet that spins around at twenty-five thousand miles an hour. To keep us from catching up with anything. "Ode on a Grecian Urn." The value in life is the pursuit, not the catching. After that, it's all downhill. I've done fucking *Richard the Third* and fucking *Hamlet*. What do I do for an encore? The *Kama Sutra*? It's all downhill from here. What am I going to do, Ned? (*sits*)

NED: There's fucking *Cyrano* and fucking *Liliom* and fucking *Richard the Second* and fucking *Lear* and some fucking Shaw and some fucking O'Neill and God knows there's some fucking lunatic tucked away in a garret this very moment writing the next perfect play for you.

JACK: I would have thought you would have taken me a little more seriously than that.

NED: It would be dangerous if we both took you seriously. Jack, everything I could possibly say to you, you know yourself. It wasn't giving up drink and working hard that gave you the desire to play Hamlet. It was the decision to do Hamlet that pushed you to shape up and, I'm sure, to love every minute of working your goddamn ass off. You're a demon when you're committed to something. It's amazing what you can accomplish when you put your mind to it. The effort of commitment, no matter to what, is the purest thing we've got going for us in this life.

JACK: That's right. We should all be committed. Commitment. Obsession. A goddamn horse race to cross the finish line on opening night. Ah, but before the gun goes off—my God, you are really part of something: A real struggle to break the back of this thing, and it's two steps forward and one step backward and there are days when you are convinced you are only half a step above imbecile and others you are absolutely blessed, and there's nothing like it, and you finally drag this behemoth over the finish line and they tell you to go do it again! Night after night recreating the same creation over and over again until you can do it in your sleep—until both you and it becomes corpses. Once I prove I can do it, I have no desire to do it again.

NED: There's a surprising amount to be learned precisely through the process of doing it over and over again. Eternal pursuit, Jack. I thought that's what you were after.

JACK: I don't know what I'm after.

NED: Jack, you're just feeling the same natural let-down everyone feels after a high point.

JACK: I know all about natural let-downs! . . . You don't think I've been miscast as a father and a husband?

NED: Not at all. Tonight is not the night to be summing up your life. Tonight is to celebrate. And there is one thing you must never lose track of in all of this, and that's what a rare gift you have. I'm sorry if that makes it seem a burden, but it kills me to see you having such a low regard for a talent that the rest of us would give anything to have.

JACK: Can I change this music?

NED: Change it, turn it off, whatever . . . (JACK lifts needle off the disk.) As an actor you seem to reside on the edge of a perpetual state of grace. Seeing you perform within that aura of grace is, for the most of us, the only inspiration available outside the cathedral.

JACK: So I'm the atheist's last hope, am I? And on the edge of what perpetual state do I seem to reside as a human being?

NED: You really are committed to being melancholic tonight, aren't you?

JACK: I just wish someone would let the world know that whatever heroic figure I may appear to be on the stage, it stops with the ringing down of the curtain. All those adoring faces. I've got to get out of this thing before I start needing those faces. (flourishing the bottle) This is the only thing I never tire of repeating. This and being with you. The only thing in your life that doesn't make sense is me. The epitaph for my tombstone shall read, "This sonuvabitch once knew Edward Sheldon." You know the only woman I can stand here in my royal tights and proclaim with full honesty that I loved her and she loved me in the truest sense of that godforsaken word was my grandmother. Mum Mum. God, how I

miss her. Why couldn't it have been her ghost up there with me tonight? The most idyllic time of my life was that period just before she died. We all knew it was just a matter of time. Out on the Sound. She rocking away beside me with one of her romances left open on her lap, dozing in the sun while I sketched my little heart out. And endless dreams floating across the sky. All wonderfully uncharted territory . . . (he laughs) A lovely day in June . . . And who's going to be by my side when I'm sitting there rocking away with a romance on my lap? . . . (turns away from NED) I guess you haven't chosen the right piece of music yet . . . How can you sleep at a time like this, Charlie! (strides to Charlie's cage and uncovers it) Morning, sport. (showing Charlie the champagne) Look what Uncle Jack has for you.

NED: Jack, don't give him that.

JACK: If it's good enough for us, it's good enough for him. Say, "I love you, Uncle Jack. I love you, Uncle Jack." (nothing) Louder. (still nothing) Say, "You're a jerk, Uncle Jack." Stubborn bird. I know you love me, even if you don't say anything. One of these days you and I are going to run away together. Fly away from all this bullshit, Charles. And why is such a pretty bird so cooped up?

NED: I would hardly say he's cooped up.

JACK: He shouldn't be in any goddamn cage. He should be out soaring with some cute little chickadee. That's what you want, isn't it, Charlie? Isn't it, sport?

NED: Charlie is a cockatoo, not a sparrow.

JACK: He may perform like a cockatoo, but inside every cockatoo is a sparrow, and that's just the way things are. Don't want you developing limp wings and going about on tiptoe, now, do we, Charlie? (opens the birdcage door) Come on out, Charlie.

NED: Jack, I don't want him flying around the apartment.

JACK: Sure you do. He's a bird. Birds are supposed to fly. It's their natural state. (*He looks to Charlie, who remains in the cage.*) A little shy, are we? By royal proclamation of the Prince of Denmark, you are now free. (*Charlie remains as before.*)

NED: Obviously, he doesn't want to come out, Jack.

JACK: Just like the rest of us. (*closes the cage door*) Give up freedom for free room and board and a few domestic trinkets. We've all been goddamn domesticated. Take away our primitive battle for survival and what have you got? (*to Charlie*) Fucking cockatoos, that's what you've got. No spirit. You don't deserve those wings, Charlie. You're a traitor to the species.

NED: Would you like him?

JACK: Would I like him if what?

NED: An opening night gift.

JACK: I couldn't take Charlie away from you. You've been together for years.

NED: Don't argue with me. You know I can't ever resist when the perfect gift gets together with the perfect recipient. It's been driving me crazy all week what I should get you. You two were made for each other.

JACK: A couple of old sparrows.

NED: That's right. Charlie's been a stuffy old cockatoo long enough.

JACK: This is on the level now? When I walk out of here, Charlie's coming with me?

NED: He can walk out of here with you, or you can fly out of here with him, Jack. I'll leave that up to the two of you.

JACK: Well, Charlie old sport, you and I are going to have some times together.

NED: But you don't have to make him into a sparrow overnight.

JACK: I'll do my best to keep him on the path. For a while. All right—time to get some sleep, sport. (*covers the cage*) You're gonna need it. (*Using the wine bottle and the champagne bottle as if they were binoculars, he looks about.*) All right, where is it?

NED: What?

JACK: (*crosses to desk*) Aha! And what have we here? (*picks up the manuscript in its folio*)

NED: Another old friend.

JACK: What are you going to do with it?

NED: I thought I'd take another crack at it. I still can't tell whether this is the best play I've ever written or the worst. And we all know what your vote was.

JACK: I never said I didn't like it. It was a little too high minded for me. Never any real sense of struggle for the character. Whenever he was about to do something "naughty," the ghost of his dear dead mother would appear in a blaze of light and music to scare him towards the right path. (*laughs*)

NED: She didn't scare him; she inspired him. She reminded him of his higher nature. The decisions were still his.

JACK: Yes, but they were so predictable. They were the playwright's decisions, not the character's.

NED: All my plays are like that.

JACK: No, they're not! You were the first to put on the stage real people with real problems. Right from *Salvation Nell* on down. Genuine conflict and wonderfully playable characters. You've stripped this down to a morality play. *Everyman and His Mother.* (*flings the folio onto the desk*) An old ham like me needs something more to strut around with. I thought you were writing a new play for Al Woods to produce this season.

NED: That's it.

JACK: But all of Broadway is out there gnashing its teeth in anticipation of the latest Ned Sheldon creation.

NED: What will all the fashionable thespians be playing for spring?

JACK: You're not upset by what I said about the play, are you?

NED: Only because there are times I feel the same way about it. I think I wrote better when I was twenty. At least then I had something to say. Or the security of ·the illusion I had something to say. The joy of ignorance. I'm becoming a sentimental sop.

JACK: You have more to say than anybody else I know.

NED: Of course . . . But do I have any more to write?

JACK: Someone in mind for the part?

NED: Don't worry. I'm not going to ask you to turn it down twice . . . Basil Sydney.

JACK: Are you serious?

NED: Why wouldn't I be serious? He and I have talked about it. It would be a good vehicle for him.

JACK: A cement truck would be a good vehicle for him. Doris Keane's husband?

NED: What has that got to do with anything?

JACK: (pacing) First you gave him your woman and now you're giving him my part. He stole your role and now he's stealing mine!

Isn't it enough you made her a star? Now this? Are you writing one for their child as well?

NED: He's right for the part, Jack.

JACK: I have yet to see anything he's right for, other than carrying a sandwich board along 42nd Street!

NED: Why are you carrying on? You had first crack at the play.

JACK: I know, but to be told that he's second choice! That's as devastating as finding out what your ex-wife's husband looks like. I just don't understand some of the things you do. I see you haven't changed the title yet.

NED: No.

JACK: Good. He deserves a play called *The Lonely Heart*. Sounds like he should have written it. *The Lonely Heart* by Basil Sydney. Christ, it doesn't even sound like a Ned Sheldon play. *The Nigger, The Boss,* even *Princess Zim Zim*— now those are titles of Ned Sheldon plays. *The Lonely Heart* is too milkish.

NED: That's a new one.

JACK: Trying to milk our emotions before we've even sat down. Jesus! . . . My God— do you know how many good actors would give their left ball to be in a Ned Sheldon play? You could open a pool hall.

NED: I was hoping for a little better monument than that.

JACK: Ned, we could exchange ghosts. What would you say to my taking it home and reading the changes. Maybe all it needs is the perspective of an old ham. Give it the Florence Nightingale touch.

NED: I'd rather you didn't. It's the only corrected copy I have.

JACK: (picks up the folio) I'll read it here, then.

NED: I want to do some more work first.

JACK: I'll come back later in the week. We could spend the entire day hacking through it. We haven't done that in ages. It would be wonderful.

NED: I need to get through it myself.

JACK: (*pause*) All right. (*puts folio on desk and picks up wine bottle*) One way or the other, though, you probably need some time away from it. Why don't you spend the day with me tomorrow? We'll only do what you're able to do, but at least we'll get out of here. You can't hibernate with this thing, Ned. You've got to give it its eviction notice. You'll probably surprise yourself once you get yourself out of here.

NED: Maybe you're right.

JACK: Of course I'm right. The two of us together are far more important than any goddamn play or any goddamn part. It's all a poor substitute for a night out on the town. From now on, more time together. Now there's a toast: More time together! (*swigs deeply from his wine bottle*)

NED: Yes, of course, more time together.

JACK: You seem a little remote there.

NED: I'm just tired is all.

JACK: You're not telling me to go, are you?

NED: Well, maybe that's not such a bad idea. It is getting late.

JACK: No stamina, hey kid?

NED: I guess not.

JACK: Am I boring you?

NED: I'm just tired. That's all.

JACK: I just want to make sure that there's

no problem when I leave here. You're always so reluctant to bring things up.

NED: (*overlapping*) Your imagination is running wild.

JACK: (*sits close to NED*) My imagination is running wild because I'm worried about our friendship. We haven't seen enough of each other lately. We don't do anything together anymore. You won't even talk to me about your play. Next, you'll be asking me for a divorce as well. I'll tell you something—our friendship means more to me than my marriage to Michael; that's how important it is. And what about you? Is that how you feel too?

NED: Yes.

JACK: That was an awfully hesitant yes.

NED: No hesitation, Jack.

JACK: Do you still love me, then? Because I love you, you sonuvabitch. I'd do anything for you. You know that, don't you?

NED: Yes.

JACK: You'd better know it.

NED: I know it.

JACK: (*rising, he kicks the hassock*) Then goddamn it, you remote sonuvabitch, get up off your ass and give me what I wanted a long time ago. I want a hug, you bastard.

NED: You and your hugs.

NED gets up with some difficulty. They hug.

JACK: Good. Now I can go pee with a clear conscience.

NED: Oh, God, don't remind me. I've been trying to distract myself for the last half hour.

JACK: We could pee.

NED: That's the coward's way out, Jack.

JACK: I can only hold my breath for so long.

NED: Well, go pee. You know where it is. I'll wait.

JACK starts to exit, then turns and crosses toward the balcony.

NED: Where are you going, Jack? It's the other way.

JACK: (*opening the balcony doors*) This way I can relieve myself and get a breath of fresh air at the same time.

NED: You're not seriously planning on pee-ing off the balcony, are you?

JACK: Sure. I do it a lot.

NED: Jack.

JACK: (*face-to-face with NED*) One pees where one has to. For God's sake, don't look so shocked. Just think back to when you were a kid and you had to go, so you peed in the neighbour's bushes.

NED: Jack, I have never peed anywhere but the toilet in my entire life.

JACK: (*a pause to take this in*) Then tonight is the night for a new pee experience. Come on—there's room for two on the balcony. (*takes NED one step upstage*)

NED: (*stops*) Jack, I will not pee off the balcony onto 83rd Street. Suppose there's someone passing underneath?

JACK: Good for the hair. Just come this way and shut up. You're such a prude sometimes.

NED: (*resisting*) I'm no prude! I just don't want to pee off the balcony onto someone's head.

JACK: It's going to make you feel better. No one is going to see us and no one is going to pass underneath us. We are allowed to look before we pee. (*takes NED upstage*)

NED: (*stopping them*) I want you to know, I'm not going to do this.

JACK: You're just coming to watch me, then?

NED: I am being dragged against my will.

JACK: No man can claim to have led a full life until he has peed off the balcony with his best friend.

NED: That is ridiculous.

JACK: Admit it. You're dying to do it.

NED: I am not dying to do it!

JACK: But a little bit of appeal there? A small inkling of fun? I know we were not put on this earth to enjoy ourselves, but certainly a little pee off the balcony is not going to hurt anything.

NED: (*pauses to consider this*) I would feel like an idiot.

JACK: Do you have to go?

NED: Yes.

JACK: Do you think you'll make it all the way to the toilet?

NED: No.

JACK: Then . . .

NED: You've made your point.

They go out onto the balcony, framed by the open balcony doors.

JACK: All right, here's what you do.

NED: I know what to do.

JACK: Pardon me. I only meant that you've got to pick out a target.

NED: I am not having a competition, Jack.

JACK: All right. Just pull it out and do it your own way. (*a moment*) Look at that, old Neddy's peeing off the top.

NED: Will you watch where you're aiming!

JACK: Relax, will you?

NED: Oh, God. I feel like I've been saving it up for three weeks.

JACK: Ohhh! It feels so good. "What would he do had he the motive and the cue for passion that I have?"

TOGETHER: "He would drown the stage with tears."

JACK: If there were more light, we'd have a rainbow for everyone to look at.

NED: Oh, my God. There's someone across the street. He's looking right up here.

JACK: He is not.

NED: It looks like a policeman. If this gets into the papers, Jack!

JACK: "Playwright and Player Caught Peeing on Police."

NED: Is he waving?

JACK: Hello, officer!

NED: Jack, come on. (*starts to cross into the apartment, buttoning his trousers*)

JACK: Making the quick exit, are we, sport?

NED: I'm afraid I can't quick anything.

JACK: Then I, Gunga Din, shall carry you inside.

NED: No one is carrying me anywhere.

Everything freezes. Then NED starts to cross toward the chaise and JACK turns upstage. Blackout.

ACT TWO

Act Two begins where Act One finished. NED continues his cross as the lights come up. He takes and lights a cigarette from the cart, removes his tie, and drapes it over the back of the chaise. JACK remains upstage, gazing out over the city. Once NED's business is complete, JACK closes the balcony doors. They are uncomfortable with one another.

NED: The sun must be poised in the wings by now.

JACK: Mmmm. My favourite time. The most optimistic period of the day . . . I wish we were somewhere with a different view.

NED: Remember the roof in Florence?

JACK: Now that was spectacular. In a muted—

NED: Florentine way.

JACK: Yes. But beautiful.

NED: There we were, overlooking the Arno River, and you kept saying, "But Ned, there's nothing like the sea."

JACK: But there is nothing like the sea.

NED: Yes, but at that moment there was nothing like sitting on the slanted roof of the hotel . . .

JACK: L'Abbazia . . .

NED: ...overlooking the Arno River, waiting for the sun to rise.

JACK: A river is running water. The sea is Seurat. The sun is setting. A calm sea, with just enough motion to break the changing light into those incredible dots of colour. The bits of blue and pink and white. It's reassuring to discover that this genius came from somewhere real. Seurat, if he will pardon my presumptuousness, is obviously a man of the sea, who views the entire world in the memory of the reflected light of a sun sliding into the ocean. His painting is filled with last glimpses . . .

They are both quiet. Then JACK starts to sing "Ch'Ella Mi Creda Libero" from Act III of Puccini's La Fanciulla Del West. *NED joins in.*

JACK: "Ch'ella mi creda libero e lontano . . ."

TOGETHER: "Sopra una nuova via di redenzione! Aspetterà ch'io torni . . . E passeranno i giorni, e passeranno i giorni. Ed io, ed io non tornerò . . ."

JACK goes out of tune on the first "Ed io," enthusiastically. They stop singing.

JACK: And what were we drinking then?

NED: I think it was something you found in a cave. You must have squeezed it from a stalactite, it was so vile.

JACK: (*lights a cigarette*) That stuff was nothing. Michael nearly fired . . . divorced me one time when we were holed up in our little sailing craft with nothing to drink and I was forced to imbibe the alcoholic fuel from her curling iron. Haven't impressed you a bit, have I? Remember why we were there? I was getting over Katherine and you were getting over Doris. What a choice of reminiscence. Ironic, hey Neddo? (*crosses to the piano for his hat and coat*) Why don't we get out of here? Go over to Child's or something?

NED: You want pancakes now?

JACK: Have a coffee. We can go see Sarah. It's been so long she probably thinks we're both dead. (*hat on*) When I start babbling about Seurat and the sea, I know it's time for some fresh air (*coat on*), a little change of scenery.

NED: (*sitting back on the chaise*) Our pee was about as much change of scenery as I can handle right now. If you're getting restless, then you go on. I'm fine here. I should be asleep anyway.

JACK: Jesus, when is this thing going to be over with, anyway? You're supposed to be getting better, not worse. What the hell kind of doctors have you been seeing, anyway?

NED: Coast-to-coast, Jack.

JACK: I've got a doctor friend who's performed absolute miracles for me.

NED: I don't need a hangover specialist to look me over.

JACK: That was nice. He's not a hangover specialist. This man is a doctor. The guy got great grades in medical school. That I know for a fact. He is not one of those high-polished society assholes who scraped through by the skin of their perfect white teeth. Those goddamn shingles they hang up should list their grades so you know if you're dealing with someone who knows his business or someone who got by peeking over someone's shoulder.

NED: Carl is a fine doctor.

JACK: Then why aren't you getting better? It's been a goddamn year.

NED: Closer to two, actually.

JACK: Two years for a tonsilitis reaction!

NED: Why don't we call it a night, Jack?

JACK: I have no place to go. I gave up my one and only home when I married Michael: my little hideaway on Fourth.

NED: Aren't you being a little melodramatic?

JACK: Probably. I don't want to go home. Call my doctor and then I'll go home.

NED: I don't want another doctor within ten miles of me.

JACK: (removes his coat and hat) What the hell is going on, Ned?

NED: There's nothing going on.

JACK: For God's sake, why do I always have to drag everything out of you? Why not this one time you volunteer the information? I'm tired of playing guessing games with you.

NED: All I said was that I was tired of seeing doctors. Is that such an unusual feeling after seeing as many as I have over the last two years?

JACK: I can't stand it when you're being heroic. Tell me, Ned.

NED: (considers for a moment, then walks to the bar) I saw Carl today.

JACK: And?

NED: This . . . thing has gotten into the bloodstream. (starts to take out his pills)

JACK: What does that mean?

NED: That there's no stopping it. A steadily deteriorating ankylosis—a sort of marauding arthritis. The curvature and stiffness will just go on unchecked. It's a condition they don't seem to know what to do with. (takes the pill, making no attempt to hide it this time)

JACK: What do you mean, "they don't know"?

NED: They don't know. It's going to spread through every joint in my body until I'm stiff as a board. Aside from that I'm in perfect health. It's definitely not fatal. It's just that at some point in the not-too-distant future, I won't be able to move a muscle of my body. Every joint will have turned to stone.

JACK: You've been sitting there all night with that on your mind?

NED: Either get rid of the pity right now or leave.

JACK: I'm just stunned, that's all.

NED: (leaning on the piano) Well, picture the possibilities. I might actually get a choice of positions. I swear that's what Carl said to me. As soon as he said it, I knew it was the kind of thing only you would appreciate. I told Carl to send me a brochure of the possible poses. Don't you find it funny? I may actually get to choose the position of my final petrification. Perhaps that's what distinguishes man from trees. That ability to choose. Maybe you could help me, Jack. What do you think of the position I'm in now? This is "the interested listener in semi-repose."

JACK: You look normal enough, if that's what you mean.

NED: That's not bad, then. You know who we need here? Bobby Jones. Now that he's finished designing *Hamlet* he can come and pose me. What do you think would be the most popular position? (indicates the poses as he speaks) Sitting-to-tea? Sitting-on-the-throne? Maybe just waiting-at-the-bar. Perhaps the poignant artiste pose would be more in character. Of course! The basic funeral position. (gradually lies back on the chaise to demonstrate) Arms folded across the chest with space in the clenched fist for a fresh bouquet of flowers every day. That would be the "he-never-looked-better-in-his-life" pose. Imagine this thing lying there motionless, and as you look at it, it suddenly speaks: "Hello, how are you today?" Quite a shock to the unsuspecting, wouldn't you say?

JACK: Ned . . .

NED: Something more classical, like "The Thinker"?

JACK: That's enough.

NED: Have I turned your stomach?

JACK: Several different directions at once.

NED: But you're the only one I can really be gruesome with. I haven't had this much fun in ages. Don't go soft now . . . You're the one who wanted to know.

JACK: Well, now I know. The first example was vivid enough.

NED: (*a considerable pause, during which NED composes himself and manages to sit up again, involving some pain and difficulty*) If I had known we were to arrive here this evening, I would have saved the Vivaldi for now . . . Please don't feel that you have to either cheer me up or give me hope. I do not want to hear in our conversation: miracle cures, faith healing, specially brewed teas, newly discovered exercises, more sun, more rain, (*rises awkwardly, using furniture from this point on to steady himself*) the restorative value of mountain air, sulphur baths, or any of it. I don't think these deletions should have any major effect on that treasure chest that is our usual source of conversation.

JACK: I find it hard to ignore.

NED: Then I apologize for not keeping it to myself.

JACK: You don't think that at some point we would have noticed. Especially if you had chosen the funeral position.

NED: Yes, but by that time I would have fully dealt with it. It's still a little new to me as well.

JACK: And if I hadn't paid my little visit tonight? You would just be sitting here yourself, dealing with it. (*NED turns away, laughs quietly.*) You don't think talking about it with someone might help.

NED: Help what, Jack? All talk would do is postpone my coming to grips with it.

JACK: I find talking to you helps me.

NED: It doesn't sound like it ever solves anything, though.

JACK: Well, if nothing else, you've certainly put *Hamlet* and me into perspective. I thought you were really enjoying yourself. You're a better actor than I am.

NED: I was enjoying myself. And I was genuinely thrilled at your success. All of that was legitimate. But what I need most is time to work this thing through alone.

JACK: How on earth are you going to keep from blowing your brains out in here?

NED: I won't be able to manage the trigger.

JACK: Unless you choose the suicidal pose.

NED: That has never been one of the options I have allowed myself to consider.

JACK: That would be the first I'd go for.

NED: (*after a moment*) No. Madness. If I wanted to give myself something to worry about, it wouldn't be blowing my brains out. Madness. Being buried alive in this body. Makes up for my not going down with Charlie Frohman on the *Lusitania*. That's when I ended up being best man at George Foote's wedding at the last minute. Fate. Saved from a sinking ship to be presented with this. It's like stepping over the banana peel and falling into the open manhole. Do you believe in the influence of the mind, Jack? The influence of the mind over the functions of the body? Do you believe a man could willfully destroy his own body?

JACK: I have often been accused of that very crime.

NED: I'm not talking about physical abuse. It's just that over the last few months my head—it's like an overloaded fuse box. It's even reached the point where I almost believe that I have somehow contrived to bring this thing on myself.

JACK: How can you think that?

NED: How? It's easy. Effortless. My thoughts have a life force of their own. But you have to admit, it's a fascinating concept. Just the opposite of faith healing which is so much in vogue these days. Faith punishing.

JACK: And what were your sins? Too many sweets? Too many holidays abroad? Too many dinner jackets? Enjoying yourself with the likes of me? Being inordinately well liked and respected? Too much success? What?

NED: I would have thought you would have taken me a little more seriously than that.

JACK: And do you think Charlie Frohman willed his own drowning?

NED: Maybe.

JACK: Then why can't I will myself to fly?

NED: Perhaps our positive yearnings aren't as "determined" as our negative ones. Jack, I'm not saying I willed this disease, that I sat down one day and decided to start turning myself into a rock. It's just that some people spontaneously recover and some people don't. I didn't. Why? I fight everything. Why didn't I fight this? . . . (composes himself) I can only assume that on some subterranean level where this kind of decision is made, I decided that this was right for me.

JACK: The body is only flesh and blood. It's

just a thing that walks and talks and sleeps and eats and pees off the balcony . . . What's so terrible about that, that you would want to turn it to stone?

NED: I don't know.

JACK: Of course you do. (pause) Doris?

NED: (regains his former control) Whatever happened between Doris and me has nothing to do with what we are talking about.

JACK: (after a moment) The curtain has descended . . . More Vivaldi? Or may I recommend more of this? (indicates the champagne)

NED: (taking his glass from the piano) Our evening of wonderful intoxication.

JACK: (pouring for NED) And more time together.

NED: Yes. More time together. (They toast each other and drink.)

JACK: To our last chance to sail to Hong Kong.

NED puts his glass down on the piano and tries to take off his smoking jacket with some awkwardness. JACK helps him and leaves the jacket on the piano.

NED: Another insane evening.

JACK: We were so close to giving it all up and disappearing.

NED: Almost.

JACK: Maybe this is the time to do it.

NED: Hong Kong?

JACK: It doesn't have to be Hong Kong. It can be anywhere. But if you're going to be cooped up, I guarantee there are better places than here.

NED: Do I close my eyes and make a wish?

JACK: No, really, I'm serious. We've talked for years about getting out of here and trying something different.

NED: This wasn't quite what I meant by something different.

JACK: I think we should do it.

NED: Then pardon me while I change into my walking shoes.

JACK: I'll haul you over my shoulder and carry you out.

NED: Why not stick postage on my head and mail me?

JACK: Ned, we've got to get out of here while we still have our dignity.

NED: Is being bedridden in New York considered undignified these days?

JACK: It has nothing to do with being bedridden. I mean, even if you weren't ill, what would you be doing? Just more of the same, over and over. We don't have our noses pressed against the window any more. We're on the inside. We've done it all. Is there ever again going to be anything that's going to give you the thrill you felt when you learned that Minnie Maddern Fiske had agreed to present on Broadway the first play of an unknown Harvard hooligan named Edward Sheldon? I'm sick of leading my life like a spooked jack rabbit except when I'm with you. What do I need this city for? Because I'm an actor? I would much rather have painted a Hamlet than performed one. I act because it's the easiest and the only way I can earn enough money to get out of here. That's why I'm saying, "Goodbye, Broadway, hello, Hollywood," because there you make more for less. You don't even have to speak loud. You just make faces all day long like all the other monkeys in the zoo. But Ned, the two of us, now . . . we'd be leaving like champions.

NED: Leaving what? This room? This city? This planet? This skin? My God—I sound like a librettist. What are we talking about? Why don't you do something from *Hamlet* and lift rather than batter me? I want some beauty. It's been your evening long enough. I want *Hamlet* and champagne. To sleep or drink some more. And *Hamlet*!

JACK: Not Barrymore? I'm giving you my best Hamlet now; aren't you listening?

NED: You're giving me your best ten-year-old. (*JACK takes a long drink from the bottle.*) I see we've chosen "to drink some more."

JACK: I, for one, refuse to go to bed while there remains unfinished a bottle of champagne.

NED: A man of principle after all.

JACK: The principles of a pirate. I am definitely a man of the sea. I was born at the wrong time. I belong with Fletcher Christian or Christopher Columbus. Yo ho ho and a bottle of . . . Mumms. Someday someone is going to cast me as a pirate, and then I shall truly not know who or what I am. Old pirates never die; they just go to Hollywood. And if there were no ink left in this world, what would you be doing to while away the hours?

NED: I could be the ship's figurehead. (*They laugh.*)

JACK: What would you *be*?

NED: A disappointment to my mother.

JACK: My number-one fan.

NED: Oh, Mother . . . When my mother was pregnant with me, she used to go to the Art Institute in Chicago and sit in front of all the Madonnas and pray that her child would be an artist. I have too many dinner jackets to be an artist. Her second choice was a grandchild factory. Fortunately, my brother and sister have taken that pressure off me, but I would have liked to have done my fair share. It would have been interesting to have a child. Children have a way of bringing you back into the world.

JACK: And of driving you out the front door as well.

NED: Why would anyone bother having us?

JACK: (*after a moment*) You really can't allow yourself to remain cooped up in this—palatial time bomb.

NED: Unless you put wheels on me, wherever I am, I will be cooped up.

JACK: But if we're there together . . .

NED: We can be here together.

JACK: No, we can't! While you're in here writing—dictating?—your plays and becoming morbid, I'll be out in California having my profile impressed into celluloid in order to entertain the imbeciles of the world. One trained monkey on the West Coast and one on the East. What are we going to do, become pen pals?

NED: No one's forcing you to go to California.

JACK: Money, Ned. That's what's forcing me to go to California. Money. Why are you so terrified of the possibility that there may just be something better?

NED: I'm not terrified of the possibility of something better.

JACK: (*opening balcony doors*) Don't tell me you've never been tempted to turn around at the height of all of your many accomplishments and say, (*crossing onto balcony and calling*) "I'm sorry; this isn't enough!"

NED: Of course I've thought that. Everyone does at one time or another.

JACK: Well, three cheers for everyone! Oh, Ned, I know places that will make you cry just to breathe the air. Places that would be spectacular in their rightness.

NED: But everyone we enjoy is here.

JACK: We'll send them all maps.

NED: Old Woolcott can bring all his pigeons.

JACK: And leave all his effete sarcasm here.

NED: A community of snobs getting some good healthy dirt on their hands.

JACK: First let's get us there.

NED: What about *Hamlet*?

JACK: Fuck Hamlet. Let him make his own travel arrangements. I'll leave behind a plaster mold of my head and they can cast it as "Alas Poor Yorick" and still keep my name on the marquee. I would be miscast as John Barrymore if I backed down now. The real Barrymore would take his brief pause for effect, raise his bottle aloft, (*he demonstrates*) and say, "Fuck it. I'm going through with it, and the hell with everything else!"

NED: And what would the real Edward Sheldon say?

JACK: He would say, "It is rather selfish and indulgent, but maybe if I just regard it as a favour to Jack . . ."

NED: All right. Where did you have in mind?

JACK: What about . . . (*he is at a loss for a moment*)

NED: Mm-hm.

JACK: What about—what about the land of Gauguin, Ned? What about that? We'd be a couple of old pirates. Bwana kings on a remote

Tahitian paradise with native boys waiting on us (*pours champagne for NED*) and the women carrying their perfect bare bosoms to us like vendors in the marketplace, oh Christ. We have enough money to have a house built on stilts along the beach. The sea, Ned. There's nothing like it, is there.

NED: No, there isn't.

JACK: The smell.

NED: The sound.

JACK: Music, absolute music.

NED: To sleep by the sea.

JACK: The waves crashing against the shore.

NED: Just washes the tension out of me every time.

JACK: Our heartbeat, our breathing, everything synchronizes with the sound of the sea.

NED: Irrevocable evidence that we did indeed, one majestic moment, rise from the sea.

JACK: Christ, we'd have that every day, Ned. The whole show. Bullfrogs and crickets at night. Rare birds to wake us in the morning. Charlie bird would love it. And your room would be overlooking the bay with a huge window, so you'd be able to see all the comings and goings. You wouldn't miss a thing.

NED: I can't.

JACK: Why not?

NED: Because I can't.

JACK: What do you mean, you can't?

NED: Because getting to the balcony (*rises and crosses to the cart to take a cigarette*) is going to be an adventure for me. I can't go to Tahiti. Allow me to be a little realistic.

JACK: I thought you agreed with me. It would be wonderful and you know it.

NED: For three days and then we'd both be bored.

JACK: How can the most beautiful place in the world be boring? It's people like you who ruined the Garden of Eden. Are you really that jaded that you can't appreciate the purity of it?

NED: Me? You're the one with the most bizarre, jaded way of life of any man this side of Gomorrah.

JACK: That's right, be sarcastic. We are both so goddamn clever, we're going to clever ourselves into a fucking hole in the ground.

NED: Jack . . .

JACK: Ned, I want to take care of you. Is that so terrible of me?

NED: What makes you think I want to be taken care of?

JACK: Well, you're sure as hell not going to be able to do it yourself.

NED: Are you proposing to me?

JACK: Yes.

NED: I know I must be the envy of all New York, but I don't accept.

JACK: Why not?

NED: Being stored away in a tropical bird cage is not my idea of fun. I know you mean well, but for once in your life would you fully consider what you're saying? There we'd be on your island and I'd be totally dependent on you and you'd be there stuck with me. How long before you got restless again? A week?

You've just opened this very evening in *Hamlet* and already you're tired of that. What would you do when you got restless? Leave me behind in Tahiti?

JACK: Of course not.

NED: Then what the hell would you do? Drag me around like a ventriloquist's dummy?

JACK: Then you come up with something.

NED: There's nothing to come up with.

JACK: So what are you going to do here?

NED: I'll give dancing lessons. (*he adjusts back onto the chaise*)

JACK: You don't let down for a minute, do you?

NED: You could put the Grand Canyon in the gap between your imagination and reality.

JACK: Just because you're too frightened to take a chance . . . I meant every word of it.

NED: You only mean things for a little while. If you don't believe me, then ask Emily . . . (*JACK picks up his bottle from the piano, drinks*) I'm sorry, Jack. That just came out. This is not a good time for me to be with people.

JACK: Too truthful?

NED: Too edgy.

JACK: Well, don't worry about it. I just got carried away and you helped me return safely to earth.

NED: Sounds like I caused a crash landing.

JACK: Just ruffled my feathers is all.

NED: I was doing what was best for me.

JACK: Of course. And we both know who

this should really be happening to, don't we? If there were any real justice, which obviously there isn't.

NED: That is not a very healthy train of thought to be following.

JACK: But that's what you've been thinking, haven't you?

NED: I never, ever even remotely suggested something like that.

JACK: But you thought it, didn't you?

NED: I couldn't live with myself if I thought like that.

JACK: (*seizing his sword from the desk*) Well, maybe it would do you good to have a thought or two like that. I mean, what did you think when this apparition staggered fourteen floors up the goddamn fire escape to make his joyful appearance and you could barely walk to the fire escape? Were you inspired by that vision? Did you think, "Ah, if only I had led the life of the degenerate, I too would be able to climb fire escapes at any hour of the day or night."? We've learned something tonight, Ned. I think it's my responsibility to set myself forth as an example to our youth. Go ahead, admit it.

NED: This was meant for me, not you. It's that simple.

JACK: And why is that? Why you and not me?

NED: Because it would destroy you.

JACK: (*touches NED with the tip of his sword*) And there we have it folks, don't we?

NED: Look—no one deserves this. It's a grotesqueness. Don't you understand I'm going to become a freak? Why are we talking about this like it's some child's toy to take turns with?

JACK: I'm glad one of us has this thing under control. Two hysterics on a night like this could be downright dangerous.

NED: One is dangerous enough.

JACK: There's not a goddamn thing I can do for you, is there? Aside from making things worse.

NED: You're not making things worse, believe me.

JACK: Don't coddle me! I'm certainly not making them better . . . You know what they say about good intentions.

NED: At least the road is paved.

JACK: Why didn't you tell me sooner?

NED: So I could avoid scenes like this. They're not good for either of us. That's why I need to keep my doors locked for a while. I don't want coming here to be unpleasant. I don't want you all forced to draw straws to see whose turn it is next to pay the obligatory visit to old Ned Sheldon. I won't have that.

JACK: I, for one, will be here so often you'll get sick at the sight of me.

NED: You sound like a small boy being brave for his father.

JACK: What the hell do you want me to be? You're the goddamn playwright! What does someone say in a situation like this? I want to make things better and I can't! Do you know what that's doing to me?

NED: Nothing that that doctor friend of yours couldn't cure, I hope.

JACK: The one time I want to hit you and you can't even defend yourself.

NED: And the one time I want to kick you in the ass and I can't lift my leg high enough.

JACK: (*pause.*) Well, I'm in the mood to cause some real damage.

NED: You need a good brawl.

JACK: A little healthy head-smashing.

NED: I shouldn't be much of a challenge. Here, (*pulling out a cushion*) why don't you bang away at this pillow?

JACK: I don't want to hit a pillow.

NED: It'll make you feel better.

JACK: I don't want to feel better. (*begins to circle the room*) It's a wonderful scenario we have here. You'll be permanently squared away against your problems. Tucked cozily into your little cocoon. And I will perpetually fly like a bird from mine. A couple of wind-up toys. I will do *Hamlet* tomorrow night and I will get drunk tomorrow night and I will rant and rave tomorrow night and what are you going to do? Spout? Have a staff of gnomes scribbling down your precious words? *The Lonely Heart, The Lonely Liver, The Lonely Kneecap!* You'd think between the two of us, one of us would have the guts to come up with something different. Well, I don't care anymore about any fucking thing. The champagne has gone flat. My stomach is completely bloated, as is my brain, and I am bored. (*smashes the glass of a picture on the wall with his sword hilt, then crosses quickly to the desk and picks up the manuscript*) You don't mind if I tear your play to shreds, do you? Just for something to do. Would that upset you? Would it be just a small inconvenience? A large inconvenience? Hey, Stony, I'm talking to you. (*he dangles the folio in front of NED*)

NED: If you insist on being upset, I would like to suggest you do it somewhere else. (*reaches for the script.*)

JACK: (*pulling the folio away*) You mean, just let things fizzle out? No dramatic gesture? I don't think so. I think two clever fellows like ourselves can come up with better than that.

(*tosses the folio to the piano bench*) Can I tear up just a couple of pages? For effect. (*Guards the manuscript by keeping his sword tip pressed against it.*) Does it make any difference to you? Does anything make any difference to you? Never out of control. Never the inappropriate gesture. Never the wrong piece of clothing. This is a wonderful arrangement we've got here. You get to do all the giving and I get to do all the taking. Well, I'm tired of playing the villain. This may come as a big shock to you, sport, but I swear, giving all the time can be just as selfish as taking all the time. Ah, if you ignore me, I will calm down. Of course. The adult and the child. Perfect.

NED: Eventually you're going to sober up—and you're not going to be happy at remembering this.

JACK: You will forgive me, won't you?

NED: You're only hurting yourself. (*JACK opens the folio with the point of his sword.*) Jack, how far are you going to take this stupidity?

JACK: (*picking up the title page*) Just the title page. You were going to change the title anyway, weren't you? I know I'd probably kill the sonuvabitch that did this to me.

NED: Is that a hint?

JACK: Have you ever had a physical fight?

NED: Why—is it time for a new fight experience?

JACK: (*impaling the title page on his upended sword*) "You take the high road, and I'll take the low road . . ."

NED: Is this how you'd have taken care of me in paradise?

JACK: Do you think I could do an entire act in one tear?

NED: Why are you doing this?

JACK: Because I feel like it. Or would you rather I tear you up? (*bringing the sword up under NED's chin with increasing pressure*) There are times, Neddo, when you absolutely reek of courage. More than we mere mortals care to witness in one sitting. You're so much more compatible with courage than the rest of us. Let's hear it for Edward C. Sheldon! Courage is his middle name. People lining up for blocks to find out what a freak thinks about while lying flat on his back! (*pushes NED completely back onto the chaise with the sword*)

NED: And you'll be right out there selling tickets, won't you?

JACK: That's right! Come see the petrified tree, ladies and gentlemen! The ship's figurehead. The basic funereal pose! (*flips the pen holder from the desk with his sword*) Here's a pen to play with, Ned. Why don't you write us one of your nice plays? "Not bad for a cripple, hey ladies and gentlemen?" An inspiration to us all. Is that what you want to be? An inspiration to us all? You can have them wheel you out onto the stage every night in whatever goddamn courageous pose you want and then you can tell us all what it's like to rise above a crisis! (*flings his sword away*)

NED: Why are you so afraid of my disease?

JACK: Because you're my glue, Ned! How dare you let this happen to you!

NED: (*pause*) Why don't you put the play away, Jack.

JACK: Is that all you want from me? To put down this pile of paper? That's all you need from me to make your life complete?

NED: That's not all I need from you.

JACK: Then what is it you need? What? Go ahead, ask me for something. Ask me for something.

NED: What? What could you possibly give me that would change things one iota?

JACK tears up the script and throws it in NED's face. It is practically a slap. The silence that follows is excruciating. Eventually, JACK picks up a bottle of champagne from the cart.

JACK: I love you, Ned. Maybe Hamlet has more to offer, but it's all I'm good for. I love you. Say it for me. Jack loves me. Jack really loves me . . . I really do love you.

No response, though JACK waits for one. He puts the bottle on the desk, and starts to exit. At the sound of NED's voice, JACK stops and holds by the victrola, facing away from him.

NED: When I was a young boy, we went on a family outing. A wonderful park outside the city. I was in the park swimming pool and I began to drown. As I was sinking to the bottom, I could actually see my parents walking away from the pool. Neither one of them saw me. All I remember thinking at the time was that I was never going to need anyone ever again. Fortunately, someone did see me and pulled me out.

JACK: You never called out for help.

NED: It never occurred to me.

The impact of this statement breaks through NED's control and he quietly begins to cry. JACK crosses to embrace NED, comforting him.

NED: (*taking his handkerchief from his pocket*) This is ridiculous.

JACK: No, it's not.

NED: My pores feel like they're starting to open again . . . I didn't even know they were closed . . . (*looking up to JACK*) So Jack really loves me, does he?

JACK: That's what the rumour is.

NED: (*nearly breaking again*) Oh, God, don't let me start up again. (*He reaches unsuccessfully for a cigarette from the cart. JACK prepares one for each of them.*)

JACK: Did I really tear up a script by the best playwright in New York?

NED: Only the best actor in North America could get away with it.

JACK: You mean there's someone in Europe you consider better?

NED: Two little tots in the nursery.

JACK: At least we get a chance to start all over.

NED: God, what I'd give for a quick glimpse into the future.

JACK: Not I, thank you. I do not want to know.

NED: I feel almost optimistic . . . Quite a night, hey?

JACK: I've enjoyed every minute of it. Two high points in the same evening. I hope I haven't used up my remaining allotment of high points all in one night.

NED: I should hope not, Mr. Barrymore.

JACK: Mr. Barrymore. Every time I'm called that, it makes me feel like the neutered headmaster of a young ladies' finishing school. (*gets his coat and hat*)

NED: Well, Mr. Barrymore, I think you can use the front door this time. Or are you and Charlie going to be flying?

JACK: What about the mess?

NED: (*beat*) Don't worry about it.

JACK: Sunday at two: *Hamlet*?

NED: Here?

JACK: If you insist.

NED: I'll be here.

JACK: (*takes this in, then crosses to birdcage and takes it off stand*) Okay, Charlie old sport, time to see the seamy side. (*starts to exit*)

NED: Good night, fellas.

JACK: Good morning, Ned. I guess we're off to breakfast. (*changes his mind about leaving via the door*) Actually, it isn't fair to climb up a mountain without a chance to climb down as well. (*steps out onto the balcony, carrying the cage*)

It keeps everything on its proper perspective. (*He balances the cage on the balcony railing and steps over onto the outside edge.*)

NED: It's still a little dark out there.

JACK: (*with the cage and his final cigarette*) I'll light the way with my aura of grace. Reflected light, Ned. Just like all the other stars.

He gradually descends the fire escape and the noise of his descent fades away.

NED: (*after a pause, quietly*) Descend gracefully, Jack.

Fade to black.

War Babies
Margaret Hollingsworth

Like many of the New Play Centre's other core writers in its early years, Margaret Hollingsworth was a recent arrival to Canada. Growing up in Sheffield and London, England, she wrote plays and worked in theatre while still a teenager before, as she thought, leaving all that behind when she immigrated to Thunder Bay in 1968. With a B.A. in Psychology from Lakehead University, she moved to Vancouver in 1972. She would earn an MFA in Creative Writing at UBC, but not before switching from fiction back to drama under the influence of Professor Doug Bankson, who also steered her to the organization he had co-founded a few years earlier. The New Play Centre premiered her one-acts *Bushed* (1973) and *Operators* (1974). *Alli-Alli-Oh*, which opened in Toronto, was rewritten for the NPC's 1977 du Maurier Festival: its sequel, *Islands*, premiered at the 1983 du Maurier. In between came Hollingsworth's first full-length plays: *Mother Country* (1980), initially produced at Toronto's Tarragon, and *Ever Loving* (1980), her popular play about war brides in Canada, at Victoria's Belfry. Both had earlier undergone substantial workshopping at the New Play Centre.

War Baby (the original title) was Hollingsworth's last play before moving to Toronto in 1984. Frustrated by the difficulty of getting exposure for her new work, she formed her own press, Act One, to publish *Endangered Species* (1988), a collection of four experimental one-acts which she described as "preoccupied with male/female relationships . . . [and] the ways in which women have been marginalized." *Alma Victoria*, her play about the wife of architect Francis Rattenbury, premiered at the Nanaimo Festival in the summer of 1990. A regular contributor to CBC radio, Hollingsworth has won two ACTRA awards for radio drama. Her non-dramatic writing includes the screenplay for a feature film adaptation of Jane Rule's *Memory Board*, and a collection of short stories, *Smiling Underwater* (1990). She has served as playwright-in-residence at the Stratford Festival (1987), Concordia University (1987), and the University of Western Ontario (1989-90).

Originally a New Play Centre/Belfry co-production, *War Baby* was revised and retitled *War Babies* before Nightwood Theatre's production at the Toronto Free in 1987. The key difference between the versions was the splitting of two doubled roles. In *War Baby*, the pregnant playwright Esme and her war correspondent husband Colin portray their own fictional counterparts, Esme 2 and Colin 2, in the play-within-the-play that Esme writes in response to the emotional warfare within her marriage. *War Babies* calls for four separate actors. The change helps clarify the various plot developments and character relationships within the non-linear structure. It also intensifies the strong female consciousness at the centre of the play, a characteristic of nearly all Hollingsworth's work. "I made the change because I liked the idea of Esme watching herself and commenting on herself," Hollingsworth explains. Published along with *Ever Loving, Islands*, and two other short pieces in a collection entitled *Willful Acts* (Coach House, 1985), *War Babies* was nominated for the Governor General's Award for Drama in 1986.

War Babies was first presented as *War Baby* by the New Play Centre and Belfry at the Belfry Theatre, Victoria, on January 5, 1984, with Nicola Lipman as Esme, Tim Koetting as Colin, Andrew Ball as the Jailor, Duncan Fraser as Jack, and Anna Hagan as both Barbara and Paddy. It was directed by James Roy with set and costumes by Willie Heslup, lighting by Pamela Loughton, and sound by Martin Millerchip.

Duncan Fraser as Jack, and Nicola Lipman as Esme in the New Play Centre production of *War Babies*. Photo by Mary Thauberger.

WAR BABIES

CHARACTERS

ESME CREARY, a playwright, age 42

COLIN CREARY, ESME's husband, a newsman, age 42

ESME 2, the character depicting ESME in the Play-Within-Play (P.W.P.)

COLIN 2, the character depicting COLIN in P.W.P.

BARBARA, around 40

JACK MACNEIL, Scottish, early 40s

CRAIG/JAILOR, age 19. The identity of this character is not immediately evident to the audience.

POLICEMAN 1, doubled by actor playing JACK

STORE CLERK, doubled by actor playing JAILOR

PADDY, doubled by actor playing BARBARA

SET

The action of the play takes place in COLIN and ESME's townhouse in a large eastern city. The set should be extremely flexible. With the help of lighting and a few props, the lower level transforms into a jail, an auditorium, a department store, a bar, a country home in western Canada. The bedroom should be on an upper level. Until the final scenes only ESME is free to cross the boundaries between real and imagined space: for example, the bedroom is off-limits to the Play-Within-Play characters until Scene Fourteen. Except where indicated, transformations from scene to scene should be accomplished without blackouts.

AUTHOR'S NOTES

The P.W.P., or Play-Within-Play, consists of fantasy scenes which grow increasingly real and urgent as the play that ESME is writing approaches its climax with the impending birth of her child. These scenes may be marked in production by lighting changes; another possibility is to place all the fictional characters on the periphery of these scenes as they are being played.

The word *beat* is used to indicate a break in the rhythm which is so swift as to allow no time for reflection. The word *pause* indicates that such time is allowed.

ESME's typewriter might well be a laptop computer. The doll is a larger-than-life rag doll.

ACT ONE

Scene One

The bedroom of COLIN and ESME's house. Darkness. We hear the voices of COLIN and ESME.

COLIN: There's nobody else in here is there?

ESME: Listen.

COLIN: There is somebody!

ESME: Yes?

COLIN: I can hear breathing.

ESME breathes deeply. Pause.

COLIN: I don't know why we have to do it in the dark.

ESME: So you won't cheat.

COLIN: Well, it's easier to cheat in the dark. Am I being punished?

ESME: No, silly.

COLIN: Let's have some music.

ESME: You have to stop while I put it on. How will I know you've stopped?

COLIN: Put the light on.

ESME: That'd be cheating. (*beat*) We'll do it together. Where are you?

COLIN: Here.

ESME: Take my hand. (*They grope their way to the tape deck.*) What do you want to hear?

COLIN: Is there a choice?

ESME: I left the Scarlatti here somewhere. Yes.

She puts tape on. Music. A high-pitched childish voice sings "Humpty Dumpty Sat On a Wall." They laugh. Music stops.

COLIN: Did you turn it off?

They go back to their chairs. Silence.

ESME: If you were blind . . .

COLIN: A blind rat caught in a wheel . . . (*loud bang; COLIN screams*) Esme! Es . . . what was that?

ESME: I dropped a stitch.

COLIN: Oh Jesus!

ESME: Aren't you used to things that go bump in the night?

COLIN: Round one.

ESME: To me.

COLIN: I'll get you next time!

ESME: Ssssh — I'm concentrating.

Silence. Alarm clock goes off.

COLIN: That's it!

ESME: One more minute!

COLIN: No — that's it. Prize for the best.

Lights come up. Late evening. They have both been knitting, and hold up the oddly shaped results of their efforts. They measure them one against the other.

ESME: How many stitches do you have left?

COLIN: (*counts*) I lost six.

ESME: I only lost three — I won.

COLIN: Mine's more perfect.

ESME: Mine's longer.

COLIN: Mine's! (*beat*) Length wasn't the criterion.

ESME: It was understood.

COLIN: Not by me.

ESME: Understanding isn't your strong point.

COLIN: What's he going to do with two scarves?

ESME: She'll tie them together.

COLIN: He'll have perfect co-ordination?

ESME: Naturally. I thought of a name today. Sandra. D'you like Sandra?

COLIN: I prefer Matthew.

ESME: How about Matthew Sandra?

COLIN: Shouldn't we be making boots?

ESME: Too advanced. We need lesson two. (*looks in book*) How to read a pattern.

COLIN: Lesson three — knitting socks for soldiers.

ESME: There's no war on.

COLIN: Perfect peace. (*snores*)

ESME: Maybe Barb'll show us when she gets here.

COLIN: Yeah — I'll bet she spends most of her time knitting when she's through with tossing the hay and whittling sticks.

ESME: That was back in the sixties. She can't still be a hippie. (*laughs*) She once crocheted a cover for her truck while she was waiting for the phone to ring. (*looks through pattern book*) You never called her. Well, she was your "lady."

COLIN: Lady?

ESME: Today she'd be called your "significant other," right? (*lets book drop*)

COLIN: Lesson four. How to be a single mother.

ESME: We're in this together.

COLIN: (*knitting*) Let's buy the bloody boots.

ESME: If you want to learn to be a mother —

COLIN: I'll learn it from you, when you've got the hang of it —

ESME: Together.

COLIN: Look — you don't have to keep feeding me tidbits to make me think I'm sitting at the table.

ESME: Is that what you think?

COLIN: I think you're trying to muzzle me.

ESME: Then go ahead and bite! (*beat*) Listen — can't we can the war games?

COLIN: What?

ESME: Can't we make out without playing games? I mean — we're grown up mummies and daddies now. When the kid comes —

COLIN: We'll roast him and feed him to the poor. You can write about it.

ESME: Not such a *swift* idea — it's been done. (*beat*) I want you to be serious.

COLIN: (*straightens face, manually poses with her*) The newsman and the playwright caught in a serious moment.

ESME: We've got to make some adjustments.

COLIN: (*adjusts pose; ESME won't go along with it; COLIN gives up*) Oh God — let's go over this when I get back.

ESME: That's one of the adjustments. (*beat*) I don't think you should go away again. (*beat*) It might be early.

COLIN: I'll be here to deliver — don't worry.

ESME: I don't think you even want to.

COLIN: Want to? Go ask the boys at the office — I'm boring them to tears on the subject. Russ Pringle even sent me a pacifier in the internal mail.

ESME: I suppose that's an internal male joke!

COLIN: Peace!

ESME: Yes, that's it. Peace. You know, I sometimes dream there's a little replica of you (*points at his stomach*) in there — curled up with a gun.

COLIN: (*laughs*) I don't have a gun.

ESME: No?

COLIN: I wouldn't bring a gun into the house —

ESME: Have you ever used one?

COLIN: No — of course not —

ESME: But in your job —

COLIN: I use a camera.

ESME: Show me some of your pictures.

COLIN: Sure.

ESME: Now. Show me some of the ones you took in the Sudan.

COLIN: Oh they have the whole file in Washington. You don't want to see them anyway —

ESME: I do. How many newsmen get to testify in Washington!

COLIN: It was nothing. I do it every day! (*ESME smiles, hugs him.*) How many non-American newsmen!

ESME: Wish I'd been there to see it. (*COLIN smiles and nods.*) Is it all desert?

COLIN: Washington?

ESME: The Sudan, silly. (*COLIN laughs.*) Supposing our pasts are stapled into our genes — yours and mine. (*rubs belly reflectively*) You know something? I feel like I'm starting out on some kind of a journey.

COLIN: Make sure I'm on board.

ESME: Oh yes.

COLIN: What's the vehicle?

ESME: A typewriter.

COLIN: (*looks at her oddly, then relaxes*) Ach — let's get back into our cruising gear, Es. C'mon. (*makes a grab for her but she gets up*) Come back here. (*pause*) Sandra?

ESME: (*downstairs now, picks up newspaper, calls up*) You finished with this paper?

COLIN: What paper?

ESME: I haven't read it.

She stands for a few moments deep in thought, looking at COLIN over the paper.

Blackout.

Scene Two

We hear a radio playing. It is a talk show. Lights up on ESME and COLIN at the kitchen table. They are finishing lunch. COLIN wears rugby shorts and shirt.

ESME: More ice cream?

COLIN: No thanks.

ESME: All natural ingredients. (*leans over and turns radio down to a background buzz; takes a drink of wine*) To us.

COLIN: To us.

ESME: If you really loved me you wouldn't let me drink, not in my condition. (*COLIN obligingly takes her glass and finishes it. ESME pours another drink for herself.*) Good game?

COLIN: So so. We lost. (*dabs his mouth with serviette*) Whoops! Another one for the wash.

ESME: Doesn't matter. (*throws her serviette over her shoulder*)

COLIN: You should use paper ones. Cut down on the work.

ESME: I like the work. (*COLIN looks at her closely.*) I do.

COLIN: You've been at it all morning. I can tell — this floor.

ESME: Scrubbed. On my hands and knees.

COLIN: You never scrub floors.

ESME: You should see what I found behind the fridge.

COLIN: You moved the fridge?

ESME: A condom.

COLIN: Esme you . . . moved the fridge?

ESME: Did you hide it from me?

COLIN: You know I . . .

ESME: Did you think I'd ask you to wear it? (*she looks at her stomach dubiously*)

COLIN: There's only another month — you know you mustn't move heavy objects.

ESME: I blew it up. It floated.

COLIN: Es!

ESME: It's okay. I didn't feel a twinge. Won't do it again. Promise. I went to the bank this morning. Opened an account for the baby.

COLIN: But he doesn't have a name.

ESME: I opened it in the name of Bump. The teller recognized me from that quiz show on TV last month — how about that? I told her there's no way I'd get away with a holdup in this city! She even asked about you — you see, you're a marked man too.

COLIN: Bump?

ESME: Bump Creary. Five bucks.

COLIN: Here — make that fifty.

ESME: Big spender!

COLIN: It's worth it.

ESME: (*restless*) Think I'll start on the den this afternoon.

COLIN: No, not the den.

ESME: Wonder what I'll find behind the desk?

COLIN: Leave it to Mrs. Price.

ESME: Oh — didn't I tell you? I fired her. She was reading our mail. (*COLIN sighs.*) The minute I decide to relax I see another cobweb, or an old sock, or . . . do you think I have a problem?

COLIN: Sounds to me like you're trying to make a goddamned nest.

ESME: Am I?

COLIN: You're reverting to the primitive.

ESME: Is that why I fixed the dishwasher?

COLIN: You?

ESME: Well, you weren't going to do it. It was dripping.

COLIN: You know my biggest fear? After this lot's over I'm gonna come home and I'm not gonna recognize my own wife. She'll metamorphose into some gigantic walking tit with a feather duster and a pair of pliers strapped round the nipple.

ESME: All the better to tighten your nuts my love. (*COLIN hugs her. ESME pushes him away.*) You stink — you and your rugby.

COLIN: We'll use paper cups and plates till . . . It's not for much longer.

ESME: Why is everything disposable?

COLIN: It isn't. (*beat*)

ESME: Anyway we can't use paper. Not with guests coming.

COLIN: I knew it, that's why you're cleaning.

ESME: It's not.

COLIN: Let me put them off.

ESME: They're on their way. The letter said they were heading down the west coast, then up the east and turning left at New York. Even Mrs. Price thought that sounded a bit vague.

COLIN: I'll track them down — if I phone around one of the wire service boys'll . . .

ESME: Oh you and your "boys." Leave it Col. They're coming.

COLIN: Why did you ask them?

ESME: Haven't we been through this?

Silence.

COLIN: Why do you keep putting me in the adversary role lately?

ESME: Do I? How interesting.

COLIN: Not for me.

ESME: I want them here.

COLIN: Well I don't.

ESME: An extended family. (*She picks up her napkin, folds it neatly.*)

COLIN: You're crazy.

ESME: Are you still in love with Barb?

COLIN: Oh don't be . . . don't get onto that!

ESME: You are!

COLIN: She was just a girlfriend. (*pause*) I haven't seen her for fifteen years, love doesn't last that long.

ESME: Is it disposable? (*COLIN turns off the radio. ESME folds his napkin.*)

COLIN: And Jack? Am I supposed to stand by while he tells me what a wonderful father he's been to your kid.

ESME: (*flinches, covers*) Well, you're best buddies.

COLIN: Were. Fifteen years ago. And Barbara was supposed to be your best friend. I haven't noticed you straining to keep in touch with her.

ESME: Maybe he'll have changed.

COLIN: Jack? You know damned well he won't've changed. I'll bet he's going out of his mind there in frontierland. He'd give his eye teeth to be in my shoes.

ESME: I can't see him wanting to be a father again. Imagine! My ex-husband — he'll be forty-two!

COLIN: I'm forty-two.

ESME: Yes, but you always did leave things to the last minute.

COLIN: Ouch!

ESME: You wish you'd been him!

COLIN: I do not.

ESME: Neither do I.

COLIN: I just don't want to talk about him that's all. He had the makings of a first-rate newsman — used to get all the plums. D'you know he broke the Six Day War? He was on the North America desk at Reuter and . . . what's he doing now? Editing some two-bit rural rag!

ESME: You think he'll be jealous of you and your war games?

COLIN: Why did you ask them, Esme? (beat)

ESME: I was scared.

COLIN: Scared?

ESME: Scared you wouldn't be here.

COLIN: The likelihood's . . . look — even if by some fluke I weren't here — we have friends. Close friends . . .

ESME: But Barb and Jack are more than friends. They're like family. Your ex-lady, my ex —

COLIN: Family. That's bull . . .

ESME: Barb was like a sister to me —

COLIN: She was just a friend. You wiped her out after she married Jack.

ESME: I love them. Both of them —

COLIN: Start living in the real world Es —

ESME: I want a family.

COLIN: We don't have a family yet.

ESME: I need —

COLIN: You don't.

ESME: I want —

COLIN: *I* don't!

ESME: I want a *family*!

COLIN: Well I don't. I don't!

ESME: (making cross on stomach) Cancel! Cancel! Cancel!

COLIN: (jumping up) If you dare to lay a finger on him . . . (They stare at each other.) Oh Es . . . why do you keep putting me in the adversary role?

ESME: Can you imagine Col? Can you imagine how it'll be in three years' time?

She looks across at the jail which begins to take shape in her mind. COLIN continues to drink coffee and eat dessert, unaware of the scene that is being played out as ESME constructs it.

Scene Three

P.W.P. A jail. COLIN 2 sits, head in hands. CRAIG enters with two cups. He puts them on a side table. Takes one, puts his feet on the table casually. CRAIG should be downstage, in a small office which overlooks COLIN 2's upstage cell.

COLIN 2:   (having watched CRAIG enter and settle himself) Well? (CRAIG drinks.) Are you expecting a guest? (CRAIG doesn't reply.) Cigarette? (pause) D'you have a cigarette? (CRAIG doesn't reply.) I don't smoke either. Battle situation. I'm used to it. I'm used to it you know. (long pause) How old are you? (CRAIG doesn't reply.) You look about six.

CRAIG: I'm nearly 20! (COLIN 2 laughs. CRAIG jams pen into shirt pocket.)

COLIN 2:   What's your name? (*CRAIG rolls down shirt sleeves.*) Going somewhere? I said going somewhere big shot? (*pause*) You and your type! (*shakes his head*) It's the same all over the world. Doesn't matter where you start out you end up the same. Twenty. I have a son you know — Matthew. (*CRAIG looks in mirror. Slicks his hair back.*) Lived in this mousehole all your life? (*beat*) I could stop anyone on the street and they'd know your name as well as they know the name of this town! (*Beat. CRAIG picks up his hat.*) Come over here and talk to me. I'll be out of here in half an hour. (*CRAIG, ignoring him, tries hat at different angles.*) I'll bet I've met your mother — your father was on the winning tug-of-war team at the carnival this year. We headlined it. (*pause*) Look lad. Give me that coffee. (*CRAIG picks up coffee and empties it into waste bin. Sits, feet on table. Drinks his own coffee.*) So this is war eh? (*CRAIG doesn't move.*) Listen — I know more about wars than you know about . . . about . . . listen — listen. (*puts head in hands*) You think I'm mad don't you? (*looks up*) I've spent half my life recording history. Is that mad? I was once holed up in a bunker in the Sudan — know where that is? Little backwater a few thousand miles from this one. We were under fire from a handful of rebels — in the mountains — I'd been taking pictures of four tribesmen . . . they came to me during a lull in the firing. One of them had blue hives on his tongue . . . they thought I could cure . . . I gave him an aspirin. They had a camel and some corn. Yes, I remember that — corn. Don't know where they came by it out there . . . worth more than the camel . . . anyway we were all ambushed. Before the aspirin could take effect. The bullets that were meant for me ricocheted off the ribs of the god-damned camel. It went down — fell on me, I could feel its bones giving way under it, like when you slide up the legs on a tripod. Don't know what happened to the corn. Anyway, somehow, somehow — I found myself in a makeshift bunker. Just me and this kid. Like you. Just a kid. Dark eyes. At first I thought he was caught in the crossfire too. Then I saw he was turning a gun on me . . . had a gun pointing at my kidneys. And his hand shaking every time a shell went off. Shaking. And I asked him for a cigarette . . . (*Mimes motion of asking when not knowing the language. Pause.*) I was on his side. I had no way of letting him know. He thought I was the enemy. I don't know why he didn't just . . . Something distracted him. I got away. When I got home I did a complete analysis of the current crisis. (*pause*) Facts. I was quoted in the U.S. Senate as a reliable witness. I left one thing out. In order to get that story — I shot him.

CRAIG: (*jerks his head up*) I don't watch.

COLIN 2:   I shot him. (*beat*) What? What don't you watch?

CRAIG: The news.

COLIN 2:   You don't watch the news.

CRAIG: It's always the same. (*takes newspaper out of desk*)

COLIN 2:   Let me see that! (*CRAIG opens up comic section.*) Let me see . . . is there anything there about me? I edit that paper goddamnit! I wanna know if I made my own front page! Is that asking too much? That's mine!

CRAIG throws paper in waste bin.

Blackout.

Scene Four

Some days later. ESME sits, staring at typewriter. Sound of typewriter offstage. The doll is propped up nearby.

ESME: Colin — (*typing continues*) Colin, where are you? Colin? (*pause*)

COLIN: (*off, over typing*) Up a tree.

ESME: I've been asking you to mow the lawn for weeks. (*pause*) Are you in the den?

(Typing stops. COLIN comes and stands in doorway looking at ESME.) Did I interrupt you?

COLIN: Look — why don't you go to bed. Write up there — any other time you're complaining that there's no time. The doctor said rest.

ESME: I can't write. I haven't been able to write since . . . *(feels her stomach)* I've only written one scene and it was set in a jail.

COLIN: Well, try something new.

ESME: What?

COLIN: I don't know. *(Wanders out of room. Sound of typing resumes.)*

ESME: Colin.

COLIN: *(off)* Go upstairs.

ESME: On my own? What are you doing?

COLIN: *(off)* I just have to finish this story then . . . then I'll mow the lawn.

ESME: Where are you?

COLIN: *(off)* I'm in the den.

ESME: He's in the den. Colin . . . I can't seem to control it. I want to write a scene set on the patio —

COLIN: *(off)* Go out there then —

ESME: You go out there — *(Pause. Types ferociously.)* When I am old and grey and full of fears . . . *(Looks across to patio where the next scene of P.W.P. begins as ESME writes it.)*

Scene Five

P.W.P. The patio. Lights dim. BARBARA, CRAIG and JACK appear in a cluster; they might sway slightly, a single unit, phantomlike. ESME

watches, fascinated. Turns back to typewriter; as she does so they stop moving. She continues to type. Lights remain on her; fade on BARBARA, CRAIG and JACK.

Lights up on patio. Hammock which was formerly empty is now bulging. JACK roams the patio. He is wearing soiled rugby clothes, the same as COLIN wore in previous scene. He has a camera. Begins to photograph the doll, whose head can be seen poking out over the hammock.

JACK: *(to doll)* Smile. Click. Don't be coy dear, I know those teeth aren't real. Smile, and again, now — present arms. *(doll's arms go up)* Eyes right, yes, sexy. *(doll's head moves)* How about a nice goose step for Uncle Jack . . . *(the leg appears)* Goosy goosy gander . . . clickety click . . . here, I bought you a present . . . *(gives doll a toy gun)* Don't tell your mother. You've got a good leg, have you got another? *(two doll's legs appear)* Ah, so, shall we dance? *(ESME 2 sticks her leg up over the hammock. JACK, still dangling the doll, examines ESME 2's ankle.)* Swollen. *(peers down into hammock)* Acutely swollen. *(dances with doll)* Oh how we danced on the night we were wed. *(thrusts doll away from him)* Did you just piss? *(whispers)* Well, she won't have to wash nappies this time around, they're all paper now — hope she'll do better with this one. Colin always wanted a nice doll for his birthday. *(dangles doll, sings)* Little Shirley Temple, she bought a penny doll. She washed it, she dressed it. Then she let it fall. *(Drops doll. Walks out laughing.)*

ESME: *(at typewriter)* She's just for practice, you're in a liberated house Jack. We've planned this child. We're going to give it the best. A happy life — a non-sexist education. We're going to take such care of this child . . . *(During this last line CRAIG has come on. He stands behind the hammock, cradling the doll, smiling at her, mocking. ESME yells, frantic, as CRAIG leaves.)* Colin — Col — where are you?

COLIN 2 enters, brings on barbecue with corn. JACK joins him at patio table. COLIN holds up glass as he did in Scene Two.

COLIN 2:   Esme doesn't drink wine.

JACK: Esme's getting boring in her old age. (*ESME, at typewriter, shakes her head.*) The lads know you're in town.

COLIN 2:   Have you played yet?

JACK: Not yet. (*sniffs himself*) They're waiting for you.

ESME: (*addressing the typewriter*) He's not playing rugby, he's only just come home!

COLIN 2:   (*talking over ESME*) I don't know if I can get away —

JACK: You'd better be there that's all. My boy's playing his first game with us today.

COLIN 2:   Craig? (*ESME shows signs of agitation.*)

JACK: Non–sexist education! My father never came near me till I was old enough to wear his soccer boots and lift a pint mug. (*pushes doll with his foot*) I'm none the worse for it. I never saw a bloody rugby ball till I came over here . . . never ate pâté on the patio and drank fancy wine. Still don't. (*leans forward confidingly*) No one expected me to be some kind of male penguin and sit on the egg for six months while the female of the species cooked pâté. (*leaning back*) And my son's none the worse for it. He was up every morning delivering papers when he was ten years old . . .

During this speech CRAIG comes and stands behind JACK. COLIN 2 does not see him. The men leave the table, CRAIG remains, seats himself. BARBARA joins him. (These changes should be slow, almost dreamlike; no one pays any attention to the bulging hammock.) ESME puts her head on the typewriter, finally looks over at BARBARA and CRAIG, and they begin to speak.

BARBARA: You're going to be nice to her. You hear me?

CRAIG: She's not my mother. You are.

BARBARA: It doesn't matter what she did. (*gets up*)

CRAIG: Barbara — I don't want to —

BARBARA: We're proud of you, your father and I. Never forget that. You're a real man!

Lights down on BARBARA and CRAIG and up on ESME who rises from typewriter. COLIN 2 and JACK resume their places at the table. CRAIG and BARBARA exit.

COLIN 2:   (*offers JACK a head of corn from barbecue; JACK pushes it away*) When I'm away I — I freeze. And when I'm back here — nothing. Not for her, not for the Bump . . . I don't feel.

JACK: Few of us can afford the luxury.

COLIN 2:   I once killed someone Jack. (*pause*) It was him or me.

JACK: On the job? (*COLIN 2 nods.*) I'm sure you made the right choice. (*COLIN 2 stares ahead bleakly. JACK puts his arm round his shoulders, old-pal style.*) We've all been there.

COLIN 2:   Don't tell Esme.

JACK: She probably knows.

COLIN 2 shakes his head. JACK reassures him. The bulge in the hammock moves.

COLIN 2:   You know what I like about you Jack? I can talk to you. It's . . . (*trails off*)

JACK: It's the job isn't it? It's no job for a man with a family, right? Since when have you thought of yourself as a married man? That's why it's lasted this long.

COLIN 2:   It was somebody's son.

JACK: We all are.

COLIN 2: (*gets up*) I'm gonna change for the game. Give me five minutes, okay?

Lights fade on JACK, alone at table, laughing. ESME exits, leaving him onstage. Slow fade to black.

Scene Six

Full light. A prenatal class in a bare room. We watch COLIN and ESME for a while. They are lying on the floor a few yards apart. PADDY enters.

PADDY: Good. Good. Now deeper. Breathe deeply. Deeper. Good girl. I can give you 15 minutes — good — (*They both follow her instructions silently for a few seconds.*) Esme?

ESME: Whoops. Fell asleep.

PADDY: Colin's doing better than you are.

COLIN: Piece of cake. (*exchanges conspiratorial glance with PADDY, as PADDY takes ESME's necklace off*)

ESME: (*to PADDY*) I was dreaming of you. You remind me of someone. Who does she remind you of Colin?

COLIN: No one in particular.

ESME: She does me.

PADDY: All right, let's start again. (*COLIN hasn't stopped.*) I want you to count to five, very slowly . . . Inhale, exhale . . .

COLIN: One, two, three, four, five . . .

ESME: We're high-risk parents. It's not just me. The sperm loses its pizzazz after the prime years. Isn't that so? How old is a man when he's in his prime? He peaks ten years before a woman even if he does play rugby. Isn't that so?

PADDY: Esme.

ESME: Well, you're the expert.

PADDY: There is no reason to suppose that yours will be anything other than a normal pregnancy provided you follow —

ESME: Listen Paddy, I don't think I can . . . go through with this.

COLIN signals PADDY not to be concerned.

PADDY: Lie back and relax. Everyone's nervous the first time.

ESME: It's not my first time.

PADDY: Our bodies forget.

ESME: Our bodies forget.

PADDY: (*soothing*) So let's remind them.

ESME: It doesn't want to remember.

COLIN: Es . . . !

ESME: (*sits up*) Look — lines. (*points to her face*) Gaps. (*She points to her teeth. PADDY lays her down.*) You know how some cats don't care for their kittens?

PADDY: That's not going to happen.

ESME: And some cats eat them.

COLIN: Cool it Es.

PADDY: Relax. Look how well Colin's doing.

ESME: Rotten Tom!

COLIN: Every sperm a bullseye! (*ESME yowls.*) See how they spray!

COLIN makes ack-ack of machine gun, sits up, sprays her with bullets. PADDY is disconcerted by this. They lapse into silence. Lie back. Breathe.

ESME: Does your husband tell you what's on his mind?

PADDY: My husband's very supportive. Like yours.

ESME: I'm being a nuisance. (*relaxes*) It's good of you to see us on our own. I suppose I was disruptive in the class. I often am . . . they throw me out of rehearsals. I have a right to stay . . . but they throw me out.

PADDY: (*adjusting COLIN's position*) Better. You're getting the hang of it. (*beat*)

COLIN: There've been studies that show that when a person imagines running, small but measurable amounts of contractions actually take place in the muscles associated with running.

ESME: Imagine that!

COLIN: The same neurological pathways are excited by imagined running as by actual running.

ESME: Imagine running.

COLIN: Physiologically.

ESME: Imagine!

PADDY: It's true. We can be in sympathy with each other.

ESME: Words!

PADDY: He can help . . .

ESME: He has all the words.

PADDY: He can help if you'd only . . .

ESME: Words.

COLIN: Shut up! I want to do this.

ESME: Words. But where are the feelings? How does this feel Bump? (*Makes a bongo out of her stomach. COLIN reaches across instinctively to stop her. PADDY calms her. She relaxes and breathes deeply.*) When we are old and grey and full of fears —

COLIN: Tears.

ESME: Fears.

COLIN: Full of tears — (*Calm, they breathe deeply.*) Tears.

ESME: Fears.

COLIN: Tears.

ESME: Schmears!

Silence.

PADDY: Are you ready? (*ESME nods.*) Now I want you to try panting. Colin, reach over and pinch. (*COLIN pinches ESME's thigh.*) That's right.

ESME: Harder. (*COLIN obeys.*) Make it hurt.

PADDY: You've prepared your song?

ESME: Forty seconds one contraction right? (*to COLIN*) Time it — ah — ah (*He is about to stop pinching in order to look at his watch. She sings fast.*)

> I love to go a-wondering
> Along a mountain track
> And as I go I love to sing
> My knapsack on my back.
> Valderee . . . (*nudges COLIN*)

COLIN: (obediently) Valderee.

ESME: Valderaa . . .

COLIN: Valderaa . . .

ESME: Valderee . . .

COLIN: Valderee . . .

PADDY: Push.

ESME: Valderahahahahaha (to COLIN)
Harder — hurt me! haaa! (yells)

PADDY: Push! — Colin, stay with it, harder
— the final contractions are enough to blast
you right across this room! Harder! (COLIN
sits up, then gets to his feet.)

ESME: (continues to sing) I wave my hat to all
I see, and they wave back to me, and blackbirds
call . . .

COLIN: See you in a few minutes . . . (to
PADDY) Need a smoke. (Exits. He can be seen
pacing on the periphery of the scene.)

PADDY: Try it at home.

ESME: (sits up and stares after him) He doesn't
smoke. (beat) I pushed too hard. (beat) I love him
you know. You mustn't think . . . we've been
together a long time. I thought we . . . knew
each other.

PADDY: You do.

ESME: What do you know?

PADDY: I sense it. An understanding.

ESME: War games. We play war games. It
helps keep the balance of power. (PADDY
laughs.) So you'd say they were necessary.

PADDY: For some.

ESME: Openness. That's necessary?

PADDY: Yes.

ESME: Well, he's not open.

PADDY: Hm.

ESME: Either he doesn't have any god-
damned feelings or he hides them so well
that . . . we used to be equals.

PADDY: Sssh!

ESME: He killed a young boy. What do you
think of that?

PADDY: Don't be silly.

ESME: You know how I found out? (silence)
I read about it in the newspaper. His paper. He
didn't tell me. Well? (silence) So what do you
think of him now?

PADDY: I'm sure there's an explanation.

ESME: Oh sure there's an explanation. It's
all in there, in the paper. He was ambushed in
the Sudan — he hid behind a camel.

PADDY: (laughs) Oh, you mean it wasn't in
Canada?

ESME: What?

PADDY: Well — in some countries life's less
important — (ESME sits back, silenced.) I don't
think life's not important —

ESME: He killed a child for a piece of news.

PADDY: I mean life itself — of course
that's . . .

ESME: That's worse than anything I've ever
done. He confessed but not to me. The irony
is that I have to be pregnant with his child in
order to have time to sit around reading
newspapers. I'm usually too busy. (beat) Is it
true that if you kill once it's easier the next time?

PADDY: I don't know. Ask him.

ESME: We have a pact. We never talk to each other about anything connected with our work. It's what's kept us together. (*beat*)

PADDY: It was probably self-defence.

ESME: He's a war correspondent. He feeds on war. I always tried to tempt his appetite. Now I don't know how to stop.

PADDY: Maybe you're making too much of it.

ESME: It used to be they thought war was what a man had to do. Now . . . (*shrugs*) Well, what does a man have to do? (*beat*) Maybe we don't need them — there's a thought. We don't need heroes any more, that's for sure. I don't want that for my child — do you?

PADDY: Society's changing.

ESME: I've changed. I wanted to try again before it was too late. (*beat*) I wasn't unkind to the first one — I just . . . I kind of abandoned him — I wonder now if I was sick — I remember feeling so claustrophobic and he was always crying — my friend Barbara had to come in and . . .

PADDY: And now you feel guilty.

ESME: Now? Always. Always . . . (*beat*)

PADDY: (*comforting*) Esme . . .

ESME: I've been wondering if I can take this on alone.

PADDY: You'll see things differently when . . .

ESME: (*pulling back*) See, I'm living with a man who kills. You know something Paddy? I don't even think I like men. They're alien beings . . . I always thought of him as my best friend, and now he feels like the enemy . . .

PADDY: He's a very nice man — you should see some who come through here!

ESME: I'm driving him away. (*beat*) What if it's another boy? It might happen . . . Oh God, what am I saying. What am I doing? He has to help me through this — he can't leave me . . . he can't go back to his wars . . . how could he . . . how could he do that? And not tell me! How many times?

PADDY: (*kneeling beside her*) It'll be all right. It'll be all right. (*strokes her hair*)

ESME: It will?

PADDY: Of course.

ESME: I want this baby you know. More than anything. I didn't last time.

PADDY: I know.

ESME: I'm so scared.

PADDY: I know.

ESME: They're going to interview us on TV. Parenting over 40. Half the people out there don't even have sex after they're 40. (*beat*) He wants a boy.

PADDY: Just relax for a while. That's it. Relax.

ESME: You know what I'm looking forward to most?

PADDY: What?

ESME: Being able to lie flat on my stomach again. (*PADDY laughs. ESME lying on the ground takes up her necklace, holds it over her stomach, making it swing in circles. Looks up at PADDY.*) You remind me of someone Paddy.

PADDY settles and soothes her, then exits to discover COLIN. Light holds on ESME during the rest of the scene, dimming slowly.

PADDY: (*seeing COLIN standing outside her office*) Oh?

COLIN: I wanted to ask you . . . you've been talking to her. (*PADDY nods.*) She's left alone more than she should be —

PADDY: You're a newsman. Must be an exciting life.

COLIN: It's not particularly glamorous if that's what she's telling you.

PADDY: Must be dangerous.

COLIN: Not really. (*beat*) So how was I doing?

PADDY: You were doing fine. (*beat*)

COLIN: I just wanted to . . .

PADDY: Why don't you sit down?

COLIN: I wanted to talk to an expert.

PADDY: I'm only a nurse Colin.

COLIN: I know. But — you're seeing women every day. Pregnant. (*beat*) Does it make a difference when they're over 40? I mean I've read about it but . . .

PADDY: She's had all the tests —

COLIN: I mean . . . is it likely to unbalance her?

PADDY: Unbalance?

COLIN: Well — I mean, what's going on with her?

PADDY: I get the feeling you two should talk more.

COLIN: We talk all the time.

PADDY: Real talk.

COLIN: I mean all I want to know is if it's normal — the way she goes on? Considering she is left alone a lot —

PADDY: Everyone reacts differently.

COLIN: I try — you've seen me try.

PADDY: Well — at least you know it's for a limited period.

COLIN: But after?

PADDY: Bliss. (*smiles*)

COLIN: Twenty years of bliss? (*Pause. ESME is seen to be listening.*)

PADDY: This is the first time for you?

COLIN: The first that I know of —

PADDY: And you're scared.

COLIN: No. I just had some questions. I don't want advice.

PADDY: Go ahead.

COLIN: Well . . . (*He trails off. Silence.*)

PADDY: Look — if you'd like me to recommend some books.

COLIN: We've read all the books.

PADDY: Then what's bothering you?

COLIN: Just now — was she talking about Craig? She had another child you know. She wasn't good at it. Parenting — that's what it's called these days isn't it? Parenting. She wasn't good at —

PADDY: I'm not a psychiatrist — I can tell you what's going on in her body, but —

COLIN: All right then, tell me that.

PADDY: There are certain hormonal changes taking place.

COLIN: That's all?

PADDY: She may seem obsessive.

COLIN: Well what about me? Are there hormonal changes in men? Is it true that a man can breast feed if . . .

PADDY: I think there have been cases, I haven't studied the literature.

COLIN: I feel like — I'm acting strange — I mean look at me — even being here, what good's it gonna do? Valderee. Is this going to go on — after it's born? I mean . . . I'm too old to be asking these questions right? Sex for instance.

PADDY: Pardon?

COLIN: That can continue of course, when she's feeding it. But will she want . . . ?

PADDY: Nothing needs to stop.

COLIN: That's what it says in the books. *(pause)* The parks are filled with grey-haired men pushing bugs.

PADDY: Buggies?

COLIN: *(nods)* But they're on their second time around. They've married their secretaries or their students. Their wives are young. Resilient. *(pause)* I find myself looking at their young wives. Is that natural? I never did it before. I always looked down on the guys who did. *(pause)* She wasn't good to the last one — said she was too young; when it was three she ran off with another man. We've had a perfectly happy marriage for 15 years. We've trusted each other, we've never been proprietary — given each other all the space. Listen, how many couples do you know who've been married for 15 years and . . . Don't tell her, I

mean — we discussed it all. I just didn't anticipate that she'd . . . change.

PADDY: Colin. I have to get back to her. *(shuffles through some papers)* Why don't you tell her what you've just told me?

COLIN: *(shakes his head)* You haven't understood.

PADDY: Then why don't you try group therapy? *(Smiles. Exits.)*

COLIN *remains, plainly horrified at the prospect.*

Blackout.

Scene Seven

Evening. Three weeks later. An auditorium. ESME is stacking chairs. She tries one on another, then reverses them. Her heart is not in the task. COLIN enters and stands behind her. She jumps. He has a bag, a camera, a briefcase.

ESME: You were out there then? *(Indicates auditorium. COLIN nods.)* I didn't notice you in the . . .

COLIN: I was at the back. Here — *(takes chairs and stacks them)*

ESME: I can do it. *(pause)* When'd you get back?

COLIN: Landed at seven.

ESME: Seven? *(COLIN nods.)* Our guests haven't shown yet. They called yesterday from North Carolina. *(pause)* So? *(pause)*

COLIN: I missed the first half.

ESME: It was a benefit. For Amnesty.

COLIN: I saw the flier.

ESME: Everyone's going for a beer at Maxine's. Shall we? (*COLIN sits on a chair, ESME on another.*) So . . . good trip?

COLIN: Usual.

ESME: We missed you. Me and the Bump.

COLIN: How's he doing?

ESME: I think he's going to miss his deadline. (*pause*) So — what did you make of it?

COLIN: What?

ESME: The reading, of course. The goddamn reading — since you were here for it.

COLIN: You knew I'd be here.

ESME: I knew you'd rush here straight from the airport?

COLIN: Yes.

ESME: And? (*pause*)

COLIN: When I left I was married to a playwright.

ESME: The theatre's dead.

COLIN: That was sudden.

ESME: It's elitist. I want to get my message across to the rag-readers and the box-watchers. Like you do. (*COLIN shakes his head.*) You know what theatre's best for? Showing pain. But nobody wants to pay to see pain: not when they see it written all over the breakfast table every morning.

COLIN: So you're going to spend your time performing for Amnesty.

ESME: I've got things I have to say. (*pause*) Doubleday's bringing the poems out in rush edition. They've asked me to do a reading in New York.

COLIN: *Poems?*

ESME: Look, it was nothing personal. I should just finish stacking these . . . chairs.

COLIN: Sit down Esme. (*ESME sits.*) *Media Mumbles* — is that what you called them?

ESME: Did you recognize that piece before I said it was yours?

COLIN: *Media Mumbles.*

ESME: Good name eh? They liked the bit about the camel — the way its legs folded. Hey — listen, here's one I didn't use — the committee didn't think it fitted the theme. All the readings had to be about torture — it's from *Maclean's* — I didn't change a word — just as she was writ in the good ol' media — (*reads*)

"Singing star triumphs.
On tour recently to promote
her recent record,
the Tennessee dirt farmer's daughter
with
the super teased hairdo
and
the remarkable figure,
needled her audience
about
her
high profile.
'I see a lot of you brought your
binoculars . . .
I know why. You don't fool me.
You wanted to see
if
these wigs
was as big
as
you thought they was.'"

Isn't that torture? — or this one . . . (*COLIN gestures that he's heard enough.*) So you see, you're not the only one who strings his words together like a third grader. (*COLIN picks up a chair and places it loudly, squarely on the ground.*) Unfair. Since I've been reading the papers I've been looking carefully at your stuff — it's way ahead of the rest. Stands out. Cross my heart.

COLIN: You try writing decent prose after you've just ploughed your way through a god-damned charnel house. What do you expect me to do?

ESME: I expect you to tell the truth.

COLIN: I tell the truth.

ESME: You tell your edited version. A newspaperman's version.

COLIN: That's what I am. You don't want me to be what I am?

ESME: I want you to stop pretending to be a hero.

COLIN: When do I ever say I'm a hero?

ESME: You maintain a heroic silence. (*pause*) Look at you now. You jerk off across the front page of tomorrow's fire-lighter, yet when you're with me you keep your zipper done up so tight you . . .

COLIN: The other guys — the other guys' wives have some sense of what they go through. (*pause*) All right then, all right — I'll talk . . . I'll come home and I'll spill it all into your lap.

ESME: No. No — you're not listening.

COLIN: Listening happens to be my job. You know what I hear? I hear a honky screaming out my most — my most intimate moments in the most public arena she can find. You're cruel Esme.

ESME: I'm not cruel!

COLIN: Maybe you don't even know what you're doing — that scares the shit out of me —

ESME: I know what I'm doing!

COLIN: Well, you don't know what you want!

ESME: I want you to stay home, that's what I want. I want our child to live with an ordinary nine-to-five father who doesn't play with guns — and if I have to shout to make you hear —

COLIN: Ordinary? Since when have you been attracted to the ordinary?

ESME: Since you got me pregnant.

COLIN: And you had nothing to do with it? Are you willing to stop banging on the typewriter and be an ordinary mother?

ESME: I already have. All I've written is two lousy scenes.

COLIN: Oh? Ordinary women produce *Media Mumbles* do they?

ESME: One in a prison and one . . .

COLIN: How do you think our kid's gonna enjoy coming home . . . coming home and finding his old man held up for ridicule in front of a gaggle of . . .

ESME: I haven't held you up. It was the media. I was . . . holding up the media.

COLIN: Held up . . .

ESME: Holed up. Bunkered.

COLIN: By a bunch of bleached women!

ESME: This is a hold-up. (*Points imaginary gun. They face each other, furious. ESME gives way first.*) They aren't bleached . . .

COLIN: Bleached middle-class women.

ESME: They aren't middle class. All right — all right your piece won't be included in the book. I was wrong.

COLIN: You were more than just wrong —
what do you think I do when I'm away?

ESME: Why do you always have to diminish
what I do?

COLIN: You don't have the first notion of
what you do. Of what you just did! That article was . . . one of the — the . . . most painful
things I ever wrote.

ESME: And you didn't show it to me. You
didn't tell me. (*pause*) So why don't we both
give up?

COLIN: I am never giving up — while
there's a job to be done and I can still do it —
I'll be there. I'll be there because I'm better than
all the rest —

ESME: And so was I.

COLIN: Then go to it!

ESME: You can bring me a souvenir back
from your next trip, to prove what you do. A
pinkie or a big toe. How about an ashtray with
"present from Santiago" on the rim, and a few
ashes in it. Human ashes. (*COLIN picks up chair,
hurls it at her. Misses.*) You could've . . . hurt the
baby. (*COLIN rights the chair, sits on it, trem-
bling.*) Well, how do I know it wasn't just a
story? That's what it was, wasn't it? Col?
You'd've told me if you'd actually — God —
I'll bet it's not the first time! I'll bet . . .

COLIN: Are you through?

ESME: You're so goddamned stoical.

COLIN: I said are you . . . ?

ESME: And I said did you shoot? (*silence*)

COLIN: Did you have a coat?

ESME: Well? (*COLIN puts his coat on.*) Bloody
hero.

COLIN: It's just a job, Esme.

ESME: Just a job?

COLIN: I've kept my mouth shut because
you never wanted into my professional life and
I never wanted into yours.

ESME: You hate the theatre.

COLIN: And you hate the real world.

ESME: That's unfair! . . .

COLIN: I come back from a bad stint, it's
like — it's like . . . it takes me a few days to
even believe in this place . . . the trivia . . . people acting plays . . . people giving poetry
readings . . . all the well-meaning people . . .
(*ESME gets her coat, cradles her stomach.*) To
believe that nothing's going on under the sur-
face — that there isn't a jail full of poor s.o.b.'s
screaming day and night while somebody pulls
the flesh off strip by strip. At first I find myself
confused . . . it takes a while to unwind and
realize . . .

ESME: What a bland lot we are. (*long pause*)

COLIN: You should just thank God that our
son's being born into a healthy environment.

ESME: What's healthy about it? Oh Col —
(*stretches out hand; he pulls away*)

COLIN: As a matter of fact I did bring you
a souvenir.

ESME: Oh?

COLIN: Tree bark.

ESME: Tree bark?

COLIN: They diaper their children with it.
(*brings out package*)

ESME: Who?

COLIN: They chew it first. (*Gives it to her. ESME drops the present. Looks around, picks up her manuscript, takes the page she has just read from, and chews on it.*) There are babies being born every second of every day out there. (*ESME chews.*) People die every day. Real death. No bags of red dye under their shirts. If they own shirts.

ESME: So what does it feel like to kill?

COLIN: You've done your share.

ESME stares at him, suddenly breaks. Sobs. COLIN approaches her, puts his arm around her. She almost chokes. He cups his hand under her chin as if she were a child. Obediently she spits the chewed paper into his hand. Laughing.

COLIN: Good job there isn't an audience.

ESME: I want you to stay home. I want you to stay home with us. We'll make it together.

COLIN: I'll see what I can do.

ESME: Maybe we could go out west. After the baby's born . . . you could get a job easily.

COLIN: I'm arranging more home leaves.

ESME: Well, Jack and Barb did it. We'll ask them to help. Jack can get you a job . . .

COLIN: (*Freezes. Looks around for a way out. Spots tape recorder.*) Is that thing on?

ESME: For the reading. (*COLIN yanks the cord out.*) For the reading, that's all.

COLIN: Jesus Esme. Jesus!

ESME: For the reading.

COLIN: You use me up. Every bit of me. You just pick me dry. (*picks up his briefcase and camera*)

ESME: Where are you going?

COLIN: To eat. Bland food, in some bland bar; maybe the bland barman'll tell me something I don't already know about all the bland people who do benefits for Amnesty.

ESME: Col . . .

COLIN: Go home. Go home and rest . . . and read Dr. Spock. (*exits*)

ESME: Colin! Don't blow it Esme. Don't blow it. (*Goes to tape recorder, turns switch and watches tape rewind.*)

Slow fade to dim light. JACK and BARB appear on periphery and remain there.

Scene Eight

P.W.P. COLIN 2 and CRAIG: the jail. CRAIG is drinking beer.

COLIN 2:   Do you know what a playwright is? (*pause*) Someone who plays — is that what you think?

CRAIG: Someone who plays.

COLIN 2:   No — you don't know. Why would you? She hasn't written anything . . . not since . . . She wasn't that well known anyway. Her stuff's too complex. Like her.

CRAIG: Why don't you just go play with yourself?

COLIN 2:   What?

CRAIG: Quit.

COLIN 2:   Quit?

CRAIG: I don't want to have nothing to do with you okay?

COLIN 2:   Well you're going to.

CRAIG: Enough!

COLIN 2: You're in charge?

CRAIG: I said that's enough.

COLIN 2: What's your name?

CRAIG: Listen . . .

COLIN 2: Name!

CRAIG: I said . . .

COLIN 2: Boss. Is that your name?

CRAIG: I said . . .

COLIN 2: Boss.

CRAIG: Now look . . .

COLIN 2: What do you know about women, Boss?

CRAIG: I don't wanna hear no more. You just go on and on.

COLIN 2: Don't keep staring at me, Boss.

CRAIG: Shit!

COLIN 2: I'll turn you round to face the wall. D'you have brown paper pasted on behind? (*CRAIG paces, not knowing what to do, not listening.*) She won this round. She won. She won every round even when she seemed to be losing. She put me in here, d'you know that? I tied myself to a desk for her. I tried to change for her. Talking to each other. There's no real contact. Nothing. Nothing. Come over here whatsyourname. Is that a gun you're wearing? Come here I said. Goddamnit don't they teach you to obey in this outfit? How come they've left you in charge anyway? How old did you say you are? When they find out who I am I'll be out of here so fast . . . as soon as they know who . . . I was. (*CRAIG makes a whimpering sound. Clenches fists.*) You think you're in love

— you try to narrow it down, you pin everything on one person — you put four walls around it. It's a fantasy . . . you can't contain it. It's a fantasy, we're always trying to contain . . . look for limits. Without limits we go mad, don't we?

CRAIG: (*leaves the office and goes into the cell, indicating COLIN 2's jacket*) Take that off!

COLIN 2: We go mad.

CRAIG: Take it off.

COLIN 2: The dumbest thing of all is trying to get it down in newsprint. That's what you'll end up as, you know. Newsprint. Thinking you know whose side you're on . . . risking your life to chase ambulances. Her stuff fed on it.

CRAIG: Take that off.

COLIN 2: Is that a gun?

CRAIG: Take . . .

COLIN 2: Look whatsyourname you . . .

CRAIG: Now.

COLIN 2: Over there they give kids guns to play with. They tell them it's a game, but it's not a game — it's war. Right? Right. Boss.

CRAIG tears COLIN's jacket off and sticks his gun in COLIN's ribs. COLIN slowly begins to unbutton his shirt. Slow fade out.

Scene Nine

ESME and COLIN's house. Later. ESME is reading Dr. Spock. She has a drink. Leans across and turns on tape recorder. We hear a recording of the final part of Scene Seven (the part of the scene before COLIN discovers the tape recorder). ESME turns it down. Reads aloud, over recording.

ESME: "A baby starts by using its head. It's a gradual process by which a baby learns to control his body. It starts with the head and gradually works down to the hands, trunk and legs."

ESME 2 walks on, arranges a copy of Dr. Spock on a lectern. ESME looks at kitchen window. A slide is projected which reads "Poet Gives Last Public Reading."

ESME 2:
    Just as soon as he's born
    He knows how to suck.
    And if something touches
    his cheek — the nipple
    or your finger for example
    he tries to reach it with his mouth.
    If you try
    to hold
    his head
    still
    he becomes angry right away
    and twists to get it
    free.
    Probably
    he has this instinct
    to keep
    from getting smothered.
    Parents ask —
    when does he learn to see?
    This is a gradual process
    like everything else.
    Provided you don't poke his little eyes out!

ESME crosses to typewriter, taking tape recorder and books with her. ESME 2 crosses to kitchen table and continues to read Dr. Spock as ESME was doing.

Scene Ten

P.W.P. Lights up on BARB and COLIN 2 sitting formally on the couch. The start of the scene has a hesitant quality as it forms in ESME's imagination.

COLIN 2:   I thought you'd still be in bare feet and bangles, Barbara.

BARBARA: That's history.

COLIN 2:   I'm glad. Nice little place. Is that a peacock on the rail? (*Looks outside. BARBARA nods.*) And mountains . . . think I'll fit in here? The interview went well. I think they'll hire me. (*pause*)

BARBARA: Yes of course, if you'd . . .

COLIN 2:   I don't want advice.

BARBARA: I'm taking a real estate course.

COLIN 2:   Real estate? You? (*laughs*) Does Esme know?

BARBARA: She just found out. (*beat*) She's jealous.

COLIN 2:   Of real estate?

ESME: (*at typewriter*) No. No not that. Try this —

ESME 2 does not look up. Shift in mood here as ESME decides what she is doing with this scene. BARB and COLIN become more intimate.

BARBARA: No. No not of real estate.

COLIN 2:   She's never jealous. (*pause*) You're still attractive.

BARBARA: Surprised?

COLIN 2:   I'd forgotten.

BARBARA: She'll be jealous.

COLIN 2:   We're not proprietary with each other.

BARBARA: But she's jealous. I know.

COLIN 2:   How?

BARBARA: Because she's my sister. She'll find out you were here last night when she comes out here.

COLIN 2:   Are we going to make a habit of this? (*BARB puts her hand on his knee.*) I'm not sure that we should. (*pause*) It'll be a help to her having you here. Since she had the baby she's agreed not to do any more public appearances.

BARBARA: Es? But that's part of her life.

COLIN 2:   It'll work out, you'll see. The country air'll do wonders.

He takes her hand, then takes her in his arms.

Blackout.

Scene Eleven

Darkness. ESME and COLIN's house. We hear COLIN putting his key in the lock and coming through the door.

COLIN: Couldn't face Chinese again — whoops, why are you sitting in the dark?

Full lights up. ESME sitting in bed.

ESME: Just wondering how to change the scene. From the big lake to the small pond. A backdrop of mountains maybe.

A mountain scene is projected onto kitchen window blind. Meanwhile COLIN takes his coat off and dumps a package on the table.

ESME: Elephant Mountain. That's a good name — it's in the atlas. I'd be able to see it through my kitchen window. Every day. Every time I yawn I'll swallow it. (*pause*) I'm writing a play about us.

COLIN: In the dark? (*goes over and pulls window blind up*) Let's have some real light on it. (*He stands for a moment in the projected image, then it is gone.*) Fried chicken okay?

ESME: (*heaving herself off the bed*) Big city tables and chairs would look different in small town kitchens. (*shifting table*) I'm going to make

you the editor of a small-time newspaper out west, like Jack.

COLIN: Me? Most unlikely.

ESME: Jack's in it too. You see I thought I'd try to put you in my position, so you'd really know how it feels.

COLIN: (*laughs*) Not pregnant! (*brings supper upstairs*)

ESME: No. It'll be three years down the road. You don't really mind if I write about you do you?

COLIN: If it keeps you happy. (*ESME looks at him, not understanding this geniality.*) We'll have it on our laps. (*supper*) Back in bed with you. Move. You're supposed to keep your feet up.

ESME: I've kept my feet up for two weeks. Is there still a world out there?

COLIN: Soon be D-Day. (*pats her stomach, removes doll from couch tenderly*) There we go Liza.

ESME: (*reaches up, takes his hand*) Love you.

COLIN: (*kisses her, undoes package*) It's not as hot as it was. I dropped by the office after I picked it up.

ESME: You're supposed to be on leave.

COLIN: Bad news I'm afraid.

ESME: Bad news?

COLIN: They want me out of here — day after tomorrow latest — Russ Pringle's come down with malaria.

ESME: Russ Pringle's come down with malaria.

COLIN: Poor s.o.b. — last year he was shot up in Guatemala, and now . . .

ESME: They want you to fly out.

COLIN: Well, I've put if off as long as I can. Is it my fault you're late?

ESME: (*lightly*) No. No. It's mine. So you're going?

COLIN: I don't have any alternative. You think I'd miss being in on this if . . . It's okay. Everything's set up. I tracked Jack down. They're heading up here right away —

ESME: You spoke with Jack?

COLIN: Yes. And I checked with the doctor. He knows the situation.

ESME: So it's all taken care of.

COLIN: As well as is humanly possible.

ESME: And all I have to do is lie back and push.

COLIN: Just keep your feet up like a good girl.

ESME: (*sticking foot up in air*) Swollen. (*beat*) What happens if I go on pushing — I push everything out — my ribs, my lungs . . . (*pause*) They strap you down you know —

COLIN: Look Es. It's not my fault. You know if I could change it —

ESME: Do you believe that having nightmares about something makes it happen?

COLIN: No.

ESME: That writing it down makes it happen?

COLIN: No.

ESME: No. It's all Russ Pringle's fault.

COLIN: It's nobody's fault. The whole Mid-East thing is . . . (*sighs*)

ESME: It's the Middle East's fault. Why don't they understand that when they sneeze in Beirut everyone in North America has to rush for the kleenex? Don't they consider how they disrupt people's lives? (*beat*)

COLIN: (*arranging paper plates*) Calm down.

ESME: Why don't they write their own history? (*pause*) Hold me Colin.

COLIN: Let's eat first. There's still some warmth here . . .

ESME: Breasts and legs.

COLIN: Es. I said I'm sorry. What else?

He takes a piece of chicken on a plastic fork and tries to tempt her. She picks up french fries and throws them at him. He reciprocates and throws a handful back. They battle with the food, laughing.

COLIN: Come on . . . come on . . . it's just like Mother used to make.

ESME: It's finger lickin' better . . .

COLIN: How does this sit on your stomach? (*aims a single french fry*)

ESME: Chicken!

COLIN makes chicken noises.

ESME: (*beside herself laughing*) Oh Jack . . . !

COLIN: (*stops suddenly*) Jack?

ESME: Oh sorry, sorry. He's on my mind that's all. (*laughs*) Did he tell you?

COLIN: Who?

ESME: Jack. (*COLIN stops battling.*) Well did he? Did he tell you who's with them? They're all together, travelling up the coast.

COLIN: Who?

ESME: Craig. Craig's coming.

Freeze. Lights fade on ESME and COLIN.

Scene Twelve

P.W.P. Lights up on jail as in Scene Eight. CRAIG is still holding the gun. BARBARA and JACK are not present. COLIN 2 and CRAIG face each other.

COLIN 2: So what is your goddamned name?

CRAIG: MacNeil.

COLIN 2: You a Mc or a Mac?

CRAIG: What?

COLIN 2: Scottish?

CRAIG: Listen . . .

COLIN 2: First name?

CRAIG: Listen . . .

COLIN 2: Listen to me boy. First name?

CRAIG: That's enough.

COLIN 2: You're in charge.

CRAIG: I said that's enough.

COLIN 2: Boss McNeil. Is that your name?

CRAIG: Enough!

COLIN 2: Boss.

CRAIG: Look . . .

COLIN 2: Name! I said name!

CRAIG: Craig MacNeil.

ESME: (*quietly*) Craig.

Blackout.

ACT TWO

Scene One A

Bedroom. ESME has the typewriter balanced awkwardly on the bed. Sheets of paper around her. She glances up, stares and as she does so . . .

Scene One B

P.W.P. COLIN 2 and ESME 2 take their places at the kitchen table. There is a view of Elephant Mountain through the window of the kitchen. The scene should mirror Act One, Scene Two.

ESME 2: More ice cream?

COLIN 2: No thanks.

ESME 2: All natural ingredients. No additives. (*COLIN 2 looks at her as if additives meant poison.*) Don't wipe your mouth on that serviette.

COLIN 2: What are serviettes for?

ESME 2: Not the linen ones. I don't want to keep washing them.

COLIN 2: You should use paper ones.

ESME 2: You said you didn't like the paper ones.

COLIN 2: Did I?

ESME 2: Yes. Yes you did. (*pause*) Isn't it true?

COLIN 2:   If I said it then I guess it must be.
Yes.

ESME 2:   Yes. that's what you said. (*She moves
some things off the table.*) You said they ended up
in soggy balls on your tongue.

Lights fade.

Scene Two A

Bedroom. ESME is still at her typewriter.

ESME: A journal, that's it. I'll have myself
keep a journal in common with all good lady
writers since the beginning of time. I'll have
nothing to write in it except that time passes.
It's a private journal, not meant for . . .

Scene Two B

P.W.P. The kitchen. COLIN 2 is holding the phone.

COLIN 2:   Barbara — is that you? Yes . . .
she's started to keep a journal. What? No,
nothing interesting, not yet . . . just a lot of talk
about mountains . . .

*ESME 2 enters deliberately, loudly. COLIN 2 puts
phone down, flustered.*

ESME 2:   Have a good day?

COLIN 2:   Tidied a few things up. Yourself?
Go out?

ESME 2:   You know I didn't go out.

COLIN 2:   I'll mow the lawn on the weekend.

ESME 2:   Yes? (*starts to stack dishes*)

COLIN 2:   Then you can take a chair outside.
Read a book maybe.

ESME 2:   Hm.

COLIN 2:   Well then the newspaper, that
doesn't take much concentration. Did the boy
deliver the paper? We ran that feature I wrote
last month. Food pricing policies in Poland —

ESME 2:   My glasses are upstairs.

COLIN 2:   Well you don't have to read it. I
doubt if anyone else will 'round here.

ESME 2:   What are you staring at?

COLIN 2:   Nothing. Nothing . . . just looking. Why have you turned that picture round?

ESME 2:   It was bothering me. It was staring.

COLIN 2:   I don't care for the back.

ESME 2:   I'll take it down.

COLIN 2:   I suppose brown paper doesn't
stare?

ESME 2:   I'll take it down now. (*doesn't move*)
Would you like it on your desk at the office?

COLIN 2:   I'm a newspaper editor, Esme, I'm
not a goddamned family doctor.

ESME 2:   Matthew called.

COLIN 2:   Oh? How is he?

ESME 2:   I don't know. He sounded . . .
strange.

COLIN 2:   Most three year olds sound
strange on the phone.

ESME 2:   I think I'll ask Barbara to bring him
home.

COLIN 2:   Don't do that. You'll freak again.

ESME 2:   I won't. I'll do better this time.

COLIN 2:   You can't confine a child to the house. You have to take him out occasionally. Are you up to that?

ESME 2:   I could try.

COLIN 2:   Give it another month. Leave him with Barbara. He's happy there with her kids. He hasn't exactly been screeching to come home.

ESME 2:   I was thinking we could turn the living room into a playground. You know. Get a slide maybe . . . we could put a swing up. Screw it into . . .

COLIN 2:   The ceiling won't support it.

ESME 2:   A sandbox.

COLIN 2:   I don't want to come home to . . . I don't want to eat my supper in a sandbox.

ESME 2:   If we had him back . . .

COLIN 2:   If we had him back you'd be beating up on him inside a week.

ESME 2:   But it . . .

COLIN 2:   (firm) That's the end of it, Esme. He stays with your sister. I'm going to read the paper — (Gets up. Softens, sits.) So, what did you do today?

ESME 2:   I listened to the radio.

COLIN 2:   And . . . ?

ESME 2:   I heard a talk-back show and I heard the news.

COLIN 2:   And . . . ?

ESME 2:   And? Somebody held up a bank. I forget where. I was thinking Col . . . (pause) Where would you buy a gun? Col . . . where would you buy a gun?

COLIN 2:   I'm going into the den.

ESME 2:   The den? I'll give Barbara a call and find out if she knows.

COLIN 2:   How many times did you call her already? You can't keep calling her. She gets fed up with it. She's threatened to move out. She'll take an unlisted number, then what?

ESME 2:   She wouldn't.

COLIN 2:   We don't want to get on the wrong side of Barbara. Why don't you call someone else if you must keep using the phone.

ESME 2:   There's no one else to call. You won't let me call you. They won't even put me through on your switchboard.

COLIN 2:   Jesus! D'you know what it's like working on a newspaper? Phones going all the time!

ESME 2:   Not out here. Nothing happens out here.

COLIN 2:   Of course they won't put you through. They can't be loading the lines down with a dozen crank calls from you every day. Pretty soon you'll be calling me up when I'm in the next room.

ESME 2:   I called the talk-back show.

COLIN 2:   (alarmed) You didn't give your name?

ESME 2:   No.

COLIN 2:   Thank God for small mercies.

ESME 2:   We talked about bank robberies.

COLIN 2:   As long as you didn't give your name.

ESME 2:   I told him about my fantasy.

COLIN 2:   Which one?

ESME 2:   About robbing a bank.

COLIN 2:   You?

ESME 2:   Yes. I want to rob a bank. To show that I can do it. To show I can still do something. There aren't many mothers who . . .

COLIN 2:   A female bank robber. I'd dare you to do it if I thought it'd help you get out of the house.

ESME 2:   He said I'd have to disguise myself as a man if I wanted to get away with it. Then it'd lose its significance.

COLIN 2:   Did you tell him about your other fantasies?

ESME 2:   No.

COLIN 2:   And did you tell him you daren't leave your kitchen? That your sister has to buy groceries and look after our child? Did you ask him how in the world anyone could rob a bank while they're sitting at the kitchen table suffering from agoraphobia?

ESME 2:   I don't *suffer* from agoraphobia.

COLIN 2:   Then what is wrong with you?

ESME 2:   Nothing. There's nothing the matter with me.

COLIN 2:   Okay. Go upstairs then.

ESME 2:   No. No . . . I don't want to. The faucet on the bath's dripping.

COLIN 2:   I told you last week. Call a plumber.

ESME 2:   It only needs a washer.

COLIN 2:   Well fix it yourself. I'm not up to it. It'll cost twice as much if I tackle it.

ESME 2:   The hot water bill's going to be astronomical.

COLIN 2:   I'll call Barbara. I'll ask her to wait here with you this once. I can't take a day off work just to sit around waiting for a damned plumber.

ESME 2:   I tried to take a nap this afternoon. I couldn't get to sleep. It scared me. The eternal dripping. Chinese water torture. I'm not going upstairs again. I'll sleep down here.

COLIN 2:   Okay. Okay, I'll do it. I'll change the washer on the bathroom tap. I'll change the washer.

ESME 2:   You will? (*pause*) The moderator said it really shouldn't be necessary to leave the house. (*COLIN is getting up and putting on his raincoat.*) Where are you going?

COLIN 2:   Out. I'm going back to the office. I have a couple of things to check out.

ESME 2:   Oh.

COLIN 2:   I won't be long — okay?

ESME 2:   Yes. Okay.

COLIN 2:   I won't take the car. I'll leave it in the drive — you might want to get out for a while.

ESME 2:   No. I don't think I will.

COLIN 2:   What are you scared of? It's been so long. When's it going to end Esme? What is it?

ESME 2:   (*shrugs, pause*) You have to understand that it's better to stay inside.

COLIN 2:   I try. Why can't you try? Try can't you?

ESME 2:   I am. Every day I try. I just can't . . . it must be this place. We should go back to the city. (*COLIN 2 sighs.*) I'll try harder.

COLIN 2: I'll fix the tap when I get back . . . okay? Oh, and by the way, Jack MacNeil is in town next weekend. I've invited him to supper on Friday. (*goes to door*) Bye. (*pause*) I said bye.

ESME 2: Yes.

COLIN 2 exits.

Scene Two C

Bedroom. ESME with typewriter.

ESME: I do understand. I do understand that telephones don't work on stage . . . but . . . just one more time. I promise I won't use it again.

Scene Two D

P.W.P. ESME 2 in kitchen dials phone.

ESME 2: Barbara? Barb . . . it's me. He just left.

Lights up on BARBARA holding her phone.

BARBARA: Don't panic. Don't panic baby.

ESME 2: I'm panicking aren't I?

BARBARA: What did he say?

ESME 2: I can't remember . . . he said . . . he said he was going to the office.

BARBARA: Then that's where he's gone.

ESME 2: Barbara?

BARBARA: What?

ESME 2: That is you isn't it?

BARBARA: Of course it's me. I've just shoe-horned Matthew into bed. He wanted to watch "The Bionic Woman."

ESME 2: Who's she?

BARBARA: A TV lady with superhuman powers. God, life was simpler when we didn't have TV. Cities!

ESME 2: This is a city?

BARBARA: Sure feels like it to me.

ESME 2: I know he didn't go to the office. Is he meeting someone? (*pause*) Barb . . . if I don't needle then there's silence. Silence and a dripping tap. It's always been . . . abrasive . . . but now it's just sandpaper on raw flesh. What if he leaves me on my own? In this god-forsaken . . . ?

BARBARA: What are you talking about? Laugh. Jees. Where's your sense of humour? You used to be a real clown. Think back to the old days in Montreal.

ESME 2: I daren't.

BARBARA: You never took yourself too seriously . . .

ESME 2: Is it because I'm visual?

BARBARA: You were a clown.

ESME 2: Yes. (*suddenly*) I've been thinking of robbing a bank.

BARBARA: That's more like it. (*laughs*)

ESME 2: D'you think it's a good idea?

BARBARA: Need an accomplice?

ESME 2: I'll surprise everyone.

BARBARA: You sure will.

ESME 2: He's inviting Jack for supper on Friday.

BARBARA: Who's Jack?

ESME 2: They used to be best buddies. (*pause*) He said he wasn't going to take the car tonight.

BARBARA: What?

ESME 2: He's taken it. I heard him.

BARBARA: I have to go now Es.

ESME 2: I won't call again tonight, eh?

BARBARA: Not tonight. (*puts the phone down*)

ESME 2: Tomorrow? Barb . . . Barb? You haven't gone have . . . ? Barb! (*Puts phone down. Walks around kitchen. Picks up newspaper. Looks at ads. Goes to phone. Dials. In odd, strained voice.*) Hello? Hello . . . I'm calling about your advertisement. Yes. How big is the bath tub? It's sold? Gold? No . . . sold . . . oh I see. No . . . don't hang up. Tell me about it anyway. You see we have a leaking tap and I thought if we were to replace the bathtub . . . hello? I mean, I wonder what we missed . . . was it a bargain? No? No . . . (*Puts phone down. Dials again.*) . . . 5932 . . . hello. I believe you have a chesterfield for sale. Yes. Gold and blue brocade? That sounds very . . . suitable. I mean it sounds nice, real nice . . . you see my husband seems to have taken a dislike to ours. I once slept on it for two weeks. He won't sit on it. How many people does it seat? (*pause*) Would that be big people or little people? My husband's a fairly small man . . . about my size. He's gone out. He said he was going to the office but I don't believe that. (*pause*) Three big people. Yes. Well, we won't be needing it just yet, but maybe . . . maybe soon. If I could call you back. It was nice talking to you. Real nice. Yes. How big is big? . . . No don't go away! . . . I have a . . . something I'd like to talk to you about . . . I suppose you don't have a gun for sale? (*Replaces receiver. Lights dim on her as she dials again.*)

Scene Three

P.W.P. 11:00 pm. Lights up on COLIN 2 and BARBARA in BARBARA's house. COLIN 2 is just replacing the receiver on the phone.

COLIN 2: I'd better get back. She's probably taken it off the hook.

BARBARA: She could be making a bunch of calls.

COLIN 2: Who to at this time of night?

BARBARA: Oh, I don't know. It could be anyone. She's lonely Colin. Lonely. (*She opens the door for him to leave.*)

COLIN 2: Okay. I get the hint. You're a good person Barb. I can talk to you.

BARBARA: Talk?

COLIN 2: Yeah — really talk.

BARBARA: Wow. That's really talking?

COLIN 2: Jesus, she's going to get out of the house. She's going to get out if I have to drag her out.

BARBARA: Just be patient.

COLIN 2: Patient! Patient! (*He roars.*)

BARBARA: (*laughing and pushing him out*) Do it at home. You'll wake the kids. Between you and that damned bird out there . . . (*walks out onto the porch with him*)

Lights down.

Scene Four A

Bedroom.

ESME: A play? Dare I have her writing a play? Yes. What the hell!

Scene Four B

P.W.P. Lights up briefly on ESME 2 arranging papers on kitchen table. She leaves. Lights down.

Scene Four C

P.W.P. Later. Kitchen. COLIN 2 (alone) dials phone. Lights up on BARBARA stumbling to her phone.

COLIN 2: Barbara? Is that you? Did I get you up?

BARBARA: That's okay, I only just got to bed anyway. The peacock's in full cry tonight. It sounds mad.

COLIN 2: I haven't even thought about bed yet.

BARBARA: (*yawning*) Lordie, it's two o'clock.

COLIN 2: I had to replace a washer.

BARBARA: That's cool Colin.

COLIN 2: She's asleep. On the chesterfield in the den.

BARBARA: Good. That's good.

COLIN 2: Listen — this is exciting. She's started to write again.

BARBARA: The journal?

COLIN 2: No . . . looks like a play. I have it right here.

BARBARA: Is it good?

COLIN 2: Good?

BARBARA: Does it make sense?

COLIN 2: I'm not an expert. The thing is she's writing again. She's hardly put pen to paper since the *Media Mumbles* three years ago.

BARBARA: Well, why don't you let her tell you about it?

COLIN 2: D'you think this is a break-through?

BARBARA: If she can finish it —

COLIN 2: Maybe she really is going to pull through this. Maybe we can straighten things out and then . . . What do you think?

BARBARA: I don't know Colin. (*yawn*) Why don't you go to bed?

COLIN 2: I'm sorry. Sorry love. I'm keeping you up. Next thing we know she'll be going outside the house and then . . . I'm being optimistic aren't I?

BARBARA: If I was optimistic I'd believe my day didn't begin at six o'clock in the morning.

COLIN 2: I'll cut the grass on the weekend.

BARBARA: Colin!

COLIN 2: Oh sorry love. I'm sorry.

BARBARA: That's okay.

COLIN 2: Oh and Barb . . .

BARBARA: What?

COLIN 2: (*very softly*) I love you. (*replaces the receiver*)

Scene Five

Bedroom. ESME is crouching over her typewriter. Phone beside bed rings. She ignores it, continues to work. Ring stops. She types. Ringing starts again. She picks up the phone. Meanwhile we see COLIN in newsroom, dialling.

COLIN: Hi honey.

ESME: What?

COLIN: You okay?

ESME: Oh —

COLIN: No pains?

ESME: No.

COLIN: You okay?

ESME: Oh. Oh — yes. I'm okay. Who were you just talking to?

COLIN: No one. I've got the newsroom to myself for a change. Just checking in —

ESME: That's cool Colin.

She puts the phone down absent mindedly, wanders back to typewriter deep in thought. Phone rings. She lets it ring. Looks at ESME 2 as she enters. Lights dim on COLIN but should not black out.

Scene Six A

P.W.P. A department store information booth. ESME 2 is in outdoor clothing.

CLERK: Can I help you?

ESME 2:   (*distracted*) What . . . oh . . . yes. Yes.

CLERK: Yes?

ESME 2:   Yes. I . . . I wanted to ask you — (*pause*)

CLERK: Excuse me . . . if you could just stand aside until you've made up your mind . . .

COLIN puts phone down. It stops ringing.

ESME 2:   Guns. I mean . . . Do they sell guns in a department store?

CLERK: (*routinely*) Fourth floor, sporting goods — now — excuse me . . .

ESME 2:   Sporting? . . . For sport? You see it's my husband's birthday. Do they sell small guns?

CLERK: Pistols?

ESME 2:   Something to fit into . . . to fit in a pocket maybe.

CLERK: You'll have to enquire from the sales clerk.

ESME 2:   Do you need a licence?

CLERK: In the sporting goods.

ESME 2:   Fourth floor? You did say fourth? How do I get there?

CLERK: (*exasperated*) Elevators to your right through menswear. (*to next customer*) Can I help you sir?

ESME 2:   Menswear? Yes. Through menswear to the elevator. (*She walks away.*) In the elevator to the fourth floor. Sporting goods. (*exits*)

Scene Six B

Bedroom. Phone rings. ESME answers it.

COLIN: Listen honey —

ESME: Col . . . I'm . . . I'm in the middle of something okay?

COLIN: That's not important. (*ESME looks at receiver in silence.*) You okay? Listen, you'll call me if there's even a twinge right? Don't go through the switchboard — Rosemary takes forever.

ESME: Rosemary?

COLIN: I'll be stuck here for a while — I've just been in with the Big Cheese — two hours would you believe — but listen — I've persuaded him to let me do a switch — I don't have to leave tomorrow! Hear that?

ESME: You don't?

COLIN: Jees — I thought he was gonna fire me on the spot —

ESME: That's great news Colin.

COLIN: I have to spend the next 24 hours briefing my replacement, so if you can just hold out that long —

ESME: So he fired you?

COLIN: I didn't say that.

ESME: And you don't mind?

COLIN: Esme, I'm not quitting the job.

ESME: But you're staying home?

COLIN: Yes. Yes. (*ESME sighs, relieved.*) Es?

ESME: How would I look in a white suit?

COLIN: Like a fucking sugar cube!

ESME: Virginal?

COLIN: We're not getting married again if that's what you're . . . the pains've started haven't they?

ESME: No.

COLIN: Listen — if Craig gets there before I make it home you'll pick up that phone right away?

ESME: He's here.

COLIN: What?

ESME: (*putting phone down*) I'm such a bitch to you Colin —

COLIN: Esme — are you there?

ESME: (*going back to her writing*) That's the secret — wait. Wait until they're nearly on top of you. Wait until you can reach out and touch them. Wait until you can see the whites of their eyes.

COLIN begins to dial again, changes his mind, is undecided, finally picks up his outdoor coat and flings himself into it.

Scene Seven

P.W.P. That evening, kitchen of COLIN and ESME's house, COLIN 2 sits at the table reading the paper. ESME 2 enters (not wearing outdoor clothes).

ESME 2:   I cooked something special tonight.

COLIN 2:   Why? Is it a special occasion?

ESME 2:   No. Not very. Pork chops in beer.

COLIN 2:   Did you use that last beer?

ESME 2:   It was in the fridge.

COLIN 2:   I've been thinking about that beer all the way home. Stuck in a traffic jam in a crowded bus thinking about that last bottle of beer.

ESME 2:   Well you're going to have to eat it now.

COLIN 2:   Why'd you have to do a special tonight anyway? You can do a special on Friday . . . when Jack's with us . . . oh and by the way, I invited Barbara.

ESME 2:   Yes. She told me. She was here this afternoon.

COLIN 2:   I know.

ESME 2:   How do you know?

COLIN 2:   She called me. She called me at the office.

ESME 2:   How come she can call the office and I can't?

COLIN 2:   Because she only calls in emergencies.

ESME 2:   What emergency?

COLIN 2:   She said she came here this afternoon. She came because you weren't answering the phone. And you didn't answer the door when she got here.

ESME 2:   I did answer the door. I let her in.

COLIN 2:   That was the second time around. She took the kids to the park and then came back.

ESME 2:   Matthew didn't want to leave.

COLIN 2:   She said she got the distinct impression that you'd been out. Did you go out Esme?

ESME 2:   Out? You know I don't go out.

COLIN 2:   You don't have to deny it. I'll be more than happy . . .

ESME 2:   It wasn't an emergency.

COLIN 2:   No — it was good news. Not an emergency. Good news. Where did you go?

ESME 2:   Nowhere.

COLIN 2:   Okay . . . it's your life . . . you do what you like. I'm happy for you that's all. It must be hell to be caged up in the house.

ESME 2:   It's not hell.

COLIN 2:   I only want to help.

ESME 2:   It's okay. I don't need any help. You and Barbara . . . everyone wants to help. You're all crowding in on me, telling me I'm sick. I guess you've told Jack MacNeil I'm sick?

COLIN 2:   Agoraphobia is a sickness. I've talked about it with several doctors. It's a perfectly treatable sickness but no one can treat you if you won't leave the house.

ESME 2:   Catch 22.

COLIN 2:   You should have something to occupy your mind. I don't know why you stopped writing.

ESME 2:   They don't ask me for plays anymore that's why. They don't invite me to conferences. My publisher's stopped calling. Everything's going on very well without me. It's like being dead. I don't exist.

COLIN 2:   You can only say no so many times Esme. After that you are dead.

ESME 2:   Anyway . . . I have got something to occupy my mind.

COLIN 2:   (pause) Well?

ESME 2:   I'm going to rob a bank.

COLIN 2:   Oh Christ.

ESME 2:   You don't think I can do it.

COLIN 2:   I don't think you can do anything much right now.

ESME 2: It's something I want to try for myself.

COLIN 2: (*sniffing*) What's that? I can smell something . . .

ESME 2: Oh. (*giggles*) I'm burning your beer! (*pause*) What were you doing at Barbara's last night?

COLIN 2: At Barbara's?

ESME 2: Yes.

COLIN 2: What are you talking about?

ESME 2: Matthew said he saw your car in the drive.

COLIN 2: Our son's going to have a more vivid imagination than his mother.

ESME 2: (*rejoining him*) He said he saw a yellow car in the drive. He said he heard your voice. Was that imagination?

COLIN 2: I should get over there more often and visit with him.

ESME 2: I was thinking. I was thinking maybe we could have the kid here and give Barbara a chance for a break. She could go to Mexico.

COLIN 2: Mexico?

ESME 2: It's a long way away. (*pause*) Matthew has a hamster.

COLIN 2: Yes?

ESME 2: He says it's prophetic.

COLIN 2: He doesn't know the meaning of the word.

ESME 2: That's what he said though.

COLIN 2: The word's not in his vocabulary. (*pause*) I hope there's nothing wrong with the kid.

ESME 2: He's okay. He just wants to come home that's all. He keeps asking Rawguts when he can come home. Rawguts the oracle.

COLIN 2: "Rawguts" needs a bigger cage.

ESME 2: How do you know?

COLIN 2: Barbara told me. And he calls it Fred.

ESME 2: When she phoned you at the office?

COLIN 2: Yes. When she phoned me.

ESME 2: Oh, so that was the emergency.

Blackout.

Scene Eight

P.W.P. Phone rings in darkness. Lights up in BARBARA's home. BARBARA is holding the phone.

BARBARA: Damn. Damn you Esme. Why don't you answer the phone any more? Come on. Come on baby. (*phone continues to ring as she speaks*) Esme, sometimes I could . . . sometimes I'd like to . . . You know Esme, last night I had this corny dream. I was driving a car . . . a white car down the centre of the road with the two front wheels straddling the white line . . . and I went over a hill, and you were standing . . . you were standing in the middle of the road in a white silk suit with a white scarf . . . reading a speech from one of your plays, a speech about a child, about a child, and I . . .

ESME 2: (*picking up the phone in her kitchen*) Hello?

BARBARA: I couldn't stop.

ESME 2: What?

BARBARA: Oh . . . oh . . . hi! It's me. You weren't answering.

ESME 2:   (*cold*) No.

BARBARA: You haven't called for a couple of days. (*silence*) I just wanted to know if you wanted me to pick up any groceries for tomorrow night? Jack's still coming eh? Do you have a menu planned?

ESME 2:   (*cool*) Colin can do it. It's his party.

BARBARA: Do you want me to come?

ESME 2:   That doesn't seem to be up to me.

BARBARA: Look Esme . . . what is it?

ESME 2:   Nothing. Nothing at all. How's Matthew?

BARBARA: He's a bit upset right now. His hamster escaped.

ESME 2:   That must be a prophecy.

BARBARA: What do you mean?

ESME 2:   Rawguts is an oracle.

BARBARA: What?

ESME 2:   Matthew told me. Very softly. When no one was listening. I hear things even when people say them very softly. When they whisper them into the telephone . . . Tell him not to be upset. (*puts the phone down*)

Blackout.

Scene Nine

P.W.P. JACK and COLIN 2 at the bar of the Royal Hotel.

JACK: And I said not Ethiopia . . . I told him I'd had enough of the Middle East. Beirut was the pits. Let them wipe each other out but keep me away from it. Too much responsibility — the wars are being fought with headlines these days — lead's out of fashion.

COLIN 2:   There's plenty of lead in printer's ink.

JACK: You were wise to pack it in Colin.

COLIN 2:   Was I? I miss the highs. Even if they were vicarious.

JACK: Nothing's vicarious in this game. Russ Pringle took a bullet in his butt. Did you hear that?

COLIN 2:   (*laughing*) Yes. Poor old Russ.

JACK: Long as they didn't hit his drinking arm eh? The opposition weren't too sorry when you quit. You were landing too many plums for our side. Didn't expect to find you in this backwater though. Bit of a comedown isn't it?

COLIN 2:   It suits — the pay's not bad. What brings you out here?

JACK: The business at Cominco.

COLIN 2:   That's all?

JACK: Isn't that enough?

COLIN 2:   Oh sure.

JACK: We've been taking some flak lately about lack of coverage out here in the west.

COLIN 2:   Rightly so.

JACK: So they've asked for a couple of features. Could take a while . . . What kind of coverage have you given the strike?

COLIN 2:   Hardly touch it. Advertisers.

JACK: (*long pause*) You know something? I don't think I'd've recognized you.

COLIN 2: No? I got a couple of teeth capped. Union dental plan.

JACK: You don't mind if I say this? I mean we used to be buddies eh? But Jesus man . . . you look like a dying duck. A dead duck . . . that's been hung a couple of weeks too long. Jesus, you'd pass for a bank clerk!

COLIN 2: I don't spend much time preening. Shall we eat? I'm sorry the arrangements got screwed up. Esme's not feeling well tonight.

JACK: Not pregnant again? Last time I saw her she was bursting at the seams.

COLIN 2: No. No . . . one's enough.

JACK: Hasn't had any Broadway hits lately then?

COLIN 2: She hasn't written anything lately.

JACK: Yes. I had heard whispers.

COLIN 2: So — how's the rugby?

JACK: Folks used to take bets on how long you two'd stay together. I still get the odd gossip hound trying to tap me to find out why the perfect couple went into hiding.

COLIN 2: We didn't. We just decided to duck out while we were on top and move to a quieter situation. Lead a more healthy life.

JACK: Sounds like retirement.

COLIN 2: Well you know . . . life in the big city was nerve shattering. We don't have the worries out here, and Esme wanted to be nearer her sister.

JACK: The glamorous sister? Didn't I meet her once?

COLIN 2: Barbara.

JACK: Come on . . . jog my memory.

COLIN 2: Oh she went back to the land.

JACK: You should give me her address.

COLIN 2: She has two kids. You wouldn't be interested.

JACK: And you are. Well . . . I'm glad to see you haven't retired completely Colin.

COLIN 2: Jack . . . what do you know about agoraphobia?

JACK: Fear of agors.

COLIN 2: Spaces. Fear of open . . .

JACK: Well, there's plenty of that around here.

COLIN 2: I guess some people get off on being confined. The prison authorities are even beginning to acknowledge that aren't they?

JACK: Are you saying that Esme . . .?

COLIN 2: Maybe it's me too. Esme and me . . . both building fences round each other. Neither of us really wanting to be here but . . . You couldn't label my malady agoraphobia. More like battle fatigue.

JACK: What are you saying? Shake yourself up man and get back into the swim.

COLIN 2: I don't think I could face up to the old life again. Esme probably feels the same. I don't have it in me any more. The rat race . . .

JACK: I don't believe you. You're always the first on the front line.

COLIN 2: They only ever sent me to the war zones. That's all I knew. That's all I wanted to know. We're defined by war . . . or its absence. Isn't that right?

JACK: You need a few more drinks. Blow away the cobwebs.

COLIN 2: Yeah.

JACK: Come on. Let's buy a couple of bottles. Take them up to my room and order a pizza. Let's tank up and then maybe we can talk sense. That woman was always a fiend.

They get up from the table and exit.

Scene Ten A

P.W.P. The kitchen of ESME's home later the same night. ESME 2 sits alone at the table. COLIN 2 and JACK enter drunkenly from darkened hallway.

JACK: *(singing to tune of "MacNamara's Band")* O ma name is Jack MacNeil and I'm the leader of the pack. I've come for Esme Creary and I want her on her back.

COLIN 2: *(calling over JACK)* Esme! Es . . . we're back. I brought you a present, Es. Have we got any booze in the house? *(whispers)* Kitchen light's on. Maybe she's still up. What time is it? I seem to have lost my watch.

JACK: One thirty.

COLIN 2: *(explodes, trying to suppress laughter)* Es. I brought Jack home. You remember? Old Jackie MacNeil? It's been a few years . . . Would you believe that? Yes it's . . . *(They burst into the kitchen.)*

ESME 2: Hello.

COLIN 2: What are you doing?

ESME 2: Just sitting.

COLIN 2: *(to JACK)* She's just sitting. At the kitchen table. The lady playwright.

ESME 2: Is there a law against sitting?

COLIN 2: Yes there is. There damned well should be. It should be a privilege. Who was it stood up to write? Hemingway was it? It's a privilege for old Russ Pringle. He had his ass blown off! *(laughs)* We got any booze? We got any beer? Well?

ESME 2: We've got some cold pork chops.

COLIN 2: How'd you like that Jack? How's that for service? You ask your wife for a beer and she offers you a cold pork chop. Jack's gonna help you. Aren't you Jack?

JACK: What?

COLIN 2: We made a bet. He bet me he could get you out of the house. Didn't you Jack?

ESME 2: You'd need a gun.

COLIN 2: Okay, so we'll get a gun!

JACK: We'll get a gun! *(laughs)*

ESME 2: *(to JACK)* What are you, a shadow or something?

JACK: Shadow?

ESME 2: *(mocking)* Shadow?

COLIN 2: I want you to have a talk with old Jack.

ESME 2: Jack can't talk. He's a shadow.

JACK: *(uncomfortable)* I don't know. I don't know Col.

ESME 2: I think I'll go to bed.

JACK: Sit down. Sit down will you? *(doubtful, tipsy)* Won't you?

ESME 2: What for?

COLIN 2: Jack wants to talk with you.

ESME 2: You've been drinking disinfectant again.

COLIN 2: Joke. That's a private joke Jack. (*plays with words*) Joke Jack! (*laughs, opens and closes cupboard doors*)

ESME 2: What are you looking for?

COLIN 2: I'm looking for some booze. There must be some sherry. Something.

ESME 2: The disinfectant's under the sink.

COLIN 2: This? (*takes out a bottle*) This is disinfectant.

ESME 2: That's what I said.

COLIN 2: I'm looking for booze.

JACK: So you don't like going out Esme?

ESME 2: No. No . . . I like it in here. On my own. In my kitchen. I like to do things on my own. Like going to bed.

COLIN 2: Sit down!

ESME 2: Goodnight.

JACK: Goodnight, Es.

ESME 2: Esme.

JACK: Goodnight Esme.

COLIN 2: She says she's gonna rob a bank. Can you imagine that? She's never been in a frigging bank for months. She's never been inside a bank. What are you gonna use Es? A knife and fork . . . a broom? A feather duster? Stick em up! If you wanna know how to hold up a bank you should talk with Jack and me. We've looked down more gun barrels than you've had . . . More gun barrels than what Jack? Go on finish it off. I've lost the knack for

the fast phrase, the fast, meaningless phrase. I've been out of the game too long.

ESME 2: Goodnight.

JACK: Don't go to bed.

ESME exits.

JACK: I told you I'd be no help Col. I told you I'd be . . .

COLIN 2: You were a help Jack. A big help. You know what I like about you? I can talk to you.

Scene Ten B

Bedroom.

ESME: (*in bed, calls*) Colin! Col! . . .

House is empty. She moves from bed, puts typewriter aside. Sits in chair as next scene is played on bed in front of her.

Scene Eleven A

P.W.P. Bedroom, following morning. ESME sits aside, watching ESME 2 and COLIN 2.

ESME 2: (*sitting on edge of bed watching COLIN 2*) Colin! (*COLIN 2 groans.*) It's eleven o'clock. (*COLIN 2 groans.*) They've been calling.

COLIN 2: Tell them I'm sick.

ESME 2: You have to go. It's only a hangover.

COLIN 2: I'm sick.

ESME 2: You've got to go to the office.

COLIN 2: It's Saturday. No right-minded person works on a Saturday. Tell them I'm dead.

ESME 2:   Please. Col. Oh Colin. Don't go to sleep! I can't call them. They won't put me through.

COLIN 2:   I don't think I want to go to work again. Ever. (*gentle snore*)

ESME 2:   Okay. So be it. So be it.

ESME 2 gets up. COLIN 2 pulls the sheets over his head. ESME 2 takes some of his clothes out of the closet. Looks at them. Rejects them. Picks up the crumpled clothes he was wearing the night before. Slowly takes off her own clothes. Exits down stairs, brushing past ESME.

Blackout.

Scene Eleven B

P.W.P. Bedroom. ESME 2 and COLIN 2. Later that day. Lights up. ESME 2 sits on the bed, as before, dressed in her own clothes.

ESME 2:   Feeling better?

COLIN 2:   No. How long does it take to get over a hangover anyway? I'm out of practice.

ESME 2:   I told them you were sick. I don't think they believed me. I called six times before they'd put me through. They're well trained. Even on Saturday.

COLIN 2:   Everyone gets sick on a Saturday morning. It's because it follows Friday night.

ESME 2:   Do they all stay in bed till Saturday night?

COLIN 2:   Don't bitch at me. Not tonight.

ESME 2:   Well the paper still came out. You're not indispensible.

COLIN 2:   Where is it?

ESME 2:   I used it to fan the fire.

COLIN 2:   Don't tell me you burned it. Good God, can't I trust you even with that?

ESME 2:   I didn't say I burned it.

COLIN 2:   Well?

ESME 2:   It got burned.

COLIN 2:   Jesus! (*gets up*) What's this then? What's this? (*picks up the paper*) Jees . . . another bank robbery? They've got to be low on copy.

ESME 2:   It was a small one.

COLIN 2:   The size is irrelevant. It's boring. It's . . .

ESME 2:   It's Saturday. It was a credit union. The banks are closed.

COLIN 2:   Repetitive. It's repetitive. Look at this. This headline's three times too long. "Lone gunman escapes with $10,000 in yellow hatchback." Well what difference does the car make? Who cares?

ESME 2:   The owner of the car?

COLIN 2:   Ach! (*puts paper aside*) Did Jack call?

ESME 2:   I don't know.

COLIN 2:   What d'you mean you don't know?

ESME 2:   I wasn't answering the phone. Not today.

COLIN 2:   Oh for God's sake. Haven't you made that thing up with Barbara yet? (*no reply*) We can't afford to quarrel with Barbara. (*sighs*)

ESME 2:   Then you'd better go over there and tell her.

COLIN 2:   I've got a headache Esme. Why don't we just sit here in silence for a while? Why don't we try sitting in silence for a week?

Blackout.

Scene Twelve

COLIN and ESME's house.

COLIN: (*entering through front door, calls up*) You okay? I grabbed a quick coffee break, jumped in a cab — (*looks around*) Well, where are they? (*goes upstairs*)

ESME is in bed with typewriter. She looks up.

COLIN: Craig — Jack. What's her name — (*takes typewriter away from bed*)

ESME: You don't remember her name?

COLIN: Barb. Oh come on Es, I haven't got time for games. I told you the situation at work —

ESME: At work.

COLIN: They're on the patio! (*Begins to go downstairs. Stops. Realizes. Turns and goes slowly back to bedroom.*) We're gonna talk.

ESME: Now?

COLIN: Now.

ESME: But you have to get back to work.

COLIN: I want some answers. First. That boy. What's it gonna do to you bringing that boy here — *if* that's what you're doing — are you really off your head? (*ESME shrugs.*) Don't smart–ass me Esme.

ESME: He's here now.

COLIN: Here?

ESME: In this room. (*rubs her stomach*)

COLIN: (*looks at her; pause*) It was just a ploy huh? And I fell for it — just a ploy to keep me from leaving town —

ESME: No.

COLIN: (*grabs her*) Es!

ESME: Please go away — I have to work —

COLIN: You have me like a puppet! You think my work's not important right? That Sudan thing — let me tell you — listen — you wanna know why I didn't tell you? I wanted to protect you! I mean . . . (*fishes for a better word*) *protect* you — you think that's funny right?

ESME: I'm not laughing.

COLIN: You . . . you're suffocating me, you know that? Years, years I've spent trying to be . . . I dunno, trying to be some kind of — Rhett Butler to please you — don't laugh!

ESME: (*overlapping*) Frankly darling I don't give a damn! Sorry, I couldn't resist . . .

COLIN: (*overlapping*) So what *am* I supposed to be. Some androgynous flunky? Is that it? Yes ma'am, no ma'am, may I borrow your panties ma'am! Why don't you make up your mind what you want?

ESME: I want you.

COLIN: And I don't want to blur the edge any more . . . I have to work damnit. It's women who have kids, not men. And why do you have to make me sound like a walking cliché . . .? (*Puts his head in his hands. ESME looks over him to where next scene is already starting.*)

Scene Thirteen

P.W.P. COLIN 2 and BARBARA in BARBARA's house. Lights up on BARBARA, transformed; no longer frowsy, she looks glamorous. She is applying the finishing touches to her make-up when COLIN 2 enters.

COLIN 2:   Well . . . here I am. Seven o'clock on the dot, just as ordered. Your friendly baby sitter. Matter of fact it'll be good to spend an hour with my son. I haven't seen him for a while have I?

BARBARA: No. No . . . he's been asking for you.

COLIN 2: I'm a lousy father, isn't that right? Tell me I'm a lousy father. I'm a lousy everything else. Haven't spoken a word to my wife for nearly a week.

BARBARA: *(lightly)* Don't let it depress you.

COLIN 2: Where are you off to then? All dressed up . . . you look stunning Barb. Almost as good as that damned bird in your yard. Hey . . . make sure you come back early eh?

BARBARA: I'm a bit late. D'you mind if I borrow the car?

COLIN 2: I walked over. I've been trying to leave it at home more . . . give her a bit of an incentive to get out of the house. I think it's working. I'll swear she's used half a tank of gas. Maybe she's improving Barb. Maybe we'll turn the corner yet.

BARBARA: Good.

COLIN 2: You two aren't on speaking terms yet?

BARBARA: No. She knows that you were here last week. She knows, Colin. I told you what that'd do.

COLIN 2: She doesn't know anything. And even if she did . . . well she's got nothing to fear has she? Ach, why don't you just make one more effort with her?

BARBARA: I think I was probably doing too much for her anyway.

COLIN 2: What do you mean?

BARBARA: Shielding her. Jack says I should let her be more independent. I mean if she had to look after Matthew and get out to the super-market . . .

COLIN 2: Jack?

BARBARA: Yes.

COLIN 2: You mean . . . but . . . he found you?

BARBARA: He told me you wouldn't give him the address.

COLIN 2: That wouldn't stop him. Damned newspaperman. Is that where you're going now? Are you going to meet him?

BARBARA: Yes . . . I am as a matter of fact. Do I have to have your permission? You were going to introduce us anyway.

COLIN 2: You'd better go then hadn't you? You don't want to keep Jack MacNeil waiting. You'd better go.

BARBARA: Are you sure you'll be okay? You just have to put the kids to bed.

COLIN 2: Oh yes. Yes. What's on TV?

BARBARA: See you Colin.

COLIN 2: Yes. Have a good time. He's a married man you know . . . always the lady killer. Never could keep his hands off . . . even in Saigon when he knew half of them were poxy . . . (BARBARA *touches his shoulder lightly, then exits.* COLIN *continues as if she were still there.*) At least I assume he's not divorced yet. Always a ladies' man . . . always. You have to be careful, young Barbara. You have to watch your step. I'm telling you this for your own good. Nobody's safe when he's around . . . double-dealing bum . . .

CHILD'S VOICE: *(offstage)* Dad! Dad!

COLIN 2: No. I didn't mean you Matthew. Your Auntie Barbara's gone out on the town. Let's see what we can do to entertain ourselves. (*Goes over and looks at hamster cage. Turns the wheel.*)

CHILD'S VOICE: Daddy!

COLIN 2 *looks over to where voice is coming from but doesn't move.*

Blackout.

Scene Fourteen A

ESME *picks up doll and hugs it, goes and sit on stairs. Looks down and sees* ESME 2 *at bottom of stairs, a dim, shadowy figure in a white silk suit.*

Scene Fourteen B

P.W.P. Early morning, dim light. COLIN 2 *is in bed.* ESME 2 *brushes past* ESME *and goes up to bedroom. She dumps a pile of boxes on the bed and is about to exit when* COLIN 2's *voice halts her.*

COLIN 2:   (*sleepy*) What's going on . . . what's happening?

ESME 2:   I'm moving my things back upstairs. (*pause*) Are you awake? I'm tired of the chesterfield.

COLIN 2:   No.

ESME 2:   You're always sleeping.

COLIN 2:   It's early Esme. Let me sleep will you? It's been a grim week. Two guys off with flu . . . What's going on? What's that you're wearing?

ESME 2:   Like it?

COLIN 2:   What the . . .?

ESME 2:   Silk.

COLIN 2:   Where did you get it?

ESME 2:   Bought it.

COLIN 2:   *You* bought it?

ESME 2:   Yup. Went shopping yesterday. Got a whole slew of new things . . . a coat, shoes, this suit . . .

COLIN 2:   You . . .?

ESME 2:   Summer is a comin' in . . . Like it?

COLIN 2:   Very virginal. The white virgin breaks the ice. Twelve days of silence!

ESME 2:   Thirteen. Barb picked it out. I was tired of wearing your clothes.

COLIN 2:   Mine? When did you ever . . . What did you use for money?

ESME 2:   Oh . . . I have money. Well? How do I look?

COLIN 2:   You could use (lose) some (more) weight. (*depending on actress*)

ESME 2:   I'll work on it.

COLIN 2:   Can't we discuss this transformation later? Breakfast time for instance?

ESME 2:   I wasn't going to let Barb leave me behind.

COLIN 2:   You're trying to tell me that you've been out of the house? Is that it? Well it had to come . . . I knew it had to come. I suspected you'd done it anyway.

ESME 2:   You did? What did you suspect?

COLIN 2:   I'm glad you got around to telling me. You certainly choose your times.

ESME 2:   Do I? (*pause*) I think we should talk. I'm better now. Matthew's coming home.

COLIN 2:   Oh no. No . . . I'm not falling for that. The instant recovery. Come off it Esme. You've tried that one before. Try some other ploy, I've given up believing in miracles.

ESME 2:   He'll have to come back. There's nowhere else for him to go. Come on, do get up. You're always in bed these days. You spend all your time in bed. You come home from work and you go to bed. You get up and you go to work and then you . . .

COLIN 2:   He stays with Barbara.

ESME 2:   Barbara's going East. Montreal. With Jack. She's leaving her kids with her mother-in-law. We can't expect her mother-in-law to take ours as well.

COLIN 2:   For a holiday? She's going for a . . .?

ESME 2:   I don't know.

COLIN 2:   When did she tell you this?

ESME 2:   Yesterday. Get up. It's going to be a nice day. We could go for a drive.

COLIN 2:   Why didn't she tell me?

ESME 2:   Why should she? She's my sister. I think we should get a new car. Something with a bit more zip in it. (*pause*) Besides, you're jealous of Jack aren't you? Get up. (*COLIN 2 groans.*) I put a dent in our old car.

COLIN 2:   (*groans*) I'm not getting up.

ESME 2:   I left it off at an auto body shop. They're going to repaint it. Red. I told them they were your instructions.

COLIN 2:   I don't want a red car. But thanks. Thanks for telling me anyway. At 5:30 in the morning.

ESME 2:   We're invited to supper at Barb's. They're leaving later tonight. Jack MacNeil'll be there. You remember Jack. We have to pick Matthew up. I just have to move this stuff . . . (*brings more boxes into the bedroom and dumps them*) Oh come on Colin. Get up.

COLIN 2 groans and disappears under the bedclothes. ESME 2 throws back the bedclothes, laughs playfully. COLIN 2 snatches them.

COLIN 2:   Give me those.

ESME 2:   Get up! (*disappears and humps some more boxes into the room*)

COLIN 2:   Oh move that stuff later whatever it is.

ESME 2:   It's dawn. "Look where the dawn in russet mantle clad . . ." *Hamlet.*

COLIN 2:   "*See* where the dawn . . ." *See* . . .

ESME 2:   I'm the visual one, not you. (*She undoes her bag and takes a gun out, very casually.*)

COLIN 2:   What's that you've got?

ESME 2:   Can't you see it?

COLIN 2:   It looks like a . . . put the light on!

ESME 2:   Well . . . you'd hear it if I pulled the trigger. Maybe I should.

COLIN 2:   A gun? Es . . . don't point that thing at me.

ESME 2:   It's all right. I haven't assembled it. It's great isn't it? Feel the weight.

COLIN 2:   N–n–n–n-no.

ESME 2:   It's light. It's called a survivor's gun. It floats in water. It's the only one that you can get that takes to pieces like this. It's really easy to assemble . . . see . . . and it fits nicely into a bag. (*begins to assemble the gun*)

COLIN 2:   Give that to me.

ESME 2:   I can't if you won't get up.

COLIN 2:   Esme! (*pause*) Esme stop that. I don't need a demonstration.

ESME 2: You need a licence for a revolver . . . or any small gun . . . Did you know that?

COLIN 2: Es . . .

ESME 2: Any gun that can be easily hidden. But not this one. This . . . It's semi-automatic . . . look.

COLIN 2: Keep it awa . . .

ESME 2: Of course. You've looked down too many gun barrels.

COLIN 2: Don't wave it around like that. Joke over. It makes me nervous. Where'd you get it?

ESME 2: Somewhere.

COLIN 2: From Jack? Jack wouldn't be so . . . put it down Esme.

ESME 2: (commands) Stay where you are.

COLIN 2: No look . . .

ESME 2: Put your hands up. (pause) I got it from a department store.

COLIN 2: You . . .?

ESME 2: Ages ago. I said hands up. Now. Get out of bed.

COLIN 2: But . . .

ESME 2: Up! (COLIN 2 obeys.) Go over to the window. Open it. Go on. Open it. I said open the window Colin. (COLIN 2 obeys.) Say after me: "Look where the dawn in russet mantle clad, creeps . . ."

COLIN 2: "See where the . . ."

ESME 2: Look . . . (She prods him.)

COLIN 2: (turning suddenly) Give me that thing. Give me that . . . (Jumps her, wrestles her briefly. The gun falls.)

ESME 2: There. It's yours.

COLIN 2: You're crazy. You're right off your head.

ESME 2: You can keep it. I don't want it anymore. Oh . . . do be careful. It's loaded. I just wanted you to unstick yourself from that mattress and take a look at the dawn . . . oh don't go back to bed.

COLIN 2: (gets into bed, puts gun under pillow) I'm going to keep this with me.

ESME 2: You're welcome. Colin. Col . . . Come out from the blankets! Col! (sighs) I've been writing a play Col. I've almost finished it in the last two weeks. It's amazing how . . . I knew I could do it and I did Colin. (pause) I'm going to have to pull myself together aren't I? Now that we won't even have Barbara. We'll only have each other. Barbara's going back to Montreal (pause) I wish you'd look in the drawers. (pause) I wish you'd look in the closet. (pause) Colin . . . the ceiling's started to come down in the living room. Where the bathroom flooded. When you fixed the faucet, remember? It doesn't matter. It really doesn't matter . . . I can live with it. I can always step over the ceiling, or I can go and sit in the yard. When you've cut the grass. I'll sit out there with a book when I'm not writing. With a book. And I'll shut Matthew in the cellar so he won't get in the way. Colin. Put that gun away. Col . . . Col! (she screams)

COLIN 2 aims the gun and fires. An empty click. He collapses like an empty sack.

COLIN 2: You bitch! I nearly . . .

ESME 2: (laughs) Of course it wasn't loaded.

COLIN 2: (near to tears) I would've . . .

ESME 2:   It couldn't have been loaded. You watched me assemble it. I didn't have time to load it.

COLIN 2:   Get out of here. Get out Esme. That's it. Go!

ESME 2:   (*laughs*) Go?

COLIN 2:   Yes. Go. Go.

ESME 2:   All right. So be it. (*laughs*) So be it. (*exits*)

Blackout.

Scene Fourteen C

Sound of a child's voice singing. "Humpty Dumpty sat on a wall. Humpty Dumpy had a great fall . . ." Lights up. ESME is discovered near tape deck. She stops tape. Walks over to stairs.

Scene Fifteen

P.W.P. Semi-dark. ESME and COLIN's house. Sound of phone ringing. It rings and rings. Unanswered. Stops. Rings again. Sound of polite knocking on outside door. Unanswered. Doorbell rings. Unanswered. Pause.

Lights up on COLIN 2. He has been in bed for several days, dishevelled. A row of dirty cups and glasses is ranked against the bed. Bed is strewn with debris that ESME 2 left behind. Typewriter on bed.

Banging on outside door increases in pitch. Door is broken in. COLIN 2 gropes for gun which is under his pillow.

POLICEMAN 1:   Okay. You take downstairs . . . I'll go up. Take it easy eh?

He brushes past ESME, not seeing her. POLICEMAN 2 (CRAIG) searches downstairs.

POLICEMAN 1:   (*bursting into room, gun pointed at COLIN 2*) Police!

COLIN 2:   Eh? (*POLICEMAN 1 relaxes his guard with the gun.*) How'd you get in? (*pause*) I'm in bed.

POLICEMAN 1:   Colin Creary? Put your hands up. (*COLIN 2 obeys. POLICEMAN 1 looks around room.*)

COLIN 2:   What day is it?

POLICEMAN 1:   You've been absent from your office for several days.

COLIN 2:   So what? What the hell are you doing in my bedr . . .?

POLICEMAN 1:   Get up.

COLIN 2:   Get out of here. What business is it of . . .?

POLICEMAN 1:   We have a search warrant. (*calls down*) MacNeil! He's up here . . . alive. Are you the owner of a vehicle, licence number PMB 083?

COLIN 2:   Why?

POLICEMAN 1:   Left in Karey's autobody shop last Saturday? (*pause*) You won't object to us taking a look around. Routine. (*Pulls back covers revealing COLIN 2 curled up foetuslike around gun.*) That gun for instance.

COLIN 2:   It's not mine.

POLICEMAN 2 enters and begins search.

POLICEMAN 1:   No. No . . . would you mind if I . . .?

COLIN 2:   I'm holding it for . . . for someone.

POLICEMAN 1 takes gun. POLICEMAN 2 begins to open drawers, throws out wads of money.

Opens boxes and bags; they are full of money. COLIN 2 sinks down under sheet. POLICEMAN 1 pulls COLIN 2 out of bed.

POLICEMAN 1: Get dressed.

COLIN 2: I . . .

POLICEMAN 1: Move! (*COLIN 2 picks up his pants.*) I said move it. Move! Here! (*thrusts shirt at him*) Think we've got all day?

COLIN 2: I've been in bed.

POLICEMAN 1: He's been in bed!

COLIN 2: For days.

POLICEMAN 1: He's been in bed for days. Move it!

He pushes COLIN 2 downstairs past ESME and out of the door. ESME goes slowly upstairs, confronts POLICEMAN 2 who is just leaving; he doesn't seem to see her. He exits. She begins to tidy away the mess of papers and money. Sits on the bed looking down on the jail.

Scene Sixteen

P.W.P. CRAIG and COLIN 2 in jail. CRAIG pushes COLIN 2 into jail with gun in his ribs. Tears off COLIN 2's shirt. Pistol whips him. Takes shirt, feels in pockets. Tosses it aside. Does same with COLIN 2's jacket.

COLIN 2: I'd like to make a call.

CRAIG: Pants.

COLIN 2: Well, it's my right isn't it? One call?

CRAIG: I said pants.

COLIN 2: What the . . .?

CRAIG: Off!

COLIN 2 doesn't move. CRAIG walks over and feels in the pockets of his pants. COLIN 2 pushes him away.

COLIN 2: What are you? Some kind of animal? (*unzips pants and allows them to fall without stepping out of them*)

CRAIG: On your knees.

COLIN 2: What?

CRAIG: Deaf?

COLIN 2: What are you some kind of . . . brute? Idiot brute? (*CRAIG pistol whips him. Forces him to step out of his pants. COLIN 2 goes down on his knees.*) This isn't happening.

CRAIG: Think you're so big? Drop those underpants. (*COLIN 2 refuses.*) Drop!

COLIN 2: Look — I don't understand.

CRAIG: What's to understand? Drop!

COLIN 2: I want to see a lawyer. (*CRAIG laughs.*) You won't get away with this. I'll sue . . . I want to see a lawyer. Now. It's my right. My right! (*CRAIG forces him onto all fours with his gun. COLIN 2 gets back into a kneeling position.*) There are no charges . . . what can they charge me with? Bank robbery? That's absurd. Attempted murder? I wouldn't hurt a fly. I love my wife. We play games that's all. Games . . . (*CRAIG kicks him back to all fours.*) Craig . . .!

CRAIG: Mister MacNeil. Say it. (*kicks*)

COLIN 2: Mister . . . Fucking mister! Mister punk, who the hell do you think you . . . (*CRAIG tears off his underpants.*) I'm clean. Clean! Listen I'm sorry. I didn't mean . . . I'm clean.

CRAIG: I can see. I got eyes.

COLIN 2: I haven't done drugs for . . .

CRAIG: Been sleeping for ten days have you?

COLIN 2:   I'm a journalist.

CRAIG: Been snowing for ten days has it? (*Turns COLIN 2 around so that he is on all fours and CRAIG is looking at his rear. Jabs his rear with gun.*) Snowbrain. Who do you think you are anyway? Pierre fucking Trudeau? (*kicks him*) Who do you think you're bigger than?

COLIN 2:   (*whimpering*) I wanna call my wife.

CRAIG: Wife? Oh, it's his wife he needs.

COLIN 2:   In Montreal. That's where she probably is. With her sister. I'll pay for the call.

CRAIG jabs him viciously. COLIN 2 spins around, wrestles with him briefly. The gun goes off.

Blackout.

Scene Seventeen

Lights come up slowly on COLIN on patio, sitting by hammock, pushing it gently. Gets up. Tiptoes into kitchen. Gets tray with orange juice and glasses. Goes back out to hammock. Picks up baby, tries to figure out how to carry tray and baby. Finally settles on baby alone. Puts tray down. Tiptoes upstairs, sees that ESME is sleeping. Puts baby to sleep in cradle (in alcove offstage). Is about to go down for orange juice when ESME opens one eye. He goes over, kneels by the bed, puts his head on her stomach.

ESME: (*soothing him*) Valderee, valderaa, valderee, valder . . .

COLIN: . . . a hahahahaha ha!

They clown, laugh, hug. Doorbell sounds. They stiffen. COLIN gets up tentatively, goes downstairs, kicks over glasses. Ignores them, changes his mind, picks up tray and takes it into kitchen. Door bell.

ESME: Colin!

COLIN opens door and ushers JACK and BARBARA in. They have aged. We see them as they are in 'real life,' an average suburban couple. JACK is blustery, BARBARA overawed. JACK has two bottles of champagne. COLIN looks out beyond them to the street.

JACK: He's down there parking the car. Is it all meters?

COLIN: Tell him I'll pay the ticket.

JACK: Ach!

BARBARA: Maybe we shoulda waited for him.

COLIN: No, come on in. (*hesitates, then shakes hands with JACK, pecks BARB on cheek*)

JACK: Sorry we're behind schedule.

BARBARA: That clutch's been acting up ever since we left . . . Is she all right?

COLIN: Fine. Fine — sick of being in bed —

JACK: She's antsy?

COLIN: Not any more.

JACK: She was like a time bomb last time. We had two false alarms — that's why I insisted on a hospital.

COLIN: We wanted to do it the natural way. Glad you made it —

JACK: Still chasing ambulances?

COLIN: Let me get some glasses —

While COLIN puts more glasses on tray, BARBARA and JACK take their coats off, look around curiously.

BARBARA: Hey Jack, come and look at the patio. Look — a hammock. (*to COLIN*) All we have on our porch is dogshit and kids' fire trucks —

COLIN: (*laughs*) Come on up and say hi.

JACK and BARBARA follow him upstairs. BAR-BARA kisses ESME. JACK takes her hand.

JACK: So?

BARBARA: How are you?

ESME: Empty.

BARBARA: (*nervous*) I know how you feel — like an overripe cheese in the plastic bag eh? I was the same with our two. I was three weeks late with Iain. (*to JACK*) Isn't that how I said I felt hon? (*ESME puts her knees down, and BAR-BARA sees that she is no longer pregnant.*) Oh! Es! (*hugs her*)

ESME: Sssh! (*indicates that baby is in next room*)

BARBARA: Boy or girl?

ESME: Girl.

BARBARA: What's her name?

JACK: Congratulations. (*shakes COLIN's hand; to BARBARA*) I told you not to get cigars! (*Kisses ESME, embarrassed, still holding champagne. COLIN is still holding orange juice.*)

ESME: No cigars?

BARBARA: So what is her name?

ESME: Cassandra.

COLIN turns sharply.

BARBARA: Nice. Kinda old fashioned.

ESME: Sandra for short —

BARBARA: (*laughs*) Oh that's better.

COLIN: (*putting down tray casually*) Well, isn't this civilized? The old gang together again after what . . .?

JACK: Years.

COLIN: So much water under the . . .

ESME: How many bridges do you have Jack? (*bares her teeth*) I imagined you with less hair.

JACK: Tempus bloody well fugits. (*pause*)

ESME: No peacock shit?

BARBARA: What?

ESME: On your porch?

BARBARA: Peacocks?

ESME: That's a relief.

BARBARA and JACK exchange glances. COLIN has walked over to the window.

ESME: (*to COLIN's back*) He's parking the car. (*to BARBARA*) Where are your kids?

BARBARA: We left them with my sister back home. We needed a break from them, eh Jack?

COLIN: Why don't you get up for a while Es? We could go and sit on the patio. Have a few pre-prandial nibblies. She was born the night before last, and we were back here the next day. She was down in the kitchen this morning making this fantastic pâté, can you believe that? Forty-two years old!

ESME: I had to do something with the placenta.

BARBARA and JACK react to this, COLIN has turned back to the window, chuckling.

COLIN: There he is! (*spies CRAIG in street*)

ESME: (*mocking*) Pre-prandial nibblies! That's for your benefit Jack!

JACK: Ach — with three kids around you learn to talk in monosyllables, eh love? (*squeezes BARBARA*)

Doorbell sounds. JACK goes down to let CRAIG in. Pauses with him by the outside door. CRAIG has luggage. Doesn't seem too eager to go upstairs.

COLIN: Well — you're still looking good Barb. (*bustles*)

ESME: What are you doing?

COLIN: Tidying up.

BARBARA: (*uneasy*) Jack was so keen to visit but I . . .

COLIN: Oh come on. I can pay you a compliment after 20 years!

BARBARA: It's the first break he's taken since he got the agency started.

ESME: Agency?

BARBARA: Real estate and insurance — it's going good.

ESME: I knew it!

COLIN: So he's given up on newsprint?

BARBARA: Ages ago — (*to ESME*) Jack and I got out your old wedding pictures before we left. Me with my matron of honour smile and mumps . . . (*blows out her cheeks, giggles*)

COLIN: That's right. I wouldn't kiss you. It's supposed to make men sterile.

BARBARA: Kissing?

COLIN: Mumps, silly.

BARBARA: And I refused to shave my armpits. Heavens, the sixties!

ESME: That's right, you did have mumps.

CRAIG bursts into the room. He is well dressed in contrast to previous scenes.

CRAIG: Dad said . . . (*Stops. Stares at ESME. She freezes.*)

COLIN: Hey! (*punches CRAIG, friendly*) Take a look at these shoulders, Es. Where'd he get them?

ESME hugs her shoulders.

JACK: (*entering*) All the better to tackle me with eh Craig? (*crouches in mock rugby tackle*)

COLIN: (*to JACK*) Still playing the old game?

JACK: Not me.

COLIN: I joined the over-40's club! (*to CRAIG*) You?

JACK: Ach — it's all hockey in our town — (*They laugh.*) Hey Craigie. This is Colin. Best man when I married your mother. Then we changed partners eh? (*pats ESME*) Very civilized. (*During this ESME is staring at CRAIG.*)

COLIN: (*to CRAIG*) So . . . are you in college?

JACK: Sure is — tell them what you're studying Craig. (*to ESME*) This'll get to you!

ESME: What.

CRAIG: Creative writing.

COLIN: You study that?

ESME: You're not in the police?

CRAIG: What?

Pause.

ESME: Your picture doesn't do you justice.

COLIN: Come on, let's drink this on the patio. (*picks up champagne*) Bit warm but what the hell. Come on Craig. Last time I saw you I coulda picked you up with one hand. Creative writing? (*to ESME*) Bring her down. (*the baby*)

CRAIG and COLIN exit. COLIN gives CRAIG tray to carry. JACK helps ESME out of bed.

ESME: You go ahead. Go on. I'm not an invalid, silly —

JACK: Sure? (*ESME nods.*)

BARBARA: Are you breast feeding?

ESME: (*nods*) I'm soaked.

BARBARA: Oh, let's see her!

ESME exits to baby. BARBARA and JACK look at each other. He puts his arm round her and indicates that they should join CRAIG and COLIN.

JACK: She likes to make a grand entrance.

COLIN and CRAIG are downstairs out of earshot of the rest.

COLIN: I shoulda been in Baghdad today.

CRAIG: Our car broke down, that's why we're —

COLIN: That car has more sense than I do, know that?

CRAIG: What's in Baghdad?

COLIN: Ali Baba for all I know! (*laughs*) Is there any room in that course you're taking?

CRAIG: You don't need a course!

COLIN: (*shrugs*) I need a bit of time to enjoy the peace.

CRAIG: Peace?

COLIN: Well, maybe it's only a cease-fire.

JACK and BARBARA join COLIN and CRAIG.

COLIN: Just talking about peace.

CRAIG: He's not going to Baghdad.

JACK: You're not giving it up, finally?

COLIN: (*shrugs*) I don't think I'm up to it right now. I feel like I've been through a bit of a war and . . .

JACK: I wondered how much longer . . . listen, they were wanting another editor on the *Gazette* back home. Chap who replaced me turned out to be a wee bit of a dud —

COLIN: No offence, Jack — I'd rather take up knitting. You know — (*draws him aside*)

During this BARBARA is stranded on the outside. CRAIG goes over to stairs and stands, undecided.

JACK: They should pension you off before you burn out.

COLIN: Got a replacement part now. (*nods upstairs, grins*)

JACK: And then they grow up.

COLIN: I watched it happen —

JACK: Aye — it's quite a sight.

COLIN: Done a bit of watching in our time eh? Did you . . . did you . . . you know . . . get to hold yours?

JACK: Sure — that's part of it.

COLIN: It was like that time in the Sudan.

JACK: What?

COLIN: My knees gave way — thought I was gonna keel over. (*JACK laughs nervously.*) I mean — see — they let me — you know, hold her before they cleaned her off — it's against the rules — there was blood. (*indicates his hands*) And I did it. She's mine. (*laughs*) C'mon, let's celebrate . . . (*They go through to patio.*) C'mon Es.

Voices only. We see their shadowy shapes, but they should not pull focus from ESME, hardly more than a murmur.

COLIN: One at a time —

JACK: Oh go on, open them both.

BARBARA: It's the best. We bought the best-

COLIN: Yea, I can see . . . whoops —

BARBARA: Oh, d'you have a cloth?

JACK: It's all right, they'll clean . . .

BARBARA: (*laughs*) Cassandra — who was it was called that?

JACK: She's dead.

BARBARA: Oh Jack!

Meanwhile CRAIG goes slowly upstairs. He stands, looking at ESME. Long pause. ESME is sitting on the bed with the baby, looks over baby to CRAIG.

ESME: Like him. Like me. You have our face. (*Indicates stomach. Laughs softly.*) It was hard as a stone. (*CRAIG approaches her slowly. She encourages him to put his hand on her stomach.*) A stone cracked open — a cave — and inside, curled up inside — life. Blind life — the wonder — the wonder of it.

CRAIG puts his arms round her neck. They embrace.

End.

Dreaming and Duelling
John Lazarus and Joa Lazarus

John Lazarus holds the distinction, according to a Playwrights Union of Canada survey, of having been the most-produced Canadian playwright of the 1988-89 theatre season. Like Sharon Pollock and David French, other major figures in the survey, Lazarus came to playwriting trained as an actor. Born in Montreal in 1947, he graduated from the National Theatre School in 1969. After an unhappy summer in the Stratford Festival company, he moved to Vancouver and performed in children's theatre, writing his first plays while on tour with Playhouse Holiday. He won *Performing Arts Magazine*'s 1971 National Playwriting Competition with *Chester, You Owe My Bird an Apology*. *Babel Rap*, an absurdist one-act comedy featuring two contemporary workmen on the Tower of Babel, first produced by Vancouver's Troupe in 1972, became one of the most popular Canadian plays of the decade. But after his New Play Centre debut, *How We Killed the Moose* (1974), Lazarus hit what he considers his low point as a playwright with *Midas* in 1977.

Dreaming and Duelling, co-produced by the New Play Centre and Vancouver Playhouse in 1980, turned his career around. It was followed by a trio of young people's plays for Green Thumb Theatre—*Schoolyard Games* (1981), *Not So Dumb* (1984) and *Night Light* (1986)—which have toured the world and played to audiences in the hundreds of thousands. Lazarus's "adult" plays, almost all concerned with the tribulations of growing up, have also enjoyed success. *The Late Blumer* (1984) ran for six months at Vancouver's Arts Club. *Village of Idiots* (Young People's Theatre, Toronto, 1985) and *Genuine Fakes* (Toronto Free, 1986) showed Lazarus ranging from Eastern European folk tale to contemporary rock 'n' roll parable. *David for Queen* (Catalyst/Theatre Network, 1988) and *Homework & Curtains* (Belfry/Touchstone, 1990) have further enhanced Lazarus's growing national reputation. Other credits include CBC radio plays, the 1980 TV movie *Jen's Place*, co-written with Michael Glassbourg, and episodes of "Lies from Lotus Land," "Northwood" and "Inside Stories."

Dreaming and Duelling is the prototypical John Lazarus drama: an adult play about the thin line between fantasy and reality, and the difficulty of being young; a young people's play for adults. Written in collaboration with his ex-wife Joa, it developed from their arguments about the motivations of two adolescent English boys who were reported in the newspaper to have fought a near-fatal duel over a girl, using wooden swords. Were they romantic, as John thought, or chauvinistic as Joa argued, with the girl just an excuse for the boys to play out their egocentric male fantasies? Joa criticized John's drafts, did rewrites, and wrote some of the dialogue. Joa Lazarus is currently "on sabbatical from writing" while raising eight children.

Dreaming and Duelling has been seen in Ottawa (Theatre 2000), Calgary (ATP), Edmonton (Phoenix), and Toronto (Shaw Festival/Young People's Theatre), where it was runner-up for the 1983 Chalmers Canadian Play Award, as well as in numerous college and university productions. It was first presented by the New Play Centre and the Vancouver Playhouse at the Waterfront Theatre on September 25, 1980, with Robin Mossley as Joel, Doug Greenall as Eric, Brenda Robins as Louise, Derek Boyes as Skelly, and Patricia Ludwick as Mrs. Thorpe. It was directed by Bob Baker, with set design by Ken MacDonald, lighting by Douglas Welch, costumes by Ken MacDonald and Pam Johnson, music by Bruce Ruddell, and fencing arrangements by Cliff Lloyd.

Patricia Ludwick as Mrs. Thorpe, Robin Mosely as Joel, and Derek Boyes as Skelly in the New Play Centre production of *Dreaming and Duelling*. Photo by Steve Terrell.

DREAMING AND DUELLING

CHARACTERS

JOEL GOLDNER, sixteen, a high-school student

ERIC CULLEN, same age, his friend and fencing partner

SKELLY, same age, very athletic

LOUISE, same age, notably pretty but for a large facial birthmark of the kind called a "port-wine stain"

MRS. THORPE, a phys. ed. and fencing teacher

SCENE

In and around a school in a Canadian city, present day. (The play was first produced in 1980, so some of the adolescent slang may call for updating.)

The settings are:

School gym, with fencing strip
Locker room
JOEL's bedroom
Bleachers at the football field
MRS. THORPE's office
School cafeteria
A park at dawn

Different designers have come up with varying ways to present these seven separate settings. Most of the set designs have involved variations on a gymnasium-with-bleachers motif.

ACT ONE

Scene One

Darkness. The sound of blades. Two white figures, their faces unseen behind fencing masks, fence in dim light. Slow motion; freezes; the amplified sound of blades sliding on each other. The movements are those of standard sports fencing at first; then they grow larger and bolder. The figures leave the fencing strip and

range across the stage. The fencing grows inspired and attractive, beautifully improvised. The fencers are as interested in creating elaborate patterns as they are in winning. Some moments of this; then one of the fencers scores a point at the other one's chest. Sound out, lights up. In full light they are ERIC and JOEL, two high-school boys in fencing uniforms. JOEL, who has lost the point, emits a loud war-whoop of ecstasy and falls on the floor in sheer joy.

JOEL: Heaven! Absolute Heaven! (*takes off mask*)

ERIC: (*taking off his own mask, laughing*) That was amazing! That was truly amazing!

JOEL: Rilly. Eric, I've had dreams about fencing like that.

ERIC: I haven't. I didn't know anybody could fence like that.

JOEL: Well, Jesus, I always knew I could, but I figured not for another five years or so.

ERIC: Well, you see, you didn't count on having a partner like me, right.

JOEL: Exactly. Exactly! (*leaps to his feet*) Eric, mon ami — I embrace you!

ERIC: Why don't we just shake on it.

JOEL: Whatever.

They shake. Enter MRS. THORPE.

MRS. THORPE: All right, you two, stop this nonsense.

ERIC: We stopped a minute ago. An' it wasn't nonsense.

JOEL: Betty, didja see us? Didja *see* us?

MRS. THORPE: I heard you. I think they heard you all the way in the office. I also—

JOEL: Good! Wake 'em up.

MRS. THORPE: I also saw you.

JOEL: Give 'em something to wonder at.

MRS. THORPE: Hey, wonder boy! Both of you! Your undivided attention! I saw you slashing all over the gym, with no thought of safety.

ERIC: There was nobody near us.

MRS. THORPE: Only because they had the good sense to get out of the way. You monopolized the whole gym.

JOEL: Yes — but — did — you — see — how — we — *fenced*?

MRS. THORPE: It's no excuse.

JOEL: Aw, Betty. you gotta admit it was brilliant fencing. It was inspired. (*to ERIC*) Wasn't it inspired?

ERIC: It was inspired.

MRS. THORPE: It's no excuse! Even if it *was* something special, and I have my doubts.

ERIC: (*to JOEL*) It was.

JOEL: It was.

MRS. THORPE: (*calls off*) Arnie! Don't make a huge sweeping curve out of it! Just come straight in! (*to JOEL and ERIC*) If I notice any greatness in you two I'll let you know. Don't hold your breath.

JOEL: Betty, inspiration just struck this gym! Like a bolt of lightning through the roof! Magic just happened here! Cullen and I came up with some genuinely supernatural fencing, and you talk about regulations. Regulations

have nothing to do with it. It's against the regulations for us to be this good!

ERIC: Yeah, right!

MRS. THORPE: (*calls off*) Arnie! Don't make a huge sweeping curve out of it! Just come straight in! (*to JOEL and ERIC*) If I notice any greatness in you two I'll let you know. Don't hold your breath.

ERIC: Thanks.

MRS. THORPE: Anyway, look, you're here to practise your one-two compound attack.

JOEL: But we know it backwards.

ERIC is already picking up his mask and épée.

MRS. THORPE: Show me.

The two boys take up guard, JOEL without bothering to get his mask.

MRS. THORPE: Joel.

JOEL gets mask, puts it on. They salute: ERIC simply touching the mask with the bell of his épée, but JOEL executing a fancy figure-eight salute that makes an impressive swish-swish through the air. They demonstrate the one-two compound attack.

JOEL: One, two, compound attack.

Performs it. Then ERIC does his silently.

JOEL: (*repeats*) One, two, compound attack.

ERIC repeats his.

MRS. THORPE: Well, not bad, but you can perfect it. (*to JOEL*) Your rear foot's still rolling forward when you go into the lunge, and (*to ERIC*) you've got to straighten your arm first and then lunge, instead of bringing the whole thing forward at once —

ERIC: Oh, I know. I know, but we got bored.

MRS. THORPE: (*confidential*) I know it gets boring. But listen, how do you think some of these other clowns feel? They're bored too, and they can't even *do* it right. You know what a pathetic bunch I've got this year.

JOEL & ERIC: Yeah . . .

MRS. THORPE: But they're trying, aren't they? Do you think it makes it easy for them to see you two leaping around like a couple of — a couple of —

JOEL: Legends.

MRS. THORPE: Maniacs.

JOEL: Ooh, strong language.

MRS. THORPE: Well, all that screaming, I mean really. This course is on shaky enough ground as it is.

ERIC: We were just havin' a little fun, Betty. Nobody else minds.

MRS. THORPE: Eric, I don't want to lose this course over a couple of screamers, okay?

SKELLY enters: large, handsome, athletic. Carries a volleyball net and a ball.

SKELLY: Hi, Mrs. Thorpe.

MRS. THORPE: Hello, Skelly.

JOEL & ERIC: (*sardonic*) Hello, Skelly.

SKELLY: Our turn, guys. Time to pack in the rubber swords.

MRS. THORPE: Skelly, will you put up the net? (*blows her whistle*) I don't want you two mucking around any more, all right? (*exits*)

JOEL: "Mucking around." Jesus Christ.

SKELLY: Oh, yeah? She catch you two doing it on the floor?

JOEL: Skelly, whenever you come in here with your big volleyballs I am a study in mixed feelings.

SKELLY: Are you, Goldner.

JOEL: On the one hand I hate seeing your grinning mug because it means fencing is over for another two days and I gotta spend forty-eight boring hours waiting for the next class.

SKELLY: Boo hoo hoo.

JOEL: And also because generally speaking you're such an asshole.

SKELLY: And you're a pervert.

JOEL: On the other hand, it's such a thrill to watch you walk in here — biceps bulging — great thighs rippling — and that lump in your pants swelling like Mount Saint Helen's —

ERIC: Joel —

SKELLY: Go to hell, you little creep! (*to ERIC*) You should stop hanging around with this weiner. You're gonna wind up just like him. Everybody knows he's a faggot.

JOEL: Only for you, Skelly, only for you.

ERIC: Joel, cut it out.

SKELLY: (*to ERIC*) You should try to screw Louise, instead of Goldner here. At least Louise is a good lay, eh?

ERIC: Oh, yeah, you know personally, eh, Skelly.

SKELLY: Course. She can't get enough of me.

ERIC: Sure, Skelly.

SKELLY: She can't. And if you don't believe me she's a good lay, you could ask practically anybody. Everybody's had her 'cept you two, eh?

As he exits we hear the school buzzer, absurdly loud and long, drowning out all conversation and thought.

ERIC: (*drowned out*) Asshole! Creep!

Buzzer finally ends.

JOEL: He hasn't, he hasn't. He's putting you on.

Scene Two

With no break in the dialogue, the scene shifts to the locker room. JOEL and ERIC change into their street clothes as they talk.

ERIC: I dunno. He's had every other chick in the school.

JOEL: Yeah, but not Louise.

ERIC: Well, Louise has had a couple of guys herself, you know.

JOEL: I know.

ERIC: Not everybody, that's bullshit, but, you know.

JOEL: I know. But she's too good for Skelly.

ERIC: *I* know that. I just hope *she* does.

JOEL: Don't worry, the woman has standards. She can resist that kind of temptation. Hell, she can resist him better than I can. Those big shoulders, that big muscular ass. I tell ya, I just go all fluttery.

ERIC: Goldner, I wish you wouldn't talk like that.

JOEL: (*cutesy*) Why not? I just can't help it, it's the way I am.

ERIC: Stop talking like that!

JOEL: Relax. You're just repressed.

ERIC: *Goldner* — Joel — My old lady calls me that.

JOEL: Right, sorry.

ERIC: Anyway, you like girls. Why don't you just stick to girls?

JOEL: "Stick to them." Apt phrase. Stick to them with Krazy Glue. Wouldn't mind sticking to somebody — anybody — male, female, animal, vegetable, mineral. Speaking of Louise, I wouldn't mind sticking to Louise.

ERIC: *You* wouldn't.

JOEL: Goddamn it, I wouldn't even mind sticking it to old Bitchy Betty. (*ERIC laughs.*) I bet old Bitchy only does it missionary style. With a stopwatch and a whistle. Hollering instructions.

ERIC: (*imitating MRS. THORPE*) "Stay on the strip! Doesn't count unless you're on the fencing strip!"

JOEL: (*laughs*) Very nice, very nice. Hey, can you imagine Bitchy in eighteenth-century France, eh?

ERIC: (*snorts*) No.

JOEL: She woulda driven them all wacko. There's old D'Artagnan, slaughtering twenty-three of the Cardinal's elite corps of crack guardsmen single-handed. An' Bitchy comes running in and hollers, "Doesn't count, your little toe's off the strip!"

ERIC: And he turns around and says, "What?" and they all run him through.

JOEL: No, no! Not old D'Artagnan. He just turns around and runs *her* through and gets back to the big boys. Ah, they knew what they were doing in those days, man. D'Artagnan and Cyrano and Zorro and Valerian. They lived it. All the time. None of this shit, marking time through two rotten days of English

Lit and Math and History before you can get down to a little real life, a little fencing. What the hell am I gonna do with my stupid boring life for two whole empty days?

ERIC: Well, gee, Joel, you could jerk off.

JOEL: You're absolutely right. Jerking off is the only thing that comes close, and even it doesn't come close. Ah, but wasn't that something, though?

ERIC: That was something else. It was like I knew exactly what you were gonna do. Every moment.

JOEL: Yeah. True communication. That was what I call transcendental fencing . . . Eric. Mon vieux. 'Ave I evair mentioned to you — ze glorious name of — Valerian L'Estomber?

ERIC: Who's he?

JOEL: Valerian L'Estomber was ze greatest swordsman in Ravolutionary France.

ERIC: No kidding, eh.

JOEL: No sheet. 'E was an aristocrat 'oo worked wit' ze peasants, as a spy on ze othaire aristocrats.

ERIC: Why do you keep talking like that?

JOEL: Also 'e was ze greatest lovaire een France as well. Kept a harem. Mostly teenagers. Girls and boys both.

ERIC: Oh, Jesus, Goldner.

JOEL: Yeah. And, mon ami, I just so 'appen to be ze world's greatest aut'oritee on Valerian. I 'ave, een my room, ze world's foremost collecksyawn of Valerian memorabilia. And you are to be ze feerst to see eet.

ERIC: Oh! Well. Excellent.

Lights fade.

Scene Three

Lights up on JOEL's room. JOEL and ERIC are looking through a cardboard carton, in and around which are items and papers about Valerian. ERIC is admiring a document on what looks like very old paper.

JOEL: See, for the coat of arms, I used only the colours that they would use. This thing took me over a week.

ERIC: The paper looks so old.

JOEL: You singe it with a candle so it turns brown. Wait. Here. Looka this. This is his brooch, for keeping his scarf on.

ERIC: Where'd you get this? Is this real?

JOEL: Glass. Cost me a quarter at the Sally Ann. It was only a quarter because there's two of the diamonds missing, see? And they're missing because zey were removed by ze priests 'oo robbed hees grave.

ERIC: The priests robbed his grave!

JOEL: Oh, yes indeedy. Valerian was a sworn enemy of the Church.

ERIC: *(approving)* All right!

JOEL: Thought you'd like that. See, it was because of this crooked bishop who used to rape the village girls, and they didn't dare tell on him 'cause he was the bishop.

ERIC: That figures.

JOEL: Yeah, so one of them went crying to Valerian. Valerian went straight to the bishop's house, walked right in, and castrated the guy with one flick of his sword.

ERIC: Aw, Joel, Jesus!

JOEL: No, no, listen. This became a big public issue. Valerian said that if he really wasn't into raping village girls, if he was a real priest, he shouldn't mind losing his balls.

ERIC: Fair enough.

JOEL: Right, so then all the village girls started coming out and accusing the guy, and then the guy co— (*hesitates*)

ERIC: What?

JOEL: Uh, committed suicide, actually.

ERIC: Okay.

JOEL: Okay. So anyway, after that the priests all hated Valerian. Especially when all the beautiful girls the bishop had raped got together and joined Valerian's harem. But anyway, the point of all this is, after he died the priests robbed his grave.

ERIC: Rilly.

JOEL: He was a great sex maniac, old Valerian. You know what he used to do when he was fencing with, like, a real enemy? He would open his pants and jerk off with the other hand. Because like you can't keep a hard-on if you're at all frightened. So this was to show that he wasn't scared, and freak the other guy out. And also I guess he just dug it. Sometimes he would keep the guy fencing until he was ready to come, and then run the poor son of a bitch through at the precise moment of climax.

ERIC: (*appalled*) Oh, Jesus.

JOEL: Yeah, neat, eh?

ERIC: Joel, that's disgusting!

JOEL: Yeah, I know.

ERIC: Okay, wait a minute, lemme get this straight here: he was working on the side of the peasants, against the Church?

JOEL: Yeah, yeah, and against the nobility. Even his own family. The only guys who knew what a spy he was were three or four contacts among the revolutionary peasants. He was a legend in his own time.

ERIC: What was his name again?

JOEL: Valerian L'Estomber. It means Valerian drops. Eighteenth-century drug.

ERIC: "Valerian — Laisse-tomber," I get it. Dumb joke, Joel.

JOEL: This is not a joke, Eric, none of this is a joke.

ERIC: I had no idea you had any of this. How come you never told me about this stuff before?

JOEL: You and I never fenced like that before.

ERIC: What are you gonna do with all of it?

JOEL: Nothing. I was thinking of starting his diary, but it'd take forever. I'd never finish it.

ERIC: You should write a book. You could make a book out of this.

JOEL: Nah.

ERIC: Oh, you should, man, you should! You got so many ideas about this guy, you could write a whole series!

JOEL: Writing some dumb series isn't the point.

ERIC: Joel, come on. You could make a fortune with this thing.

JOEL: It'd wreck it. It'd turn it into work. Besides, people wouldn't understand it. They'd think I was a total nut case.

ERIC: I don't.

JOEL: You, mon ami, are diffayront. Most people think you're supposed to outgrow all this swashbuckling crap when you're eleven. So then tell me, how come it's so terrific to pretend you're Sylvester Stallone and Don Johnson and all those dorks? The entire high school is stocked with cheap imitation Rambos. That's supposed to be okay. But to make up your own? To make up a Valerian? Ho, boy. They'd think I was crazy. That's why they're so fucked up. They're afraid to admit their fantasies.

ERIC: Like their sex fantasies, eh.

JOEL: No no no, any fantasies. Sex fantasies are just like all the others, only you sort of jerk off in the background. Right?

ERIC: I dunno.

JOEL: Sure. People aren't ashamed of the sex, they're ashamed of the fantasies. But the thing is that everybody fantasizes. Everybody lives in this dream movie in their heads. This is a fact.

ERIC: Everybody? Come on.

JOEL: Absolutely. Every moment of their lives. Nobody in history has ever woke up and actually noticed the real world — ever.

ERIC: Oh, Goldner. Just 'cause you're like that you think everybody is. I don't have any fantasies. So there goes your whole idea.

JOEL: Biggest fantasy of all! Course you do, everybody does. It's because our lives are shit, you know. If we ever woke up and saw the real world we'd all puke. I swear, you know, the only time I think clearly is when it's Valerian. Rest of the time I'm all mixed up. Whenever nothing's happening in my mind, Valerian just appears and takes over.

ERIC: (suddenly sits up, alarmed) Jesus.

JOEL: What! What is it!

ERIC: I never thought about it before. I never noticed what it was.

JOEL: Told ya! So what is it? Tell me it.

ERIC: Never mind.

JOEL: I told you mine. I even showed you my props.

ERIC: It isn't the same. This isn't a fantasy. It's just something I think of.

JOEL: So tell me!

ERIC: Joel, it's none of your business.

JOEL: Of course it's my business!

ERIC: No! It is *none* of *your business*! I'm the one who decides that! Not you! So just *back off*, Joel!

JOEL: Well, all right. Holy shit, I didn't mean to cause you a traumatic experience or nothing. (*puts props back in box*)

ERIC: When Valerian did his spying—he didn't do it with anybody else?

JOEL: Nevaire.

ERIC: Wasn't there ever one guy who was like a longtime connection? Like a sidekick?

JOEL: Ay sidekeek? Valerian does not deal wit' ze sidekeek. 'E works always alone. Zere ees no one 'e can trost.

ERIC: Not even a peasant?

JOEL: What are you getting at?

ERIC: You know, like Sancho Panza. Like Tonto. A faithful companion.

JOEL: He has a dog named Marcel.

ERIC: A guy, a guy! A guy he can trust! Why are you being so dense?

JOEL: It just isn't his style.

ERIC: Aw, come on, Joel. What if somebody asked? To be his sidekick.

JOEL: Uh–uh.

ERIC: Some real smart peasant.

JOEL: He can fight off a hundred men singlehanded. What's he need a sidekick for?

ERIC: Doesn't he ever need somebody to talk to? Just to talk to? He has all these terrible secrets stuffed into his head. Doesn't he ever get lonesome, Joel?

Beat.

JOEL: He would have to be a great swordsman.

ERIC: Yeah, of course.

JOEL: Don't interrupt. Nerves of steel. Nerves of steel. And he would have to know the countryside like the back of his hand.

ERIC: He could be a, whaddaya call those guys. A highwayman! A highwayman! That's how he meets Valerian: he robs him. They have this fantastic swordfight. And Valerian knows a fantastic swordsman when he sees one, so he hires the guy.

JOEL: Cullen, that is simplistic.

ERIC: Why? Where's your imagination, Goldner? This is good! It's night time on the high road. And along comes Valerian on his horse, riding full throttle.

JOEL: (*pained*) *Full throttle?*

ERIC: Suddenly this guy jumps down on him from a cliff and knocks him off his horse and Valerian falls on his ass.

JOEL: Hell, no! Valerian always lands on his feet! Like a cat.

ERIC: Okay, but so does the other guy.

JOEL: Well, okay, maybe.

ERIC: Yeah, so he knocks Valerian off his horse and the horse runs away.

JOEL: Ze horse of Valerian does nevaire run away!

ERIC: Okay, so the horse sticks around. But his lantern goes out! (*Turns off light — a home rheostat dial. Moonlight from the window.*) Valerian's lantern goes out! It's pitch, pitch black, they can't see each other at all!

JOEL: Okay — so — so they stand there on the highway. So?

ERIC: (*slow motion mime*) They *draw their blades.*

They do so.

ERIC: They salute.

They salute: ERIC's direct, JOEL's a figure-eight.

JOEL: So how are they gonna fence each other, it's dark.

ERIC: Uh—There! Ha! I can hear your footsteps. The highwayman lunges at the sound of the footsteps— (*does so*)

JOEL: And Valerian parries him. (*does so*) He parries him. 'Cause he heard the guy's blade swooshing through the air—no, wait, a blade doesn't swoosh on a forward lunge. Shit.

ERIC: Yes it does! It does to these guys. Supersensitive hearing. Supersensitive hearing. Both of us.

They listen.

JOEL: I can hear your breathing.

They listen.

ERIC: I can hear yours.

JOEL: So they fence. (*slow-motion mimed fencing*) And then—Valerian the Cunning—holds his breath.

ERIC: So does the other guy.

JOEL: Ah shit, Eric. If they both hold their— (*stops, listens*)

ERIC: Wha?

JOEL: Sh!

ERIC: What?

JOEL: Sh! Sh sh sh. (*They listen. In awe.*) I can hear your heart beat. Eric, I can hear your goddamn heart beat.

They listen.

ERIC: Not from there.

JOEL: Yes. Yes.

ERIC: *I can't hear my—*

JOEL: *Sh!*

They listen.

ERIC: Yeahh.

JOEL: Yeah.

ERIC: And yours. I can hear yours. Jesus.

JOEL: Two hearts beating as one. God damn.

ERIC: The two greatest swordsmen who ever lived on this whole planet.

JOEL: Yeah.

ERIC: Alone together.

JOEL: Yeah.

ERIC: In the pitch black night. On a road, somewhere in France.

JOEL: Destiny.

ERIC: So what do they do?

JOEL: They fence. (*slow-motion mimed fencing*) They fence all night long—

ERIC: Yeah.

JOEL: Not a word is spoken.

ERIC: Excellent.

JOEL: Just ze two 'earts beating — ze 'eavy breathing in 'armonee — ze boots scuffling on ze ground — ze slash and slice of ze blades.

ERIC: They miss each other by inches.

JOEL: Quarter of an inches.

ERIC: Eighth of an inches.

JOEL: Fantastique! All night long, peetch black, and nobody gets ze hit!

ERIC: And zen — wait a sec — (*goes and turns up the wall light*) Zen ze sky starts to get light in ze east.

JOEL: Yes. Yes. Ze sun starts comeeng op. We begin to see each othaire. Hold it, hold it. Perfect. Just the outlines at first.

ERIC: We slowly stop fencing.

JOEL: But of course. Because now eet ees too easee for us.

ERIC: And we get ze good look at each othaire.

JOEL: What's the highwayman look like?

ERIC: Uh — okay — he's wearing brown soft leather. Like, uh, like whatsit, calfskin.

JOEL: And a linen shirt? A rough old yellow shirt? With the neck open.

ERIC: Yeah, yeah. And one of those sort of Australian cowboy hats where they stick up one side and put a feather on it, you know? And a flower on his sleeve.

JOEL: He's sort of short and wiry. In his forties.

ERIC: Yeah, yeah, right, that's great. Also he has a grey moustache and, um, a ragged purple velvet eye patch.

JOEL: An eye patch? Uh, the guy is blind in one eye and he's a great swordsman?

ERIC: What the hell, why not?

JOEL: Well, depth perception, you need depth perception.

ERIC: Oh. Uh. Well. Uh, why'd ya think he had to develop supersensitive hearing!

JOEL: (laughs) Touché!

ERIC: Okay! What does Valerian look like?

JOEL: Very tall. Slendaire. Pale skeen, but healthy, yes? Green eyes, ze incradible green eyes. Ze long straight nose, ze black beard. All dressed een black and white, and buckles of silvaire, wit' lace on ze shirt.

ERIC: That's great. So we just look at each othaire for a while. And ze sun ees comeeng op. (turns light up further)

JOEL: (bows) Zees ees indeed an honaire. I am Le Conte Valerian l'Estomber.

ERIC: (bows) Compôte des Eglantiers. 'Ighwayman for ze Ravolution.

JOEL: Who des what?

ERIC: Compôte des Eglantiers. It's French for rose hip jam.

Beat.

JOEL: Okay. Compôte—eef I may address you as, uh, Compôte—I greet you as a mastaire swordsman.

ERIC: Ah. Monsieur le Conte. Eet ees good to be appreciated.

They shake hands. Lights fade.

Scene Four

A football field. Late afternoon sunlight. JOEL and ERIC recline on the bleachers, eating peanuts and watching the offstage cheerleaders. We hear the cheerleaders run through one of their cheers, off.

JOEL: Poetry in motion, eh . . .

ERIC: Yeah . . .

JOEL: Pale, creamy thighs — oh, God. I want, I want. Me want woman!

ERIC: The wiggly number! They're gonna do the wiggly number. Lookit, lookit!

JOEL: I see, I see. (shouts at the cheerleaders) Go for it!

They watch, open mouthed, slowly chewing peanuts in a stupor of lust, as the wiggly number is practised offstage. They sigh.

ERIC: Aren't they excellent looking, Joel? All of them. Just ace.

JOEL: All of them everywhere.

ERIC: Even the ugly ones.

JOEL: There's so *much* in the world! An' they all go walkin' and talkin' and practisin' their cheers as if it didn't matter. Why can't we have just a little bit? What harm would it do?

ERIC: Why can't we have a whole lot?

JOEL: (*in agreement*) All right!

ERIC: I have this cousin? He has two girl friends? They're both so cute it hurts to look at them.

JOEL: Heartbreakers, huh.

ERIC: And he does it with both of them! And guess how old he is.

JOEL: Eleven.

ERIC: How'd you know?

JOEL: What? He is? I was joking!

ERIC: Yeah. It makes me sick, what we're missing.

JOEL: Eleven. Really. My God.

ERIC: Those girls hardly have tits yet.

JOEL: This new crop of kids is incredible. Eleven.

Silence.

ERIC: Know who I really want, eh.

JOEL: Yeah.

ERIC: Boy. Any time, eh.

JOEL: Yeah. Me too.

ERIC: (*sighs*) No, but I really — I really.

JOEL: Me too.

ERIC: I mean, you know — if she can go and have some of the jerks she's had — I mean she *likes* me! She really likes me a lot.

JOEL: She likes me too.

ERIC: Yeah, well.

JOEL: Well what? She does. (*mutually annoyed pause*) Ha! Wiggly number again.

They watch sadly.

ERIC: Ah, you can have 'em. I just want Louise.

JOEL: I merely want all of them. Every single one that ever lived. I mean that's all I ask. Please Mister God sir, thank you very much.

ERIC: Mister God, eh? Lots of luck.

Silence.

JOEL: Valerian 'ad 'ees own cheerleading team, n'est-ce pas. For ze fenceeng matches. Valerian eenvanted ze cheerleading, you know zis?

ERIC: No sheet.

JOEL: Leetle-known heestorical fact.

LOUISE enters behind them, unnoticed, carrying books and a clarinet case. The first thing people observe about LOUISE is a large purple splotch covering part of her face; it is called a port-wine stain. Otherwise she is notably pretty.

JOEL: (*continuing*) Twelve 'and-peeked feefteen-year-old milkmaids from Brittanee. Crème de la fuckin' crème. Valerian chose zem and trained zem 'eemself. When zey deed well, 'e rewarded zem wit' a fuck per cheerleader.

JOEL and ERIC are highly amused.

ERIC: Uniforms! What were their uniforms!

JOEL: Uniforms: silk striped knee-socks — little satin slippers with bows — and white fur pompoms. Oh, and little white velvet collars.

ERIC: That's it?

JOEL: Zat ees eet.

LOUISE: Absolutely pathetic.

JOEL: Oh my God.

ERIC: Hey! How are ya doing! Come siddown.

LOUlSE: You guys are just pitiful. I come all the way over here just to sit with you, and what do I find, you're making up gross stories about naked cheerleaders.

JOEL: How — how long were you here?

LOUISE: Oh, long enough, Joel, long enough.

JOEL: Oh, God.

ERIC: Siddown, siddown, join us.

LOUISE: Join you? Forget it. You go join your naked cheerleaders.

ERIC: You're not really mad, are you?

LOUISE: Am I? If you talk about Roz and the other girls like that, how do you talk about me? Ah, the hell with this. (starts to leave)

ERIC: No! We don't! I mean, we're not talk-ing about real girls at all. It's just a made–up story.

JOEL: Eric.

ERIC: It's about this guy who lived hundreds of years ago.

JOEL: Eric!

ERIC: He was this great swordsman and spy, and he — (JOEL kicks him.) Ow! What was that for! Jerk!

JOEL: Just shut your mouth, okay?

ERIC: Well, okay! You don't have to kick me!

JOEL: Looks like I do, asshole!

ERIC: Go to hell!

LOUISE: On second thought I think I'll join you after all. (Sits. Silence. To ERIC.) You finished with my trig notes? (He finds the notes and hands them to her, silently.) Oh, come on now, boys, kiss and make up. (no answer) So, Joel, I hear you're gonna be a porno writer when you grow up. "Pompoms and Perverts," by Joel Goldner.

ERIC: (laughs) Told ya! I told him he should write a book.

JOEL: Fuck off.

LOUISE: Oh, we're just teasing you. You're so cute when you blush.

JOEL: Bugger off.

LOUISE: Same colour as me.

JOEL: Bugger off, I said.

LOUISE: Oh ho, that's it, eh. Worst insult in the world.

JOEL: No. (gets up to move away)

LOUISE: Oh, come on, siddown.

JOEL: No, no, that's all right, I'm studying, okay?

JOEL sits down at a distance from the other two, opens his textbook. Silence. LOUISE and ERIC watch JOEL pretend to study; LOUISE turns to ERIC; they smile at each other; he offers the peanuts.

ERIC: Nuts to you?

LOUISE: Don' mind if I do, big boy.

They eat peanuts.

ERIC: So how's Band?

LOUISE: Oh, good, really good. We're doing a thing by George Gershwin. I have a great solo. Right at the beginning, I am the first sound you hear. I have to slide up about three octaves like a trombone. Actually I'm a bit nervous about it.

ERIC: The thing you were practising Thursday?

LOUISE: Yeah.

ERIC: That was great! Anyway, you're the best clarinet player in the school. So you keep telling me.

LOUISE: True.

JOEL: *(with nose in book)* Best frog dissecter in Bio Lab.

LOUISE: That's me, gorgeous and talented both.

ERIC: Excellent.

LOUISE: Rilly.

JOEL: *(with nose in book)* "In the poison clouds of Eepers and the muddy torment of Vimy, the name of the Canadian Armed Forces shone forth as a symbol of courage, endurance, and resourcefulness under stress." Says so right here.

LOUISE: You two always work together?

ERIC: Who, him? He just follows me around.

LOUISE: You two make quite a team.

ERIC: Why, you jealous?

LOUISE: Jealous? Of him?

ERIC: 'Cause if you're jealous, there's a good double feature on Friday at the Waterton. Wanna go?

JOEL: "Lasting benefits of the First World War: an increase in mining and shipbuilding, and a boom in airplane manufacture." Boom!

LOUISE: Boom.

ERIC: Just us. Not him.

LOUISE: No thanks.

ERIC: No thanks. It's always no thanks. Why not, Louise?

LOUISE: Well, I don't wanna discuss it right now, eh?

JOEL: Introduction of daylight-saving time! Hot shit, what a great war!

ERIC: Uh, Joel?

JOEL: You guys are missing a terrific war here.

ERIC: Joel, do you think we could be alone for a few minutes?

JOEL: We're alone.

ERIC: Joel, I'm tryna be nice, will ya fuck off, please?

JOEL: I can stay here. It's a free country. Thanks to those who fought and died.

ERIC: (*to LOUISE*) All right, then, we'll go over there. Come on.

LOUISE: No way. I'm not traipsing over there just because of Joel.

JOEL: Good for you. You tell him.

ERIC: Okay, we'll discuss it right here, then!

LOUISE: Forget it!

ERIC: Aw, come on, gimme a break! He can listen. Like it's all friends here. Even if he is being a pain in the ass.

JOEL assumes listening position.

LOUISE: All right, I give up. What?

Pause.

ERIC: You go out with other guys, You even — uh — I mean you even —

LOUISE: Well.

ERIC: What I mean is, you won't even go to a movie with me!

LOUISE: Make me sound like the school sleaze or something.

ERIC: No, no, it isn't that. It's just that — I mean it's only a movie!

LOUISE: Oh, Eric. God.

ERIC: Why won't you go out with me, Louise? What turns you off so much? I got bad breath?

LOUISE: No.

ERIC: So why?

LOUISE: I dunno. I like it the way it is.

ERIC: You like it the way it is.

LOUISE: Yeah. I don't want to spoil it.

ERIC: Louise, going to some movie isn't going to spoil it.

LOUISE: No, eh? You know where that stuff leads. Groping in the dark!

ERIC: "Oh, Eric, it's been a lovely evening, let's not spoil it."

LOUISE: Yeah! (*pause*) Oh, I dunno. You're my friend, that's all. You two are like the only two guys I don't have to worry about.

ERIC: Louise, if you like somebody, that's why you're supposed to go out with them.

LOUISE: There's lots of reasons.

ERIC: Okay, what if I stopped being your friend? Would you go out with me then?

LOUISE: Don't be silly. Even if I did it wouldn't be worth it.

ERIC: No?

LOUISE: Believe me.

JOEL: "Four hundred twenty-four thousand Canadian lads went overseas, of whom over sixty thousand did not return." "Did not return," isn't that delicate.

ERIC: Louise, you got everything backwards.

LOUISE: Yeah?

JOEL: "Did not return," I love that. They stayed in France an' opened a hardware store.

ERIC: Completely backwards. I'm not talking about a sex thing. Why can't we just go out!

LOUISE: You don't want to just go out.

JOEL: I *said*, "They stayed in France an' opened a hardware store."

From offstage comes the sound of football practice ending.

LOUISE: (*gathering her things*) I gotta go. Football's breaking up.

ERIC: You know, they just go out with you because they think you're easy.

LOUISE: (*angry*) I am. I'm easy, they're easy, it works out fine.

ERIC: They think you're easy because you know why.

Brief pause.

LOUISE: I'm late for Band.

ERIC: They think you're afraid to say no because of it.

LOUISE: Well, then, I just proved that they're wrong, didn't I, Eric, eh?

ERIC: Well — Skelly says everybody's had you except me!

JOEL: And me.

Pause.

LOUISE: Oh, guys, that is a load of crap.

ERIC: Of course it's crap, I'm just telling you what Skelly's saying.

LOUISE: No, I mean he didn't say that.

ERIC: Yes he did!

JOEL: Yes he did! I was there. He also said you can't get enough of him.

LOUISE: Did he, now.

JOEL: (*indicates offstage*) Uh, 'scuse me. I mean, perchance we ought not to have spoken.

LOUISE: No, no, that's okay.

ERIC: Speak of the devil an' there he is.

LOUISE: Hey, Skelly! Skelly, comere a minute!

They wait.

ERIC: What are you gonna say?

LOUISE: Oh, I'll think of something.

Enter SKELLY, in football gear.

SKELLY: Hi, turkeys. Whaddaya want, Honey?

LOUISE: Skelly, everybody hasn't had me. Practically nobody's had me, and you know it.

SKELLY: Uh — no, I didn't mean, uh — sorry.

LOUISE: Sure as hell not you, anyway, huh? Even with you nagging and practically trying to rape me and generally making an ass of yourself.

SKELLY: (*sees JOEL and ERIC enjoying this*) Yeah, Louise, let's forget it, eh?

LOUISE: You know I wouldn't sleep with you if you were the last guy on earth.

SKELLY: 'At's okay, Louise. You're just talking like this 'cause you're having your period. Only chick I know has her period right on her face. See ya. (*exits*)

ERIC: Skelly! *Skelly!*

LOUISE: Siddown.

ERIC: Skelly, take off that football gear and I'll slaughter you!

JOEL: Run after him!

LOUISE: Eric, siddown. Sit down sit down sit down!

ERIC: He can't say that to you. I can't let him do that.

JOEL: Let's go after him. We'll both take him.

LOUISE: For God's sake leave it alone!

JOEL: It is your honour! We must avenge your honour!

LOUISE: Aw, please, no avenging, okay? No honour, okay?

JOEL: We can handle him.

LOUISE: Joel, that is not the point!

ERIC: How can you let him just walk away?

LOUISE: That kind of stuff goes on all the time. Haven't you noticed?

ERIC: Yeah, but not like that.

LOUISE: Oh, no, not like that, no, it's always different. Some little kid asks why my face is dirty, or once it was, uh, "God has marked you because you have sinned" — or they just give you this *look*. What are you gonna do? Kill everybody who even stares at it?

ERIC: Maybe.

JOEL: Yeah!

LOUISE: Eric, you were staring at it this morning in Geometry! I saw you!

ERIC: Was not. I was looking at you.

Beat.

LOUISE: Oh. (*beat*) Listen, it isn't the thing itself. It's everybody reminding me that it's so important, okay?

ERIC: Okay.

LOUISE: Everybody's so afraid that I might forget for a split second that I have it. You know something, my father never even kisses me on this cheek.

JOEL: Parents.

ERIC: Well, I think he's crazy. I would kiss you anywhere.

LOUISE: Well, thank you.

JOEL: Anywhere, huh.

LOUISE: Oh. Oh, very funny, Eric.

ERIC: I didn't mean it like that! (*to JOEL*) And you know it, creep! I didn't mean that.

JOEL: Well, I thought it was fairly amusing.

ERIC: (*to LOUISE*) I was trying to be nice. Every time I try to say something nice to you, it comes out like a dirty joke.

LOUISE: Not every time. I gotta go, I'm late.

ERIC: Listen — I'm sorry.

LOUISE: For what? Everything's peachy keen. You're making points, Eric.

Brief pause. She kisses him. Exit.

JOEL: Wow . . .

ERIC: (*bitter*) Points. Points!

JOEL: Eric, she kissed you.

ERIC: Who the hell wants points?

JOEL: It was just like the movies.

ERIC: How many points before she goes out with me?

JOEL: She kissed you, you dork! On the mouth! Did you not perchance notice?

ERIC: I noticed.

JOEL: What ingratitude. What a waste.

Brief silence.

ERIC: I'd like to punch that son of a bitch out, I really would.

JOEL: My dear fellow, do be realistic. He would cream you.

ERIC: I don't care, you know? It'd be worth it if I could just get a couple of good ones in.

JOEL: So go for it.

ERIC: You heard her. She doesn't want any avenging.

JOEL: Cullen, if you want to go after the guy, go after him. Don't let her stop you.

ERIC: Big shot. Why don't you do it?

JOEL: Me? Jesus Christ, I don't wanna go after him, you think I'm crazy? But at least I'm not using her as my excuse not to.

ERIC: It's not an excuse. I care about what she wants, that's all.

JOEL: As you wish.

Brief pause.

ERIC: You were sure hot on going after him a minute ago.

JOEL: Ah, with you, mon ami, with you. But alone, that's another story. Only a maniac would go after Skelly alone. A maniac or — wait a minute.

Beat.

ERIC: Oh, wait a minute!

JOEL: Ah, eet ees all comeeng clear to me now. Clearlee zis ees a job for —

ERIC: Hold on!

JOEL: I got it, I got it. Ze lady Louisa bears ze birth mark of ze Royal House of, uh —

ERIC: Joel —

JOEL: Charlebois. She bears ze scarlet heart shape on ze left cheek.

ERIC: Yeah, yeah —

JOEL: And along comes ze Baron von Skelly, an' 'e insoolts ze lady right in front of Compôte!

ERIC: Aw, Joel —

JOEL: So! Compôte bursts in on ze orgy at Valerian's place and reports ze insoolt. Valerian challonges ze Baron von Skelly to ze duel at dawn. Only when zey 'ave ze duel, 'e does not keel heem, or even wound heem. 'E merely cuts up 'is cheek wit' a t'ousand tiny cuts. Skelly keeps trying to parry 'im, 'e even knows where Valerian ees aimeeng, but Valerian ees so fast zat he keeps comeeng een on ze cheek, wit' little flicks of ze point.

ERIC: That's enough!

JOEL: "Zat ees enoff!" cries out Skelly: "I 'ave satisfaction!" But Valerian says, "But I do not, yet," which ees like a joke, because as usual 'e ees mastoorbateeng wit' ze othaire hand; zis ees driving Skelly crazy wit' fear and lust! And when 'e ees finished, 'e 'as carved out ze little phaleek symbol on Skelly's cheek, zat 'e weel wear for ze rest of 'is life. Ze ponishment to feet ze crime!

Pause.

ERIC: You through now?

JOEL: (*with a small flourish*) But of course.

ERIC: Listen. I don't want that to be a Valerian story. I don't want that in with the others, all right?

JOEL: In what?

ERIC: I want that one thrown out, okay?

JOEL: My dear boy, you and I can't throw it out. It isn't "in" anything. Except our heads. Now that it exists, you can't make it not exist any more.

ERIC: Why not? Who makes the rules? That's your rules!

JOEL: No, it's a law of nature. Honest, Eric. Sometimes I make up Valerian stories that right away I realize they're the pits. But it's like this one, we're stuck with it. We can't make it go away.

ERIC: Garbage. Of course you can. What do your parents do, anyway? The big shot journalists. Do they keep everything they write?

JOEL: Leave my parents out of it. They're just newspaper writers, they're hacks.

ERIC: I bet they throw most of it out, don't they? Or the editor does.

JOEL: Cullen, I have no idea how my parents work and I don't care. They don't tell me anything about their work anyway, you know that. What they throw out and what they keep. They don't let me in on fuck all.

ERIC: Oh gee whiz gosh, Goldner, don't get excited or anything.

JOEL: We aren't talking about them, we're talking about my brilliant story of Valerian's revenge.

ERIC: Crappy story.

JOEL: Brilliant or crappy doesn't matter. The point is, as soon as I invented it, it belonged to the world. It is immortal.

ERIC: What! Immortal! Horse shit! Nothing is immortal! Nothing!

JOEL: Stories are. Ideas are. They don't have bodies, so they can't die.

ERIC: Oh my God, Joel, you sound like a minister. We're gonna die and Valerian's gonna die with us.

JOEL: I dunno. I dunno. It seems to me that if you invent an idea — even if you never tell anybody — the idea's still there. It's been created. So somehow it's still around after you're gone. And zat is why we cannot cancel zem, n'est-ce pas.

ERIC: Look. Jerk. If anything is gonna be immortal it oughta be people. And if people can't, then nothing else should. You can't have all these cute little ideas floating around like pixies in the sky while human beings hang themselves in the garage.

Pause.

JOEL: Uh — 'scuse me — but what brings this up now?

ERIC: Something I ate, okay?

JOEL: Oh, Jesus. It's a year. Isn't it.

ERIC: Next week.

JOEL: Next week! Jesus! Why didn't you say anything?

ERIC: Who cares?

JOEL: Whaddaya mean, who cares? *I* care!

ERIC: You forgot.

JOEL: Yeah. True. I'm sorry.

ERIC: Oh, I don't mind you forgetting, I mind my old lady. 'Cause like the thing is, to me it's still like it just happened.

JOEL: How?

ERIC: Oh, I dunno.

JOEL: Tell me.

ERIC: You know when we had that fencing match yesterday? I kept wanting to tell him about it. Like I kept thinking, "I gotta remember to tell Dad about that" — and then each time I would remember that I can't. And I still do that, all the time, every time something neat happens I make a mental note to tell him, and — I still do that.

JOEL: So what's the thing about the old lady?

ERIC: Ah, she's forgotten all about him. She goes out on dates, for God's sake.

JOEL: Is that bad?

ERIC: She screws.

JOEL: So is that bad?

ERIC: Well, she never says his name, it's like he was never alive. She hasn't even said anything about it coming up to a year. The guy has been demolished. So if you can demolish a guy who was alive, you can demolish a stupid story that makes fun of Louise.

Brief silence.

JOEL: Eric, will you do me a huge favour? Tell me what happened —

ERIC: No —

JOEL: — at the funeral?

ERIC: No.

JOEL: Oh, please. It's been a year. Eric, that funeral's been driving you crazy. Whatever it was, it can't be as bad as some of the stuff I've imagined.

ERIC: Huh! I'll bet.

JOEL: Let's honour the anniversary. Let's break the silence.

ERIC: Just forget it, will ya?

JOEL: You want to tell me. I can tell you want to.

ERIC: Just drop it, Joel!

JOEL: Just drop it.

ERIC: Yeah.

JOEL: Just like your mother.

ERIC: (*without conviction*) It isn't the same.

JOEL: Well. I wouldn't know. You decide if it's the same.

Pause.

ERIC: You got to promise never to tell anybody.

JOEL: I swear.

ERIC: And don't interrupt. If you screw around with this, I'll kill you.

Pause.

I was really upset even before the funeral. 'Cause I'd read about what they do to the carcass, how they drain out the blood and put in embalming fluid, whatever that is. And they put *make-up* on their face. So already I was pissed off. And in the car on the way there everybody was sobbing and snorting and wailing about what a great guy he was. That killed me. Nobody ever told him that when he was alive. When it might have done him some good. No, they saved it up till he killed himself, and then they all told each other.

So I was really steamed when we got there. And we went in, and I knew he would have make-up on, but I wasn't ready for what he looked like. I almost didn't recognize him. He looked so beautiful. Like pretty. He looked like a woman.

And then, during the eulogy — you know what the minister did in the middle of the eulogy? Checked his watch. He checked his wristwatch. This guy baptized me, right, he was in charge of our youth group, I always thought he was God's personal best friend. And I look at him and he seems like just this jowly old businessman checking his watch while he's making a cheap speech.

And then, as we're filing out at the end, my mother tells me I should kiss my father for the very last time. Very last time, I love that, I'd never kissed him since grade one. And I leaned over him, and he really smelled good. I expected some kind of chemical smell, but he smelled so nice. So I kissed him. And he wasn't chilly or stiff or anything, it felt like he could have been alive. And — I suddenly realized — look, I think I told you enough.

Pause.

I realized I was getting this — I already had this really enormous hard-on, if you laugh I'll tear you to bits, you tell anybody this and I'll kill you, I had this huge rod, and I pulled away from him real fast and looked around. And my mother had this sly, kind of sexy look on her face like she'd caught me at it and she thought it was funny. And I looked at the minister. And boy, the look on *his* face. Like he was ready to send me straight to Hell. And I wanted to say, "I loved the guy, at least I loved him. What did

you do? You checked your damn watch!" But I didn't say anything. But that's when I quit the Church, man, that moment. If that's the best they can come up with when somebody dies, forget it. And if you laugh, I'll slaughter you.

Silence. The light has changed, ideally without our noticing it, from late afternoon to the beginning of a burnished autumn evening, with long shadows.

JOEL: Eric, that's a beautiful story.

ERIC: Kind of sick, eh?

JOEL: Everything's kind of sick, somewhere along the line. Look, Eric, it's not such a terrible thing. I mean, everybody gets hard-ons at the wrong time.

ERIC: Not like that.

JOEL: I get them at all *kinds* of weird times.

ERIC: Not like that!

JOEL: Hey man, we're teenage boys, it's part of the deal. I wouldn't worry about it so much.

ERIC: Just don't tell anybody.

JOEL: I won't. But there's nothing wrong with it.

ERIC: I only told you because, uh —

JOEL: I'm *glad* you told me.

ERIC: Because you wanted to know what I was mad about.

JOEL: Right.

ERIC: Well, that's what I'm — that's what I was mad about. The funeral. And then my mother forgetting about it, like, now, after a year.

JOEL: Also you were pissed off at my Valerian-and-Skelly story, right?

ERIC: Right. Right. And also Skelly insulting Louise.

JOEL: Of course. And let's not forget the fact that Louise won't go out with you —

ERIC: Yeah, right, that's a good one.

JOEL: And, oh, jeez, what else? We could throw in the general stupidity of history books.

ERIC: Yeah. And the fact that everybody's gone home and we're both late for supper.

JOEL: (sighs) And also the smell of the evening air, yes?

ERIC: What's wrong with the air? The air is excellent.

JOEL: Yeahh — This is shaping up to be one of those long autumn evenings that can drive you crazy with wanting — and needing . . .

ERIC: Wanting and needing, yeah, you got it. And — and you don't even know what it is you want and need. Right?

JOEL: Exactly. Exactly. Zere ees so much to choose from, is zere not, mon vieux.

ERIC: Zere sure fucking ees, mon vieux.

The lights fade.

Scene Five

The gym. Sounds of students fencing, offstage. Enter SKELLY with volleyball. Checks the equipment room door and finds it locked. Glances off at the fencers. Proceeds to practise with his volleyball: batting it against the wall, bouncing it off his head, dribbling it like a basketball. But he is distracted by the fencers. Slows down, stops, watches. Imitates — rather well — the en garde posture, the parry, the lunge.

Returns to volleyball play. Enter JOEL and ERIC in fencing gear, carrying their épées and masks.

JOEL: Just over here where there's a little room, okay? I'm sick of bumping into Arnie and those guys.

ERIC: Oh, yeah, well, look what's over here, eh.

JOEL: Oh, that. Well, perhaps eef we eegnore eet, eet weel go away. En garde.

SKELLY: Okay, ladies, pack it in.

ERIC: When the buzzer goes.

SKELLY: "When the buzzer goes." (crossing away) Hey, Mrs. Thorpe? Mrs. Thorpe?

JOEL: (low, to ERIC) Just warn him. Warn him. Go for it.

ERIC: (low) She wants me to leave it alone.

JOEL: (low) That's an act she puts on. She wants you to slaughter him. She's testing you, Eric.

ERIC: What?

SKELLY: (coming back) Where's Thorpe, anyway? We gotta start some *real* athletics here.

JOEL: She went out for a few minutes.

SKELLY: Aw shit, do I have to watch you guys? I'm gonna go check out the girls' hockey next door. (Goes to the doorway, stands watching offstage.)

JOEL: Testing, Eric, testing.

ERIC: Joel, she *means* it.

JOEL: Okay, you wanna go on being her friend? Her palsy-walsy? Fine.

ERIC: Hey, Skelly. (*SKELLY looks back.*) You make any more cracks about Louise's face, and I'm gonna put a few cracks in yours. Okay?

Pause. SKELLY comes back to JOEL and ERIC.

SKELLY: Oh, Eric, you got me real scared.

ERIC: And also don't go around pretending you've screwed her when everybody knows she won't let you within a mile. Just makes you look like a real jerk. Okay?

SKELLY: Eric, I was only trying to give the kid's reputation a boost. I mean, face it, she looks like she's been puked on, eh?

ERIC: Okay, Skelly. Okay. You and I have a date.

SKELLY: Ooh, you thavage!

ERIC: Yeah, yeah. Lunchtime in the lane behind the drug store. We got a date. You and me.

SKELLY: Oh, Cullen, are you gonna poke me with your rubber tip?

ERIC: No, Skelly, I'm gonna take you on with my bare hands.

SKELLY: Uh, hold on there, just a second there. You challenged. That means I get to choose the weapons. And I choose épées.

ERIC: Are you kidding? You got no training.

SKELLY: Why? You think you're so hot with these things? I been watching, I got the idea. Epée is easy. You just have to be fast like this.

Grabs JOEL's épée out of his hand. For the rest of the scene, the sound of the offstage fencers may reflect their response to the action.

JOEL: Hey!

SKELLY: En garde! (*takes up a good en garde position*) I'll take you on right now! En garde!

ERIC: No.

SKELLY: Chickenshit! Thorpe isn't even here! En garde!

ERIC: I want a real fight.

SKELLY: Chickenshit! I'll give you a real fight! (*pokes at ERIC with the épée*) Touché! Touché!

ERIC: (*parrying*) Cut it out.

SKELLY: Come at me! Come at me!

ERIC: You don't have a mask.

SKELLY: I don't need one. Touché! Touché! (*pokes and jabs*)

JOEL: Zat weel do. Geev me ze waipon! (*grabs ERIC's épée.*)

ERIC: Gimme that!

JOEL: Zis is a job for Valerian!

He swooshes through his figure-eight salute and engages SKELLY's blade.

SKELLY: Well, all right. I'll take you instead, Goldner.

ERIC: Not instead!

JOEL: Mon Baron, I am at your sairveece.

SKELLY lunges. JOEL parries, lunges and scores.

JOEL: Touché, Mon Baron.

SKELLY: Yeah, eh? Interesting. All right, now, this stuff is easy.

Lunges again. JOEL parries and scores with a "Touché," and returns to garde. SKELLY shifts from side to side, studying angles. He lunges again. JOEL parries and lunges, but this time SKELLY parries him successfully, lunges and scores.

SKELLY: Hah! Touché yourself, dipshit!

JOEL flails angrily at SKELLY, which makes it easy for SKELLY to score again.

SKELLY: And touché again! I got it now, no sweat.

JOEL: *(enraged)* You got notheeng! Ambayseel! 'Ow dare you!

Charges at SKELLY, slashing with the épée as though it were a sabre. Having lost his temper he is now quite splendid. Scores again and again, bellowing furious "Touchés." SKELLY may still manage a point or two; if he does, it enrages JOEL further and pushes him into more violent swordplay. Chases the now-defensive SKELLY around the gym. SKELLY, backing away, grabs the tip of JOEL's épée.

JOEL: Coward!

Whips the blade out of SKELLY's hand, hurting him; continues to poke him around the room. Ad-libs from SKELLY, ERIC and the offstage fencers. MRS. THORPE enters, unnoticed.

SKELLY: Awright! God almighty, I give up!

JOEL: Nevaire beg mercee of Valerian! Touché!

SKELLY: I give *up*, damnit! *(throws down épée)* I'll take Cullen at lunchtime!

ERIC: Okay, good!

SKELLY has turned partly away from JOEL, considering the fight to be over. But JOEL whips his blade back over his shoulder for a backhand cut across the side of SKELLY's head.

JOEL: *(a war cry)* Louisaaaa!

ERIC: No!

SKELLY turns, sees the threat, covers his face. But MRS. THORPE has stepped in behind JOEL and grabbed the tip of the épée.

JOEL: *Fuck off!*

Spins around to pull it away, and sees who it is. The buzzer goes, loud and long as before. The characters are frozen in position. The buzzer finally ends.

Blackout.

ACT TWO

Scene One

MRS. THORPE's office. JOEL and SKELLY sit side by side awaiting their doom. MRS. THORPE enters, angry, holding the épée.

MRS. THORPE: How could you be so stupid? Even in your stupidity you're amazing, you surpass everybody. Nobody else in the whole school could have come up with something so — brilliantly self-destructive. You're a raving genius, you little brat, sometimes I hate your guts. How *could* you? Do you know how long I had to fight to get a fencing programme in this school? Five years! Five years of fighting the bureaucracy, so that you can wipe it out with one slice? No way, pal. No thank you. Not on your wretched little life. *(no answer)* Joel, you say something, open that little mouth of yours so maybe I don't have to kick you out, okay? Do yourself a favour.

JOEL: Hah! You thought I was really gonna! Boy, did I have you fooled —

MRS. THORPE: Don't you lie to me. Just don't, you little — you're in enough trouble. Do you have any idea how many rules you broke out there? Don't add lying, okay? I felt you pull on this thing. You lie to me and I have no choice, you're out.

JOEL: Betty, we were just fooling around.

MRS. THORPE: I just told you. What did I just say?

SKELLY: Uh, no, Mrs. Thorpe, we really were just fooling around. Joel was showing me a few moves and it got weird.

MRS. THORPE: What is this, nursery school? I can't walk out for five minutes without my kiddies crippling each other? People get blinded by these things! (*holds the épée in front of JOEL*) Look at this thing! Look at it! You don't think the rules apply to you, that's your problem. You're above it all. I hope you realize I have to kick you out of fencing.

JOEL: What? You wouldn't! You wouldn't!

MRS. THORPE: I will not let this fencing programme go down the tubes because of you. Nothing can justify what you were gonna do.

JOEL: What about Skelly? He broke the rules too!

MRS. THORPE: What's the fight between you two? I want to have it out. (*no answer*) Oh, Lord, the boring old schoolboy code? How quaint.

SKELLY: Um, okay, look. A lot of it was my fault. (*They look at him in some surprise.*) You know this girl Louise? She has this big mark on her face?

MRS. THORPE: I know Louise.

SKELLY: Well, I said something really sh — uh, really rude to her. And so then we got into this argument. And like I'm the one who wanted to use the épées. And so we had this fight. And so — uh, that's all.

MRS. THORPE: Joel? Is that what happened?

JOEL: Basically, yeah.

MRS. THORPE: Well. I can understand a fight — it isn't all right, but I can understand it. Perhaps I can even understand why you might grab your épées and do it in the gym — unforgiveable, but I can picture it happening. But what makes no sense at all is you attacking an unarmed, unmasked boy with an épée blade. Now can you explain that to me, Joel? (*no answer*) Joel, I need to know that you know the seriousness of what you did. If I can believe that, then maybe, just maybe, I won't have to kick you out of fencing. (*no answer*) Joel, I need an answer.

JOEL: I can't say anything! You just said yourself nothing can justify it, so how can I give you an answer? You see, I'm stuck, aren't I? Whatever I say, I'm hung up on your stupid rules!

MRS. THORPE: Okay, then, never mind my rules, let's put them aside. I want to know your rules.

JOEL: *My* rules?

MRS. THORPE: Look. Sometimes different people follow different rules. And then we get into a kind of, uh, moral confusion. What you did makes no sense according to my rules. So does it make any sense according to yours?

JOEL: Well, sure it does. Of course it does.

MRS. THORPE: How?

JOEL: A man insults the honour of a lady. He will not apologize. There is only one solution. Revenge at the point of the sword.

MRS. THORPE: Revenge at the point of the sword. Where does this rule come from?

JOEL: From me.

MRS. THORPE: Joel, there's something behind all this. You and Eric are involved in some kind of play-acting, or —

JOEL: No! There's no play-acting.

MRS. THORPE: Oh, yes there is. You two have some kind of ritual, some special thing —

JOEL: We're your best fencers, that's all! That's our special thing. We talk to each other through our épées, we make those goddamn blades *speak*. It's like nothing else. We don't *need* anything else. You just don't understand.

MRS. THORPE: Oh, yes, I understand. I've been there, I know how wonderful that feeling is. And people like you and Eric and I are lucky to be able to experience that. But Joel, we can't have that feeling all the time —

JOEL: Why not!

MRS. THORPE: Because you have to live in the real world.

JOEL: Aww —

MRS. THORPE: And that can be exciting, Joel! That can be the best challenge of all! Because it means you can have that feeling — and control it. But to do that, you have to have discipline. Do you understand that?

JOEL: Of course.

MRS. THORPE: Because that is the most important rule. When you hold the épée you're holding your own discipline in your hand.

JOEL: Agreed.

MRS. THORPE: Okay! Okay. As long as we know that, we're clear with each other. Now I just need to know from you — that you would never do anything like that again.

JOEL: Of course I would. (*she stares*) I maintain my rules.

MRS. THORPE: No. No, wait. Joel, haven't you been following me? I am looking for an excuse to keep you in! Don't make it impossible!

JOEL: You said that if I showed you that I knew how serious it was, you'd keep me in. Well, I showed you. I know how serious it was.

MRS. THORPE: But you would do it again!

JOEL: That's how serious it was!

Beat.

MRS. THORPE: I give up. You want out this badly, well then, you're out.

JOEL: I don't want out!

MRS. THORPE: If you're going to go by your own cockeyed rules, I just —

JOEL: You're going back on your promise!

MRS. THORPE: Can't you see? I have no choice!

JOEL: Put me on probation!

MRS. THORPE: Oh, sure, and as long as you don't blind anybody, you can stay? Joel, you're capable of anything.

JOEL: I'm your champion! Me and Eric! You practically said so yourself! We could get to the Nationals within four years!

MRS. THORPE: (*grimly*) Three.

JOEL: And that isn't even the main thing, that's nothing.

MRS. THORPE: That's right.

JOEL: I see it in your face when you watch us practise. You know how good I am.

MRS. THORPE: You're not as good as you think you are. But you're good enough so that I could wring your little neck for the way you just blew it. What a waste! You have more potential than the rest of the class put together and you waste it on Errol Flynning around the place like a madman. You're the kind of kid that's got gifts that other people break their backs trying to duplicate, but for you it's just a gift, that's all, so you throw it away. You waste it all on silliness, on games, on staring out the window, worlds away somewhere. Your other teachers all say the same thing —

JOEL: Stick to the subject! You're gonna kick me out of Fencing for staring out the window during Trig?

MRS. THORPE: Maybe it'll wake you up!

JOEL: This is just a power trip! I fence your way and I'm teacher's pet. I fence my way and you break your promises and squash me like a bug.

MRS. THORPE: That wasn't fencing, that was assault!

JOEL: You tricked me into confessing and then broke your promise! You're just doing this to prove I'm not your little pet. And the reason you got to prove it is because I am.

MRS. THORPE: You watch it.

JOEL: 'Cause if I weren't, you'd have me expelled completely. But you don't have the guts to expel me, because — *you love* me — and you don't have the guts to keep me in, because I scare you! So you go halfway, right, you kick me out of the only class that matters and you keep me in the rest of this boring goddamn school. Typical!

MRS. THORPE: Clean out your locker. Leave your gear in the equipment room.

JOEL: *(falls on his knees)* Please, Betty, don't kick me out of fencing, okay? I won't blind anybody. I'll stay on the fencing strip. I won't have any more honour. I'll be a good boy, I'll do whatever you say. Please don't kick me out. It's all I got. There's nobody else in town can teach me to fence.

MRS. THORPE: And Skelly, you're off the volleyball team for the year.

SKELLY: Yes Ma'am.

JOEL: You like this, eh? You getting off on this?

MRS. THORPE: Joel, I'm making an appointment for you with the student counsellor.

JOEL: Fuck the student counsellor!

MRS. THORPE: I don't know what your problem is, and I don't have whatever is required to —

JOEL: Don't bore me with excuses! You gonna kick me out, kick me out! I'm not interested in your cheap excuses! *(exit)*

MRS. THORPE: Joel! Joel!

Blackout.

Scene Two

The lunchroom. Cafeteria sounds. ERIC and LOUISE are sitting at a table. ERIC has his lunch in front of him, and LOUISE is carrying a couple of books: she has come to talk with him.

ERIC: So then Joel's winning, eh? I mean he was really wiping the guy out, it was amazing. I've never seen Skelly lose at anything before.

LOUISE: How exciting.

ERIC: Well, it — well, anyway, then Skelly throws down his épée and says he gives up, and so then Joel goes really crazy. And then he tried to hit him with it, and —

LOUISE: What? Wait a minute. Joel tries to hit Skelly *after* he drops his sword?

ERIC: Yeah.

LOUISE: Across the face.

ERIC: Yeah. But anyway, Thorpe stopped him, and that was that.

LOUISE: How did it start?

ERIC: There was this — argument.

LOUISE: About me.

ERIC: Well. Skelly said some more stuff, eh.

LOUISE: I see. So then Joel comes to the rescue? That figures.

ERIC: It happened really fast. I tried to stop it.

LOUISE: Did you, Eric? Did you really?

ERIC: Yeah!

LOUISE: Thorpe managed to stop it.

ERIC: Thorpe is Thorpe. (*beat*) Well. Maybe I coulda done better. Maybe I coulda really stepped in there.

LOUISE: Maybe.

ERIC: But I didn't know how serious it was gonna get. I didn't know it would end up with Joel getting kicked out and everything.

LOUISE: Joel getting kicked out! That's what I mean! That's all you think of! What about me, Eric?

ERIC: I thought of you.

LOUISE: Did you think of me turning into the laughing stock of the school? All over again? How long do you think it's gonna take, Eric? Before the word spreads they were fighting over Purple Face? Word's already out. It's gonna be just like it was when I first got here. That's really funny, you know: when I first got here, you and Joel were practically the only people who didn't make a big deal about my skin. And now they're finally getting used to me around here, finally treating me like a human being, and look who starts a whole new fuss! That's all they need! Everybody'll be talking about me, they'll start in with the *jokes* — (*Brief pause. Possibly tears.*) Did you think about that. Did you think about what it'll do to me.

ERIC: (*feebly*) I tried to stop them.

LOUISE: I gotta tell you. I'm scared you're gonna get like Joel.

ERIC: How's that?

LOUISE: Insane.

ERIC: Oh, come on, Louise!

LOUISE: Eric, you got to stay away from him for a while. Just avoid him for a while.

ERIC: Avoid Joel.

LOUISE: You hear your tone of voice? It's like I said to do something horrible. Listen, it would be good for you. It might even be good for him.

ERIC: Louise, he's my best friend. He gives me the only real fun in my life. My only fun these days is fencing an' horsing around with Goldner.

LOUISE: Well, that sounds pretty weird right there.

ERIC: Okay, you give me some fun in my life and maybe I'll stay away from Joel.

LOUISE: Fuck you.

ERIC: I'm sorry, I was just kidding.

LOUISE: I don't trade myself.

ERIC: I know, I was kidding!

LOUISE: Yeah, right, you were kidding. Exactly. You were kidding just like he does. You learned this crap from him.

ERIC: I am *not* like *Joel*. You're just making something up! Look, did I get in the fight? Did I try and cut up Skelly? Did I get kicked out of Fencing?

LOUISE: No.

ERIC: So I'm a little bit more together than he is, okay?

LOUISE: Okay. I mean I know that. But I'm just afraid of — (*hesitates*)

ERIC: (*gently*) Yeah, what? You're afraid of?

LOUISE: I am afraid of losing you as a friend. You are just about my only real — male friend. Every other boy is either — I don't know — they want sex — or they see my skin is weird, so they think I'm *all* weird . . . This is embarrassing. (*beat*) I don't want to ask you to choose between me and Joel. But I'm afraid of losing you. And I'm not gonna keep you by screwing you. And — if you're gonna stay friends with Joel, I don't know what to do.

ERIC: I'm not gonna just dump him. You expect me to just dump him? You think that would be fair?

LOUISE: No. I know.

ERIC: I mean he's got feelings too, you know. He just lost *his* only fun in life. He isn't just some vicious maniac or something, you know, the guy is hurting.

LOUISE: I know. I know. (*SKELLY has entered and now arrives at their table.*) Oh, God. What do you want?

SKELLY: Uh — Listen, Honey, uh —

LOUISE: Don't call me that.

SKELLY: Okay. Uh — like that stuff about your period and everything, eh? What I said there? Like, uh, that was really sleazy, eh? And, uh, it was just 'cause I was pissed off. But, uh, like I'm sorry I said it, okay?

LOUISE: Well, my goodness me. Okay. Okay, great.

SKELLY: Course I still think you're a bitch for not goin' out with me, eh.

LOUISE: (*smiles*) You're a great man with an apology, Skelly.

SKELLY: (*pleased*) Yeah?

LOUISE: What brought this on?

SKELLY: Nothin'. It started a lot of shit and I thought it was crummy, so I'm saying I'm sorry, okay?

LOUISE: Okay.

SKELLY: Whaddaya think, I'm scared to fight Cullen?

Brief pause.

LOUISE: To fight Cullen?

SKELLY: Yeah. All this shit started when Cullen and I were gonna have a fist fight.

LOUISE: Oh.

SKELLY: (*to ERIC*) So I'm lettin' you off, okay? (*ERIC does not respond.*) Yeah, good, I wouldn't wanna damage you anyway. (*Gently punches ERIC on the shoulder.*) Hey, can you fence as good as Goldner?

ERIC: I dunno.

SKELLY: That guy's fuckin' amazing. But crazy? Jesus, that guy's crazy. You shouldn't hang around with him too much, you know, it might be catching.

LOUISE: Gee. Just what I was saying.

SKELLY: Yeah, eh? (*awkward pause*) Well, hey, I feel better. (*exit*)

LOUISE: (*staring at ERIC, who stares at his plate*) You tried to stop them! You tried to stop them! You bloody liar! You started them!

ERIC: He kept saying these things about you.

LOUISE: What about what *I* said?

ERIC: You didn't hear what he was saying behind your back.

LOUISE: I heard what he said in front of my face. He said I have a birthmark that looks like menstrual blood, which it does. So what!

ERIC: And you expect me to just ignore that!

LOUISE: Skelly is an amateur. *I* thought of that period thing *years* ago. I thought of worse. You'd be amazed. I used to lie in bed crying my stupid head off, making up the worst things anybody could think of. Skelly's jokes are nothing.

ERIC: Okay.

LOUISE: What about what *I* said? Did you even remember what I told you? And Joel? How I didn't want — Jesus.

ERIC: I remembered.

LOUISE: Well, then, obviously what I want isn't important.

ERIC: I figured you were just — (*hesitates*)

LOUISE: What? You figured I was what?

ERIC: (*small voice*) Testing me?

Pause.

LOUISE: That's it. It's too late. It's too god-damn late. (*stands*) You're already lost, you know. You've already turned into a — a — a little plastic model Goldner. That's what you are. A little toy Goldner.

She runs out, leaving ERIC angry and miserable. Lights fade.

Scene Three

The locker room. JOEL sits on the bench, brooding, holding his fencing glove. Gets up and opens ERIC's locker. It is full of ERIC's street clothes, books, and sporting gear bag. Opens his own locker. It is empty, except for two wire clothes hangers. After a moment ERIC enters in his fencing gear, warm and fatigued.

JOEL: Hi, whatcha cover today?

ERIC: (*proceeds with locker-and-clothing biz*) What do you care?

JOEL: What do you mean, what do I care? Tell me what you covered.

ERIC: You walk past me in the hall today, you don't even say hello —

JOEL: You didn't say hello either!

ERIC: I had a reason!

JOEL: Well, Jesus, so did I!

ERIC: Fine, then, leave me alone.

He continues with locker business. Brief pause.

JOEL: Well, Jesus, Eric, Bitchy kicked me right out of my whole life, what do you expect? Can't a man have a day or two to recover? I had to be alone with my thoughts. I had to shed a private tear for my loss, okay?

ERIC: Fine, sure, go be alone with your thoughts.

JOEL: What are *you* so pissed off at!

ERIC: (*stops business, looks at JOEL*) Louise hates my guts. She hates me. She thinks it's all my fault. She won't talk to me any more. All right? All right, Joel? You got me in enough trouble?

JOEL: *I* got *you* in trouble! Listen, Cullen, none of this would have happened if you hadn't offered to fight Skelly in the first place!

ERIC: That's right! And I wouldn't have offered to fight him if you hadn't said she was testing me!

JOEL: She was!

ERIC: *No! You're wrong!* It's possible, you know! It's possible for the great Goldner to be wrong!

JOEL: Of course it's possible. But you could have said I was wrong *then*. You could have decided she wasn't really testiing you *then*. And you didn't. You made the challenge. You started the fight. And if you hadn't started it, none of it would have happened, because God damn it *I* don't have the balls to challenge god-damn Skelly to a fist fight! I don't mind you blaming me. But you're only entitled to blame me for *half*. (*silence*) Right? I'm right, aren't I?

ERIC: Yeah.

JOEL: So enough bullshit, tell me what you covered.

ERIC: (*sighs*) All right. We reviewed compound attacks: the one-two, the double and the low-high. And also attack combinations. Oh, and we did something new in épée.

JOEL: Something new! Terrific! What! What!

ERIC: It's called the enveloppement. Take it easy.

JOEL: Show me it! Right now, right here!

ERIC: It's about the épées? There's no épées?

JOEL: Shit. Wait a sec. Here!

He grabs the two wire clothes hangers out of his locker, gives one to ERIC.

ERIC: Uh, Joel?

JOEL: (*straightening out his hanger*) En garde.

ERIC: (*begins straightening his own*) Joel, am I gonna have to do this every time?

JOEL: Just show me. En garde. (*takes up garde position*)

ERIC: Joel, I'm not gonna do this for you after every class.

JOEL: Yeah, well, we'll see, just show me.

ERIC: Listen, I just wanna make it clear —

JOEL: *Just show me! Just fuckin' show me! Show me what you learned, you fucker!*

Pause.

ERIC: Okay, just calm down.

JOEL: Show me and I'll calm down.

ERIC: Okay, take it easy. En garde.

JOEL: Come on.

ERIC: Yeah, okay. Do a lunge on my exposed line of sixte.

JOEL lunges quickly and pokes ERIC in the chest.

ERIC: Not so fast! Do it slow motion!

JOEL returns to garde and repeats the lunge in slow motion.

ERIC: Now instead of the regular parry of sixte — I catch your tip on my bell — or I would if these things had a bell — (*does these moves as he speaks*) And I go around your blade once — or I would if these things were long enough — twice — and then lunge. (*does so*)

JOEL: And I leap back and disengage and come in under you and score. (*does so quickly*)

ERIC: No, no, you wouldn't have time if it was real speed.

JOEL: Why not? Valerian once dodged back and forth like that, nine times in two seconds.

ERIC: Leave Valerian out of this! She didn't teach us the defence yet! The defence is next time! All we learned today was the enveloppement, all right?

JOEL: Yessir.

ERIC: So lemme show it to you faster. En garde.

They perform the enveloppement at close to fencing speed, but they cannot engage properly; the hangers bend and are too short.

ERIC: This is stupid, we have no control with these things.

JOEL: Go back in and sneak out a couple of épées!

ERIC: Oh ho, forget it. Come on. You try it now.

They perform the sequence again, this time with JOEL taking the offensive role.

JOEL: Again. (*They repeat it.*) Again! (*They repeat it. The hangers are impossible.*) Again! Shit!

The hangers get caught on each other, and JOEL hurls his noisily against the lockers.

ERIC: (*cringing*) Will you bloody calm down!

JOEL: How do you expect me to learn anything with these things?

ERIC: I don't.

JOEL: These things are no damn good!

ERIC: (*throws his away*) Of course not! It's obvious.

Silence. JOEL sits on the bench. ERIC returns to his locker.

JOEL: (*dejected*) Who's your new partner, anyway?

ERIC: Arnie.

JOEL: Very funny.

ERIC: Arnie! Arnie's my new partner.

JOEL: Arnie! That klutz! That wimp! Has he learned which end you hold it by yet?

ERIC: He's doing his best. The guy's learning.

JOEL: Learning? Eric, some things you can't learn. What you and I can do out there, you can't learn.

ERIC: He's not interested in that, Joel. He's interested in fencing.

JOEL: That asshole doesn't know what fencing means!

ERIC: He doesn't run around the place like a lunatic! He doesn't break all the rules and get everybody else into shit!

JOEL: I must tell you, Eric, I was really ashamed of you during that fight. That was unworthy of Compôte, *standing around* like that.

ERIC: Compôte? What does Compôte have to do with it? What about real live people, Joel? What about you, even! You know, Valerian's doing great, eh. *He* wasn't kicked out of fencing.

JOEL: He was. He was better zan ze mastaire heemself. Zey could not stand for zat.

ERIC: Of course. But did it matter to him?

JOEL: Certainly not. He was above all zat.

ERIC: Yeah, right, but it matters to you, doesn't it? (*no answer*) Yeah. He's got you doing his dirty work for him. That's the whole problem.

JOEL: The whole problem, as you put eet, ees zat Skelly was not worthy to be cut up by Valerian, zat ees all. Eet ees getteeng so zat Valerian must look far and wide for ze worthee opponents. Indeed, eet may be zat ze onlee man left for heem to fight ees hees own man, Compôte.

Pause.

ERIC: Look. You keep going too far with this Valerian stuff and I don't know if I'm gonna be able to stay your friend, Joel.

JOEL: Don't you threaten me! So now I'm supposed to choose between you and Valerian? Don't push me to it! I'd take Valerian over you any day!

ERIC: Yeah, I guess you would. The two of you deserve each other. Don't you care how this affects anybody else? Like Louise, for instance?

JOEL: Ah yes, Louise.

ERIC: Yeah, that's right, Louise! You can't just use her like that, I'm not gonna let you. I care lots more about her than you do.

JOEL: You do not! I love Louise!

ERIC: You love the stain. You love the stories you make up about her. You don't care about her.

JOEL: I'm crazy about her, I dream about her all the time! Jesus Christ, I got kicked out of Fencing for the sake of her honour!

ERIC: You got kicked out for the sake of being a bloody maniac! You don't care about her!

JOEL: I care!

ERIC: Is that how you prove it, embarrassing her like that?

JOEL: You want proof? You want proof? Here's proof!

He slaps ERIC's face with the fencing glove.

ERIC: What the hell is that? Is that supposed to hurt, or what?

JOEL: I hereby challenge you to a duel.

ERIC: Duels. This isn't a story, asshole!

JOEL: A duel with real, pointed épées. A real duel to the real death.

Pause.

ERIC: You're completely nuts.

JOEL: And you are a coward!

ERIC: Maybe I'm just afraid of what *I* could do to *you*, Goldner.

JOEL: Did I say any different?

Pause.

ERIC: Nobody fights duels to the death!

JOEL: People been doing it for hundreds of years.

ERIC: Well, people don't do it nowadays.

JOEL: Maybe that's why nowadays is nowadays. Maybe that's how you define nowadays, eh, Eric? Nowadays is that age when people are not ready to die. Nowadays is the age of cowards. But if you and I do a duel, then it's all changed. Then, people fight duels nowadays! And so nowadays becomes a different age! Because of us, because of you and me! Ah, Eric, think of the power. Holding our destinies in our own hands. Ze powaire and ze gloree!

ERIC: The power and the glory, eh.

JOEL: We would fly through the clouds. Like shafts of light through the clouds, you and me, we would shine, we would shine. We would be legends in our own time. Compôte — legends in our own, sweet time.

Pause.

ERIC: What if you win? Eh? Aren't you scared of winning?

JOEL: Why?

ERIC: Well, Joel, the trouble with this duelling thing is, somebody's gotta win, right? If I win, you get to fly through the clouds, you get to shine and everything, you got no problems. But what happens to you — if *you* win?

JOEL: They would have to lock me away. Because I would be so glorious they couldn't let me walk around loose. They would lock me up — and then they'd tear down the prison walls trying to get in with me.

ERIC: Well, it's been real swell talking to ya — (*starts to go*)

JOEL: So you gonna think about it?

ERIC: Joel, I don't believe this! I'm not gonna fight a duel with you! This is the craziest thing I ever heard!

JOEL: 'At's okay, Eric. Listen, you don't have to fight this duel. I mean I can't force you, now, can I?

Silence. The lights fade.

Scene Five

The lunchroom. LOUISE sits eating lunch and reading. Enter JOEL.

JOEL: Hi.

LOUISE: Go away.

JOEL: I think it's time we had a little chat.

LOUISE: It's time you got outa my life. Go away.

JOEL: Yeah, I've been hearing that that's your attitude. (*sits*) I think you're being very unfair to me.

LOUISE: *I'm* being unfair to *you*!

JOEL: Yeah. I don't think you understand all the implications of this fight I had with Skelly.

LOUISE: (*stares at him, open mouthed*) I don't understand?

JOEL: I mean, here I avenged your honour, for one thing. Also I protected Eric from getting mashed up in a fist fight — I wiped out Skelly, shamed him, defeated him —

LOUISE: What do you want, Goldner?

JOEL: Well, for starters, I want you to thank me.

LOUISE: You want me to thank you.

JOEL: And I want you to stop badmouthing me all over the place.

LOUISE: Thank you, Joel. Thank you so much. For making me the biggest joke in the school. I walk into French this morning and everybody blushes and giggles and all the conversation stops. I'm a celebrity! You know what I've started doing? Just like when I was a kid. I sit like this. (*sits with hand covering stained cheek*) I made a vow on my birthday I'd never sit like that again. And now you got me doing it.

JOEL: *I* got you!

LOUISE: I had this thing licked, you little creep, and now it feels like I'm thirteen all over again.

JOEL: I would have thought you could handle it.

LOUISE: You don't think at all, Joel. You just do what you damn well feel like.

JOEL: Look, Louise, if you couldn't handle the consequences, you shouldn't have been testing us in the first place.

LOUISE: Testing! (*beat*) You really got him, don't you. Right under your thumb. Did it ever occur to either of you that I just possibly meant what I said!

JOEL: Maybe you *think* you meant what you said.

LOUISE: Oh, but you know better, eh, Joel? You know the inside of my mind better than I do, eh? That's one of your best tricks, eh?

JOEL: Well, Louise, you're a lot like me.

LOUISE: Whoa, hey, I am nothing like you. You are like nothing on earth.

JOEL: Oh, you won't admit it, but you're a lot like me. Manipulating Eric, stringing him along, giving him points —

LOUISE: It isn't the same!

JOEL: And you're good at it. So don't just assume I'm gonna wind up with him. You might just steal him away from me.

LOUISE: I might — just — Do you realize what you're saying?

JOEL: Zat you and I are ze rivals for Com — for Eric.

LOUISE: Joel, are you really gay? Are you gay or or what?

JOEL: I'm a what. That's what I am, I'm a what.

LOUISE: Oh, for Christ's sake! Look. Joel. (*enter ERIC, who listens*) I'm not a — a tester, or whatever it is you're calling me. I don't even know what you're talking about! I really don't understand! I just seem to wind up in this — this situation — and I don't know why. Whether it's something about me, or *what* it is.

Pause. Her genuine bewilderment has finally got through to JOEL.

JOEL: Oh. Well. You know — maybe — maybe you manipulate unconsciously. Maybe it's your beauty that manipulates.

LOUISE: My what?

ERIC: What is this?

JOEL: See, you don't know your own beauty. 'Cause you think the stain takes away from it. You don't see how much it adds to it. It lifts you above the ordinary pretty girls. Because you're beautiful two different ways.

You have the beauty of a woman, and you also have the beauty of a design, an abstract painting. I bet you catch a glimpse of it in the mirror sometimes. But then you go away from the mirror and you forget. It's too bad you can't see it all the time like I do. You show us how a woman can also be like a — a map of a foreign country.

ERIC: Don't listen to this crap —

LOUISE: Sshhh.

JOEL: So your beauty manipulates us. Because you don't know your own power. Like — like a fencer in a fencing class, eh! He thinks it's just a sport, the épées have rubber tips, just play-acting. But then he stabs the other guy — or the other guy stabs him, or both, it doesn't matter — and he realizes the épées were sharp all along. He just never noticed. That's like you.

Silence.

LOUISE: I better go now.

JOEL: So you see, that fight with Skelly—I don't hold it against you.

This breaks the spell for LOUISE.

LOUISE: You don't hold it *against* me? *You* don't hold it against *me*?

JOEL: You don't know your own strength.

LOUISE: How big of you! It was your own damn fault, and you go around forgiving everybody! How kind!

JOEL: My fault? That's right! When in doubt, blame Goldner, everybody else does! I'll tell you whose fault this is! I'll tell you, I'll fucking tell you!

LOUISE: Forget it, I'm not interested —

ERIC: Mine, right?

JOEL: Yeah. Eric's fault. And my fault, okay, sure, and, but also, but also, it's Skelly's fault, and it's your damn fault, Louise, and don't pretend it isn't. And it's Bitchy's fault, boy is it ever Bitchy's fault. And Eric's parents and my parents and the buggered-up school system, and the goddamn government, and, uh, the ad industry, and pollution and war and TV and, um, and, um —

ERIC: What the hell are you talking about?

JOEL: I am *placing blame.* It is the fault of the twentieth century.

ERIC: Oh.

LOUISE: You think any other century was any better?

JOEL: But of course! The eighteenth!

LOUISE: Yeah? Was that Valerian's?

JOEL: (*staring at ERIC*) Son of a bitch.

ERIC: What? Why?

JOEL: (*ineptly attacking ERIC*) You told her! You told her, you son of a bitch!

ERlC: No I didn't!

JOEL isn't much of a fighter without an épée in his hand; ERIC is holding him off.

JOEL: You told her! You told her, you bastard, you told her!

ERIC: *You* told her! She's overheard it, you been shooting your mouth off!

JOEL: You told her, you broke a sacred trust!

ERIC: Tell him I didn't tell you!

LOUISE: He didn't tell me.

JOEL: (*turns on LOUISE*) You know something about good little Cullen here? Cullen isn't all that pure and clean and clear minded, you know! He's just as twisted and warped and fucked up as I am!

LOUISE is quickly gathering up her things.

ERIC: Joel —

JOEL: He can tell you about Valerian, I can tell you a little something too, you know!

ERIC: Shut up!

LOUISE is running off, JOEL pursuing her, ERIC pursuing JOEL.

JOEL: Ask him about trying to fuck his daddy in the coffin!

LOUISE is gone. Pause. JOEL turns back to ERIC.

JOEL: Little poetic license there.

ERIC: I oughta fuckin' accept your challenge! I really oughta!

JOEL: Yeah, you should, Eric — but you won't, will you? 'Cause you don't *do* things, do you, Eric? You didn't do anything about Skelly —

ERIC: I tried!

JOEL: And you didn't do anything about your mother — and you didn't do anything about your father, did you? Before, or after!

Pause.

ERIC: Okay. Okay. You got your duel, you bastard. You want a duel? You got a duel.

Pause.

JOEL: Get two épées out of the equipment room. Don't hide them, just carry them out as if you were allowed to. Get them to me. I'll sharpen the weapons tonight. In the basement. With my father's tools.

ERIC: You sleazy little fucker, you have this all worked out, don't you?

JOEL: In the meantime we shall try to act normal, yes? Come on, Eric. Come on. Lemme walk you to History.

ERIC will not go with him. JOEL shrugs, exits. ERIC slowly follows. The lights fade.

Scene Six

Early morning in a park. Grey lighting. Perhaps fog. A crow caws. JOEL enters. He is chilly; carries the two épées wrapped in a black cloth. He does warm-up exercises. ERIC enters.

JOEL: Morning.

Pause.

ERIC: I came to tell you I'm not gonna do this. I'm not going through with it.

JOEL: Why, Compôte, but this is not like you.

ERIC: Last night I kept dreaming you and I were duelling. I kept waking up 'cause my body would go into a full lunge. Lying there in my bed. I'd wake up in a full lunge. And I knew it'd gone in — but I couldn't tell if it had gone into you or me. And I didn't care.

JOEL: Right.

ERIC: And that's the part that's evil. That we don't care which of us gets it, as long as one of us gets it. That's the evil part.

JOEL: Right.

ERIC: So, Joel, I've decided I'm not gonna —

*JOEL tosses him an épée. ERIC catches it reflex-
ively, by the handle. He regards the tip.*

ERIC: Jesus, you weren't kidding. I'm telling you, I'm not gonna do this, Joel.

*JOEL approaches ERIC, who takes a step back. But
JOEL holds out his hand.*

JOEL: I will love and respect you still, Compôte. We will still be brothers in arms.

*After a moment's hesitation, ERIC takes JOEL's
hand — but JOEL pulls ERIC into a tight embrace.
Pause for a moment, and then ERIC pushes JOEL
away. As JOEL springs away, he is already en garde.*

JOEL: *En garde,* Compôte!

ERIC: I won't fight you!

JOEL: Coward! *En garde!* Defend yourself!
(lunges)

ERIC: *(parrying)* There's nothing to defend!

JOEL: *(punctuating his taunts with lunges, as
ERIC parries)* No honour left to defend, then?
Still the coward, Compôte? Still afraid to fight
the Baron, afraid to face your father, afraid to
fight me? Afraid? Afraid? Afraid!

ERIC: *Stop it!*

*ERIC joins the duel; they fight. Soon it is fast and
furious. Then JOEL lunges, and ERIC replies with
an enveloppement and lunge. They fight on for a couple of strokes but then JOEL suddenly steps back and
lowers his blade. Brief pause.*

ERIC: All right, good. Look, you win, okay?
You win this duel, you win the whole thing,
it's over. It's over. There's nobody left for you
to fight with, you've beaten us all, Skelly and
Louise and Thorpe and me, okay? You're the
winner and still champion, okay? Congratulations, okay?

*JOEL takes a step towards ERIC. His knees buckle
and he collapses. He holds his stomach. There is a
significant amount of blood.*

ERIC: Oh, God. Oh, my God. Aw, no. Oh,
my God.

*He goes to JOEL. JOEL is holding onto himself and
moving about on the ground. He coughs, moans in
pain.*

ERIC: I didn't see this. I swear, Joel, I didn't
see it. It happened when I wasn't noticing. It
all happened when I wasn't —

JOEL: It hurts — oh, Eric, it hurts —

ERIC: I know. I know. Look, I'm going for
help. I'll be back.

*He starts to get up. JOEL grabs him and holds onto
him.*

JOEL: No! Don't go! I am frightened, Com
— I mean — I'm scared, Eric. Eric. I'm scared.

ERIC: I know.

*He grabs the black cloth, tries to stop JOEL's bleeding
with it. It doesn't seem to help. JOEL's pain is increasing. The sunlight is growing stronger.*

JOEL: This — isn't what I thought it would
be like — I thought — that it would be like
Valerian — but — it's just like — real life —
only worse —

ERIC: I know.

*He is holding JOEL in a kind of Pièta pose in his
arms.*

JOEL: I thought — this duel would turn —
my life — into Valerian's —

ERIC: No. No, it doesn't work like that.

JOEL: Instead — I turned his life — into mine
— and — I took you down with me too —

Forgive me. Eric. I'm sorry, man. I screwed up. Forgive me.

JOEL dies in ERIC's arms. The morning sunlight comes through fully.

ERIC: (*weeping*) Yeah, right. Easy for you to say. You shoulda taken me all the way with you, Goldner. You shoulda. All right, then, let's see you fly through the clouds now, Joel. Like you said you would. Let's see you do it. Shine for me if you can, Joel. Let's just see you shine for me if you can.

End

SOMETHING RED
TOM WALMSLEY

The great majority of playwrights to emerge from the New Play Centre have been university-educated men and women who came to the organization with middle-class backgrounds and the credentials of polite society. Tom Walmsley has not been the only exception to this general rule, but he has been the most highly visible. Born in Liverpool in 1948, he moved to Oshawa with his family when he was four. The eldest of six children, Walmsley dropped out of grade ten, making his way to Vancouver by 1967. In the interim, he worked for a while on the assembly line at General Motors. "That was the bottom; the worst thing I've ever done," he would tell *The Globe and Mail* in 1980. He was including in this assessment the felony crimes and heroin addiction of his six years of life on the streets in the late '60s and early '70s, the experiences that would provide the sometimes very raw materials for his writing.

Walmsley's first writings were poems. A collection called *Rabies* (1975) was published on the day his first play premiered at the New Play Centre. He had entered the play, *The Working Man*, in a contest sponsored by the Victoria Community Arts Council and adjudicated by Pamela Hawthorn. Though she awarded it only third prize, Hawthorn was struck by its authentic dialogue and strong theatricality, and she invited Walmsley to put it through the New Play Centre workshop process. In a 1987 retrospective essay, Hawthorn listed among her most vivid New Play Centre memories the day when "Tom Walmsley first sat down over coffee, gave me *The Working Man*, and informed me that he was 'keeping a low profile' for certain 'legal reasons.'" *The Working Man* premiered at the same 1975 du Maurier Festival as Tom Cone's *Herringbone*. In 1977 it appeared at Toronto Free Theatre in a double-bill with *The Jones Boy*, which Walmsley wrote at a Banff Playwrights Workshop and refined through the New Play Centre.

Meanwhile, he had published his second book of poetry, *Lexington Hero* (1976), and in 1978 the New Play Centre premiered *Something Red*. That same year he won the Pulp Press Three Day Novel Contest with *Doctor Tin* (1979), described by *The Globe and Mail*'s Jay Scott as "a psychedelic, sado-masochistic bi-sexual rewrite of Raymond Chandler."

In 1982 Walmsley moved to Toronto where all his subsequent plays have premiered. They include the comedy *White Boys* (Tarragon, 1982), a runner-up (along with *Dreaming and Duelling*) for the 1983 Chalmers Award; *Getting Wrecked* (Theatre Direct, 1985), a musical about teenage alcohol abuse, winner of the 1986 Dora Mavor Moore Award for children's theatre; and *Mr. Nice Guy* (Necessary Angel/Toronto Free, 1986), a play about wife abuse in a middle-class home, co-written with Dolly Reisman. Since then Walmsley has worked on the film script of John Schlesinger's *The Believers*, and on adapting his own plays for the screen.

Something Red epitomizes the brutal naturalism that made Walmsley's plays of the 1970s such a shock to Canadian audiences: the booze, drugs, sex and explosive violence; the detailed explorations of the limits of machismo and the fatal attractions of sado-masochism. In a 1978 review titled "Uncanadiana at Last," Tom Shandel of Vancouver's *Georgia Straight* called it "the most powerful piece of dramatic writing to have emerged in this country up to now." *Globe and Mail* critic Ray Conlogue told Toronto audiences to see the play if "you like to be scared till your knuckles go white."

Something Red has been produced by Toronto's Tarragon (1980), Ottawa's Theatre 2000 (1980), the Manhattan Rep at New York's Westbeth Theater (1986), and in French translation by Théâtre de la Manufacture in Montreal (1985), with a tour the following year. The play was originally published by Virgo Press (1980). *Something Red* was first presented by the New Play Centre at the Vancouver East Cultural Centre on October 6, 1978, with Michael Hogan as Bobby, Tom McBeath as Alex, Rosemary Dunsmore as Christine, and Michelle Fisk as Elizabeth. It was directed by Kathryn Shaw with set by Richard Cook, lights by Marsha Sibthorpe and costumes by Christina McQuarrie.

Michael Hogan as Bobby, and Michelle Fisk as Elizabeth in the New Play Centre production of *Something Red*. Photo by Glen Erikson.

SOMETHING RED

CHARACTERS

BOBBY

CHRISTINE

ALEX

ELIZABETH

SET

The stage is on two levels, showing BOBBY and CHRISTINE's apartment downstairs, ALEX and ELIZABETH's upstairs. A stairway, only partially visible to the audience, connects the two apartments. The entrance to each apartment is centre stage. Stage left downstairs is a couch, chair, coffee table and two end tables. Far stage left is a component stereo set. Upstage, immediate stage right is the hall cupboard. The kitchenette is downstage from here, with a long bar facing three bar stools. The bar contains a sink. Far stage right is the entrance to the bedroom.

The upstairs apartment covers only a third of the downstairs. There is one chair to the left of the entrance. The upper stage cuts diagonally right from there. Stage right upstairs holds a small bookshelf. Far stage right holds the entrance to the bedroom and against the right wall, a couch.

ACT ONE

The play opens with a darkened stage. BOBBY is pacing around in the dark, lighting a cigarette he has rolled from butts. There is a Hendrix record playing, the needle stuck in one of the grooves. There is the sound of a key in the entrance door, which opens partway and is stopped by a chain. CHRISTINE reaches in and unlocks the chain.

CHRISTINE: Why are all the lights out?

She turns on the lights.

BOBBY: It got late behind my back, I guess. I was starting to think you got hit by a truck.

CHRISTINE crosses, avoiding BOBBY's attempt at an embrace. She takes the needle off the record. BOBBY goes to the door and replaces the chain.

CHRISTINE: I had to go all the way out to Burnaby.

BOBBY: I made you a pot of tea, but probably it's cold.

CHRISTINE: They're delivering the TV Monday. I told the guy you'd be home for it. Throw this one out the window and I'm throwing you after it.

BOBBY: Hey, feel this muscle.

CHRISTINE: I'm going to drop dead if I ever come home and find this place tidy.

BOBBY: Tell me if this isn't the most amazing right arm you ever grabbed onto.

CHRISTINE: Amazing. How about using those amazing arms to clean up around here while I get out of these things?

BOBBY: Now you're talking — let's get you out of these things.

CHRISTINE: Don't even think about it, Bobby.

BOBBY: You want me to make some more tea for you?

CHRISTINE: I've been drinking it all day.

BOBBY: Alex called a couple of minutes ago. They're coming down.

CHRISTINE: Shit, is it that late?

BOBBY: A little nudge before they get here would put the roses in your cheeks.

CHRISTINE: It'd take more than that to put roses in these cheeks after three hours on the bus.

BOBBY: Okay, listen now. I mean, I'm sorry, but what can I tell you? I'm lying down having a nice time, listening to a little music, and when I look up there's three people dressed like pickles dancing on the screen. Now, I admit, I shouldn't have given the thing the heave, but it just hit me wrong. It was the booze, I guess. That TV was pretty old anyway.

CHRISTINE: Those things cost money, you know that?

BOBBY: Just like everything else. It was the booze, really.

CHRISTINE: Then maybe you should stop drinking.

BOBBY: Birds fly, fish swim, I drink.

CHRISTINE: Will you get some of this stuff cleared away? Please?

CHRISTINE exits to the bedroom. BOBBY makes a half-hearted attempt at tidying up — probably nothing more than crumpling a newspaper or moving a few beer bottles to the kichen counter.

BOBBY: So how'd it go today, generally?

CHRISTINE: Oh, all right. They say I'm a good worker.

BOBBY: They tell you that just so you'll work your ass off for them.

CHRISTINE: It beats working at Eve's. I really was working my ass off, there.

CHRISTINE comes out of the bedroom, either without her skirt on or without her blouse, still changing.

BOBBY: Your outfit was cuter, though. Lady, I do like the way you look without that dress.

CHRISTINE: For that, you get a kiss.

She gives him a small kiss, but BOBBY takes her in his arms and turns it into a long one.

CHRISTINE: You know what'd be nice? Don't get too wrecked tonight. We can have a nice time after they leave.

BOBBY: Kid, it's a date.

CHRISTINE: Do you want to take a run up to the liquor store?

BOBBY: They're bringing it with them.

CHRISTINE: Do you think we should get some snacks? They had some, last time.

BOBBY: I think you ought to sit down and take it easy.

She sits, or is sat down by BOBBY. There is a copy of Play It As It Lays *by Joan Didion somewhere close at hand.*

CHRISTINE: Have you been reading this?

BOBBY: I took a look at it today. It's dogshit. The people got lots of bread, they can do anything they want. But their lives seem to be empty. Fuck that.

CHRISTINE: Oh, I thought it was pretty good. I started that other thing, but all it's about is a guy thinking. I'm going to have to dig up something new.

BOBBY: Get Alex to give you his novel.

CHRISTINE: I didn't think he was finished.

BOBBY: He'll never be finished.

CHRISTINE: What do you know about it?

BOBBY: I know it'll be dogshit.

CHRISTINE: That's a nice way to talk about your best friend. What did you do with yourself today?

BOBBY: Let's see. I got up . . . had some cereal, we need some more. I drank about a gallon of coffee . . . uh, played a record . . .

CHRISTINE: I mean besides that stuff.

BOBBY: Well, I played music for a couple of hours, did my exercise, took a bath . . .

CHRISTINE: All right, all right.

BOBBY: And I wrote you a poem. Do you want to hear it?

CHRISTINE: No.

BOBBY: It's called "For Christine."

"I kissed you this morning
after drinking all night,
You stood sleepy-eyed at the door.
You rise for your job
at the first day-light
and I wish that you'd rise no more.
So I thought just for fun
I'd put on my gun
and butcher the swine by the score.
But for every six bastards
who'd die by my hand
There'd always be sixty-five more."

It's listening to the birds and things, I guess. Puts me in the mood.

Pause.

CHRISTINE: You can't keep doing this, Bobby.

BOBBY: Yeah. I've been thinking about it, today, you know. I got to get some bread. Have a couple bucks in my pocket, maybe help out with the food and rent. Like, if I pick up four or five hundred, we could ride on that for a while, right? Or even something like a hundred a week. Fifty, even.

CHRISTINE: It'd beat sitting around in the dark.

BOBBY: I mean, I'm not talking about a straight job. I might be able to get some sort of thing, you know, a few dollars here and there. You can sometimes get a deal like that.

CHRISTINE: Well, I never heard of one. I don't mean go out and get a job, but wouldn't you just like to go out? Take a look at the mountains, once in a while? Or maybe join a gym or something. It just seems to me . . .

BOBBY: I could bang old ladies with blue hair. What d'you think? Would you be willing to shell out a few bucks for a nice, young stud if you were old and blue?

CHRISTINE: Isn't that what I'm doing right now?

BOBBY: What kind of fucking talk is that?

CHRISTINE: It's a joke, I guess.

BOBBY: I mean, how do you think that makes me feel? Jesus.

CHRISTINE: It was supposed to be a joke. Really. I'm tired and I said that without thinking.

BOBBY: All right.

CHRISTINE: The way I meant it was, you really are a nice young stud. See? It was supposed to be nice.

BOBBY: All right that does it, let's fuck.

BOBBY pulls CHRISTINE down onto the couch. Laughs, etc., mauling, tickling. There is a knock on the door.

CHRISTINE: Shit.

BOBBY: Get it.

CHRISTINE: It's only Alex.

BOBBY: Get it. (*swats her on the ass*)

CHRISTINE straightens her clothes and opens the door to admit ALEX and ELIZABETH.

ALEX: Hello, sunshine.

CHRISTINE: Hi, stranger. Hi, Elizabeth.

ELIZABETH: How goes it?

BOBBY: Whoa, there he is. Looking just as pretty as the last time I saw him. (*Fakes punches to ALEX's head. ALEX retaliates by pretending to attack BOBBY with one of the bottles he is holding.*) Turned into a dirty fighter behind my back. (*to ELIZABETH*) Hello, you little devil.

ELIZABETH: Hello, you thug. Shot anyone lately?

CHRISTINE: My God, two bottles?

BOBBY: Lots of liquor there, boy. I didn't think you were a man who could hold his drink.

ALEX: Hey, hold *this*. (*cups his hand around his crotch*)

BOBBY: Make me an offer.

CHRISTINE: We'll need ice.

CHRISTINE takes the bottles, goes behind the counter and prepares the drinks while ALEX and ELIZABETH sit in the living room talking to BOBBY.

BOBBY: We could guzzle it right from the bottle.

ELIZABETH: Let's not become animals until later in the evening.

BOBBY: Promises. (*looks at ALEX, sizing him up*) Now, am I imagining things, or have you grown in the last week?

ALEX: I was just about to ask you if you'd shrunk.

BOBBY: (*making as if to attack ALEX*) Well, you ornery bastard.

ALEX draws imaginary gun, shoots BOBBY.

BOBBY: Now *that's* dirty fighting.

ALEX: I'm too tired for Marquis of Queensbury.

BOBBY: That's the trouble with trying to enjoy yourself with you worn-out workies.

ELIZABETH: Ah, complaints from the energetic unemployed.

BOBBY: Well, by God, looks like I'm going to have to take you both on.

ALEX: It's nice to see you've come through another week of peril and adventure unscathed.

BOBBY: I went out . . . when was it? Monday, Tuesday, I don't know. Got drunk and passed out on the bus. That's about it.

ELIZABETH: It's good to hear you're preserving your health.

ALEX: So you finally found a bar where you feel safe.

BOBBY: What are you talking about? Those other bars weren't my style, that's all.

ALEX: I know what you mean — they had people in them.

BOBBY: The only thing that scares me is kryptonite. (*some vocal reaction from ALEX*) But this bar I went to — I don't know the name, but the only people in the place were a couple of rubbies and some guys from the post office. So, yeah, I figure, it's a nice, safe place to drink. You get a little uptight, drinking in here all the time.

ELIZABETH: Oh, I know what you mean. Anytime I stay in the house for three or four months it tends to depress me.

CHRISTINE: Here we go. (*Brings the drinks over on a cookie sheet, which she places on the coffee table.*) Take the one with the crack, Bobby.

BOBBY: What for?

CHRISTINE: Because I've got the one with the chip.

ALEX: I'm ready for a couple.

BOBBY: Listen, let's have the bottle over here so we can take a hit when we want it.

BOBBY goes to the counter and brings the opened bottle back to the couch. ALEX is sitting on the chair, ELIZABETH and CHRISTINE on the couch. BOBBY sits next to CHRISTINE.

ALEX: Your boy seems to have worked up a thirst.

CHRISTINE: Yes, for a change.

ELIZABETH: Did you ever notice how violent drinking sounds? A hit. Hit me.

ALEX: Give me a belt. Or better yet, a slug.

BOBBY: Yeah, I could use a shot. You're right, kiddo. Listen, let's have a toast. That's not violent, that's breakfast. Here's to . . . you're quitting your job soon, right?

ELIZABETH: Next week is my last.

BOBBY: To Elizabeth's last week. Looking at you, kid.

They drink.

BOBBY: Awful fucking stuff.

CHRISTINE: I like a sweeter drink, myself. Except you throw up.

BOBBY: I don't know why the hell I drink, I can't stand the taste of the stuff. Then when I don't drink, I know why I drink.

ELIZABETH: And why do you drink?

BOBBY: I like getting drunk.

CHRISTINE: (*at the same time*) He likes getting drunk.

BOBBY: Thank you, sweetheart.

CHRISTINE: I know your heart, Bobby.

ALEX: I like getting drunk, too. We've been out just about every night this week and the people we've been seeing, I mean, they're nice enough, but when they ask you if you want a drink they mean one drink. And it's always wine. You toss it down and they say. "Would you like some coffee?" As though you'd just chug-a-lugged a twenty-six and want to sober up a bit. It's murder.

ELIZABETH: I've been showing off this gracious lad to all my friends who've been deprived of the pleasure.

BOBBY: You've been taking my partner around meeting fruits?

ELIZABETH: You liberal son of a bitch.

ALEX: Go back to calling them gearboxes, Bobby, it sounds tougher.

BOBBY: Bite my big salami.

ALEX: Make me an offer.

BOBBY: I'm warning you, boy, don't pass out around these guys, know what I mean?

ALEX: Wake up in the morning without my cherry?

BOBBY: Or pregnant.

ALEX: A bun in the buns, you mean? My God. Hey, you folks didn't hear about Elizabeth's accident.

ELIZABETH: What a twisted sense of association.

ALEX: A few nights ago at the Y, she sits down on a piece of glass in the shower room. Had to have stitches.

CHRISTINE: Gee, do you want me to get you a pillow?

ALEX: Sitting down doesn't bother her. Other things give her all kinds of trouble, eh, honey?

ELIZABETH: Are you sure you don't want to be more graphic?

ALEX: Oh, I think we'd have to go a lot farther than that to shock these jaded specimens. Is anybody blushing?

CHRISTINE: There's this girl at work that puts a big piece of foam rubber on her chair because she's got this boil on her bum. She's really uptight about people knowing.

BOBBY: Everybody in the world is weird about their own ass, except me.

ALEX: ' You and the gearboxes.

ELIZABETH: How are you finding the job, Christine?

CHRISTINE: Oh, you know, it's a job. I don't mind it too much.

ALEX: Listen, the fat man came up to me today and held up some wool. He asked me what colour it was and I told him, orange. He held up some more and I told him, red. Then he held them both out and asked me which was which. I thought it was some kind of primitive I.Q. test.

BOBBY: Being a creel boy sounds pretty exciting, all right.

ALEX: What happened was someone replaced the spools of red for spools of orange. The weaver couldn't tell until he'd done about three yards of rug. So they had a rug half red, half orange. Had to scrap the whole thing.

CHRISTINE: Did they think it was your fault?

ALEX: It looked that way. Wasn't too long ago I would've walked right off the job, after a routine like that.

BOBBY: I'd have ripped his dentures out for him.

ALEX: Gee, I wish I were half the man you are. Now, I'm about to tell you something, so pay attention, I don't expect you to know it on your own. A job is a place where you show up at a certain time and put in eight hours work. Can you grasp that?

BOBBY: Kind of like going to school, you mean.

ALEX: Oh, you remember school, do you?

BOBBY: I got a sort of memory of it. Do you have recess?

ALEX: Oh yeah, we've got that. We've got lunch hour, too, and a cafeteria.

BOBBY: And if you fuck up do you get the strap?

ALEX: No, you get the boot.

BOBBY: It doesn't sound like much fun.

ALEX, ELIZABETH, CHRISTINE: (at once) It isn't.

BOBBY: Whoa, horsies.

BOBBY pours himself a fresh drink, or at least picks up the bottle to do so.

ALEX: I see you've managed to get past the taste.

BOBBY: Decent stuff you've brought over, for a change.

ALEX: You'd drink piss if you thought there was alcohol in it.

BOBBY: And you'd drink piss if you thought it came from your boss, right?

ALEX: You know what you can take a bite out of.

ELIZABETH: Now *you* say, "Make me an offer."

BOBBY: You're learning there, junior.

ELIZABETH: Where's the arsenal tonight?

ALEX: Yeah, aren't you afraid a crazed newsboy might throw himself through the door even as we sit here?

CHRISTINE: It's in the bedroom. That's the peak danger period, sleeping.

BOBBY: All right, all right.

ELIZABETH: So now you can settle down for a little television with your knife and club near at hand. That must be a comfort.

CHRISTINE: And his gun, don't forget.

ELIZABETH: Did you move the TV?

BOBBY: No, the fucking thing . . .

CHRISTINE: It's broken.

BOBBY: Who's ready for another one?

Whoever wants a drink will hold out their glass while BOBBY pours.

CHRISTINE: You're going to get hammered. How's that for violent? Smashed. What was that awful stuff Roger and I drank one time? Something Greek, not ouzo. Anyway, we were drinking it and it didn't even feel like getting drunk, but like we were high. So I was on my way to the bathroom, I thought I felt pretty good and I just suddenly had to lie down. I lay right down on the kitchen floor. Roger came in and saw me and started laughing and right in the middle of a laugh he threw up, it just jumped right out of his mouth about three feet, right against the refrigerator. I'm not kidding, three feet.

ELIZABETH: Must have been a bad year.

BOBBY: You know, a long time before Alex and me ever heard of scotch we used to knock back all that sweet, cheap red shit. That stuff is mainly good as a laxative. One night we were lying around, an awful goddamned night. Anyway, we got an empty bottle of what? Port?

ALEX: Something terrible.

BOBBY: And you know how empties are never really empty, there's always a little puddle in the bottom? Well, we pour it out and it fills a large tablespoon. We take Larry's syringe, this other guy who's living with us, and we shoot half a spoon of red wine each. It was the same feeling you get when you drink wine in the afternoon — your mouth tastes awful, your tongue is thick and you've got a bit of a head. Well, we get that feeling instantly. Awful stuff to shoot, too. You can hardly tell when you've hit blood.

ELIZABETH: When in God's name was this?

ALEX: That was when? A couple of years ago, I guess. Just before Bobby decided to go back east and get into all sorts of new trouble.

BOBBY: Before you decided you were better off working for the Man. That was around the time Dennis and I hooked up. God, it was great. Nuts, but great. I swear to Christ me and Dennis knocked over every grocery store in the West End. Half the fucking city was after us.

CHRISTINE: That doesn't sound so great to me.

BOBBY: And do you think we could keep our hands on a dime? We had to rip off Welfare at the same time just to go on living in fleabags.

CHRISTINE: I've had that and you can keep it.

BOBBY: Not like I had it, you didn't. It's nothing like the fucking same, what I did.

ALEX: Listen, Bobby, remember that time I sold those bikers those oregano joints? These guys came into the bar the next day, Bobby and I were sitting there, and they marched right over to us. I figured we were on our way to the hospital. The guy says, "Listen, that dope you sold us. Can we get a pound?"

ELIZABETH: I'm afraid my adventures would sound somewhat pale by comparison.

CHRISTINE: Believe me, you haven't missed anything.

BOBBY: Hey listen, Alex, let's you and me go out and get into trouble.

ALEX: What kind of trouble do you get from a couple of rubbies and some postal workers?

BOBBY: More than you get in this place.

CHRISTINE: We should all do something together. I don't mean go out, but play a game or something.

ELIZABETH: We could move all this up to our place and watch some TV.

ALEX: The second part of that movie's on tonight. You know that thing about the Queen? But I guess you probably missed part one.

BOBBY: I guess we probably did.

CHRISTINE: Are there any other good movies on tonight?

BOBBY: Aw c'mon, this is the weekend, for Christ's sake.

CHRISTINE: I don't think we've got your kind of energy, Bobby.

BOBBY: Why are women always tired at night?

CHRISTINE: We work all day.

BOBBY: Right.

CHRISTINE: Would anyone be up for Scrabble?

CHRISTINE gets up and crosses to kitchen area, rummaging through cupboards.

ELIZABETH: Be warned, I excel at Scrabble.

BOBBY: I'm glad all that education's good for something.

ALEX: Easy does it partner.

ELIZABETH: Oh, that's just his way of saying he's fond of me. Isn't it, Bobby?

BOBBY: You're as cute as a button. I mean, you know what I mean?

ELIZABETH: God, I wish I had this man's ability for self-expression.

CHRISTINE: Where did I put it? It's been months. Bobby, where's the Scrabble game?

BOBBY: Come on, forget it, all right?

ALEX: We could go bowling. Take the liquor in pop bottles.

BOBBY: What is this, a conspiracy?

ELIZABETH: What would you like to do, Bobby?

BOBBY: Oh, I don't know. Get drunk.

BOBBY shadow-boxes, something he does whenever the mood takes him.

ALEX: Getting ready for the champ?

BOBBY: Just warming up in case Elizabeth gets out of hand.

CHRISTINE: I still like the idea of Scrabble. Would you really hate it?

BOBBY: All right, darling. To show you what a sport I am, we'll play. It's up in the closet. Maybe I'll come up with something better later. (*sits back on the couch*)

ELIZABETH: You notice he knows the exact location of the game.

CHRISTINE: That's because he keeps his gun there. I couldn't stand having it by the bed, I was afraid he'd shoot me. Then he stashed the ammunition because he was afraid I'd shoot *him*. Now the gun's in one place, the bullets are somewhere else and it takes him ten minutes to get it all together. (*puts the game on the coffee table*)

BOBBY: Well, if a blind guy shows up and decides to beat the door down with his cane, I'm ready for him.

ELIZABETH: At least you're developing a sense of humour about it.

BOBBY: It's either that or go nuts.

CHRISTINE: We all pick a letter to see who's first.

BOBBY: What are we trying for — a low letter or a high one?

ELIZABETH: Are you going to persist in pretending you've never heard of this game?

BOBBY: Well, I'm in with an *E*.

ALEX: *R*.

ELIZABETH: *C*.

CHRISTINE: I win, a *B*. I pick my letters first. Then it goes, Elizabeth, Bobby then Alex. So you guys switch around.

They re-arrange themselves.

BOBBY: How come I'm not getting excited about this?

ALEX: If you think of anything more exciting, tiger, we'll do it.

ELIZABETH: How was your day today, Bobby?

BOBBY: I did fuck all.

ELIZABETH: Doesn't that ever wear you out?

BOBBY: Sure does.

ALEX: It's like having your very own Marcel Proust downstairs.

ELIZABETH: The man with the memory but has misplaced his quill.

BOBBY: Kid, you do say a mouthful.

CHRISTINE: Well. I've got a word already. *Top*. That blank letter's supposed to be an *O*.

ELIZABETH: My God, you're using your blank letter for that? Hang on to it, Christine. Can't you make anything else?

CHRISTINE: Don't look at my letters.

ELIZABETH: Or even change it to *Tip*. Or *Tap*.

ALEX: She's made her word, leave her alone.

CHRISTINE: Who's going to keep score? Alex, you're good with numbers.

BOBBY: Who knows a dirty joke?

CHRISTINE: Are you getting that way already?

BOBBY: Just trying to keep from falling asleep. I'm lousy at this game.

ALEX: At work the guys are still telling jokes you hear in the sixth grade. It's unreal.

BOBBY: Listen, I heard one in the bar the other night. Just about killed me.

CHRISTINE: Is it filthy?

BOBBY: No, no. It's the story of my life, I think. Also, why I'm lousy at Scrabble games.

ELIZABETH: Brace yourselves, everyone. *(puts down letters)*

BOBBY: What kind of fucking word is that?

ELIZABETH: *Dotage*, darling. It means senility.

BOBBY: Well I never heard of it.

ELIZABETH: I'm shocked. It's a real word, I assure you.

CHRISTINE: I'll get the dictionary. *(looks around for the dictionary, which she will find in the closet)*

ALEX: It's a real word, Bobby.

BOBBY: Isn't there some kind of rule that everyone has to know the word you make?

ELIZABETH: I'm afraid not.

BOBBY: Oh man, I don't know about this. All I can make is *Hat*. You got all the good letters.

ELIZABETH: There may be a new word you can make, now that my letters are down.

CHRISTINE: *(dictionary in hand)* Here we go, let's see. *D*.

BOBBY: Forget it, Christine. It's just you and me who've never heard of it.

ELIZABETH: Weren't you going to tell a joke about Scrabble?

BOBBY: No, I said why I'm no good at it. But when I heard this thing, I thought, "Now that's the story of my life." I mean, kind of. In a way. It's funny as hell anyway. There's this clown, right, he plays nightclubs all over the world and his whole act is he insults people. So this guy goes to see him and the clown picks him out of the audience. "Hey you," the clown says, "stand up." Guy stands up. The clown says, "Are you the donkey's head?" Guy says no. "Are you the donkey's tail?" Guy says no. "Well, if you're not the donkey's head and you're not the donkey's tail, you must be the donkey's ass." Well, everyone laughs and the guy thinks, I'm gonna get that clown. So he goes to some big university and takes a five-year course in quick sayings and snappy comebacks. Then he travels all over the world till he finds where the clown is playing. The night before the show, he reads every book in the library on quick sayings and snappy comebacks. He's ready. He goes to the show and after all this time, the clown recognizes him. "You, stand up." Guy stands up. "Are you the donkey's head?" No. "Are you the donkey's tail?" No. "Well if you're not the donkey's head and you're not the donkey's tail, you must be the donkey's ass." The guy says, "Oh, yeah? Well FUCK YOU, CLOWN."

CHRISTINE: That isn't funny, for God's sake.

BOBBY: Maybe you had to hear this guy tell it. Anyway, I feel like that guy. The guy who says fuck you.

ELIZABETH: Perhaps you should elaborate on that some other time.

CHRISTINE sits beside BOBBY, looking at his letters.

CHRISTINE: Hurry up and make a word.

BOBBY: I don't want to play this. It's a drag.

CHRISTINE: You're just mad about Elizabeth's word.

BOBBY: Go fuck yourself.

ALEX: What's the matter, sweetie, got the rag on?

BOBBY: No, but you better tell your new friends that *you* do.

ALEX: Those guys used to keep you alive at one time.

CHRISTINE: You know these guys, Bobby?

BOBBY: He means fruits. Alex is just jealous they used to pick me.

CHRISTINE: Are you serious? You fucked guys?

BOBBY: No, no.

ALEX: What do you think he is, queer?

BOBBY: I let the odd guy blow me for a couple of bucks.

ALEX: And he means a couple.

BOBBY slugs ALEX in the shoulder.

ELIZABETH: You're like that corporal in the army. He runs up to the captain and says, "Captain, the camp's full of queers. I tasted shit on the sergeant's cock."

ALEX: Come on folks, this is a Scrabble game.

CHRISTINE: Put down *Hat*, Bobby. There's an *E* there now. You can make *Hate*.

BOBBY: I quit. (*he gets up from the couch*)

ELIZABETH: Now don't become a poor sport. I won't have it. Just sit down and make a word.

BOBBY sits.

CHRISTINE: He'll do it for you.

BOBBY: She's a guest. What are you giving me a hard time for?

ELIZABETH: No one's giving you a hard time. Just behave.

ALEX: If he doesn't want to play, leave him alone.

BOBBY picks up the Scrabble board, dumps the letters into the bag, tosses the board down. CHRISTINE probably slaps his legs.

BOBBY: Listen, let's all get drunk and to hell with this, all right? I still say me and Alex should go out and get into trouble.

ALEX: Now why is it my pulse isn't racing at that prospect? Come on, Bobby, let's just relax, hoist a few, and forget about going out. It's been a long week for the rest of us. I think we're a little old to pretend every night is Hallowe'en.

BOBBY: Well, in that case, I'm going to dance with your old lady. (*to ELIZABETH*) Will you have this dance, you rascal?

CHRISTINE: Don't be a fool, Bobby.

ELIZABETH: If you find some nice music.

BOBBY: Help me pick something out.

ELIZABETH goes with BOBBY to the stereo, where they look through the records.

ALEX: Maybe you and I should go and do the town, Christine.

CHRISTINE: Don't think I'm not tempted. He's trying to make me mad.

BOBBY: I heard that, honeybunch.

ALEX: Besides going out and getting into trouble, what would you like to do, Bobby?

BOBBY: I told you. Dance.

ALEX: Besides that.

BOBBY: I have a short poem on this subject.

CHRISTINE: He wants to kill people.

BOBBY: Not that poem. I'll find it. Dig up some music there, Elizabeth.

CHRISTINE: You don't have to bother, you know. Why don't you just sit down?

ELIZABETH: Is it really going to bother you if we dance?

CHRISTINE: I guess not. I just thought we could all do something together.

BOBBY keeps his poems on various pieces of paper in a pocket of his jeans. He looks through them, finding the right one.

BOBBY: Here we are. It's called "For Christine." They're all called that, in fact.

"I'd like to drink for a week with the sailors,
break someone's nose,
lose my shoes
wake up in San Francisco
without a nickel, wondering
what now?
And you say to me:
do you want coffee
or do you want tea?"

Pause. No reaction from the others — ALEX and ELIZABETH are perhaps embarrassed.

CHRISTINE: You know what I'd like?

BOBBY: What?

CHRISTINE: (*to ALEX*) If you'd read from your novel.

ALEX: Give me another month or two and you'll be able to read it yourself.

CHRISTINE: But you could read us a little part now.

BOBBY: Almost finished the monster, have you? I didn't think you'd get a chance to write, running around with college kids.

ELIZABETH: That's a nice crack.

BOBBY: Not you, sweetie, not you. (*to ALEX*) Drink?

ALEX: Absolutely. (*BOBBY pours him one.*) I don't spend all my time meeting people, Bobby.

BOBBY: No, you spend most of it changing wool. So is this book just about yourself? Like, is that the book?

ALEX: Well, I'll tell you. It's about a guy who spends all his time lying around getting hung up. (*CHRISTINE laughs.*) But this guy wants to be a writer. One nice spring day when he's almost thirty he meets this beautiful, witty, blue-eyed university student on the beach. And she changes his life for him.

ELIZABETH: She sounds like a wonderful woman.

BOBBY: You think anyone is interested in that?

CHRISTINE: It sounds interesting to me.

BOBBY: Seems to me it's what the guy did before he met this woman that's the interesting part.

CHRISTINE: He's not writing the book about you, Bobby.

BOBBY: And am I talking to you?

ALEX: I'm sorry man, living in thirty different furnished rooms and picking up a welfare cheque once a month doesn't sound interesting to me.

BOBBY: Funny way of looking at it.

ALEX: You know, the first time you ever met me I told you I was writing a novel. I've been telling people that for twelve years and now I'm finally doing it. No social workers at the door, no cops, no more being broke all the goddamned time.

CHRISTINE: Believe me, I know what you're talking about.

BOBBY: What's the matter, Elizabeth, can't you find a record?

ELIZABETH: I'm sorry, literary discussions always enchant me.

ALEX: Curly headed student reforms street boy.

BOBBY: Street boy? Creel boy, you mean.

ALEX: Something bothering you, man?

ELIZABETH: Here, you impatient brute. We have music. (*puts record on*)

CHRISTINE: Ignore him, Alex. He hates people who work for a living.

BOBBY: Hate to see what it turns them into, that's all.

The music starts. ELIZABETH goes to BOBBY and they dance.

ALEX: Do you feel like dancing?

CHRISTINE: If we're going to dance, then let's go out. This is stupid.

BOBBY takes a swig from the bottle.

CHRISTINE: Don't be a pig, Bobby.

BOBBY leaves ELIZABETH and goes over to CHRISTINE.

ELIZABETH: God, you're the same with dancing as you are with Scrabble.

BOBBY: Say you'll be mine, my little muffin.

CHRISTINE: Are you drunk already?

BOBBY: I'm begging your company on the dance floor. The woman I love.

CHRISTINE: Wouldn't you rather go somewhere and dance?

BOBBY: Absolutely. And I'd rather not have a warrant out on me and people wanting to break my legs. I'd rather be rich. I'd rather be someone else. Will you dance?

CHRISTINE: Since you ask so nicely, I will. (*gets up and dances with BOBBY*)

ELIZABETH: (*to ALEX*) Will you have this dance, handsome?

ALEX: I've been on my feet all day. Why don't you sit down here and we'll pretend we're dancing.

She sits next to him. ALEX wraps his arms around her.

ELIZABETH: You reformed street boys are all alike.

ALEX: Did that embarrass you, that stuff?

ELIZABETH: Not at all. (*they kiss*)

BOBBY: Hey there, cop your nookie at home.

ALEX: Cop my joint.

BOBBY: Hey, there's an idea. Let's get a foursome going here.

CHRISTINE: Will you be nice?

ELIZABETH: Always the life of any party.

ALEX: On top of everything else, you've got a great little body.

ELIZABETH: You're not in bad shape yourself, for a man of your advanced years.

BOBBY: Can you believe this? Kids nowadays, I'm telling you.

ALEX: Don't go letting some engineering student catch your eye now, will you? Or some understanding professor. Promise me, okay?

ELIZABETH: I may not have to. (*to BOBBY*) Are you planning to hog that bottle all evening?

BOBBY: Help yourself.

ALEX: How do you mean, you may not have to?

ELIZABETH: There's a way of avoiding engineering students altogether, it seems to me. Unhand that bottle, sir.

ALEX: How do you mean?

BOBBY: All right, change your partners.

BOBBY lets go of CHRISTINE and grabs ELIZABETH.

ELIZABETH: Do I have to go through this every time I want a drink?

CHRISTINE: Come on, Alex, it's kind of nice once you get into it.

ALEX gets up. Tentatively begins dancing with CHRISTINE.

BOBBY: Right from the bottle, kid. You can do it.

ELIZABETH takes a large swallow from the bottle.

ALEX: You have a plan for being inconspicuous on campus?

ELIZABETH: I have a plan for being invisible.

BOBBY: He's right, you've got a great little body.

ELIZABETH: It's so nice to be thought of as more than just another fine mind.

ALEX: I'd like to hear your plan.

BOBBY: What plan? (*ELIZABETH whispers in his ear.*) Well, far out. Far fucking out.

ALEX: (*taps on BOBBY's shoulder*) I'd like to cut in here, Gene Kelly.

BOBBY: Right you are, boy.

BOBBY lets go of ELIZABETH, grabs ALEX and begins dancing with him.

ALEX: You come here often, stud?

BOBBY: Every night for the rough trade. (*grabs at ALEX and they break*) Listen, we're all going to drink another toast.

ALEX: Let's not get started on toasting everything. We'll be blasted out of shape in twenty minutes.

BOBBY: This is a big one. Grab your glasses everyone. Say when, sweetie. (*pours liquor into ELIZABETH's glass, nearly filling it to the top*) Uh . . . any time you feel like. Okay.

ELIZABETH plugs her nose and drinks the whole glass down — or at least a substantial portion of it.

BOBBY: Hey, the toast, wait a second, there. Good God, y'all.

CHRISTINE: I don't know if that's a very good idea.

BOBBY: Best idea of the night. All right, hold out them glasses.

CHRISTINE: Count me out.

ALEX: If you're thinking of repeating her little stunt, count me out, too.

BOBBY: Well by God, I knew it. Man brings over two bottles and all he's got stomach for is an eyedropper full. Are me and your girlfriend the only ones with balls in this place? No offense, sweetie. (*ALEX begins to drink.*) Hold it, hold it, I'll race you.

They square off, then begin gulping down their drinks. ELIZABETH may join the race.

ALEX: Holy fuck.

BOBBY: Did you win?

ALEX: Holy *fuck*.

CHRISTINE: Drinking like that can kill you, you know.

ALEX: It doesn't surprise me.

BOBBY: Doesn't exactly sneak up on you, does it? Well, goddamn it, we forgot the toast. Have to do it all over again.

CHRISTINE: Go do it by the hospital this time, so I don't have to drag you there.

ALEX: I think I'm going to sip the next one.

BOBBY: Well, shit. (*pours drink*) Another one for Elizabeth for quitting school. At least, not going back.

ALEX: What the fuck is that supposed to mean?

ELIZABETH: I'll drink to it.

ALEX: Is this a joke or something?

BOBBY: Folks don't make jokes when they're dancing with Bobby.

CHRISTINE: I wish we had some ginger ale or something.

BOBBY: Scotch and ginger ale? Christ.

CHRISTINE: Just the ginger ale. I don't like the taste of this.

ALEX will probably choose this moment to take the needle off the record.

ALEX: Did you tell him you weren't going to register?

CHRISTINE: Register for what?

ELIZABETH: I guess you all had to know the truth, sooner or later. I have to go and register my tits as dangerous weapons.

BOBBY: Do they take prints of them?

CHRISTINE: That's pretty good. What's my most dangerous weapon?

ALEX: You're not going to register at school?

CHRISTINE: You know, plugging your nose does make it taste better.

ELIZABETH: That's right. I'm not going to register at school.

ALEX: I think we'd better talk about this when we're alone. Ten points for picking the worst possible time to bring up a subject.

CHRISTINE: What's my most dangerous weapon, Bobby?

BOBBY: Me. (falls down next to CHRISTINE and grabs her)

ELIZABETH: What's grosser than an academic? That's a riddle.

ALEX: How about his drunken students?

BOBBY: Wait a second, what was the question?

ELIZABETH: Alex already answered it: the only thing grosser than being a teacher is being a student.

ALEX: That isn't what I said.

ELIZABETH: Do you know, I'll be twenty-five years old by the time I finish. Twenty-five and still in school.

CHRISTINE: I wish I had that much school. I really do.

BOBBY: Well, I sure don't. Now when I was your age, I was doing — what? Something crazy. I was married and divorced by that time.

ELIZABETH: Maybe I'll do something crazy.

ALEX: Yeah? Look where it got him.

BOBBY: Now where's that coming from, man?

CHRISTINE: Anyway, didn't you already finish school last year? I mean, I never was too sure why you were going back. Not that I think it's a bad idea.

ELIZABETH: That was my B.A. This would be my M.A.

CHRISTINE: Is there a big difference?

ELIZABETH: No, it just means I could turn around and teach another group how to become school teachers.

BOBBY: Kind of like a circle jerk.

ELIZABETH: From the mouths of babes.

ALEX: All right, has everyone finished making their little jokes about this?

BOBBY: What's the matter, Alex, got the rag on?

ALEX: Maybe the two of us should talk about how smart an idea this is later.

BOBBY: Christ, you never even finished high school.

ELIZABETH: You've had a life, and you've still read all the books I have. Now why can't I have a life too? Why should I stay in school forever? None of you did.

CHRISTINE: All we've been is on the bum. Anybody can do that.

BOBBY: Not what I did. Not everybody can do that. (*goes over to ELIZABETH*) You want to help me rob a candy store, sugar?

ELIZABETH: I don't know, think I'd be good at it?

ALEX: Why don't you just butt out of this, Bobby?

CHRISTINE: The point is, you've got a future. Instead of just a lot of memories.

BOBBY: What are you, her mother?

ELIZABETH: You can say that now, because you've got the memories, you've settled down. (*to ALEX*) You've settled down.

BOBBY: Not me.

ELIZABETH: I've been settled down since I was about sixteen. You don't know what that's like. Right from home to this.

BOBBY: From Daddy to Alex, huh?

ALEX: Fuck you. You don't even know what you're talking about.

BOBBY: Just a joke.

CHRISTINE: All I can say is I wish my biggest problem was as small as yours.

ELIZABETH: Thank you so much for your kind support.

BOBBY: Everybody take it easy.

CHRISTINE: You're just drunk. That's your big problem.

ELIZABETH: I need another one.

BOBBY: Coming up.

ALEX: She's had enough.

ELIZABETH: Gee, getting kind of stuffy in here, isn't it?

CHRISTINE: Maybe all of us shouldn't drink anymore.

BOBBY: (*pours himself and ELIZABETH another drink*) Or any less. Here's to me and Elizabeth knocking over candy stores.

ALEX: You know, this could turn into an early night. I mean a really early night.

ELIZABETH: I think I'd rather rob a bank. It's got more class.

CHRISTINE: Why don't you just keep quiet?

ELIZABETH: Am I not allowed to joke, either?

BOBBY: What's bugging you?

CHRISTINE: I think this whole conversation is stupid.

ALEX: I second that.

BOBBY: Well, then why don't you two run off and have your own party? (*puts his arm around ELIZABETH*)

ALEX: Why don't you leave her alone?

BOBBY: Me? Christ, it's you who's acting like you got a poker up your ass.

ALEX: This whole thing should never have come up.

BOBBY: Why don't you just let her enjoy herself, for a change?

ALEX: What the hell is wrong with you, man? Do you have some kind of beef with me? Quit trying to piss me off.

BOBBY: Better slow down there, partner.

ALEX: *You* can fucking slow down.

CHRISTINE: Both of you settle down.

BOBBY: Stay out of this.

ALEX: Come on, it's time to go.

ELIZABETH: Let's all just relax and get drunk.

ALEX: Don't you think you're drunk enough?

BOBBY: Go ahead, Elizabeth, go put him to bed. He's tired out from changing all that wool.

ALEX: I'm getting tired of your stupid cracks about my job.

BOBBY: I'm tired of hearing about the stupid job. Fuck off, before I get mad.

ALEX: I'm really scared.

CHRISTINE: Will you both shut up? What the hell is wrong with everybody?

ELIZABETH: It looks like we're going to have to go.

BOBBY: You oughta be scared, man. You oughta be.

ALEX: Pardon me if I don't puke with fear.

ELIZABETH: Well, you're both scaring me, so let's get out of here.

CHRISTINE: Sit down, Bobby. Take it easy.

ALEX: I was going anyway.

BOBBY: Sure you were.

CHRISTINE: Bobby . . .

ALEX: Oh, yeah? I don't have to take any . . .

ELIZABETH: (*talking over him*) For the love of God, let's go. Goodnight, goodnight, everybody. See you later.

They exit.

BOBBY: Now what turned him into such an asshole?

CHRISTINE: It was her, that little smartass.

BOBBY: What the hell's wrong with you?

CHRISTINE: I'm getting a little tired of her always hanging on to you. "God, you don't know what it's like always having money." Poor little her. You know, I just don't think she's an honest person. I don't trust her.

BOBBY: Well at least they left the booze.

CHRISTINE: She thinks she's cute, too. I don't think she's so cute.

BOBBY: Well, I'll tell you who I think is cute.

CHRISTINE: You think *you're* cute.

BOBBY: By God, that does it. Let's fuck.

He throws CHRISTINE over his shoulder and carries her into the bedroom. As the lights dim in the downstairs apartment, ALEX and ELIZABETH enter their place upstairs. ELIZABETH goes directly to the sofa, looking like someone suddenly feeling the effects of too much alcohol. ALEX closes the door, turns on the lights and pulls off his shirt. He is wearing a T-shirt underneath.

ALEX: What an asshole. I should've taken a swipe at him. Everytime we see him, he manages to piss me off some way. He doesn't scare me. And always trying to break my balls about my job. Just because I'm not in the hole he's in. I don't know how she puts up with that bastard, I really don't. Well, fuck it. See how he likes staying in that place and seeing nobody. I mean it, I'm not going down there anymore. (*boots the chair*) Why the hell you'd decide to tell your plans to that asshole is beyond me. Don't I deserve some kind of break? If you've got something on your mind, tell me, don't bring it up around those morons. All right? That was a hell of a time to bring up anything important. What I'm saying is, let's talk about the personal stuff at home. Is that too much to ask? Is it?

ELIZABETH reacts on the sofa in some way, perhaps leaning over and holding her stomach.

ALEX: That's what you get for swilling it down the way you were. Shit. We should have brought a bottle back with us. We got anything around here? (*pause*) We got anything here to drink? (*exits to the kitchen, is gone for a few seconds, then returns with a half or two-thirds of a bottle of wine*) Look, I'm not trying to take it out on you, all right? But still, that's not the kind of thing to bring up around other people. Not that I think that it's such a horrendous idea. So you don't get your M.A. You've got lots of options. What's the matter, are you feeling sick?

By this time he is sitting beside her. ELIZABETH takes the wine bottle and has a large couple of swallows.

ALEX: That's the way. We'll have our own party. I'll tell you what — let's finish this thing off, then we'll play spin the bottle. The adult version. (*He tries for an embrace, but ELIZABETH moves away, quickly.*) Let's not do this again, all right? You know, up until Bobby and I got into it, that was one of the nicest evenings we've had in a long time. Is that what's been bugging you so much the last while? Going back to school? You should have told me about it, we could have talked. It isn't that big a deal. Why don't we just cuddle up a little bit? I'll be careful with your cut.

ELIZABETH begins to cry.

ALEX: Hey, honey, what's wrong? Take it easy now.

ELIZABETH once more takes the bottle from ALEX and takes a big drink.

ALEX: Maybe that's not the best thing to do right now.

ELIZABETH: What is the best thing to do, Alex? You tell me.

ALEX: About what? Has this school thing got you really hung up?

ELIZABETH: Going to school, not going to school — who cares? Who can it really be important to, except a goddamned school kid?

ALEX: It's important to you.

ELIZABETH: I'm a goddamned school kid. You know something? I don't know what to do, when to do it or why. Nothing. I don't know a thing.

ALEX: It's just the booze brought all this on.

ELIZABETH: I'm not crying about school. I'm not crying about that. I don't know. I don't know what to say or how to say it.

ALEX: Now, I have trouble believing that.

ELIZABETH: Do you know why I do the things I do?

ALEX: All right, why do you do the things you do?

ELIZABETH: I don't know.

ALEX: Maybe you could use a little coffee. Maybe we both could. What do you say? Mixing drinks probably wasn't such a hot idea. Will you be okay if I leave you alone?

ALEX exits briefly and returns. We can see ELIZABETH struggling with herself.

ELIZABETH: It just looks like a series of boxes. All I've ever had and ever will have.

ALEX: What are you talking about?

ELIZABETH: Did you hear me tell an interesting story downstairs, while everyone else was telling theirs? I don't have any to tell.

ALEX: Don't be ridiculous. That's just us sitting around bullshitting.

ELIZABETH: At least you've got things to bullshit about.

ALEX: And so do you. The kind of stories we tell, that's just like two old guys talking about the war. They skip all the ugly parts. Do you know what it was really like, back then? One time I lived in the Ford Hotel for about seven months. I had a can of Raid for the roaches, and every once in awhile, a fly would come in through the window. Well, as soon as one did, I'd get up and shut the window so it couldn't fly out again. Keep in mind, this is a grown man I'm talking about. I'd chase the fly around, spraying Raid at it, and then I'd watch it die. Then I'd open the window again. Seven months. Are you trying to tell me you don't have a better story than that?

ELIZABETH: What'd you do after the seven months?

ALEX: Bobby showed up and we took off to California. See. You always hear the second part, never the first part. Now, getting together with you showed me there was a better way of doing things — a better way than killing flies and waiting for somebody to show up and save you.

ELIZABETH: (laughs) It's so ridiculous, isn't it? I thought it was getting together with you that showed me there was a better way of doing things.

She continues to laugh, then suddenly gags, puts her hands over her mouth, and rushes offstage.

ALEX: Are you okay? (*follows her*) Do you want me to come in? Honey, are you okay?

(*A moment or two, then ELIZABETH enters followed closely by ALEX.*) Are you all right? Do you feel better now?

ELIZABETH: Worse. A thousand times worse.

ALEX: Come on, that water should be about boiled by now. A cup of coffee will fix you up. Things won't look so bad in the morning. (*stops and hugs her*) So that's what made you so upset? Not having enough adventure in your life?

She breaks from him and walks into the kitchen.

ALEX: *Now* what's bothering you?

ALEX leaves the stage and the lights go down. Lights come up in the downstairs apartment as BOBBY enters from the bedroom, his pants still open. CHRISTINE is a couple of beats behind him.

BOBBY: Well, I guess that about does it. I'm ready for the glue factory. I never thought I'd see this day come to pass.

CHRISTINE: It's just the booze, champ.

BOBBY: Christ, I didn't even have that much. It wasn't too long ago I could've drank both bottles and still worn you out besides.

CHRISTINE: I'll give you a rematch tomorrow, how's that?

BOBBY: Losing it in the clutch. Might as well take me out and shoot me, I guess.

CHRISTINE: Guys are all alike. The first time you can't get it up, you panic.

BOBBY: Now that's nice talk, really nice. You've seen them come and go, have you?

CHRISTINE: That's right, I forgot. You thought I was a virgin.

BOBBY: Yes, indeed. Cherry of the massage parlour.

CHRISTINE: You sure didn't have any trouble getting it up that time.

BOBBY: Any time I've got to shell out fifteen bucks to spend twenty minutes alone with a woman, I get it up pretty fast.

CHRISTINE: Poor Bobby. You didn't know the fifteen only covered the rub down.

BOBBY: I was counting on you to lose your head once you saw the monster stand up and stare at you. Now it looks like all it wants to do is stare.

CHRISTINE: Believe me, most of them spend more time staring than they do standing.

BOBBY: Maybe you ought to keep another guy around as a pinch-hitter. Get Roger out here.

CHRISTINE: He had one of the great one-eyed stares of all time.

BOBBY: That's something I'll never understand. Why would a woman live with a guy who couldn't jump her at least twice a day?

CHRISTINE: It isn't that important to some people.

BOBBY: Sure it is. They just lie about it 'cause they can't do it.

CHRISTINE: Well, a lot of times you just take what you can get. Haven't you ever been with someone who didn't like it as much as you?

BOBBY: When they're with me, they start to like it.

CHRISTINE: The gearboxes, too?

BOBBY: I wish that bastard would have never brought that up. Me doing that was the same as you working in the massage joint.

(pause) Say, you think maybe that's what's happened? The little guy's gone queer on me?

CHRISTINE: I kind of doubt it.

BOBBY: Yes sir, you sure got yourself a bargain. The one thing you keep me around for, and now I've lost it.

CHRISTINE: You think that's why I keep you around?

BOBBY: Well, you tell me. If I was footing the bills for some asshole who throws TV's out the window I'd get rid of him pretty quick.

CHRISTINE: I was mad when that happened, but it really isn't that big a deal. It was pretty old. I can kind of understand it, too, you know, you stuck in here all the time, getting nervous. But I'll say one thing for you, tiger. At least when you're that uptight you take it out on the furniture. You don't decide to knock me around.

BOBBY: Any guy that hits a woman is just afraid to fight men.

CHRISTINE: I could give you a list of guys to tell that to.

BOBBY: Give me that list and I'll do more than just tell them.

CHRISTINE: You're such a big, tough character, aren't you? I think you're just a pussycat. I know it, in fact.

BOBBY: At last someone's got the straight goods on me.

ALEX comes banging on the door.

CHRISTINE: Who is it?

ALEX: Alex, it's Alex!

BOBBY: For Christ's sake.

CHRISTINE *unlocks the door and ALEX barges in. He runs at BOBBY, catching him off balance, and they both go down smashing the coffee table. ALEX falls over BOBBY and lands on the couch, perhaps breaking the end table or the lamp on it, as he tries to keep his balance. BOBBY is the first one on his feet.*

BOBBY: What the fuck are you doing?

ALEX *charges off the couch, tackles BOBBY and they go down again. They wrestle around until BOBBY gains a superior position, getting ALEX in a headlock. BOBBY hits him in the face, hard, two or three times with his free hand, then stands up leaving ALEX in a heap.*

BOBBY: You're going to get hurt, man. I mean it.

ALEX *stumbles to his feet in the vague direction of BOBBY, who grabs him and throws him onto the couch where he pins him with a knee on the chest. BOBBY grabs a beer bottle from the other end table and raises it as though to smash ALEX in the face.*

CHRISTINE: Don't, Bobby!

BOBBY: (*backs a step or two away from the couch*) Try me again and I'm putting the boots to you.

ALEX: That wouldn't bother you a bit, would it?

CHRISTINE: What is going on here?

ALEX: Shall I tell her?

ALEX *gets up and moves behind the chair. CHRISTINE is close to BOBBY, hampering his movements.*

BOBBY: Listen, if you've got something to take up with me, let's do it outside. Get the fuck out of here while you can still walk.

ALEX: Your boyfriend's been having a little affair with my lady.

CHRISTINE: What? (*grabs BOBBY by the shirt*)

BOBBY: Let's go out on the lawn, you and me.

ALEX *gets as far away from BOBBY as possible.*

CHRISTINE: Is this true? Bobby, is it?

ALEX: He gave her that cut on her ass.

BOBBY: You're going to die for this.

ALEX: (*gets to the door and opens it*) I'm gonna kill you, Bobby. I swear to Christ. (*exits quickly, slamming the door*)

CHRISTINE: You gave Elizabeth that cut on her ass? What's he talking about?

BOBBY: Ah, he's nuts. I broke my god-damned hand.

CHRISTINE: Have you been fucking Elizabeth? Look at me.

BOBBY: Look at *me*. I just got attacked by a maniac. A lot of help you were.

CHRISTINE: It's true, isn't it? You've been doing it to her.

BOBBY: I need a drink.

CHRISTINE: (*grabs him and turns him around*) God damn you, have you been fucking her?

BOBBY: You want to just calm down for a second? (*pause*) Once. One time. I was drunk.

CHRISTINE: You son of a bitch.

BOBBY: It happened weeks ago. It didn't mean a thing.

CHRISTINE: And what about the cut? What the hell was that?

BOBBY: I had the knife open on the bed, the time we did it. She rolled on top of it. It was an accident.

CHRISTINE: She got that cut this week. You did it to her here, in our bed.

BOBBY: Aw, look.

CHRISTINE: Did you have it out so she could use it on you? Give you the kind of pain you like in bed, instead of me having to claw you up with my nails every night? Is that why you had the knife out, Bobby? So you could work out your sick fantasies?

BOBBY: I told you, it was an accident.

CHRISTINE: Was fucking her an accident, too? Fucking her in my apartment.

BOBBY: I was loaded. She doesn't mean a thing to me.

CHRISTINE: Get your stuff and get out.

BOBBY: Come on baby, give me a break.

CHRISTINE: Get out or I'm calling the cops.

BOBBY: Christine, don't do this.

CHRISTINE: You fucking bastard. How could you? How could you do it to me?

BOBBY: Can we talk about this? I mean, can we just sit down for a second?

CHRISTINE: I'm giving you five minutes to get out.

BOBBY: Listen to me. I love you. Please just listen to me for one minute. I mean, I love you, you know? I did it to her a couple of times. I was drunk and I was stupid, that's all. She means nothing to me.

CHRISTINE: How much am I supposed to take from you? All you give me are your god-damned awful little poems. You don't do anything, Bobby, nothing. Just wreck my TV set and drink all the time.

BOBBY: Look, I'm sorry. I was going to tell you.

CHRISTINE: What? That you were fucking that little cunt while I'm killing myself to keep us alive?

BOBBY: It was the booze. I'm going to quit drinking.

CHRISTINE: It's you, that's all it is. You're twisted. You just don't give a shit.

BOBBY: Look, it isn't true. Come on, now.

CHRISTINE: God, I hate you. I wish I could kill you.

BOBBY: Okay, look, I'm going to tell you something. You make me leave and that's just what you're going to do. I'm a dead man out there, Christine. Now, I told you, I made it with her twice and I'm sorry as hell about it. Do you want me to die for that?

CHRISTINE: I don't believe that stuff, it's just an excuse. Nobody's going to kill you.

BOBBY: They got Dennis. If they wanted him, they want me. I was behind the house. I could hear him screaming. They'll bust my knees. Okay, they don't kill me, they cripple me. This is no bullshit. I was there. They'll use bats on my knees.

CHRISTINE: Good.

BOBBY: You want to see me get it because I got drunk two times? You don't mean it.

CHRISTINE: Will you stop bullshitting? You've been fucking Elizabeth, not getting drunk. Fucking another woman. I've taken everything from you, but I won't take that.

BOBBY: And you're always saying you love me, you love me. This is how much you love me. I fuck up one time and you want to give me the heave.

CHRISTINE: You've been fucking up since I met you. Four months I've been paying the rent, the food and your liquor. Just so you can turn around and do this to me.

BOBBY: You think I haven't been trying to find a way out? Christ, you want me to go out and get some donkey job and that's okay, fair's fair. How am I supposed to do it? I can't even use my own I.D., there's a warrant out for me, don't forget. So what am I supposed to do about that? If the guys downtown don't nail me, the cops will.

CHRISTINE: You're a grown man, it's about time you acted like one.

BOBBY: Easy to say when you don't have my situation.

CHRISTINE: Yeah, you and your god-damned terrible pain, like nothing has happened to anyone else. I've had a life. I've had a situation. I managed.

BOBBY: I know all about it. You're always hitting me over the head with what a hoot you and Roger used to have. How the hell do you think that makes me feel? You know, you may have to take it, but you dish out plenty too.

CHRISTINE: You bastard, you don't even know what it was like, me and Roger, you won't even let me talk. I know about every bimbo you ever stuck it into. You and your amazing life. I don't think you're so amazing.

BOBBY: I'm really glad you said all of this, you know that? It's nice to know how you really feel. And you say you love me.

CHRISTINE: And what did you ever do except just say it? Nothing.

BOBBY: You just blow me away, you know that? All your fucking talk, but the first time there's trouble you pack everything in. Just like with your kid.

CHRISTINE: You cocksucker.

BOBBY: I never was too crazy about that, you know. Leaving your kid, coming out here, living like a whore.

CHRISTINE: Roger's family has money. They'll take care of my boy, you prick. You don't even know the situation.

BOBBY: How can a woman leave her baby? And go to work in a massage parlour?

CHRISTINE: I'm calling the police.

BOBBY: That'd be your style, all right.

CHRISTINE: You never thought leaving him might have fucked me up, instead of everything just fucking *you* up? Do you ever think maybe I feel pain, that things are hard on me?

BOBBY: As long as there's colour TV sets you'll be happy. As long as there's things left to buy. But you couldn't buy me, could you?

CHRISTINE: Anyone can buy you, you come cheap.

BOBBY: Well, I'll tell you, I'm not leaving. Not tonight. I don't have a cent and I got nowhere to go. You might as well get the cops, they're going to nail me pretty quick if I'm walking the streets all night, anyway.

CHRISTINE: I'm not kidding, Bobby. I'll call them. This is my place. I want you out.

BOBBY: In the morning. I'll sleep in here tonight. Now listen, I figure if you're ready to see me get my knees busted or go to jail just because of something that didn't mean anything anyway, you'll at least give me a head start. All I want to do is stay here till the morning. Then I'll be gone like a cool breeze. How about it?

CHRISTINE: All right, then I'm going out. (*goes to closet, gets her coat, gathers up her purse*) I don't even want to be in the same room with you. But in the morning, first thing, you'd better be gone. I mean it.

She exits. BOBBY goes to the door and chains it.

BOBBY: Sweet Jesus Christ.

BOBBY paces around the apartment wildly for a moment or two, goes behind the counter, yanks open a drawer, checks the change jar. There is less than a dollar in change. Takes a box of ammunition from the same drawer, looks at it for a minute. Then goes to the closet, reaches up behind clothes, and takes down his gun. It is at the very least a .38. Goes back to the counter, flips the cylinder out on the revolver as if to load it. The whole idea defeats him. He lays the gun down, a beat or two, then goes to the telephone and dials enough digits to indicate a long distance call.

BOBBY: Hello, Mom? Yeah, it's Bobby. I'm out on the coast. Yeah, right. So how are things there? What did you tell them? Well listen, don't let them know I'm out here, okay? So how'd Dad take it? Well, the money he put out for bail, see, I've got a job here and I'm going to pay it all back. It takes awhile, right? I had to, Mom, it was either that or go to jail. No, it wouldn't be better. Listen, I just wanted you to know I was okay, like that. This job, see, I'm going logging and they won't pay me for a month. I need boots, all that kind of stuff, so I was wondering — no, I don't want to talk to him. (*pause*) Hi, Dad. Look I'm sorry about that. I was just saying to Mom I'm going to pay you back, I got this . . . But I'm going to set it straight by you . . . look, I'm sorry, really, sorry . . . don't be this way, listen . . .

He slowly hangs up the phone.

BOBBY: Oh, God. Fuck it, what do I care?

He begins crying, his face in his hands.

Blackout.

ACT TWO

BOBBY is sitting on one of the stools, toying with the gun. The entrance door is suddenly opened and stopped by the chain, snapping BOBBY around.

ALEX: Open the door.

BOBBY goes to the door, kicks it shut and removes the chain. Walks away. ALEX opens the door.

BOBBY: The fuck do you want?

ALEX: You're going to have to kill me, this time.

BOBBY: Get out of here before I shove this up your ass.

ALEX: Go ahead and try it.

BOBBY: I mean it, man. I don't have the time for you.

ALEX: (*slams the door and runs over to BOBBY*) Get up, you son of a bitch.

BOBBY grabs ALEX by the shirt-front and manhandles him, holding the gun as though about to club him.

BOBBY: It looks like I'm going to have to crack you over the head with this thing and put you to sleep.

ALEX: If I had one of those, you wouldn't be alive right now.

BOBBY: Here. (*hands ALEX the gun*) Save us both the energy.

BOBBY backs up a few feet, grinning, mocking ALEX. Raises his hands. ALEX stands holding the gun, undecided. When it is obvious that he can't use it, BOBBY gently removes the gun from ALEX's hand. Takes a step or two away from him, then suddenly points the gun at ALEX and pulls the trigger three or four times. The hammer clicks on empty chambers. ALEX drops to the floor, arms wrapped around his head.

ALEX: Shit!

BOBBY laughs, doubling over. Finally controls himself and, grinning, flips the cylinder out to show ALEX the gun is empty. Goes to the box of ammunition and puts a single bullet into one of the chambers. Closes the cylinder.

BOBBY: Now try it when it's loaded.

He hands the gun to ALEX, who doesn't take it. BOBBY spins the cylinder once or twice and hands the gun over again. ALEX stands there, not touching it.

BOBBY: I'll make a deal with you. You pull the trigger, and if that's where the bullet is, I'm dead. But if it don't go off when you squeeze it, I'm going to take the fucking thing and smash out all your teeth with it. Fair? (*ALEX hesitates, not taking the gun.*) Take it and go shoot your old lady with it.

ALEX quickly grabs the gun, holds the barrel to his temple and pulls the trigger. There is a click.

BOBBY: What the fuck was that all about?

ALEX: I want to see you die, or I'll die, I don't care which.

BOBBY: Listen, if you really want to kill yourself, I'll put the other five in to make sure you don't miss.

ALEX: Let's see what you're made of. (*lays the gun down on one of the stools*) Let's see you do what I just did.

BOBBY: Don't be an asshole.

ALEX: If you've got any guts, you'll do it.

BOBBY: Don't you talk to me about guts, junior.

ALEX: That's how we settle it. Pick it up and do it, tough guy.

BOBBY: This is all on account of a little nookie?

ALEX: You're scared right out of your mind, aren't you?

BOBBY: I've had loaded guns pointed at me before.

ALEX: Yeah, I'm sure you and the boys did this kind of thing all the time.

BOBBY: I'll tell you something, man. If you want to go right down the line on this thing, I'm ready. I got nothing to lose. I'm just saying it's stupid.

ALEX: (*picks up the gun and thrusts it, butt first, at BOBBY*) Are you in or out?

BOBBY takes the gun, thinks a moment, then manages to raise it quickly to his head and pull the trigger.

BOBBY: There. Nothing to it. I'll tell you something Alex, this thing'll blow your face right away. I mean, rip your head right off your shoulders. (*ALEX reaches for the gun, which BOBBY holds away from him.*) Hold it, hold it a second. What am I supposed to tell them when you blow your brains out?

ALEX: That's your problem . . .

BOBBY: Well, fuck that, man, you're going to put me in a weird spot with the cops.

ALEX: Jesus, don't you ever get tired of using that goddamned warrant as an excuse?

BOBBY: Excuse for what? Who's making excuses?

ALEX: That warrant's the reason you don't work, the reason you don't go outside, now it's your reason for chickening out.

BOBBY: (hands ALEX the gun) I hope you do blow your brains out.

ALEX: You're pathetic, do you know that? Can't even set foot outside the door. If Christine wasn't paying the bills you'd be down at the hostel with the rest of the old rubbies.

BOBBY: At least I don't run out of here every morning to go kiss ass at some god-damned factory, creel boy.

ALEX: What *do* you do? Nothing, except wreck other peoples' lives. What've you ever done except wreck me, from the moment I met you?

BOBBY: I got you out of your lousy room where you were always crying yourself to sleep. You used to have balls, Alex.

ALEX: Why? Because I wasted a lot of time with you standing on highways with my thumb out? Real life takes balls.

BOBBY: Yeah, tell me about it. Working in a factory takes more guts than making it on the street. Playing ball with them is braver than doing it on your own. That's what they try and tell you, and you bought it. It's a fucking plot.

ALEX: You think it takes balls to lock yourself up in a room and drink yourself to death? Trying to impress everybody with your past. That's all you've got. Look at yourself, for Christ's sake.

BOBBY: You copped out to the first school kid you met with hot pants. You're a real man, all right.

ALEX: Keep her out of this, you son of a bitch.

BOBBY: You know, a few nights ago I had her tied down to the bed, arms out here, legs out here. I got my knife to cut her loose . . .

ALEX: No one in the world would convict me if I shot you right now.

BOBBY: Go ahead. I'll make it easy for you.

BOBBY turns his back. ALEX hesitates a long moment, then holds the gun to his own head and pulls the trigger. BOBBY looks quickly over his shoulder as he hears the click.

ALEX: Fuck, this thing has a loud click.

BOBBY: You bastard, trying to shoot me in the back.

ALEX: I had it pointed at my head.

BOBBY: I didn't see it. How do I know where it was pointed?

ALEX: What do you want me to do, take two in a row?

BOBBY: All right, you turn your back this time.

ALEX: Fuck off, Bobby. If you don't have the guts for this, just say so.

BOBBY: I'm just saying you could have pointed it anywhere. Maybe it was pointed at me, how do I know?

ALEX: If you want to start at the beginning again, let me tell you, I'll do it.

Pause.

BOBBY: How many we took? Shit. Now, listen man, are we really going to kill ourselves over this thing? Don't forget, maybe I did have a little thing with her, but she was still fooling around on you. You're going to die over a woman like that?

ALEX: Or see you dead, yeah.

BOBBY: I was drunk and didn't even know what I was doing, the first time. I swear to God that's true.

ALEX: What about the second time? The fifth time?

BOBBY: She never meant a thing to me. Now look, you're the best friend I ever had. Why don't we just walk out of here and be gone like a cool breeze? Go to New Orleans or some place, pack all this shit in. You're not cut out to be a factory worker, man, you know it. Why don't we dump the ladies and go? Doesn't that sound a little more like it?

ALEX: It sounds like an old re-run. It sounds like nothing at all. It never was a party out there for me. I was never winding up in all those strange beds. Do you know something? I've never even had the clap. I've made love to four women in my entire life. Not five hundred. Four. And none of them felt like supporting me. I never knocked over a grocery store when I was broke, any more than I knocked guys down who pissed me off. Being out on the street again doesn't tempt me.

BOBBY: You'd rather be working all day, sleeping all night and catching a little TV in between? How the hell does that look better than taking off down south? It's nuts. How can you keep on with that bullshit — just because you're writing a fucking book? That pretty well do it for you?

ALEX: I don't expect you to understand it.

BOBBY: You oughta try understanding what it's like if you didn't have it. If you didn't have that book, you'd be just where I am. You are, anyway, you just don't know it. The difference between you and me is I don't kid myself about a pile of scrap paper.

ALEX: I'll tell you the difference — I don't have people to look after me. I can't lock myself in a room and spend all my time getting hung up. What makes life any tougher on you than on anybody else? It's hard on everyone.

BOBBY: Oh yeah, I can see that, all right. I can see how hard it is on your fucking girlfriend, bopping over to Europe, working for the summer, putting in a little time before she goes back to school. Yeah, life's a bitch, all right.

ALEX: Don't blame Elizabeth, just because you can't make it.

BOBBY: Right now, I wish I'd never even heard of her, believe me.

ALEX: No, Bobby. You wish I'd never heard of her.

BOBBY: Yeah, something like that, I guess. I never thought I'd see the day when you'd let a woman come between us. You've meant more to me than any woman everr did.

BOBBY is squatting beside ALEX, who is sitting in the chair. During his last couple of lines, BOBBY has put his arm around ALEX's shoulders. ALEX reaches up and puts his arm around BOBBY.

ALEX: Well, you don't mean anything to me anymore. (*shoves BOBBY, sending him sprawling on the floor*) I've spent the best part of the last ten years bailing you out of trouble. And what do I get for it, except a kick in the balls? Thank you very much.

BOBBY: (*getting to his feet*) Well thank *you* very much. I can't fuck up one time, everybody gives me the boot. Jesus Christ. You know what I'm going to do? (*pause*) All I can think about now is what I did. I guess because I don't do anything now. I'm an ex. Ex-thief, ex-husband, ex-factory worker. All the things I did, and I was lousy at all of them. Everybody I ever stole anything from knows it's me who stole it. The first time Dennis and I ever robbed a place, we got thirty-two dollars. I didn't even know you could lift up the tray in the cash register. Working, I could never cut it. I just get too uptight when I'm doing it. I'm a lousy worker, too. Christ, I don't know. Like all the time I've put in on that street, for what? It was just hanging around. Just a little of this, a little of that. Hanging around. See. I'm not saying I'm blaming anyone, but still, some fucking life that is. I mean, some fucking life.

ALEX: Other people sure seem to think it's been a hell of a life.

BOBBY: Yeah, well I used to think so too, but now, it all looks like shit. Like, it isn't just Elizabeth's life that drives me nuts, it's Christine's too. And she's had fuck all. She's been through every number I've ever done and beat me at it. Yeah, I guess that's how I look at it. Beat me at it. Shit. It just isn't worth it, man, none of it. Even when Christine and I are having a fairly good time, like if we've just made it — I don't know — we'll be laughing, and right in the middle of it I'll hear a noise outside the door. A creak, anything. And then all I can think about is broken legs. I think, what am I laughing at? I'm going to get my legs broke. Like Dennis.

ALEX: Is that what you're blaming it all on? You're waiting to pay penance for something that happened back then?

BOBBY: No, no, if it happens I can handle it. What goes around, comes around, right? It isn't Dennis so much, it's the guy we did. (pause) See, I know just what it's going to be like. Flowerpots. That's what it reminds me of, when you drop a flowerpot full of dirt on the sidewalk and it just kind of spreads out. That's what his legs looked like everywhere we hit them. They say when you do that to a guy, he'll faint. Well, sometimes they don't faint. He screamed like a woman, then cried like a baby. Christ. And Dennis, he was just a kid. I was behind the house burying dope when they came and got him. I could hear him screaming. And I didn't even go back in the house,

I could imagine it. Except I didn't know it was his legs, then. I thought they'd killed him. (pause) I'm sorry. That's all. I'm sorry my old man had to sell the car because I jumped bail. Just sorry for fucking everyone up. (ALEX takes a mouthful of whisky and spits it out at BOBBY's feet, then gets up and walks away.) One thing I'll say, sex was great. Fuck it. I don't care. I really don't.

He raises the gun and pulls the trigger. A click.

BOBBY: Jesus Christ, if you did that every morning before breakfast, it'd really keep you on the ball, wouldn't it?

ALEX: You'd run out of luck one day.

BOBBY: That happens, anyway.

ALEX: I was sure you were going to get it, then. It seemed like you had to. Fifth shot. This is it. It has to be.

BOBBY: It's a possibility, all right.

ALEX: Well, if I make it, the next one's going to be a bitch.

BOBBY: Don't you think we've gone about far enough on this thing?

ALEX: You ever see a man get shot in the head? No, don't tell me.

BOBBY: Look, man, you impressed me, all right? You took two shots. I took two shots. We take any more and one of us winds up dead. It isn't worth it.

ALEX: I'm not trying to see who racks up the most points. The deal was, we do this until somebody loses.

BOBBY: All because of your girlfriend getting a little on the side? Christ.

ALEX: You don't have any idea what you've done to me, Bobby. Not a clue. You don't even know what she means to me.

BOBBY: Whatever she means, it isn't worth your life.

ALEX: That's exactly how much she's worth to me. I wouldn't even have a life, but for her. I finally got a place to come home to and a reason for putting one foot in front of the other. That's what you fucked up for me.

BOBBY: Well, she's not dumping you, is she? You still got her. Christine's giving me the heave.

ALEX: What have I got? Something you stepped into and dirtied, just like you've dirtied everything else. You just can't leave me alone, you've got to jump in and put your hands all over anything I've got. Always the big hero, the centre of attention. Well, I've about had it with you. (*They are side by side on the couch by this point. ALEX tries to move toward the gun where BOBBY dropped it, and is dragged back.*) You'd love it if I just crawled out of here right now, wouldn't you? Just so you'd have something else to hold over my head. Well, I'm here to beat you, Bobby. Once and for all.

BOBBY: Alex, all I'm saying is we could both say good–bye to this town. Kind of start out all over again.

ALEX: What you're really saying is you've got no one to look after you anymore. How does it feel? No more reliable Alex to drop everything and run with you, or to pay your hotel bills while you're out scaring old ladies with your gun. That's all I've ever been to you, isn't it? Somebody you could use. Christine, everyone. No one means a thing to you. Do they? It's all one person, the world, one face.

BOBBY: Why don't you scoot on home and help your girlfriend change her bandage?

ALEX: That's what's so unbelievable about you. How much you hate me, yourself, everything. But especially how much you hate her. The time you must have put in with her, the things you did, but still you really hate her guts, don't you? Is that why you did those things to her?

BOBBY: You don't even understand the trip. You don't know what you're talking about.

ALEX: Why did you hurt her, Bobby? What was in it for you?

BOBBY: Go home, man. Leave me alone.

ALEX: What's the matter — is the man with nothing to lose losing his nerve?

BOBBY: (*grabs ALEX as though he may hit him*) I've been with you shot for shot, you smug little prick, and I don't have all your broken-heart bullshit going for me. Don't talk to me about nerve.

ALEX: I don't have the time for any more mysteries, that's all. Why did you give her the cut?

BOBBY: You got to be in a situation like that to know what it's like. It's like . . . like being right on the edge of losing control. Like the thing you're doing has the control. I don't know. The more I hurt her, the more she wanted to be hurt. And the closer I got to her. A thing like that, it can make you close. The thing that scared me was the feeling that eventually I was going to kill her. I felt that. (*pause*) Anyway, I had her tied to the bed one night and I wanted to cut her loose, so I just grabbed my knife. She panicked, just like an animal caught in a trap. But after that, she told me she liked the idea of me running the knife over her, like I could use it at any second. So I did it. Then she said, if I wanted to cut her, I could cut her. I was just moving the knife over her, almost like I was watching somebody else's hand, and when I got to that spot, I just kind of twitched my wrist. I forgot how sharp the knife is.

ALEX: That's your idea of being close to someone? Tying them up and slashing them?

BOBBY: It isn't like that, man, it isn't like that at all. Listen. I had to get drunk afterwards. See, I didn't want to keep on doing that to her, right? I didn't even want to keep on fucking her. I mean it. But like . . . I'll tell you something. It's weird, but I thought I was the other way. Like, that I'd like her to do me. That's how the whole thing came up. But she wanted to get done. So I did her. It's all the same thing. You know what I used to think of? Both of us walking into a big flame, burning and making it at the same time. Dying.

ALEX: Do you love her?

BOBBY: Naw, she drives me nuts.

ALEX: Christ, it wasn't even love, but you've had things with her I've never had, never will have.

BOBBY: Weren't even listening, were you? You don't care what she wants. Just why you don't want it and why that's better than wanting it. Just like the rest of your fucking life. I can see why you'd want to kill yourself — you've never gone whole hog on anything in your life. At least when I was a bad guy, I was really a bad guy. But you're not even a real good guy. You asshole. You don't really want anybody to die, you just like the way it sounds when you say it.

BOBBY gets up, walks over to wherever the bottle is. ALEX, yelling, dives for the gun, holds it to his head, pulls the trigger. BOBBY dives towards ALEX, trying to stop him. There is a click. ALEX drops the gun, crawls and runs offstage, gagging. BOBBY slowly gets to his feet, picks up the gun.

BOBBY: Well, kid, let's see what you're made of.

ALEX staggers in from the bathroom, stays in the kitchen area. If the sink works, he will shove his head under the tap. Otherwise, he'll just try and recover.

ALEX: My whole body released everything at once. Do you have anything I can clean the bathroom with?

BOBBY: Yeah, over in the . . . listen, fuck the bathroom, okay?

BOBBY laughs, ALEX joins in slightly, leaning over, head bowed. BOBBY suddenly levels the gun at ALEX's head, hesitates and lowers it. ALEX is oblivious.

ALEX: I did it. I really did it.

BOBBY: You think you could do it right now? If you were me?

ALEX: I couldn't be any surer than I was that last shot. I *knew* I was going to die.

BOBBY: You're a tough character all right.

ALEX: I think I am, you know. I really think so.

BOBBY: I played your little game with you and my luck ran out and I can take it like I'm supposed to. Stick around. It's going to happen.

ALEX: But you're *supposed* to be tough. I'm just the patient scribbler, working for a living. But I did it. I really did it.

BOBBY: You think you've backed me down?

ALEX: I'm not concerned with you any longer. Shoot yourself or don't, it's your decision. I made my point. (*goes to the door and opens it*)

BOBBY: I must have missed it.

ALEX: Goodbye, Bobby. (*exits*)

BOBBY: You're going to miss the ending, Alex!

BOBBY tries vaguely to take his shot, then collapses onto the couch.

BOBBY: Jesus. I want to die, but I don't want to kill myself. Isn't that the story of my life.

The lights go down in the lower apartment and come up on ALEX standing in the doorway of the upstairs apartment, wet, bruised and exhausted. ELIZABETH calls to him from offstage.

ELIZABETH: Alex? Where have you been? (*enters*) God, I really didn't want you to find out that way. What happened, did you have a fight? God, I didn't want that to happen. I'm sorry. You see, it wasn't a question of him . . . the real problem is me. He was just the end result.

ALEX: Tell me why you did it.

ELIZABETH: It was just . . . it gave me something I needed. I don't know how to put it exactly, but it gave me something I didn't have. I don't mean *he* did, do you understand? But the situation . . . oh, Alex, it made me feel free.

ALEX: Oh Jesus. Nothing is going to change what happened.

ELIZABETH: It wasn't because I don't love you . . .

ALEX: I guess I can almost see how it happened. You've got to do a lot of digging to get past all his stuff, to find out what you're really dealing with. It took me ten years.

ELIZABETH: But you see, that's what I'm saying. It wasn't because I was attracted to Bobby, or thought I'd be better off with a man like him . . .

ALEX: What does it matter?

ELIZABETH: It matters to me.

ALEX: Sometimes you can take drastic action without knowing what it really means.

ELIZABETH: I *know* what it really means. It was a way out of the little box I've squeezed myself into. It's that simple. No matter what you think of it, what he and I had gave me a feeling like I was alive. I need that feeling. I'm not trying to hurt you, Alex, but you need to understand it. I need out of this.

ALEX: If there's a way out of this, then go ahead. Go ahead.

ELIZABETH: I have to be on my own for a while.

ALEX: When I was a kid, my old man used to really grill me over school work, put me right through the wringer, until I turned into the best behaved kid in the school. Then one day I heard him tell a buddy of his what a rough little bastard he'd been at my age. And he said, "I think Alex is too timid for that." Yeah. And I thought, "What the fuck does he want?" What the fuck do you want?

ELIZABETH: I just tried to tell you. Aren't you listening?

ALEX: You know what I just did? We took Bobby's gun and put one bullet in it. We didn't know where the bullet was. Then we took turns holding the gun to our heads and pulling the trigger.

ELIZABETH: You're not making any sense.

ALEX: It takes you a long moment after you hear that sound to realize you're still alive. That the gun didn't go off. And every time it was his turn I hoped that the bullet was there. And at the same time I hoped it wasn't. Five shots, and we always missed the bullet.

ELIZABETH: Why in God's name would you do something like that?

ALEX: Because we had to, that's all. It was a fight. I won.

ELIZABETH: It sounds insane. How could anyone win?

ALEX: Yeah, how could anyone win? I took all my shots. He still has one to go. He's trying to get up the nerve to take his last shot.

ELIZABETH: He's down there now, with the gun?

ALEX: He won't pull the trigger. What difference would it make if he did?

ELIZABETH: You can't mean that. I'm going down there.

ALEX: Go ahead, I don't care. I really don't care. (*ELIZABETH exits the apartment.*) What the fuck does everybody want?

ALEX lies down on the couch, finished. Lights down, coming up downstairs. ELIZABETH opens the door which for once BOBBY hasn't bothered to lock. He reacts quickly, pointing the gun at her and nearly startling her out of the apartment. He lowers the gun when he realizes who he is dealing with, and ELIZABETH fully enters, tentatively, closing the door behind her.

BOBBY: How am I supposed to kill myself with all this traffic? Hello, you little devil.

ELIZABETH: You shouldn't play with guns when you've been drinking, Bobby.

BOBBY: I've had a hell of a day, baby.

ELIZABETH: I think that's true all 'round. I heard about your little game.

BOBBY: Yeah. I got to kill myself.

ELIZABETH: You know you don't. No one expects you to be that tough, Bobby.

BOBBY: Christine's giving me the heave.

ELIZABETH: So you're going to shoot yourself? Some tough guy.

BOBBY: It's not just that. The whole thing is pretty complicated. This kind of thing wears you out, you know that?

ELIZABETH: I'm not surprised.

BOBBY: I mean the woman thing. Poor Christine. She always ends up with losers. She mothers losers, I guess. I mean, not just that, but you know what I mean, right?

ELIZABETH: It's a hell of a way to treat your mother.

BOBBY: I treat my mother pretty bad, too. I'm a bad guy I guess.

ELIZABETH: Do you have any violin music I can put on as a background to all this?

BOBBY: Go fuck yourself.

ELIZABETH: Never at a loss for a witty retort. Listen, champ, I think you'd better call it a night. You're going to feel a little silly remembering this in the morning.

BOBBY: I'll be dead in the morning.

ELIZABETH: Don't be stupid about this now.

BOBBY: Listen, I'm serious. (*Holds the gun to his temple with both hands, then lowers it.*) You know something? You got to have one thing that makes everything else look like shit. That's how I used to feel about armed robbery, before it started scaring me. Everything scares me now. Dogs. Heights. Liquor. I scare myself. But armed robbery. Christ. Everything else was dogshit.

ELIZABETH: There must be something you feel that way about now.

BOBBY: You.

ELIZABETH: I'll take that as a compliment, being favourably compared to armed robbery.

BOBBY: You don't know it, but it is. Hendrix on guitar. You know what blows me away? That he even existed. Everything's so square, you wouldn't even think he'd be allowed. Like coming. It's so good, you don't think they'd allow it. Yeah, that's about it, I guess. Robbery, Hendrix and you.

By the time he's finished talking, BOBBY is very close to ELIZABETH, touching her.

ELIZABETH: All right, stud, are we about ready to call it a night? I can't stay down here. Come on now, give me the gun and I'll put it away.

BOBBY: I love you Elizabeth.

ELIZABETH: Then you won't mind doing me this little favour, will you?

BOBBY: I don't mind doing you, period. I love doing you.

ELIZABETH: Am I going to have to wrestle that evil little weapon out of your hand and force you into bed?

BOBBY: Okay, yeah. Force me into bed. Christine's gone for the night.

ELIZABETH: You're dreaming, Bobby.

BOBBY: (*runs his hands over her breasts and upper body, kissing her*) Christ, I love you. How am I going to see you again? I'll have to phone. We'll meet someplace, right? I got nowhere to live anymore. Or maybe I'll kill myself. I forgot that part.

ELIZABETH: (*gently disengages herself*) How drunk are you, Bobby? I want you to listen to me. Don't call my place. I'm moving out. You understand? I'm not going to live there anymore. I'm not sure where I'm going to be.

BOBBY: What's that? Are you going someplace?

ELIZABETH: I'm not staying in this town, Bobby. I'm leaving. Do you understand what I'm telling you? Don't call me.

BOBBY: Listen, take me with you.

ELIZABETH: I don't think that's a very good idea.

BOBBY: Sure it is. Look, I'll get a job someplace, you know? Or some kind of a deal where I can pick up a few bucks on the side. I'm not kidding.

ELIZABETH: I'm not taking you with me, Bobby. I can't. Let's not even discuss it, all right? It's impossible. But I'll miss those big bloodshot eyes of yours, you little devil.

BOBBY: Jesus, Elizabeth, I can't live without you. I mean it.

ELIZABETH: Christine's thrown you out before. Things will work out.

BOBBY: I need you.

ELIZABETH: You're drunk. All we are is a case of amazing sex. Don't go kidding yourself.

BOBBY: No, I mean it. I love you. Really, really love you.

He begins to cry. ELIZABETH goes to him.

ELIZABETH: Not this, now.

BOBBY: I'm going to blow my fucking brains out. Now there's nothing to stop me.

ELIZABETH: Don't use that one, Bobby.

BOBBY: (*holding her tight*) Come and lie down with me, Elizabeth. At least do that.

ELIZABETH: Bobby, please . . .

They have a long kiss.

BOBBY: I'm never going to see you again. Five minutes, that's all.

ELIZABETH: You're too drunk. It isn't a good idea.

BOBBY: You always said it made you feel free. That's a beautiful thing to tell somebody.

ELIZABETH: What is it about you, anyway? Always bringing out the worst in me.

During the following, until they exit, BOBBY will run the gun over ELIZABETH's breasts, down her thigh, and finally bring the barrel up between her legs.

BOBBY: You know how it made me feel? Like I was standing on the edge of something red. It always reminds me of something red. Like being on the edge of a big red saucer and you're always getting closer to the middle.

ELIZABETH: You're loaded, Bobby.

BOBBY: Come and lie down. Five minutes.

ELIZABETH: What if she comes home?

BOBBY: She won't. You ever see it that way? Like a big red saucer?

ELIZABETH: No. I don't know.

BOBBY: And you finally get to the middle.

ELIZABETH: I don't want you to do me, Bobby. Not now.

BOBBY: Just lie down with me. I want your body again.

ELIZABETH: Just a few minutes. I'll do something nice for you. But I've got to go.

BOBBY: Christ, you feel beautiful.

They enter the bedroom, arms around each other. A few seconds pass, then CHRISTINE tries the entrance door and finds to her surprise it is open. She enters, closing the door behind her. She has two styrofoam cups of coffee which she places on the floor, then removes her coat. Goes to the record player, takes off the record, takes out her favourite album and puts it on. "The First Time" by Roberta Flack. Sits, letting the music go through her. Slowly, BOBBY enters the living room. CHRISTINE looks up when she's aware of his presence, and turns the record down. She will take the needle off either at the song's end or close to it.

CHRISTINE: What's this all about?

BOBBY: What? What do you want?

CHRISTINE: Why do you have the gun out?

BOBBY: I don't know. It's a joke.

CHRISTINE: Oh. You're not thinking about shooting somebody, are you?

BOBBY: Yeah, that's right. I got to shoot myself.

CHRISTINE: How much have you had to drink?

BOBBY: Lots. Lots and lots. I got trouble hearing.

CHRISTINE: You weren't going to kill yourself just because I threw you out, were you? That's not too bright.

BOBBY: I pretty well have to.

CHRISTINE: No, you don't. Now listen. I've been thinking it over and maybe you don't have to go. I'm saying maybe.

BOBBY: Go where?

CHRISTINE: Maybe we should talk about it in the morning.

BOBBY: No. (*walks over and sits next to her on the floor*) Do you believe in God?

CHRISTINE: Drunk as a skunk, all right.

BOBBY: You do it and you pay for it, right? What goes around comes around. I mean, sometimes you have to set that up for yourself. There's no other way. Like, if your luck's too good. You see what I mean? Like me being behind the house when they came. Too much luck. You do it and you do it and you do it and nothing ever happens.

CHRISTINE: Have you had anything else besides the booze?

BOBBY: Listen, listen. When he took that fifth shot, I knew he was going to get it. He had to, it never happens to me. Don't you see? My old man put up my bail, I was only in for two days. All that kind of thing.

CHRISTINE: I see, I see. You've been too lucky.

BOBBY: Kind of. Not that, exactly.

CHRISTINE: Maybe you just live right. I brought you some coffee. (*goes to get the coffee cup*)

BOBBY: No, no. Stay here. Don't leave.

CHRISTINE: We could lie down and talk. (*hands BOBBY his coffee*)

BOBBY: I've done it all now, Christine, I really have. Now I got to do this thing.

CHRISTINE: Now listen to me, Bobby. I was really mad about Elizabeth, and I still am, but I'm not throwing you out. We'll talk it over in the morning. Things are going to have to change some, but it'll be all right. All right?

BOBBY: It'll never be all right.

CHRISTINE: Do you want to leave? Is that it? Because I'm telling you you don't have to.

BOBBY: You don't understand it.

CHRISTINE: Sure I do. I've thought it all over and, you know, maybe we should get out of the city. You smashing things up all the time around here, I think things have been getting to you. Probably that little bitch was getting to you. Now, I don't like what went down with you and her, but I can handle it. I think I can handle it. One thing, we have to move out of this place for sure.

BOBBY: I'm a dead man, Christine.

CHRISTINE: Bobby, will you stop it? I told you I'll take my lumps, all right? Aren't you even listening?

BOBBY: You never want to get hurt in bed. Why not?

CHRISTINE: Why the hell should I? Just because your girlfriend likes it?

BOBBY: No, no, but how come? I like it, sometimes.

CHRISTINE: And I do it to you, sometimes. You know something, I've been hurt everyplace else, in bed I like to enjoy myself. Weird, huh?

BOBBY: You know what it is, doing that to somebody? It's like doing yourself. You know what they like 'cause you like it and it's good for them because you're doing it to yourself. It's like one person, like putting halves together. Two people, then one person. But it isn't like pain. It's like freedom.

CHRISTINE: Bobby, please, I don't want to hear about how great it was for you two in bed, okay? Don't do this to me. I'm telling you we can stay together. Don't you even give a shit?

BOBBY: You get into it that far enough, you're just watching. Watching your hands do things. You can see something red kind of out of the corner of your eye, then you're there, right in the middle of it. Like a big red saucer.

CHRISTINE: Christ, you're unbelievable. (*begins to exit to bedroom*)

BOBBY: No, no, don't do it, stay here.

CHRISTINE: I'm not listening to any more of this shit. You don't just nail her, you've got to talk about it. You just keep on getting crazier, Bobby, maybe I'm just kidding myself.

BOBBY: Listen, it's like settling the score with yourself. You're too lucky and you settle up, even it out. Maybe that's all it is.

CHRISTINE: What? Having someone hit you so you feel better about what you did? You're bullshitting yourself, Bobby. You know, you've done a couple of things to a couple of people and they survived it. My baby's back in Toronto because I let that asshole adopt him. I let my baby go. You think that feels good? Bad things have happened to me and I've done some bad things, too, and I still don't like getting hurt in bed. You like it and you do it and she liked it and you did it to her and that's all. Just a weird trip. Don't go saying that's all part of your goddamned awful little life, too. Maybe you'd better stay out here, after all.

BOBBY: Christine, look at me.

CHRISTINE has almost reached the bedroom door when BOBBY's words stop her. She turns and looks. BOBBY shoves the gun into his mouth and pulls the trigger. The styrofoam cup explodes in his hand, spraying coffee. Shock slams BOBBY onto his back, on the couch. The gun has not fired.

CHRISTINE: You sick bastard.

She enters the bedroom.

BOBBY: How could we pass it? I got to do it for sure, now.

CHRISTINE screams from the bedroom. Comes out, very shaken. BOBBY holds the gun to his head and pulls the trigger. A click. Another click.

CHRISTINE: What in God's name have you done?

BOBBY: No, no. What's wrong with this thing?

He runs to the ammunition case and begins loading the entire cylinder.

CHRISTINE: What have you done to her?

BOBBY: She said it herself, no matter how great it is, you got to go on living when it's over. But you don't. It's love, too. I loved her. I don't care if you know it or not.

He raises the gun to his head, pulls the trigger once, twice, three times. Three clicks. He aims the gun at CHRISTINE.

CHRISTINE: Don't, don't! Don't shoot me!

BOBBY pulls the trigger. A click.

BOBBY: Maybe the bullets are duds. Maybe the firing pin's broken. I don't know enough about guns.

CHRISTINE runs out of the apartment.

BOBBY: What am I gonna do now? The fuck am I gonna do? Ripped off.

He throws the gun at the door.

A pause.

BOBBY: Luck. (*pause*) And isn't that the story of my fucking life.

End.

UNDER THE SKIN
BETTY LAMBERT

At the time of her death from cancer at age fifty, already a veteran of a quarter–century of playwriting, Betty Lambert was the New Play Centre's most promising dramatist, on the verge of a career breakthrough. Born in Calgary in 1933, she came to Vancouver in 1952. With a B.A. from UBC in English and Philosophy, she began writing radio plays for CBC in 1958. More than thirty were produced during her lifetime, three of them published in *West Coast Review* (1985), including *Grasshopper Hill*, 1980 ACTRA Award winner for best radio drama.

Lambert's first stage plays were written for tours by Holiday Theatre, the children's wing of the Vancouver Playhouse. *The Riddle Machine* (1966), which toured Canada, the U.S. and Europe, concerned a spaceship full of children fleeing their destroyed planet. Her first adult play, *The Visitor* (Vancouver Playhouse, 1970), was a failure. But her second, the sex comedy *Sqrieux-de-Dieu*, had great critical and commercial success. Along with new work by Tom Cone, Sheldon Rosen, Sharon Pollock and others, a scene from *Sqrieux-de-Dieu* had been staged as part of the New Play Centre's Collage 3 (1973). In 1975 the NPC produced the full play, directed by Richard Ouzounian. He remounted it at Festival Lennoxville in 1976 and again the next year, touring eastern Canada and to the National Arts Centre. Lambert's program biography for the original production read: "Having written many unsuccessful serious dramas and children's epics, Betty has decided to come out of the closet and write heterosexual smut. Fortunately, she has tenure at SFU."

Simon Fraser, where she taught English from 1965 until her death, was the setting for her satirical *Clouds of Glory*, produced by the New Play Centre in 1979. The same year saw the publication of her novel, *Crossings*, published in the U.S. as *Bring Down the Sun*. But it was *Jennie's Story* (1981) that brought Lambert to national attention and established her as a major talent. Written in what she called "female tragic form," the play plots an Alberta farm girl's gradual awareness that she has been unknowingly (and legally) sterilized at the behest of the priest who had seduced her. Commissioned and first produced by the New Play Centre, *Jennie's Story* was subsequently done in Toronto (1983), Calgary (1984), Ottawa (1986), and New York (1987), and was both a Chalmers and Governor General's Award runner–up.

Lambert's last play, and her best, was *Under the Skin*, produced posthumously by the New Play Centre in 1985 and published along with *Jennie's Story* by Playwrights Canada (1987). Based on a 1980 crime in a Vancouver suburb, the play centres not on the six–month–long secret abduction and sexual assault of the young girl by her male neighbour, but instead on the relationship between the girl's mother, the neighbour and his wife. The profoundly disturbing result, Lambert's glance into the darkness of the human heart, is a distillation of her own deepest fears: Maggie in the play is a projection of Betty Lambert, middle–class English professor and single mother of a teenage daughter.

Under the Skin was also produced by Upstart Crow, first at New York's Perry Street Theater (1987), then at the West Coast Ensemble Theater in Los Angeles (1988) where the *L.A. Weekly* described the audience "drawn breathlessly into the terrifying emotional maze." The Toronto production at Theatre Passe Muraille (1989), a Chalmers Award finalist, was directed by Susan Wright who had starred in the original *Sqrieux-de-Dieu*.

Under the Skin was first presented by the New Play Centre at the Waterfront Theatre on November 5, 1985, with Alana Shields as Maggie, Wendy van Riesen as Renee, and Dwight McFee as John. Directed by Pamela Hawthorn, with set design by Paul Ford, lighting by Marsha Sibthorpe, costumes by Judy Hayes and sound by Patrick McMullen.

Alana Shields as Maggie, Wendy van Riesen as Renee, and Dwight McFee as John in the New Play Centre production of *Under the Skin*. Photo by Glen Erikson.

UNDER THE SKIN

CHARACTERS

MAGGIE BENTON: An assistant professor at the nearby university. Divorced. Comfortably off. Mother of Emma. Comes from secure class, and is initially unaware of RENEE's fears and envies.

RENEE GIFFORD: Pronounced Reenee. 36, thin, too made-up, too consciously feminine. Wracked with   self-doubt. Sensual. Took an evening course but does not have a degree. Presently married to JOHN. Her first husband, Nick, left her for someone younger; her children are Joanie, 9, and Dougie, 11.

JOHN GIFFORD: About 40, good looking in a squarish way: that is, he's square-set, not fat. Wears glasses. Looks something like the Reverend Jimmy Swaggart: has some of the same physical movements and the same intense self-absorption.

SET

We open on a stage that is only partly revealed. It is the kitchen of the Gifford family. It is middle class and affluent. We see it from the vantage point of the workshop, which is down the hill. We see a patio on stilts. Sliding glass doors lead into the kitchen. A door leads offstage to a hallway, and upstairs, and to the front door.

The kitchen has all the latest equipment: a microwave, a waist-high oven, matching fridge, cuisinaire set, dishwasher. The cupboards and table and chairs are wooden, and finished with verithane. There is a degree of familiar clutter—Joanie and Dougie have put up their drawings on the fridge with magnetic buttons or ladybugs. The fridge ejects ice cubes. Things are clean but just a touch off—there's a kind of embarrassing tastelessness. There are, for instance, no pottery objects, such as MAGGIE would have—everything has a sort of Woolworth's glaze finish. Things are a bit too bright and shiny. The canister set is labelled, for example: COFFEE, TEA, SUGAR, FLOUR, and so on. A kitchen that tries too hard but doesn't quite make it. A bit like RENEE herself.

TIME

181 days, from Spring to Fall.

Scene One

From the kitchen, people can see the sound, the greys and blues of a spring morning, the bright thin light of a morning of terror.

MAGGIE: (*sits at table*) So then he said, "Well, Mrs. Benton, we don't have unlimited manpower." I said, "Look, I called up yesterday and they told me she was off the computer printout." My god, the incompetence! I told him, I said, "Look, I phoned yesterday and she wasn't *on* the computer printout."

RENEE is making tea. She reaches up for cups and saucers from her built-in china cabinet. All the cups and saucers are single patterns—they don't match. They are displayed proudly through glass. There are also china knick-knacks in the cabinet, and a wine decanter in the shape of a Mexican, a souvenir of her honeymoon.

MAGGIE: You   always   look   so— finished . . . in the morning. My god, I don't think I've showered for two days. (*smells herself*) Shh! Yech! "She was off the computer printout," I said.

RENEE: What did he say?

MAGGIE stares ahead of her. She is in a state of frenzy, trying to wrestle the world to her will. She is full of outrage, furious with the police, but beneath the outrage and the apparent grasp of the situation, she is living in terror. Occasionally she slips into that terror.

MAGGIE: He said . . . they didn't have unlimited manpower . . . he said they'd put her back on the printout.

RENEE: Well, so did you check yet to see if she's on it today?

MAGGIE: No. I didn't check it yet.

RENEE gives MAGGIE her tea. Goes to the wallphone. Listens to see if JOHN is on the phone in the workshop. Dials from a number written on a cute memo square, plastic, beside the phone. She checks one of the many hanging pots for wetness of soil as she waits.

RENEE: Have you heard from Graham again?

MAGGIE: No. I should go home in case he calls.

RENEE: Have your tea. I think you should eat—Hello? Yes, this is Mrs. Gifford, Mrs. John Gifford? I'm a neighbour of Mrs. Benton's? Yes. Yes. Apparently yesterday's printout of missing children did not contain Emma's name. I just wanted to make sure Emma's name is on today's printout. Yes, yes, I'll hold. *(to Maggie)* They're checking.

MAGGIE: I can't believe the incompetence. I cannot believe the sheer incompetence. *(picks up stale old toast from a plate beside her and eats it)* I said, "Who is your superior?" You know what he did? He sighed. He sighed. He said, "Look, Mrs. Benton, we don't have unlimited manpower," and he sighed as if I were boring him. *(laughs)*

RENEE: Yes? Oh it is? Okay, thank you very much. You can understand how she feels. Yes, okay, yes. Thank you. Yes I will. *(hangs up)* He said would I keep an eye on you and I said I would.

MAGGIE: And when they were looking yesterday, they were making jokes. Didn't John say that?—when they were out in the bush they were making jokes about it?

RENEE: Not about that. Just jokes. People do that. To keep up their spirits.

MAGGIE: John said though, they were laughing. *(eats another piece of toast absently)*

RENEE: Let me make you some, fresh.

MAGGIE: No, I'm not hungry, I can't eat.

RENEE: *(annoyed)* They've done all they could, Maggie. John himself has been out every day. You've got good friends.

MAGGIE: Yes, I know. *(furious)* Why shouldn't they look? If it was their kid, I'd look. I'm not grateful, why should I be grateful? It's only what's human.

RENEE: They don't even know you, you're new here.

MAGGIE: I'm human, they owe me that, they owe Emma that, to look. Fuck them. I've been here four years!

RENEE: That's new to them.—They've been out for a week, and she's probably just off with some guy she picked up with.

MAGGIE: What? Jesus Christ, Renee.

RENEE: I don't think you're in any position to take the name of the Lord in vain.

MAGGIE: "Some guy she picked up with"?

RENEE: You live in a dream world. Things like that happen.

MAGGIE: Not to people like us.

RENEE: Yes, to people like you, who says you're safe? Why should you be safe?

UNDER THE SKIN 221

MAGGIE: We're talking about Emma, remember Emma? Emma with the big crush on the Holy Ghost? Emma whose big bible was Anne Frank . . . (*hands over heart*) "I truly believe than everybody has some good in them" or crap like that while some SS was fucking her . . . Oh Jesus! No, she'd phone me, if she met someone and she was off with him she'd phone me, say she had to save him or some shit, she'd phone me. Oh god. Oh god. She would have phoned me.

RENEE: You're blind about that girl. You're blind, she was asking for it. (*staring out front, towards the workshop*) The way she carries on, with John.

MAGGIE: She misses Graham.

RENEE: All right, I won't say anything. You're too upset right now. But you'll see, she'll phone from San Francisco, she'll ask for a ticket to fly home.

MAGGIE: I know I'm a burden to you.

RENEE: Oh god, it's been a terrible week, let me make you some food. Our nerves are all ragged. That's all. That's all it is. I had a bad night.

MAGGIE: I'll go home in a minute. I'll go home. I've got to take a shower. No, I don't want anything. Please don't make me anything. You've been good friends to me, I know I should feel grateful, I'm sorry I can't feel grateful, I think you should be good friends.

RENEE: (*staring out*) If it were Joanie I'd be mad.

MAGGIE: Yes, I thought I'd go mad at first. Isn't it funny.

RENEE: I said to Emma that time, I said, "Emma, for god's sake, you've got to use a feminine deodorant now you're menstruating because men can smell it."

MAGGIE: I've never in my life had to ask for favours. The police treat me as if I'm boring, a boring mother. I said, "Who is your superior?" and he sighed.

RENEE: And she should have worn a brassiere, just for practical reasons, your breasts start to sag and Emma was full bosomed for her age.

MAGGIE: Don't do that.

RENEE: You need to eat. You've been picking at Joanie's leftovers.

MAGGIE: Do me a fucking favour and stop using the fucking past tense. Sorry. And I don't want eggs, for christ's sake, Renee, just let up on me, I don't wear a brassiere either, for christ's sake.

RENEE: You're swearing all the time now.

MAGGIE: I know. It's an alternative to screaming continuously.

RENEE: You were into a symbiotic relationship.

MAGGIE: (*laughs*) What's symbiosis anyway, I thought it was something to do with moss.

RENEE: Symbiosis is when you get so dependent on someone you can't live without them.

MAGGIE: I thought it had something to do with fungus. I though the fungus lived off the tree and the tree got something from the fungus, and they were both better off.

RENEE: What would a tree get from a fungus?

MAGGIE: He sighed. He just gave this big sigh as if I were phoning about someone's dog peeing on my lawn.

RENEE has been boiling an egg and toasting bread. Getting it ready, cutting the toast into strips.

RENEE: John says he'd bet anything that Emma's just gone off with some guy.

MAGGIE: (*as RENEE serves it to her*) Why do you keep saying that? Emma's never in her life done anything remotely like that. My mother made egg toast that way. (*begins to eat hungrily*) I know I'm horrible, I know I'm ungrateful, I can't stand myself either. Yeah, Mom made them just like this, I'm glad she's dead, she'd die. (*laughs*) It'd kill her. (*laughs*) I didn't even want an egg.

RENEE: You may not have noticed, but Emma's growing up.

MAGGIE: She's only 12 . . .

RENEE: She'll be 13 on Wednesday.

MAGGIE: (*overcome with terror, clutches herself*) Oh my god, oh my god. (*RENEE comes over to hug her.*) No, don't touch me, I can't stand it if anyone touches me, I'll go to pieces, don't. (*RENEE, behind MAGGIE, draws back in disgust.*) She's dead. She's dead.

RENEE: Don't be silly.

MAGGIE: That's what he said to me, that officer, "Mrs. Benton, you must prepare yourself for the worst." (*laughs*) How the fuck do you prepare yourself for the worst. I can't bear it.

RENEE: You've made that girl too much in your life. (*MAGGIE is breathing hard.*) Children leave us all some day.

MAGGIE: Not like this they don't.

RENEE: Well, at least you've eaten something. (*takes plate away from MAGGIE*)

MAGGIE: I didn't even think I was hungry.

RENEE: Sometimes I think it'll be nice when the kids go and John 'n' I are alone. John 'n' me, I mean.

MAGGIE: (*absently*) No, you were right the first time, it's *John and I.*

RENEE: Last time you said it was *John and me.*

MAGGIE: That's 'cause it was in the objective case, you said something something with John and I, and that should be *John and me.* A lot of people do that, they get upset about their fucking usage and over-correct, like saying *I feel badly.*

RENEE: I thought that was right, *I feel badly.*

MAGGIE: No, it's *I feel bad.* Who gives a shit.

RENEE: Well I do, I don't want to sound like an illiterate.

MAGGIE: Christ, even my chairman says *I feel badly.* "Maggie, I can't tell you how badly I feel."

RENEE: (*putting dishes in washer*) Did I tell you how Dougie busted in on us last Sunday morning? (*laughs*) God! I was sure I'd hooked the door. I have this routine, go to the bathroom, put in my diaphragm, hook the door . . .

MAGGIE: They said she was on the computer printout, eh?

RENEE: I told you.

MAGGIE: I better go, Graham could phone.

RENEE: You'll have to go back to work, it's no use just waiting around the house, it's better to have a routine, it gives you something to hold on to.

MAGGIE: I know people have been good, I am grateful. (*tearful*) People have been really good. It's just the police seem so blasé . . . I said to that young one, the one who came the first night, "You never think this sort of thing will happen to you," and he just looked away as if I'd said something . . . disgusting. That's the thing, they make you feel so disgusting.

RENEE: When Nick and I broke up, Nick and me, I said, "No way the kids're gointa be my life," I went out with John three months before I ever told him I had kids.

MAGGIE: (*flaring*) Why should I be made to feel disgusting! Fuck them!

RENEE: You better hold it down when John comes in, he can't stand a woman with a mouth, we'd go to his place, and I'd say I had to be home because all my stuff for work was there, in a way though it worked out, he got really jealous, thought I was married and had to get back to my old man. (*She laughs. MAGGIE sits and stares.*) Well, I've been lucky I guess.

MAGGIE: Sometimes I think just come and tell me she's dead. That way I know she's not suffering.

RENEE: Why do you keep on about that? Why should she be suffering? Kids run away . . . it's common knowledge kids run away with men . . . time means nothing to them . . . she's off with some guy . . . she isn't even thinking of you.

JOHN Gifford comes in through sliding doors. Goes to MAGGIE, embraces her. MAGGIE starts to cry. Holds onto his arm awkwardly.

JOHN: There there. There there. We're doing all we can.

RENEE looks on impassively.

She'll be found, she'll be found, Maggie, I know it. I feel it.

RENEE: (*neutral voice*) I've got your breakfast ready, it's in the oven. Juice?

JOHN, hugging MAGGIE, rocks her back and forth, kisses her hair. MAGGIE, head thrown back, gives herself to this comfort. JOHN looks down at MAGGIE's thrown back face. Moment of stillness. He bends down and kisses her full on the lips. RENEE turns abruptly and opens oven door. Puts on mitt. Reaches in for plate of pancakes and bacon. Places them on the table. JOHN now moves toward RENEE to kiss her on the lips. RENEE avoids him. Goes to fridge for juice. JOHN pulls her around firmly, smiles at her, kisses her on the lips.

JOHN: Good morning, Renee.

RENEE: (*looks at him*) Little early for it, isn't it?

JOHN: Hmmm. Think so?

RENEE: What's gotten into you?

JOHN: What's gotten into you—lately? (*laughs; starts to eat with appetite*) I picked up the Fraser kids this morning. Hitchhiking. Not a care in the world. Right out there. I stopped the van and told them to get in . . . I said, "You kids haven't heard about Emma Benton." They won't hitch again in a hurry. Pass the syrup, would you?

RENEE: Oh those Fraser kids, they do what they want irregardless. I've told Joanie not to bring the girl over here anymore. Who needs it.

JOHN stares at the cupboard under the sink which RENEE has opened to get some cleanser.

JOHN: When are you going to clean that cupboard under the sink? God it bothers me . . . all that crud . . . you are really a scumbag housekeeper, Renee . . . my mother used to say, "Look in a woman's cupboards if you want to know how she keeps herself."

RENEE: Oh your mother—

JOHN: Keep off my mother. (*mild*) Any coffee?

RENEE: (*pouring coffee*) Her cupboards are clean, oh yes, compensation . . .

JOHN: Quit that phony baloney crap. It's *regardless*.

RENEE: Pure compensation, overcompensation . . .

JOHN: My mother was a clean woman.

RENEE: Well, she's not so clean now.

JOHN: It's *regardless* not *irregardless*, ask the college professor here.

RENEE: (*sing-songy*) She's rotten . . . rotten . . . she is rotten . . . and the worms are crawling in her eyes . . . (*MAGGIE gives a high laugh.*) Sorry.

JOHN: You're sick.

RENEE: Sorry, Maggie, I didn't think . . .

MAGGIE: I should go.

JOHN: Give her a brandy.

RENEE goes toward the liquor cupboard.

MAGGIE: I should be home in case the police call. And Graham said he'd call. (*RENEE pours the brandy into an ordinary glass, puts it in front of MAGGIE.*) No, if I drink I won't be any good for the rest of the day.

JOHN: Maggie? I'm going to say something for your own good. —Drink up. (*waits until she raises the glass to her lips*) Go back to work.

MAGGIE: I can't.

JOHN: You can.

MAGGIE: No. You don't know. They're so beautiful. You walk into a lecture room and there they are, so young and so beautiful and so full of life. All that joy. All that life.

RENEE: All the sex. Eighteen-year-olds are nothing but walking bags of hormones.

MAGGIE: Yes. All that, yes, sensuality, that sheer joy at being alive and being able to move and laugh and sing. (*drinks*) I look at them sometimes and their sheer . . . beauty overwhelms me. The skin, pimples and all . . . it just radiates. Sometimes I come out of a lecture so high . . . just on them, the way they are. And every year they stay the same age and only I get older. I would see them all go up in flames in the fiery furnace, just to have her back. I would see them torn to pieces. I would see the world go mad. I would bring down the sky.

RENEE: You think I wouldn't. For Joanie and Dougie? You think I don't love them like that?

MAGGIE: I could kill.

RENEE: She's just off with some hulk. You didn't see her, she was always rubbing up against John.

JOHN: Keep your mouth off Emma. I'm telling you. (*to MAGGIE*) We're all just upset and worried.

MAGGIE: (*gets up*) Thank god for good friends, I do really . . . I mean to feel grateful . . . I will . . . it's just right now . . .

JOHN: 'Sallright, no need to say a word. Anytime, Maggie, I'm here. (*walks her to sliding doors, arm around her shoulder*) Try to get some rest. And think about it, going back, work's the only salvation, it's an old clinker but it's true.

MAGGIE: Yes. (*comes through the doors, onto patio, walks down steps; exits*)

JOHN watches her go. His gaze rests on the workshop. He turns and goes back into kitchen.

JOHN: Joanie's been mucking about with my things again, will you tell her to leave my stuff alone.

RENEE: She only borrowed a hammer.

JOHN: She put it back in the wrong place. I have everything exactly where I want it, everything has a place . . .

RENEE: Just to put a poster up, in her room.

JOHN: Are you listening to me? I don't think you're listening to me. I don't care what Joanie wanted the hammer for. She could have crucified the next-door neighbour's cat for all I care. Does that penetrate your brain at all? I don't care what the hammer was used for. I do not like your brat using my things.

RENEE: Oh my, what a gruffy bear this morning. What a gruffy bear. Ooooh oh, he has the grumps this morning, he has, he has, oh my what a big *EEyore* bear this morning.

JOHN: (*looking out the sliding doors*) You know what she said one day? (*short laugh*) She said, "My mom's going to take me to get birth control when I'm sexually active." (*laughs*)

RENEE: What?

JOHN: Are you deaf?

RENEE: Who said that.

JOHN: Emma.

RENEE: Maggie was asking for trouble. That's all. Just asking for it.

JOHN: "Sexually active"!

RENEE: Maggie was always too free with that girl.

JOHN: Why don't you shut up.

RENEE: Grumpy bear this morning, grumpy bear.

JOHN: Just keep your brats out of my workshop. —Oh yes, she said that, for all her big religious talk. "My mom's going to take me to get birth control when I'm sexually active." I said to her, "Emma, you've got a big surprise waiting for you, the world isn't like that, everybody nice and good, the world is just waiting for people like you, everybody's out for number one."

RENEE: Oh kids get religious at that age. I wanted to be a nun when I was 13—

JOHN: I don't want to hear about how you wanted to be a nun. I've heard that story a thousand times. That is completely irrelevant. What are you trying to prove? Can't you keep your mind on the subject for two minutes?

RENEE: I was only saying that kids're often religious at that age, Emma was no different, it was just a phase . . .

JOHN: And you keep your mouth off Emma. Do you hear me? You keep your filthy mouth off Emma. She's not like you, you're a born whore, do you hear me? Renee? Do you hear me? —Do you understand me? Renee?

RENEE: Yes.

JOHN stares at her. RENEE turns and starts to put dishes in the washer. JOHN gets up, moves toward her, stands behind her.

RENEE: I've got work to do.

JOHN pulls up her skirt and moves in to her, pushing her down over the washer.

Go to black.

Scene Two

The darkened kitchen. Late spring. A figure against the sliding doors pounds on the jamb. The figure pounds again.

MAGGIE: (*calls*) Renee? Renee? Renee!

RENEE appears as a silhouette in the kitchen doorway, turns on the patio lights, recognizes—after a brief hesitation—MAGGIE. Goes to the sliding doors and opens them.

RENEE: What is it, what's happened?

MAGGIE: I heard her.

RENEE: What?

MAGGIE: I heard her, heard her crying out to me. I heard her calling me. "Momma, Momma." Somebody's hurting her.

RENEE: It was a dream.

MAGGIE: No. I wasn't asleep.

RENEE: You were asleep. (*MAGGIE sits down at the table. She is disheveled, in an old robe.*) I'll get you a drink. (*does so*)

MAGGIE: I heard her.

RENEE: It was only a dream. (*stares out at the workshop*)

MAGGIE: It was real, I could hear her. (*She's shaking. RENEE gives her the drink.*) Today one of my students came to see me. She wanted to complain against one of my T.A.'s. He's not marking the essays. He's just giving grades. No comments. I said I'd mark it. —That's the son of a bitch who faked his footnotes. (*brief laugh*)

RENEE: It's good you're back at work.

MAGGIE: Other people's children. I hate them. (*drinks*) I hate them for being alive and well.

RENEE: No, it's good for you to be back at work.

MAGGIE: People keep saying that to me. It's good I'm back at work. Whatshisname across the hall, he said, "You must have a steel trap for a mind." (*laughs*)

RENEE: You've got to think of yourself.

MAGGIE: Why is that. (*RENEE sighs. MAGGIE gulps the drink, looks at RENEE.*) Such a sigh. Why such a sigh? Am I disturbing you?

RENEE: Well, you make me . . . well, impatient. It's been two months.

MAGGIE: God yes, it's been two months, at least! I should be well over it by now. (*RENEE sighs. MAGGIE puts down her drink; gets up.*) Yes. You're right. It's boring. I should be able to handle it myself. (*starts for the sliding doors*)

RENEE: No. Don't go.

MAGGIE: (*pauses*) Were you asleep?

RENEE: No. —No.

MAGGIE: Everything's so clean. For once in my life the house is completely organized. No mess at all.

RENEE: Life goes on.

MAGGIE: I feel I should be screaming down the street. I feel I should be tearing the world apart. The cherry blossoms're out. Everything's alive. I should pass and the grass should wither. (*laughs*) Everything hurts my eyes.

RENEE: Life goes on.

MAGGIE: (*laughs*) That's what's so unfair.

RENEE: I've never been one to brood. When Nick and I broke up, I said that's that, and I let him go. I went out and I met new men and

I met John and I said Nick's over and done with. I opened my fingers and I let him go. I've shed enough tears for that bastard, I said. — You're young, you're still attractive.

MAGGIE: Who are we talking about, what are we talking about, a child isn't a man, you can always get another *man*.

RENEE: You've had an education. You're independent. I never had the opportunities you've had, if something happened to John we'd be done for . . .

MAGGIE: Oh Renee, it's not the same—

RENEE: What do you know about it? What the . . . christly hell . . . do you know about it. You've never had to struggle.

MAGGIE: I'd take a child over a man anytime, a man you can get anywhere, a child is . . . a child . . . you give birth to a child . . . what the fuck are we talking about . . . I put myself through university, it wasn't any free ride let me tell you . . .

RENEE: . . . you've had it all given to you, how much did that chesterfield cost? and you didn't even think twice, you didn't even wait till the sales . . . you just bought it . . . saw it and bought it . . . you saw it and you wanted it . . . do you know how long it took me to get a kitchen like this? I was raped once you know.

MAGGIE: You never told me that.

RENEE: I don't tell you everything.

MAGGIE: What did you do about it?

RENEE: What could I do? I'd known him, we'd been to bed together, Nick was working nightshift then, and I started this thing with David. Then we broke up. One night he came to our place and he beat me up and raped me. I didn't dare scream because of the baby. That was Dougie. I was afraid to tell Nick. I couldn't tell Nick, how could I tell Nick? He'd have said

I let him in on purpose. Well, I did let him in, he knocked on the door and I thought, Oh, it's just David and I let him in, you wouldn't think to look at him . . . I didn't get my period for three months, I was terrified I was pregnant. If I was pregnant I'd have had to tell Nick, he'd have had to sign the form, wouldn't he? And then I'd have had to tell him and he'd say I let David in, I asked for it.

MAGGIE: It's a nightmare. The whole world is a nightmare.

RENEE: But life goes on, you forget.

MAGGIE: Life goes on and on and on, and it has no business going on. —I could hear her crying out for me. Sometimes I think my ears are just dead to the sounds in the air. That the air, the real air, is alive with screams of pain and terror. The abattoir across the inlet. The screams of dying fish on hooks. All the suffering of the forest. And the deep deep sea. And that what I do, what we all do, is learn to close our ears to the real noise of the night.

RENEE: Shut up. (*MAGGIE looks at her, astonished.*) Just—shut—up.

MAGGIE: What is it? Renee? What is it? (*MAGGIE gets up slowly. Holding her breath, crosses to RENEE. Takes her by the shoulders and shakes her once.*) What is it?

RENEE: She's dead. Emma's dead. Face it. Emma's dead.

MAGGIE stares at RENEE and then howls. RENEE, caught by her pain and by real affection and empathy, clasps her and rocks her, crying as well, rocking back and forth.

RENEE: I know, I know, oh god, oh dear god, it's not true. It's not true.

JOHN enters through the sliding doors. He stands there, his back to us. The women look at him.

Go to black.

Scene Three

Mid-summer. On the patio. Deck chairs, table, umbrella shade, flowers in baskets and pots. MAGGIE and RENEE in summer clothes, drinking tall drinks. RENEE looks very good in shorts and top. MAGGIE is slumped in rumpled jeans and t-shirt. JOHN comes up from the garden, bare to the waist, in jeans.

JOHN: Whew! (*takes drink from RENEE and downs it*)

RENEE: (*arch*) Oh my, what a greedy bear, oh there he goes, stealing my honey! (*laughs at him*)

JOHN: Get me a drink.

RENEE: Oh no please . . . no please today . . . oh he hates to do the garden . . . he hates the sunshine . . . he hates nature . . . what a gruffy bear . . .

JOHN: Get me a drink, Renee, do I have to send you a telegram? —Can you get it through your head I might be thirsty?

RENEE: My lord and master. Yes, sire. You command and I obey.

She gets up and archly wiggles herself in slavelike obeisance in front of him. Raises her hands and palms them prayerfully.

JOHN: Move! (*pulls up chair and sits down*)

RENEE: God, sometimes I could kill you. (*goes into kitchen through sliding doors*)

JOHN looks at MAGGIE. MAGGIE stares ahead of her. Drinks.

JOHN: You look like shit, Maggie. —I'm telling you for your own good. You look like shit. Fix yourself up, for chrissake. —When you going back to work.

MAGGIE: It's my research semester.

JOHN: So do some research.

MAGGIE: Get off my back, John.

JOHN: Forget it, forget her. She's off with some asshole, she's having the time of her life, she's not thinking about you, you'll get a phone call from Timbuktu, Bail me out, Mom . . .

MAGGIE: No. Not Emma. She wasn't like that.

JOHN: She was like that. She was like that. She was always out in the workshop, rubbing up against me. Oh it's natural, I guess, and she missed her dad. But she was asking for it, rubbing up against me. You know what she said one day, she said, "My mom's going to get me birth control pills when I'm sexually active." Sexually active!

MAGGIE: You think that was wrong.

JOHN: Was that true then? Did you actually say something like that? To a 12-year-old? Boy. Maggie. Shit.

MAGGIE: What're you going to tell Joanie?

JOHN: Joanie? What have I got to do with Joanie? —She's not my kid. That's Renee's business.

MAGGIE: She's your kid now.

JOHN: (*suddenly enraged*) Joanie has nothing to do with me. I am nothing to her. We're not related.

MAGGIE: I'm sorry, I didn't mean anything.

JOHN: I didn't even know she *had* kids. Asked her to marry me, and then I find out. Shit.

MAGGIE: Well, you're her stepfather now.

JOHN: I never bargained for her brats. She pulled a fast one on me there.

RENEE: (*comes out with a drink for JOHN*)
There you are oh lord and master. I told Maggie she has to get out of the house, all she does is sit and watch TV. (*sits down and drinks*) That's all I *can* do as a matter of fact. Can you believe it, Maggie, this old cheapskate won't even fix our TV. I've been after him for three weeks now. All it needs is for him to take it into Jenkins', but will he make the effort . . . noooooh. (*drinks*)

JOHN: It's summer, what d'ya need TV for in the summer?

RENEE: Well, *I* like it at nights, when you're working.

JOHN: I've had the cable turned off anyway.

RENEE: You've what? You've what, John?

JOHN: The TV's busted, I had them turn off the cable for the summer.

RENEE: Aw John, aw John, aw . . . I *like* my TV.

JOHN: You like your fuckin' soaps.

RENEE: Oh what a gruffy bear he is this morning, oh my what a gruffy bear!

JOHN: Listen, I want you to tell Dougie to keep outa the workshop.

RENEE: Oh my, what a gruffy bear, what's the poor kid done now?

JOHN: He's been messing with my paint.

RENEE: Well, he was doing this sign for the circus. (*to MAGGIE*) You know, the kids're so cute, they got this circus going and Dougie was supposed to be the clown and he wanted to make this sign . . . a dime to get in . . .

JOHN: He moved my things. I have a place for everything and everything has a place.

RENEE: And Susie, from across the road? She's supposed to be the trapeze artist . . .

JOHN: Just keep your brats outa my workshop. Do you hear me, cunt?

RENEE: (*looks at MAGGIE quickly, laughs uneasily*) There's no need to talk to me like that. Not in front of Maggie.

JOHN: Maggie knows you're a cunt. Listen, Maggie? You know the other day, when you were talking to the police again? (*laughs*) And you said we live in the cul-de-sac off the highway? You know what Renee did after you left? She looked it up in the dictionary, only she didn't know how to spell it.

RENEE: I was telling Maggie, she'll turn up . . . she's just off with some guy . . . if it was anything else, we'd have heard. No news is good news, you've got to keep hoping.

MAGGIE: Emma wasn't like that.

RENEE: Mothers're the last ones, Maggie, she was always at John, rubbing up against him, wasn't she, John, you tell her . . .

MAGGIE: She was on this big religious kick. She was always quoting those last lines from Anne Frank at me, what are they . . . oh jesus . . . "because in spite of everything . . . I still believe . . .(*choking*) . . . that fucking people are really good at heart."

JOHN: Yeah but those aren't the last lines in the book.

MAGGIE: Yes, the last lines in that book, she was a little girl who hid out from the Nazis, in Holland, only they found her, and she kept this diary . . .

JOHN: I know the book you're talking about, Maggie, just because I'm married to a cunt doesn't mean I'm a cunt. I know the book and I'm telling you, those aren't the last lines in the book.

MAGGIE: Well, they're the last lines in the movie or something. Who gives a shit.

RENEE: I was on a religious kick when I was that age . . . it's sublimation . . .

JOHN: It's what?

RENEE: Sublimation.

JOHN: What's sublimation?

RENEE: Oh John, you know what sublimation is. (*laughs and looks at MAGGIE*)

JOHN: No I'm just an ignorant guy, Renee, I never went to no college course in psychology at night school.

RENEE: Well, sublimation is when you put your sex into something else . . .

JOHN: Oh, is *that* what that is. (*throws a glance at MAGGIE who smiles weakly.*)

RENEE: Oh John, don't be such a bully . . .

JOHN: Me? I'm just trying to get an education, you know what it's like, living down the street from a college professor, I mean she just about pukes when she hears you going on sometimes, Renee, don't you know that?

MAGGIE: That's not true, John . . .

JOHN: She's laughing at you, for chrissake, Renee, don't you know that, you cunt? (*Silence. MAGGIE starts to get up. JOHN pulls her down, roughly.*) Sit. Sit. Jesus. It's hot, it's just the heat and if it's not the heat it's the humidity. (*laughs*)

RENEE *and MAGGIE do not laugh.*

MAGGIE: I'm not laughing at her.

JOHN: She makes you throw up, Maggie. She makes me throw up.

RENEE *gets up abruptly and goes inside. MAGGIE twirls her glass around. Reaches into her pocket and takes out a cigarette package.*

JOHN: You want to kill yourself?

MAGGIE: Why do you do that? Why do you talk to her like that.

JOHN: She's illiterate.

MAGGIE: Oh for crying out loud. (*lights up*)

JOHN: You want cancer?

MAGGIE: What're you trying for, John, the Archie Bunker lookalike prize?

JOHN: That's how you see me, isn't it, a redneck bastard.

MAGGIE: You're the one with the hangup about class, John.

JOHN: Oh yeah? Listen, I see you, every time she drops some clanger, you wince, I see it.

MAGGIE: No you don't.

JOHN: I see you. When you first moved in, I saw you, this big polite act . . .

MAGGIE: Renee's my friend, she's been good to me, if it hadn't been for Renee these last months I would have gone insane.

JOHN: You looked at us like we were bugs . . . you looked at those plaques Renee's got in the kitchen like they was shit . . .

MAGGIE: They're just not my kind of thing.

JOHN: Oh. "Not your kind of thing," eh?

MAGGIE: No. People have different tastes, John.

JOHN: Your kind of thing is some old pot made by some hippie down in White Rock. Right?

MAGGIE: Right.

JOHN: You don't like me much, do you? Truth now, Maggie. Truth time.

MAGGIE: (*drinks, looks at him, smokes*) No.

JOHN: (*laughs*) But I turn you on, don't I?

MAGGIE: Yes.

JOHN: Yes. But you hate my guts.

MAGGIE: You're not important enough to hate, John. I merely despise your type.

JOHN: My type eh? What type is that, Maggie?

MAGGIE: Renee said it. The bully. The little bully. You push her around because she's helpless and can't do anything about it. You push her around but if anybody stands up to you you back down.

JOHN: You think I'd back down to you?

MAGGIE: I know it.

JOHN: (*long pause*) Fuck you, Maggie.

MAGGIE: Don't you wish, buster.

RENEE: (*comes out, all made-up; brightly*) Listen, I've put some spare ribs on, let's all have spare ribs, never mind him, Maggie, he's such a gruffy bear when he hasn't had what he wants, you know . . . it was Dougie's fault, wasn't it, John? Dougie burst in this morning, I'd forgot the lock on the door, and Dougie bursts in this morning, you should have seen this gruffy bear . . . (*looks at JOHN and tentatively sits on his knee*)

JOHN: (*sits for a moment then shoves her off*) Get off me, you whore. (*gets up*) I'm going to the shop. (*stalks off*)

RENEE looks after him, eyes wild.

Go to black.

Scene Four

The fall. MAGGIE and RENEE in the kitchen. MAGGIE is wearing a new outfit: pants, top, boots. She has had her hair done. She smokes. RENEE looks drawn and haggard.

MAGGIE: And the chairman says he could understand that I was upset. Upset! I say, "Look, Benny, I've got an 18-page paper here, 17½ pages of which are copied word for word from a book!" And Benny says I'm vindictive. He says, "However, I can understand what you are feeling." I said, "Look, Benny, this has nothing to do with Emma. This has nothing to do with the fact that Emma is still missing. That's irrelevant. This has to do with a simple case of fucking plagiarism. This fucking student has fucking well plagiarized her term paper, in a fourth-year course, in Shakespeare . . ." "She didn't even copy from a good critic," he says. Thought that would make me laugh. Then he suggests I see a good doctor.

RENEE: What're they going to do about the student?

MAGGIE: Oh, I'm contracted to lecture to her. If Miss Shitface turns up on Monday, under the terms of my contract, I must lecture to her. "Listen," I told Benny, "if that bitch turns up in my class on Monday, I will puke all over her, direct from the podium." —Then he says, "She's built like a brick shithouse." That's what he said — "built like a brick shithouse." The chairman of the English Department! That's the sort of simile he uses for a woman.

RENEE: Maybe you shouldn't have expelled her from the class. Maybe that was a bit harsh.

MAGGIE: Harsh! Harsh! I'd like to string her up from her tits. How's about a drink, Renee?

RENEE: Oh yeah, sure. (*turns and gets bottle, etc. from cupboard*)

MAGGIE: You okay?

RENEE: Sure. Fine. Why?

MAGGIE: I don't know. You on a new diet again?

RENEE: No.

MAGGIE: No, people get away with everything these days, they're not wicked, they're just suffering from social maladjustment. Benny said something like that, he said the woman was emotionally disabled or something.

RENEE: Well, maybe she was! (*hands her a drink*)

MAGGIE: (*half-laugh*) Whaaat?

RENEE: You don't know why she did it. You don't *know*.

MAGGIE: I know. She wanted a good grade so she cheated. She thought it was worth the risk.

RENEE: Maybe it's not so simple, Maggie, maybe she was desperate. Maybe she couldn't write her essay and got desperate.

MAGGIE: Tough shit.

RENEE: Well, how would you know! You can always write whenever you want, maybe she needs your compassion . . .

MAGGIE: Maybe she needs my boot in her butt. I said to Benny, "What has her being built

like a brick shithouse got to do with anything?" And he kept calling her a girl. "The *girl* has emotional problems," he kept saying. I looked her up, she's twenty-fucking-eight.

RENEE: Well, maybe she does have emotional problems.

MAGGIE: You think that excuses her?

RENEE: Well, sometimes people don't always understand the things they get caught up in, and they just, you know, get caught up in them, and they just do it, they don't work it out, like, ahead of time, they just find themselves sort of in the middle of it.

MAGGIE: I don't know, it's like saying Hitler had a bad day.

RENEE: People get caught up in things!

MAGGIE: Then they should get un–caught. You get in a bad situation, you walk away. You just . . . walk fucking . . . ay-way.

RENEE: Please stop using that word. It's bad in front of the children.

MAGGIE: The children are not present, Renee.

RENEE: Well, you don't watch your mouth even when they're here. —I can't walk away! How can I walk away!

MAGGIE: I wasn't talking about John.

RENEE: Weren't you? He said you had a fight, he said you hate him. He says misery loves company, you'll try to get me to leave him, well, you can cut the crap, Maggie, just because you're lonely and frustrated . . .

MAGGIE: I've never interfered between you and John . . .

RENEE: Oh haven't you! Oh! haven't you . . . last week, when I was showing you that new dress, you got that look on your face, I could just tell what you were thinking—

MAGGIE: Because you were doing this cringing whelp act . . . you were cringing away—

RENEE: What . . . what act?

MAGGIE: Like a cringing whelp . . . a dog—

RENEE: That's another thing—

MAGGIE: "Oh John, I got this really cheap, see? See how cheap it was and I really do need it, oh you gruffy bear." Jesus—

RENEE: I do not sound like that!

MAGGIE: And you'd changed the sales tags—so he wouldn't know what you paid for the fucking dress!

RENEE: I do not sound like that!

MAGGIE: You sound like that!

RENEE: (panting) You don't understand.

MAGGIE: I understand.

RENEE: No. You don't. You don't understand.

MAGGIE: What is he, good in bed?

RENEE: Jealous?

MAGGIE: (small laugh, gets up) Maybe. That's it. Maybe. If a man came into me now he'd corrode in bile. He'd dissolve. I'm full of spleen. —Sorry. Sorry. Sorry. It's none of my business. It's none of my business. People don't know about married couples. I don't know about you and John. What really goes on. I can't talk.

RENEE: (still furious) No. You can't.

MAGGIE: No, I can't. I don't know, maybe you're right, it's this thing affecting everything. It's true, I can't stand the way he treats you. That's true.

RENEE: You don't understand. I like it.

MAGGIE: Do you?

RENEE: Yes.

MAGGIE: Okay. Look, I'll water the plants, don't worry. I'll take care of things.

RENEE: All right.

MAGGIE: (pauses, then goes and embraces her) Have a good time, have a great holiday.

RENEE: (stiffly, unyielding) Thanks.

Go to black.

Scene Five

The darkened kitchen. The hall light shines through into the kitchen. MAGGIE is at the sliding doors, key in lock. Opens doors, slides them back. She is in a housecoat. Switches on the light over the sink. Gets watering can and spray bottle from beside the sink. She measures hyponex into the watering can. Starts to water and spray plants. She moves about the house, then returns to the kitchen. Suddenly she bends over, grabs herself.

MAGGIE: It's like living with a stone at your centre. Emma? Emma? I wish they'd find you dead. Yes I do. I wish it would just be over. I wish I could bury you and it would just be finished. I want my life to start again. I'm sorry. I can't mourn you, I can't grieve. I've just become mean minded. Small and petty and mean minded. I resent everyone their life. I resent Renee on a holiday in California, soaking up the sun, swimming. I resent her happiness. I resent her children. I grudge her that she has John to make love to at night. I grudge her that I can't love anyone until I know where you are. I grudge everything. I'm sorry. Be dead. Be something. I can't stand it anymore. *(turns and waters the plants)*

MAGGIE goes out into the hall, presumably upstairs. RENEE comes in from the hall, carrying bags. Stares wildly around, as if expecting some terrible devastation. She looks wild, crazed. JOHN comes after her, carrying a polystyrene freezer container and a food hamper.

JOHN: Why'd you run like that, you crazy or something? You coulda fallen and hurt yourself.

RENEE: She's watered the plants.

JOHN: She tells me to come home the middle a our friggin' vacation and that's why? She's afraid her friggin' lesbian friend's gonna forget to water her friggin' plants?

RENEE: I was sick. I had to come home.

JOHN: She was sick. You are sick. You're crazy. I should have you put away in the funny farm. *(turns to go out, crosses to sliding doors)*

RENEE: Where're you going?

JOHN: To the car. To get the resta our stuff. You left a lot of junk in the car.

RENEE: Don't wake Joanie, I'll get Joanie. I'll carry Joanie in.

JOHN: She's awake, she come in after me . . . she's upstairs.

RENEE: *(goes to hall, calls)* Joanie?! Joanie?! You in?! You upstairs?! *(No answer. She calls.)* Dougie?! Are you in, did you come in?

JOHN: They're dead on their feet, driving all day 'n' all night like maniacs.

RENEE stands there as if she can't remember what they have come home for. She reaches out to a plant, touches its leaf. It is still alive.

RENEE: She took care of my plants.

JOHN: Ladybird ladybird
Fly away home,
Your house is on fire
An' your children alone. *(laughs)*

RENEE covers her ears.

JOHN: You disgust me. You're old. You're getting old. You fill me with disgust. I can't touch you, you make me want to throw up. *(turns and walks toward the sliding doors)*

MAGGIE comes in from the hall. RENEE gives a small scream. JOHN turns, stops.

RENEE: What are you doing here? What are you doing here!

MAGGIE: I was upstairs. I was watering your plants. What's happened? Has something happened?

RENEE: What did you say to them, what did you say?

MAGGIE: What? What?

RENEE: What did you say to my children?

MAGGIE: What? John?

JOHN comes back, shoves RENEE into a chair, gets her a drink, shoves it under her nose, forces her head back.

RENEE: *(drinks, chokes)* No. I don't want it.

JOHN: You're hysterical. Can you hear me? You're hysterical. We're halfway down the coast of California and she says we gotta come home. Ladybird, ladybird, fly away home . . .

RENEE: Stop it.

MAGGIE: Renee, what happened?

JOHN: Nothing happened.

RENEE: Nothing happened. We just drove and drove, farther and farther away. Away. We just kept on driving . . .(*laughs*) Now we're home.

MAGGIE: Was there an accident?

RENEE: My life is an accident. (*laughs again*)

JOHN: Drink that. Drink that all down.

RENEE: (*to MAGGIE*) Oh hate me, for god's sake, hate me.

MAGGIE: Oh Renee, I don't hate you. (*MAGGIE crosses to her and tries to hug her, but RENEE cannot bear her touch.*) I love you. You're my friend. I would have gone mad these months without you. You're my friend, my dear friend.

RENEE: No. No . . .(*sobs*)

MAGGIE: Why, why did you come home, what happened?

RENEE: Nothing. (*with terror*) Nothing happened. We just drove further and further away. I watched the signs going past . . . Sacramento . . . San Francisco . . . Carmel . . . I watched the signs going past . . .(*a long shuddering sigh*) I had to come home.

JOHN: She didn't like the signs. So she ruins a vacation. I guess it's the Change, I guess she's into the Change, you into the Change yet, Maggie?

RENEE: Why don't you check things out, John. Why don't you check things out. Maybe somebody's broken in. Maybe something's happened.

JOHN: (*small laugh*) Nothing's happened.

RENEE: You haven't checked your workshop, John, maybe something's gone, maybe something belongs to you is gone.

JOHN: Nothing's gone.

RENEE: Maybe it's gone.

JOHN: So, Maggie, sit down, have a drink, we haven't seen you in a long time, any word?

MAGGIE: What?

JOHN: Any word on Emma?

MAGGIE: You'd have heard first thing, John.

JOHN: Sure we would, sure we would, I know that. (*Small laugh. MAGGIE sits down beside RENEE. Looks at JOHN who goes to cupboard, pours a drink for MAGGIE.*) You get it out of her, Maggie, you're her best friend, you get it out of her, why she decides to ruin a perfectly good vacation. Here. (*Hands MAGGIE the drink; she takes it cautiously.*) What you two got going anyway, she can't leave you for a couple of weeks, what you two got going anyway, eh? (*laughs*) O don't give me that look, Renee, I heard about these intellectuals, they swing both ways, eh, Maggie, eh? You swing both ways, don't you?

MAGGIE: (*looking at RENEE who hasn't touched her drink*) Listen, are you okay? —If you want I can stay for a bit.

JOHN: Ooooh ho ho ho, oooo, I get it, I get it, I can take a hint, oooh ho, yes, I can take a hint, don't mind me, I'm leaving, I'm leaving. (*He goes to sliding doors. RENEE stares after him. Rigid.*) I know when I'm not wanted, I know when I am not wanted, yes sir. I'll leave you two girls together for girl talk, yes sir, I will leave you two girls together for a little old heart to heart.

MAGGIE: Renee? What is it?

JOHN: What is it, Renee, tell your best friend in the world, eh? Why don't you, eh Renee? She's your best friend in the world. Maggie, you should watch out, people who come between husband and wife get their face punched out sometimes. (*holds up hand*) Unh, oh, no no, just kidding, eh? Just kidding. You know the kids missed Disneyland? The kids missed Disneyland. We got all the way to Santa Barbara almost and she says we gotta turn back. "We gotta turn back, we gotta go home." (*laughs*)

MAGGIE: Well, I'm glad you're back, I missed you.

JOHN: Missed me, Maggie?

MAGGIE: Missed you both. Having you here. You know, I came over every day to water your plants. It was scary. I felt I had to come. I don't know why. I just felt I had to come and check things. It was a bit freaky.

JOHN: So.

He walks over to the cupboard and opens it. Takes out a couple of chocolate bars. Reaches into drinks cupboard, takes bottle of vodka. RENEE watches him. JOHN takes down a package of chips. RENEE watches him.

JOHN: Well, I got some stuff to do out in the workshop. (*goes to sliding doors, looks at RENEE, walks out, slides door to*)

MAGGIE: Listen, if you feel bad about what happened, before you left, don't—I've been a drain on you, I know. I've thought about it a lot while you've been gone. I'm too dependent on you, I know that, I'm going to be different. Listen, whatever the reason, I'm glad you're back. I missed you. (*RENEE turns and looks at her.*) What, what is it? Renee?

RENEE: You're a fool. You're a fool you stupid cunt. You disgust me.

MAGGIE: You're tired, you're exhausted, let me help you—

RENEE: Get out. You stupid whore. You cunt. Get out. (*starts to laugh and then sob*)

MAGGIE puts her arm around RENEE and tries to help her from the room. RENEE pushes her away and goes into hall.

Go to black.

Scene Six

Mid-October. On the fridge, children's drawings of witches and jack-o'-lanterns are held up with magnetic buttons. RENEE comes in. It is early dusk. She comes to the sliding doors and looks out. Now she turns and goes to the fridge, starts to get vegetables out of the bin. She gets a piece of meat and she begins to pound it with a wooden mallet. Seasons it, puts it into a casserole. Puts in onions. Looks up, holds herself, comes again to the sliding doors and looks out. Picks up the telephone and presses the intercom button. Waits. Looks again to the sliding doors. Waits. Presses down the receiver button.

RENEE: Hi. It's me. Just about to put the meat into the microwave, thought I'd . . .(*listens*) John— (*listens*) John, the last week or so you've bitched about everything being overdone or cooked too much, I'm just about ready to put this stuff into the microwave, I thought I'd give you plenty of . . . It's time to quit work! No, I did not. No, you did not. No. No, I never heard you tell me not to phone the shop. No. No. I told you, no. (*turns and stares out the sliding doors*) No, this isn't some new idea she's put into my head. I said, I haven't seen Maggie in weeks. John, I know you're busy out there, what I want to know is, what are you doing? You haven't shipped out a chesterfield in a month! —Okay, okay. I am minding my own business, I have to feed a family, don't I? Jenkins phoned again yesterday and said where was his armchair, that came in last August. You haven't even paid the hydro! I told you, Maggie hasn't even been here in . . . five weeks now. This is me, me, Renee talking. All I'm saying is, the dinner's going into the microwave, so could you be in here on time tonight? (*Lifts her finger off receiver button. Presses intercom button. Waits. Looks toward sliding doors. Waits.*) John? It's just me, I thought

I'd tell you, dinner's going into the microwave now. —I didn't think you'd mind just this once. Well, you haven't eaten your dinner the last few . . . all right, John. All right, all right, all right I won't, no I won't. I'm sorry. I'm . . . sorry.

Slowly she puts the receiver back onto the wall hook. Lifts receiver again. Dials three numbers. Puts receiver back onto hook. Puts casserole of meat into microwave. MAGGIE knocks at sliding doors. Slides them back.

MAGGIE: Hi.

RENEE: Oh. Hi.

MAGGIE: (*halfway in*) How are you?

RENEE: I'm all right. You?

MAGGIE: So so. —Well, just thought I'd see how you were, saw your light on . . .

RENEE: Want a drink?

MAGGIE: Well . . .

RENEE: He's out in the shop.

MAGGIE: Well, maybe a quick one.

RENEE: Guess you've been pretty busy—

MAGGIE: I've been pretty busy . . . (*They laugh. RENEE makes her a drink.*) I've missed you.

RENEE: Yeah. Well. It's just one of those things. (*hands her the drink*) We really don't have that much in common. I took a couple a courses but John's right, I'm not in your league.

MAGGIE: John's not always right, Renee.

RENEE: Yeah, well, that's another thing; you always saying stuff like that, it could break us up, you know? John and I. John and me, which is it anyway?

MAGGIE: (*looks at her drink, puts it down*) Yeah. Well. Guess I better be going. (*starts for sliding doors*)

RENEE: How . . . are things?

MAGGIE: Shitty. Oh, I get up, I move, I go to work, I lecture, I even make jokes. Time goes by. I don't hear her screaming anymore.

RENEE: What?

MAGGIE: Sometimes at night I thought I heard her scream.

RENEE: Stay and have your drink.

MAGGIE: Was that what it was, my buttin-sky stuff about John?

RENEE: Oh, you meant well . . .

MAGGIE: No I didn't. Maybe I didn't. Maybe what happened has made me so paranoid about men. I don't know.

RENEE: Only it came to a choice kind of, between you and him, he.

MAGGIE: (*breaks into a laugh*) Him. It's him, you had it right the first time, why don't you just relax, you'll be okay, you have a feel for language, you know.

RENEE: Do I?

MAGGIE: Yes. —You always pretend to be so stupid, Renee, it kind of pisses me off, if you want to know.

RENEE: Oh yes?

MAGGIE: Yes. I mean, if it's time for truth games, I might as well tell you, this habit you've got of putting yourself down all the time, and this invidious comparison stuff you're into about me, it really pisses me off.

RENEE: Invidious comparison. I don't know what that means.

MAGGIE: You know what it means. Look. If you wanted an education, a formal education, you could get one, what's stopping you? Don't put it off onto . . . no, I know what you're going to say . . . but this house practically runs itself and you could go in, even for day courses. John's always around anyway, you don't have to worry about Joanie and Dougie, there'd always be someone home for them.

RENEE: (*a shrill laugh*) You don't know what you're talking about.

MAGGIE: If you're that unhappy, leave him. Oh there I go again. Boy. Put my foot into it everytime, it's just, I can't stand seeing you take it from him, I just can't stand it, it's horrible, it's so degrading. —I mean, have you got the TV fixed yet? No, no? There you are, you see? You were begging him to let you get it fixed how long ago, and just because he's out in the shop day and night doesn't mean you have to go without TV for you and the kids, I mean why doesn't he let you watch his set in the shop? I mean, it's crazy the way you have to beg for everything?

RENEE: What?

MAGGIE: The way you have to beg for everything, the way you have to cringe and grovel, and *apologize* for every blessed thing, you think I didn't hear you apologizing for spending so much on Joanie's school shoes.

RENEE: What TV?

MAGGIE: Your TV, haven't you got it fixed yet?

RENEE: No, you said he's got a TV in the shop, what TV?

MAGGIE: The one he took in last summer. He's got it hooked up to your cable line. I know because he bragged to me, he didn't have to pay twice, he knew how to hook it up, said he could hook it up to Pay-TV with some aluminum foil.

RENEE: John's got a TV in the shop?

MAGGIE: Oh, I don't know. I'm out of line I guess. I'm sorry. I said to myself, Keep your mouth shut, don't say a word, and here we are, right into it again.

RENEE: I didn't know about the TV.

MAGGIE: Well, he's gotta be doing something in there, he's in there day and night, isn't he? I guess he watches the TV in there.

RENEE: We have a good marriage. You have no right to say anything about our marriage.

MAGGIE: You have a rotten marriage.

RENEE: Get out of here. I didn't ask you in. I curse the day you moved next door. I curse you.

MAGGIE: What is it, Renee, tell me what it is.

RENEE: We were happy until you came. We were happy.

MAGGIE: He treats you like shit.

RENEE: He's right about you, you're green with envy.

MAGGIE: The day I envy you a man like that prick—

RENEE: You're dying for it. (*MAGGIE laughs.*) Don't you dare laugh at me, you big shot . . . you think you're perfect—

MAGGIE: Oh go to hell, go to hell. I've missed you, I've missed you terribly.

RENEE: Last week, Dougie was late home from school. The bus came and he wasn't on it. I was watching from the window, and I saw the bus come and drop off the Fraser kids, but Dougie wasn't on the bus. Joanie was going to be late because she had band practice, so I knew she'd be late, but Dougie was supposed to be on the bus. I phoned the school and Mrs. Duncan had kept him late. —She said she didn't know he was supposed to come home on the bus. She said it was inexcusable of her. She apologized. —Dougie walked all the way home from school. He got here, he was half crying, he had run all the way the last part, he knew I'd be worried sick about him. He had run all the last part, he could hardly breathe.

MAGGIE: The terror.

RENEE: Yes. And that was just a few minutes. Less than 15 minutes before I got Mrs. Duncan on the phone. That was . . . and all these months, you . . . (*MAGGIE nods, holding herself in.*) It's true, I've always been jealous of you, it's true, you seemed to have it so good, you were so lucky, you were so free.

MAGGIE: (*stiffens although RENEE does not notice*) Fortune's child.

RENEE: (*unaware of the change*) Part of me was glad when you were brought down.

MAGGIE: That's the basis of most dramatic literature. They love it when Oedipus falls down, you know, they get a secret nasty thrill when they know he's slept with his mother. (*small laugh*)

RENEE steps away, realizes she's gone too far. The two women look at each other. The hostility reflares.

RENEE: Well, I wouldn't know, I don't have your advanced knowledge of dramatic literature.

MAGGIE: (*closes her eyes*) Oh shit. Here we go again. I've lost my child, Renee. I've lost my child. My child could be anywhere, terrible

things could be happening to her right now, while we fight out this old story about who's got the better education . . . I don't believe you sometimes.

RENEE: I don't believe *you* walk in here, you haven't even stopped by in five weeks—

MAGGIE: Jesus, the last time I was here you called me a cunt.

RENEE: You bust in here, you try to get between me and John, what've you got against John anyway?

MAGGIE: Let's not get started.

RENEE: You've got something against him, you've looked down on him from the first, you have, I can remember that first night, after we'd been talking for a couple of weeks, and I invited you over—

MAGGIE: Emma and me.

RENEE: (*small smile*) Isn't it *Emma and I?*

MAGGIE: (*stares at her*) No, actually, that was the objective case.

RENEE: Oh was it?

MAGGIE: Yes, it was. Personally, I don't very much give a good fuck about the objective case, but it comes naturally to me, while the ablative absolute does not.

RENEE: Oooh ho.

MAGGIE: You want to know what I've got against John, you really want to know? That night, that night when we had dinner together, he put you down for every single thing you did, he put you down and he smiled this small little complicit smile at me as if I'd understand why he was doing it. This small little you-and-me-babe smile at me.

RENEE: What kind of smile?

MAGGIE: You-and-me-Babe, we-know-the-kind-of-dumb-bitch-we've-got-here smile.

RENEE: No, that other word. I don't understand what you say! You do it on purpose!

MAGGIE: What word?

RENEE: You know what word! How am I supposed to go out into the world? I can't make it without a man! I can't, I don't have your chances.

MAGGIE: Shit shit shit, Renee, that's shit and you know it's shit, and I won't have this envy, this rotten fucking envy, I won't let it eat away at you and me, I won't, I won't! (*goes to her, but angrily, and puts her arms around RENEE*)

RENEE: You're trying to bust us up. (*tries to resist MAGGIE's embrace*) It's true what he says, you're just trying to get in between us, you're making me think things about him, it's you . . . (*starts to sob*) Oh god, oh god. (*MAGGIE is holding on grimly.*) Oh god, oh god, oh I can't bear it. I can't stand it, Maggie, I can't live . . . (*buries her face in MAGGIE's breast*)

JOHN appears at sliding doors, watches. Opens the doors. MAGGIE starts, begins to draw back guiltily, then reaffirms her embrace of RENEE, and stares defiantly at JOHN. RENEE, at first, is unaware. JOHN comes in and stands silently, watching. Grins. RENEE, after a moment, senses his presence, and moves away. MAGGIE looks at her in fury.

RENEE: It's almost ready. Dinner. —I'll get you a beer.

She goes to fridge and gets JOHN a beer, opens it. Gets a glass. MAGGIE stands still, looks at JOHN. He grins at MAGGIE. RENEE holds out glass of beer to JOHN, who doesn't take it. RENEE puts it down on table beside the place setting.

MAGGIE: I'd better go then. (*Comes toward sliding doors, but JOHN is in her way. She pauses.*) Excuse me.

JOHN raises his hand abruptly. MAGGIE winces and cowers.

JOHN: (*laughs*) What's the matter, Maggie, I was just going to take off my cap. Dja think I was going to hitya? She thought I was going to give her a knuckle sandwich, Renee. Didja see her? Jeezus, Maggie thought I was goingta give her an old knuckle sandwich, the old one-two, what's the matter, Maggie, got a guilty conscience? I was just taking off my cap, see?

MAGGIE: Just let me get by, please.

JOHN: I ain't stoppin' ya, Maggie, who's stoppin' ya? You can get by.

RENEE: Let her get by, John.

JOHN: Another country heard from— another cuntree heard from, get it, Maggie? You're the big professor, you should like wordplay, another cunt tree, get it?

MAGGIE: Why do you always do that, John? Talk like a moron when I'm here.

JOHN: (*laughs*) Do I, talk like a moron, Maggie?

MAGGIE: Yes. You speak perfectly good English and then I come over and suddenly it's Dogpatch Time.

JOHN: Dogpatch Time, eh? That's pretty good, ain't it, Renee? Dogpatch Time.

RENEE: Let her go, John. Just let her go.

JOHN moves suddenly aside, with a sweep of his cap.

MAGGIE: I know you, John, I know you from when I was a kid in Winnipeg, there was this boy there, Norman Stewart, he used to grab the little ones and give them an Indian Wrist Burn. (*exits*)

JOHN turns and watches her go. RENEE, behind him, closes her eyes. JOHN very casually closes the sliding doors. Crosses to table and sits down.

JOHN: Well? You said supper was going to be ready.

RENEE: (*with an effort, goes to microwave and gets out the food*) Oh. I'm sorry, I forgot the vegetables.

She puts in the vegetable dish. Punches the computer. Puts the casserole on the table.

JOHN: (*politely*) No beer?

RENEE goes to table and gets the beer and lifts it toward him.

JOHN: Thank you. (*He refuses to take it. RENEE is forced to put it down beside him on the table beside his hand.*) Well. So you and your friend have made up, eh? That's good. I like for you to have friends. Bosom buddies again eh? (*small laugh, lifts casserole dish*) My my, what's this?

RENEE: Lasagna.

JOHN: Lasagna. My my. Lasagna. What'd the kids have?

RENEE: They ate before.

JOHN: I didn't ask when they ate, Renee, I asked what did they eat? There's a grammatical distinction. There's a semantic distinction, which I am sure your dear friend Maggie could elucidate upon. What did they eat, the children?

RENEE: Peanut butter sandwiches.

JOHN: Peanut butter sandwiches. And I get lasagna. Excuse me, Renee, but this is not really anything so fancy as lasagna, this is hamburger and macaroni. No. Come here and look at it, Renee, this is hamburger and macaroni.

RENEE: (*as bell dings*) The vegetables are ready.

JOHN: It never fails to amaze me how you cannot understand what I am saying to you. Did I inquire about the state of the vegetables? Did I? Did I.

RENEE: No.

JOHN: No, I asked you to kindly step over here and look at this dish, which you claim is lasagna. Step over here, Maggie. (*RENEE crosses to table.*) Bend over and look at it, Maggie.

RENEE: Please.

JOHN: Look at it, Maggie.

RENEE: My name is Renee.

JOHN grabs her by the neck and pushes her face into the casserole.

JOHN: That is shit. This is shit, that's what it is, you give me shit to eat, you filthy bitch.

RENEE: You don't give me any money! (*backs away, teeth chattering, but ferocious*) You never give me any money, that's all I got in the freezer, that's why the kids don't even get hamburger, and you got a TV in the workshop!

JOHN: What?

RENEE: You heard me, you got a TV in the shop. (*grabs a tea towel and tries to wipe her face*)

JOHN: I got a what?

RENEE: (*standing against the sink*) If you touch me, I'll do something.

JOHN: I don't think I heard you right, Renee. I got a what in the shop?

RENEE: A TV.

JOHN: Oh? How you know that, Renee?

RENEE: I had to go in today. To get a washer.

JOHN: Oh yes? A washer? A washer for what?

RENEE: For the sink. For the bathroom sink. The tap in there.

JOHN: A washer. For the bathroom sink.

RENEE: I don't need to bother you for a washer put in, I can put one in myself. I don't need to worry you for that.

JOHN: Which tap is that, Renee?

RENEE: The one in the bathroom. It's leaking.

JOHN: I gathered it was the one in the bathroom. You told me that before.

RENEE: The one in the shower. The right one.

JOHN: The right one?

RENEE: I mean, hot, the hot one.

JOHN pushes back his chair. RENEE jumps.

JOHN: (*crosses to her, smiles*) Don't give me any of your lies, Renee. You weren't in the shop.

RENEE: Yes, I was. I was.

JOHN: No, Renee, you were not.

RENEE: I saw it.

JOHN: (*backhands her casually*) No, Renee.

RENEE: (*falls to her knees*) O don't oh don't oh don't . . . the kids'll hear again . . . oh god . . . (*JOHN kicks her in the stomach.*) Oh don't John . . . I'm sorry . . . oh god . . .

JOHN: (*pulls her up by the hair*) Okay Renee? Okay? Now you tell me the truth, Renee. I have to do this when you lie to me. You know that. I have to hurt you when you lie to me, Renee, now you tell me.

He knees her in the chest. Catches her as she falls back, keeps her upright.

RENEE: Maggie.

JOHN: Ah, Maggie told you. Yeah. She saw me take it in.

RENEE: It isn't fair.

JOHN: What? Did I hear you make a comment?

RENEE: The kids don't have TV.

JOHN: You're an old whore, Renee, and I can do what I like with you and you'll take it, because you're an old whore and I'm the last chance you've got for a real man. That's true, isn't it? Renee?

RENEE: I'm not an . . . oooh.

JOHN: Yes, you are. Say it. (*pulls her hair back*)

RENEE: —I'm . . . an old—

JOHN: Whore.

RENEE: Whore . . . and   you're   the last . . . chance I got—

JOHN: For a real man.

RENEE: . . . a real man . . .

JOHN: Now, Renee, I'm going to have to punish you, you know that, don't you? You know I've got to punish you now, don't you? Yes. Okay. Take it out. Go on. Take it out. (*RENEE sobs. JOHN pulls her hair backwards until her face is close to his crotch.*) Go on, Renee, don't make it hard on yourself. (*laughs*) Make it hard

on me. (*RENEE reaches up and unzips him.*)
That's a good girl. That's a good girl.

Go to black.

Scene Seven

Hallowe'en night. The workshop.

A very small area of the workshop is visible. We can see a bit of the work bench. The tools hanging on a perforated board. Nothing is out of place. There is a plastic filing cabinet arrangement for nuts, bolts, etc. Immediately to one side of the work bench and lathe is a piece of the floor, painted a bright blue. On top of this floor area are plastic jugs filled with various fluids: oil for wood, paint thinner, etc.

Slowly, the lights are brought up on RENEE looking at the area, from the penumbra. She looks at the workshop. She cannot see a TV. She is wearing a housedress, and has made herself up carefully: neat and clean and ordinary looking.

She comes into the light. Stands in front of the lathe. She touches the lathe, the tools, the filing cabinet of small items. Turns away, then turns back. She looks at the plastic jugs on the square of blue painted floor. The floor is painted a slightly brighter blue than the surrounding area. She turns away again. Can't think why she is bothered. Starts away. Stops. Turns back. Something else was there before. What was it? She looks around. Yes, something else had stood there. She goes over to the jugs. She bends to lift one. It does not come away. It is glued to the piece of flooring which she sees now is a wooden plywood slab, fitted into the floor.

Behind her a silhouette . . . the figure of a man, as if in a doorway. RENEE straightens up. Does not turn.

JOHN: (*comes in*) Looking for something?

RENEE: You know that tarnish-free stuff? I was looking for that tarnish-free stuff.

JOHN: Why would I have tarnish-free stuff?

RENEE: I needed it for my rings. (*holds out her hands*)

JOHN: Gold doesn't tarnish.

RENEE: Not my wedding ring, this ring, the one Dougie gave me.

JOHN: The one Dougie gave you.

RENEE: It's turning my finger green! (*laughs, shows him*)

JOHN: (*refuses to look at her hand*) I don't like you messing around in the workshop.

RENEE: Where's the TV?

JOHN: What?

RENEE: Where's the TV, John?

JOHN: I took it back. I was watching it too much, I wasn't getting my work done. — Listen, don't worry, I'll get the kids' TV fixed. I'll take it into the shop today. Is that what's bugging you?

RENEE: Is that Jenkins' armchair?

JOHN: Oh yeah. I had to wait for this part.

RENEE: You had a nightmare again last night.

JOHN: We got a good life, Renee, you and me, we got a good life for us 'n' the kids. We got our ups and downs but we're a lucky family, you know that? We got our health. I got this little business, it'll start picking up again, I know I'm good at what I do, I'm good with my hands, the thing is, you see, I'm really like everybody else. That's what you don't understand about me, Renee. I'm just like anybody else. I know you judge me, yes, you judge me, you have always judged me! —But I am just like any man. Just like any man. I have my pride, Renee, you can't undermine a man's pride in his manhood, that's what you have done.

RENEE: How did I do that?

JOHN: A lot of couples, they can't talk things over like we can, they have a communication problem, we don't have a communication problem, we talk, you and I. —A man sometimes has problems that way, that's all. It's quite natural. You ask any psychologist.

RENEE: I am not complaining about that, have I ever said anything about that?

JOHN: You're not an educated woman, Renee, you don't understand these things, a man goes through many stages in his life. Many stages in his life. There's a book called that: *Stages in Life's Way* or something. By Kierkegaard. Have you read *Stage in Life's Way*, by Kierkegaard? Did you realize that if God exists, Renee, it is our duty to deny him? —Have you read Heidegger? Have you read Jaspers? I'm an educated man. I've had to educate myself. You know Dostoyevsky once said that only if you could rape a 10-year-old girl could you say you were truly free. Free of all morality. It's conventional morality that holds us back, Renee. I married you although I knew you were a conventional woman.

RENEE: Why would anyone want to?

JOHN: I married you knowing full well there would be areas of my life you could not enter, areas in my life you could not understand, but you married me, you took an oath, for richer or poorer, for better or worse, we are one flesh, Renee. Why would anyone want to what?

RENEE: Rape a 10-year-old girl?

JOHN: You don't understand the concept, Renee. Listen, listen, you know what Maggie said that time about Emma—

RENEE: Emma?

JOHN: You know what she said, how Emma believed what Anne Frank believed, how she used to say those lines ". . . because in spite of everything, I still believe that people are really good at heart"? You know. Maggie quoted that to us, she said Emma believed that. But listen! Maggie said those lines were the last lines in the book. —They're not. No. And I've heard that from other people too, people say that all the time, that those're the last lines in the book, but they're not. You know what Anne Frank talks about at the end of the book? No, those lines come earlier, a couple of chapters, I think, no, what she's talking about at the end of the book is how she can't be good, how she knows she can't ever really be a good person. People don't like to know that Anne Frank knew it, and what she says at the end of the book is she could be good, yes, she could be, "if only there weren't any people living in the world." Something like that, I haven't maybe got it exact: I could be good if ". . . there weren't any other people living in the world." That's what it says at the very end of that book. —You see? Do you see, Renee?

RENEE: She wasn't a good person? Anne Frank wasn't a good person? So it was okay what they did to her?

JOHN: It makes me tired sometimes, Renee, to try to make you understand a philosophical concept.

RENEE: You're trying to say Anne Frank wasn't a good person?

JOHN: That's right. Nobody is, Renee, that's what I am trying to convey to you.

RENEE: So she can be raped?

JOHN: What? What are you talking about, Anne Frank wasn't raped.

RENEE: You said this guy said you should rape a 10-year-old girl.

JOHN: Oh, no, that was just an example of the act that would be a defiance . . . would spit in the face of God, which is the duty of a free person. You see, Abraham should have given God the finger. You know. You have heard of Abraham, Renee.

RENEE: Yes.

JOHN: When he took up poor little Isaac to the mountaintop, and God said "Kill your only son," and you can imagine how difficult that was, Sarah was 99 when she had him, how old was Abraham? I don't know, who cares, don't get me off the track, the point of all this is, Abraham should have refused to obey God.

RENEE: But there was a ram in the thicket.

JOHN: What—? Yes, but how did Abraham know that?

RENEE: He had faith.

JOHN: (laughs) A lot of good that did Anne Frank. Listen, if you want to know the truth about Emma, that was her trouble, she believed in people, she trusted people, Maggie taught her to trust people, that was her trouble. In a way, the person who teaches her that lesson is a saviour, an educator, yes, an educator, she could be grateful the rest of her life. Even Moses said you should rape the young girls. In Numbers. You didn't know that, did you? Oh yes, when they were going against some tribe, he said kill off all the older women, the ones who are dirty already. That means the ones who have done it with men. But then take the pure girls for yourself. Moses understood that that's what women really want. That's what you want, isn't it, Renee?

RENEE: I thought I did.

JOHN: Oh you did. You loved the rough and tumble, admit it.

RENEE: Yes. I admit it.

JOHN: Then you think you're a married woman, you get all respectable and you pretend you don't want it. But I remember.

RENEE: Only, it wasn't like it is now.

JOHN: Sure it is. —You and I, we get along, Renee. You can't follow me everywhere, that's only natural, you don't have the education, and to tell you the truth, you're just not as bright as I am, but that's okay. I'll look after you. —Only. Renee? Don't come into the workshop anymore, okay? Okay, baby? I like to keep things a certain way. Anything you want you ask me for it. I'll get it. In fact, hey wait a minute—where is that tarnish-free? I did have it, I had it for something on that armoire I was doing—just a moment. Aha! (gets the tarnish-free bottle and hands it to her) You were right, kiddo, this time you were absolutely right, it was here all along!

RENEE: I can't believe anybody said that, rape a 10-year-old girl, I want to read that book where he says that.

JOHN: Okay. I'll get it for you. It's down . . . in the basement.

RENEE: Where?

JOHN: Downstairs in the basement, in that box my mother sent over. I'll get it for you, but it's really a sort of metaphor you know. It doesn't mean literally.

RENEE: You took back the TV eh?

JOHN: Yes. Months ago.

RENEE: Okay. (turns to go)

JOHN: Don't worry. I'll take the one in the house in, I'll take it in this aft. The kids'll have it tonight.

RENEE: It's Hallowe'en tonight. They'll be out tonight.

JOHN: Hallowe'en eh? Jesus, time flies, doesn't it, it's quite warm still though, Indian summer eh?

RENEE: Yes. (*pauses*) That'd be nice though, John, if you could do that, for the kids. —I miss it too, the TV.

JOHN: Okay okay. A promise is a promise. Okay?

RENEE: Okay. (*goes out*)

JOHN looks after her. Turns and looks down at the jugs on the plywood slab. Now he looks out after RENEE.

Go to black.

Scene Eight

Hallowe'en night. The kitchen. RENEE is preparing bowls of candies, apples, pennies, for the children. From the front room the sound of the TV can be heard.

RENEE: (*briskly*) Dougie? Joanie? Now you can listen to that TV anytime. —You're going out tonight, do you hear me? I didn't put hours into those costumes for nothing. Now you get ready. I'm coming in and turning that TV off in 10 seconds. I'm not kidding. 10 . . . 9 . . . 8 . . . 7 . . .6 . . . 5 . . . 4 . . . 3 . . . 2 . . . 1! — (*The sound of the TV goes off. She turns back to get the bowls. As she goes out into the hall the ring of the doorbell is heard.*) See? They've started already!

Door opens. Children's voices: "Trick or treat!"

RENEE: (*off*) Well! Don't you look horrible! Oooh! You scare me sick. Oooh . . . what a face! Here, please take it and go away . . . (*Laughter from children. Door shuts. She reappears in kitchen.*) Oh I forgot the pennies for Unicef. Joanie? Joanie, are the kids still taking pennies for Unicef? Joanie, answer me when I talk to you. (*goes into hall for a moment, comes back*) I thought they were.

She looks at telephone. Picks it up. Then, puts it down firmly.

Okay. I'm coming. (*goes out; off*) Yes, that's good, yes, oh that bag's big enough, oh all right. (*comes back to kitchen, gets a big plastic bag, takes it out to hall*) Now I want you two sticking together, no, Dougie, I do not want you leaving your sister, No, listen to me! I don't care, you are not to leave your sister. Joanie? I am not listening to any of that, things're going to be different around here from now on, I'm not taking any lip from you, no! And back here by nine at the latest. Joanie, do you understand me? All right. All right. Yes, you look lovely. Yes. I love you. Take care. Don't get sick! (*Door opens.*) Listen, don't bother Mrs. Webb, she's sick. Yes. She's dying. So don't go up to her place, okay? Okay.

Door shuts. RENEE comes back into the kitchen. Sits at the table. Gets up, goes to stove, puts on kettle. Doorbell rings. She goes out. Door opens.

Hello! Don't you look wonderful! Here you are.

Children's voices. "Trick or treat!" Door shuts. RENEE comes back. Sits at table. Stares out through the sliding doors. Kettle sings. She gets up and turns it off. She doesn't make tea. Stares out the sliding doors. Doorbell rings. She almost doesn't respond. Then does. We hear door open: "Trick or treat!"

Oh my! My goodness, oh that's really ugly, Bennie. Oh I'm sorry, it's not Bennie, I thought maybe it was Bennie Fraser from down the street, but you can't be Bennie, you're too disgusting.

Laughter. Door shuts. She comes back and stares out the sliding doors. Laughs. Goes to the telephone.

(*on telephone*) This is Mrs. John Gifford. 1600 Ashcroft Road. My husband is going to commit suicide. He's in his workshop. He's locked himself in with a gun. —1600 Ashcroft Road. That's just off the highway. A sort of lane. A cul-de-sac. Never mind. You just turn off the highway about five miles from the park, going east. 298-6009. Twenty minutes ago. Yes he did.

Hangs up the receiver. Goes and sits at the table. Folds her hands and rests them on the table. Stares out the sliding doors. MAGGIE appears at the sliding doors. RENEE starts, then sees who it is. MAGGIE knocks tentatively, then opens the doors.

MAGGIE: Hi! I thought I'd come help. I brought some stuff. (*She has some Hallowe'en goodies with her in a bag. She goes to RENEE's cupboards and takes down bowls to put her stuff in.*) Listen. I've got an apology to make. Listen, Renee, I'm sorry. I think I set you up for something. I think when I left here the other night I got him mad and I knew he'd take it out on you. It's been bugging the hell out of me. I don't even know why I did it. I knew he'd take it out on you. He did, didn't he? (*Doorbell rings.*) Oh let me get it. I put out all the lights at my place. (*goes out into hall*)

Door opens: "Trick or treat!"

(*off*) Hi! Oh my! Oh what a gruesome pair! Oh Jeez, Renee, you should see these two! Oh where did you get *that!* Yuck.

Laughter. Door shuts. RENEE sits staring at the sliding doors, her hands clasped.

MAGGIE: (*comes back into the kitchen*) At first I thought I couldn't stand Hallowe'en and then I thought, Oh hell, I'll just go over to Renee's. Are the kids collecting for Unicef this year?

RENEE: Mmm-hmm.

MAGGIE: He did take it out on you, didn't he? And I knew it. Jesus, I'm such a shit.

RENEE: (*small laugh*) You did me a favour. Now he'll do anything for me. I've got something on him, now he can't do enough for me, he got the TV fixed.

MAGGIE: Oh. That's good. I guess. What did you have to pay for it?

RENEE: (*small laugh*) Plenty. (*Doorbell rings.*) Too much.

MAGGIE: (*going to the hall*) Let me get this one, eh?

RENEE: Too fucking much.

Children's voices: "Trick or treat!"

MAGGIE: (*off*) Ooooh . . . You look wonderful. Just beautiful. My goodness. Oh you're a real stunner. Does your mother know you're out?

RENEE makes an hysterical sound. The first break she's made.

MAGGIE: (*off*) There you are. Bye now. (*Door shuts. MAGGIE comes back to kitchen.*) God, they're so cute. *Walpurgisnacht.* All Saints' Eve. How we make the horrible ordinary. How we transform it, make it comic and cuddly. Human beings!

RENEE: Wal what?

MAGGIE: *Walpurgisnacht* . . . it means night of the witches. Something like that.

RENEE: Oh.

MAGGIE: Night of the female bitches. Oh the old chthonic underpinnings of this society . . . I love Hallowe'en really. I always did, as a child. We don't really have enough times to let go . . . ritual times of release . . . I guess Christmas is the time we really let go . . . remember how drunk we got last Christmas? . . . how disgusted Emma was with us?

RENEE: I remember John kissed you, under the mistletoe.

MAGGIE: Yes.

RENEE: You seemed to enjoy it.

MAGGIE: Well, you can be attracted to a man . . .

RENEE: Then you got into this thing about open mortgages.

MAGGIE: Oh yes, jesus. (*Doorbell rings.*) You want to go?

RENEE shakes her head. MAGGIE goes into hall. Opens door: "Trick or treat."

Aw . . . aw, Renee, you should see these ones . . . there's a ghost and a skeleton and a monster mummy . . . is that what you are, a monster mummy? Oh my . . . here you go . . . Bye now. Bye. (*Door shuts. MAGGIE returns, shakes her head.*) Normalization of our deepest terrors. That's part of it.

RENEE: You started in about how you had this open mortgage and John didn't know what you were talking about. And he said he'd paid off more than half of the house and you said how long had he owned it and he said 10 years and you said if he didn't have an open mortgage that would probably be impossible. And he got out the contract and you showed him, he hadn't been paying off the . . . what did you call it . . . the principal? He hadn't been paying off the principal at all, he'd just been paying off the interest, keeping just ahead of it really, and you said unless he got himself an open mortgage he couldn't pay off at his own rate, he was at the mercy of the mortgage company, and he was furious with you, did you know that? And he went down to check it out and you were right, and he couldn't even get an open mortgage, there weren't any and he said you must have done something fast, no, pulled a fast one to get an open mortgage, and then you came over and he said, Show me, and you did, you showed him. —God he hated you for that. And every month he would sign the damn cheque and he would figure it out, how much off the principal and it was only 18 dollars or something, it would drive him crazy. And then you bought that chesterfield. —I think that's when he started to go down.

MAGGIE: Go down . . . what is it, Renee?

RENEE: Oh yes, he started slacking off on his work, you know, and he spent so much time out in the shop. But nothing was really getting done. Oh everything was tidy. He organized everything. He spent hours, days, organizing screws and bolts and stuff. It was crazy. That was about February. The thing was, I always knew about the shop, it was in the house description when we got the place, so I always knew.

Doorbell rings. RENEE gets up and goes out to hall. Door opens. Children's voices: "Trick or treat!"

RENEE: Here you are.

MAGGIE gets herself a drink from cupboard. Gets ice cubes from fridge. Sound of door closing.

RENEE: Get me one too, would you?

MAGGIE: Sure. (*makes her a drink*) You're in a mood tonight.

RENEE: Night of bitches. (*small laugh*)

MAGGIE: I don't get what you said just before, about the house description. You said something and I didn't quite—

RENEE: Tell me about Emma.

MAGGIE: What?

RENEE: No, you think you know someone, you live beside them for a few years, but you don't know them, tell me about Emma, who was she?

MAGGIE: Emma was a 12-year-old girl. She hated it when I got the divorce. The sun rose and set on Graham. It didn't matter what I said or how I felt, and the truth is, Graham isn't a bad man, I just didn't want him anymore. And, and, and, she was religious . . . she had this big religious streak . . . probably connected with puberty . . . she prayed for people . . . she believed everyone has good in them . . . I don't know, I probably encouraged that . . . we had a talk once and I said if there's a choice . . . and you could choose between the one who fools and the one who's fooled, it's better to choose the one who's fooled, because then you've put your bet on humanity, and that is like inertia . . . it starts something . . . people respond to trust . . . oh god, I may have made her a walking target for some creep.

RENEE: How would you describe me, if somebody asked, if I were dead or something and somebody asked?

MAGGIE: (sips drink) Well. I'd say, you were my friend. Your name was Renee, short for Maureen, Gifford. You'd been married once before, had two kids. Were raped once. Met John, married him, but I guess that's just data isn't it? Well, I'd say you had a good sense of humour, and a quick wit, but you were frustrated, you felt inadequate about your education, you felt inferior to other people, and it niggled at you because you knew if you had a chance you'd be okay. —No, I'd say you were a woman torn between things. Torn. Not knowing which way to go, and caught in the middle.

RENEE: Is that what you'll say?

MAGGIE: Well, it was a bit off the cuff, I'm sure I could work up something better if I had to do your eulogy. I'd say, Renee was a good friend to me.

RENEE: Is that what you'll say.

MAGGIE: You planning on going somewhere?

RENEE: In the end, we're all just part of someone else's scenario, aren't we? I'm real to you as the neighbour who stuck by you when your daughter went missing. That's what it comes to, I'm just a character in your scenario. Someone you tried to help out, because she wasn't liberated. Someone who had a yen for education but was "torn."

MAGGIE: Well, you asked for it quick. I . . . you mean more to me than that.

RENEE: But even with Emma, in the end it's not Emma who's real to you, it's what you said wrong to her, what you did wrong, that's what's real . . .

MAGGIE: Oh Emma is real. —Oh yes. Emma is real. Although sometimes now I can't remember how her faced looked. She had a mole right here (indicates thigh) . . . I used to notice it when I did her diapers . . . and then of course in the last years she's been so modest, she never let me see her naked . . . I never saw it . . . Sometimes I think her god wants me to curse him and die. But I won't, I won't, won't give her god that satisfaction, won't admit her god exists. Not even to curse him. A twist on Job. But you're right—she's becoming somebody in my *scenario*. Jesus I hate words like that.

RENEE: (drinks) I have all these vocabulary entries from my one venture into higher education.

MAGGIE: Oh, when your child is taken from you the world ought to end. The world ought to end. I ought to have died from the pain of it. (Takes out pack of cigarettes and lights one. RENEE reaches over to the cupboard and pulls out an ashtray for her.) That's what's so surprising, I went on living. It's not as though I had hope left. No, it's not as though I have hope left. Not now. I think, by the summer, I knew she had to be dead. She would have called me. One night, that was the night you came back. I came over here to water your plants. I thought I heard her calling me, I think she must have died that night. She felt so close.

RENEE: Do you hate the person?

MAGGIE: There's a line in the Bible, something about, whoever hurts a child, better he should have a millstone around his neck and be cast into a pond or something. I guess I think that about him. Can you imagine, living with that, having done that, all your life? You'd be better off dead.

RENEE: What if it's a woman?

MAGGIE: A woman? No, it couldn't be a woman.

RENEE: Why not? Why not. Women are equal to men, aren't they?

MAGGIE: No, a woman couldn't hurt a child like that.

RENEE: I thought you were the big women's libber.

MAGGIE: No, it wouldn't be a woman. A woman would feel what it was like. She would feel . . . empathy. No. No woman would do that to a child. To another woman.

RENEE gives a small laugh. Doorbell rings.

MAGGIE: (*hesitates*) Want me to get that?

RENEE: Okay.

MAGGIE goes out to the door. Door opens. Murmur of male voices.

MAGGIE: (*re-enters*) It's the Mounties.

RENEE: What do they say?

MAGGIE: They want to talk to you. Oh jesus, the kids!

RENEE: (*gets up slowly, stands there*) You see what they want.

MAGGIE goes back into hall. Murmur of her voice and male voice.

MAGGIE: Mrs. Gifford asked me to take a message.

RCMP: Well, we've been out to the workshop, it was open, but there's no one inside.

MAGGIE: The workshop? Are the kids in the workshop?

RCMP: No, it was Mr. Gifford she was worried about, I understand.

MAGGIE: Mr. Gifford?

RCMP: Mrs. Gifford put in a call to us about half an hour ago, but we've checked and there's no one in the shop. The lights are on but there's no one around. Actually, maybe she should lock up, it's Hallowe'en and the kids get up to things on Hallowe'en.

MAGGIE: (*comes back into kitchen*) They say there's nobody in the shop.

RENEE: I phoned the police. I told them I thought he was going to kill himself in the shop.

MAGGIE: What? My god, what? Renee.

RENEE: That's what I told them. What are they doing now?

MAGGIE: They've gone.

RENEE: Gone! They can't go. Tell them to go back! (*gets up, grabs MAGGIE*) Go on, tell them to go back!

MAGGIE: But he's not there!

RENEE: (*runs out into hall*) He's there! (*Door opens. Shuts. She comes back.*) They've gone. They drove away. (*starts to rock herself back and forth*) I want you to know . . . I loved him . . . I loved him. (*reaches for the telephone, dials*) Yes, this is Mrs. Gifford again. Yes, I called you before. Your men have just left. They were here and they just left. Get them back. No, stop them, and get them back. No, my husband's there. He's there. No, there's a trap door in the workshop. There's a room, under the shop. Yes, there's a sort of air raid shelter under the shop. He's got another room down below. — It's a plywood slab painted blue. There are jugs of stuff on top of it. They're glued. They stay on the slab when you pull it up. It's a secret room. It's on the house description. Yes. Yes. —Thank you. Yes, I'll hold. (*does not turn*)

MAGGIE is staring at her. Puts down her drink. Gets up slowly. Turns and looks out toward us, through the sliding doors.

RENEE: Yes, yes? John Gifford. Yes. Yes. Yes, that one, Mrs. Benton lives next door. Yes. —Yes, yes, it's a secret bunker or something. A plywood slab, painted blue. There're jugs of stuff, turpentine or something, on top, but they're glued down, so when you pull up the slab they don't fall off.

MAGGIE: (*turns and looks at RENEE*) I hope you live a long time, Renee. I hope you have a long long life.

RENEE: Forgive me.

MAGGIE: Never.

She turns and goes to the sliding doors, slides them open, and runs out into the night toward the workshop.

RENEE: Yes. Yes, I'll hold on.

Dim spot on RENEE's face, hold briefly, then go to black.

THE IDLER
IAN WEIR

Ian Weir's professional stage career has been closely tied to the New Play Centre. Born in 1956 in Durham, N.C., he was raised in Kamloops, B.C., where his teenage version of *Robin Hood* was produced by Tom Kerr's Western Canada Youth Theatre. Weir moved to Vancouver in 1978, earning a B.A. in English from University of British Columbia and later an M.A. from the University of London. In 1979 he began selling radio plays to the CBC and BBC, among them *Sacking*, a play about Alaric the Visigoth and Attila the Hun. Though Weir's *Gildengrim the Great* was given a staged reading at the New Play Centre's 1982 du Maurier Festival, and an adaptation of one of his CBC plays, *Oedipus Gunslinger*, was produced at Seattle's Empty Space Theater in 1985, he remained essentially a radio dramatist until the New Play Centre production of *The Idler* in 1987.

The success of his first full-length stage play prompted Weir to begin writing directly for the theatre. The result has been New Play Centre premieres of *The Delphic Orioles* (1988), a comic drama about a graduate student baseball team, and *Bloody Business* (1990), a comedy-thriller about Dracula in the Okanagan. Weir has also written episodes of "Lies from Lotus Land," "Beachcombers" and "Northwood" for television, and a novel for young people, *The Video Kid* (1988). His syndicated humour column appears in eighteen newspapers across Canada.

The Idler began life on CBC radio, making the transformation to stage play via workshops with the New Play Centre's Paul Mears, who has directed each of Weir's three NPC premieres. The play was based on a newspaper article about a father's grudging admiration for his educated sons who were all on welfare, none of them doing anything formally "useful." Like Weir's other stage plays, *The Idler* takes a comic view of self-delusion, the crassness of modern life, and the personal myths we create to help sustain our sense of dignity and worth. Citing it as one of Vancouver's ten best shows of the decade, *Vancouver Sun* critic Lloyd Dykk wrote: "In the Eighties, when it seemed that everybody was prosperous and enthralled to the notion that they were immortal, it became important to hear reminders to the contrary . . . . Ian Weir made that contrary figure funny, touching, and heroically his own man. You felt the pain of the have-nots." *The Idler* won Vancouver's 1988 Jessie Richardson Award for best new play, and has since been produced by Western Canada Theatre in Kamloops, Toronto's Theatre Plus, and the Resource Centre for the Arts in St. John's.

The Idler was first presented by the New Play Centre at the Waterfront Theatre on September 18, 1987, with David Marr in the title role of J.J. Davenport, Duncan Fraser as Wilfred Grimshaw, Kim Kondrashoff as Guy, Ted Cole as Bobby and Murray, Norma Matheson as Susan, and Wayne Yorke as Jason. It was directed by Paul Mears and designed by Ken MacDonald with lighting by Gerald King.

David Marr as J.J., Duncan Fraser as Grimshaw, and Norma Matheson as Susan in the New Play Centre production of *The Idler*. Photo by Martin Keeley.

THE IDLER

CHARACTERS

J.J. DAVENPORT, 30

WILFRED GRIMSHAW, early 60s

GUY, late 20s

BOBBY, early 20s★

MURRAY, his twin★

SUSAN, early 20s

JASON, late 20s

(★ It is intended that BOBBY and MURRAY be played by the same actor.)

SCENE

Vancouver. The present.

SET

The set can (and probably should) be minimal, but the playing area must be fluid, and be capable of suggesting three separate locales. ONE is the squalid apartment shared by J.J. and GRIMSHAW: a desk, a couple of chairs, and two entrances—one leading to the outside hallway, and one leading to an off-stage bedroom. TWO is the living room of the ramshackle house shared by GUY, BOBBY and MURRAY: a chesterfield, an armchair and two entrances — a front door, and a door leading to the rest of the house. THREE is an open space which needs to serve (at various times) as the Sunshine Cafeteria, the beach, the pub of the Blackwater Hotel, and a sea-cliff.

In the original production this was effectively facilitated by conflating the two primary playing areas. The "core" of the J.J./GRIMSHAW apartment was a slightly raised platform (with a writing-desk) upstage centre, but the scenes in the apartment spilled over into (and utilized the same furniture as) the space representing the living room of the house. In other words, the two living areas shared the same central portion of the stage, while a table downstage right served as both the cafeteria and the pub, and an open area downstage left served as the beach and the cliffs. All of this was set against a backdrop of whimsically cockeyed cut-outs of ramshackle urban buildings, which served admirably to establish the slightly off-centre reality of the play itself.

As far as possible, the movement between the scenes should also be fluid. Rather than blackouts (except where indicated or absolutely necessary) I would favour music-bridging, employing eighteenth-century music to complement the mock-Boswellian tone of the Biography which "frames" the play.

ACT I

Scene One

Lights up on the apartment. (Note: The downstage area is set for the Sunshine Cafe: a table and chairs.)

GRIMSHAW is seated at the table, pen in hand, composing. He is little more than sixty, but looks older, the result of a forty-year relationship with the bottle. His appearance is seedy, but his manner—and especially his voice—retains a certain faded elegance, even a lyricism.

Beside him is a mickey bottle of gin from which he sips occasionally.

GRIMSHAW: "The Life and Times of J.J. Davenport," by Wilfred Grimshaw.

He considers this for a moment, and takes a reflective sip. Then he crumples the paper and throws it into a wastebasket. Tries again.

GRIMSHAW: "The Davenport I Knew," by Wilfred—

J.J.: (calling from the bedroom) Wrong tense.

GRIMSHAW: What?

J.J.: I'm not dead.

GRIMSHAW: (considering this for a moment) True. (crumples paper, tries again) "The Davenport I Know," by W. Grimshaw. (disgustedly) The Davenport I know, the chesterfield I am acquainted with, the love-seat and I are as ships that pass in the night . . . (crumples paper) How can you write a serious biography about a man named after living room furniture?

J.J.: (from the bedroom) "Grimshaw's Life of Davenport"?

GRIMSHAW: What?

J.J.: (from the bedroom) "Grimshaw's Life of Davenport."

GRIMSHAW: By Grimshaw. Yes. Not bad. A bit redundant, but no harm in having two Grimshaws in the title. Just to stress the point that Grimshaw — while not the titular hero of the work — is not a man to be overlooked. Although this is precisely what large segments of society have been doing for decades. Right!

He resumes composing, energetically.

"Grimshaw's Life of Davenport," by Grimshaw, an account of the life and times of two gentlemen of leisure. "Gentlemen," because they are men of culture, and "leisured" because they are not men of work. In actual fact, two men of Welfare, or to be more precise two men on Welfare . . .

J.J. enters from the bedroom, with a flourish. He is the epitome of second-hand clothing-store flamboyance—a long scarf, a somewhat tattered vest and long hair.

J.J.: (declaiming) Welfare, Sir? No, think not of it as Welfare. Think of it as a pension from the Crown, for the benefit of those who would not squander their intellectual energies on unrewarding employment. Unrewarding employment, sir, is the most pernicious form of idleness.

J.J. looks toward GRIMSHAW for a reaction. GRIMSHAW motions him to continue.

J.J.: Ah . . . (resuming) What, Sir, would Socrates have chosen, had he been offered a choice between Welfare and night-shift at the Seven-Eleven? Sir, Welfare offers the man of intellect the opportunity to live the life of the mind. And the mind is its own place, as the Poet observes—it can make a heaven of hell, and a hell of heaven. Although not, perhaps, a heaven of the Seven-Eleven.

GRIMSHAW: Well done!

J.J.: (pleased) You think so?

GRIMSHAW: Splendidly done.

J.J.: Great. Then let's go. (starts toward the door)

GRIMSHAW: What?

J.J.: We've made a start — that's enough for one day.

GRIMSHAW: But—

J.J.: (exiting) Come on, Wilf. There are things to be done!

GRIMSHAW shrugs, then stands and puts on a jacket. Starts to the door. Turns back, fetches the mickey bottle, puts it in his pocket, and exits. Lights down on the apartment.

Lights up on the Sunshine Cafe. BOBBY and GUY, seated at the table. Both are dressed rather shabbily. BOBBY is still quite boyish-looking, and exists in a kind of genial fog. GUY is considerably harder—and, unlike BOBBY, he is very bright.

At present, he is hunkered down in nihilistic boredom.

BOBBY: So, what are we gonna do today?

GUY: I dunno. What do you want to do?

BOBBY: I dunno. We should do something.

GUY: Why?

BOBBY: I dunno.

GUY: Can't you say anything intelligent, for God's sake?

BOBBY: (*vaguely*) Sure.

GUY: Before we do anything, we've got to find some bread.

BOBBY: What?

GUY: (*sharply*) Money.

BOBBY: (*a sudden thought springs to mind*) Real estate.

GUY: What?

BOBBY: (*animated, for the first time*) That's what I was going to tell you about. This guy I seen on television. Real estate.

GUY: What are you talking about?

BOBBY: The guy on the television. He's offering this course — he teaches you how to make a million bucks in real estate.

GUY: Real estate?

BOBBY: For sure. It's really simple — it's beautiful. The idea is, you buy a house really cheap, from some guy who's just lost his job, or something. And then you sell it at a really major profit to someone else. You see? And then, with the money you've made, you buy a bigger place, and then you sell it at a bigger

profit. You just do that three or four times, and you've got a million bucks.

GUY: Oh, yeah?

BOBBY: You can't miss. Guy, we've got to look into this.

GUY: Yeah?

BOBBY: Seriously. You just buy a piece of property . . .

GUY: How?

BOBBY: What?

GUY: How? Where do you get the money to buy the first piece of property?

BOBBY: Oh, you don't. You buy the property without the money.

GUY: Oh, yeah?

BOBBY: Absolutely. This is the beauty of high finance. You buy the property without any money . . .

GUY: How?

BOBBY: (*impatiently*) Well, this is what they teach you in the course.

GUY: Oh.

BOBBY: I mean, they've got to teach you something, don't they? I mean, if they didn't have anything to teach you, nobody would take the course. Everybody would just be out there selling real estate.

GUY: Twenty-five million Canadians, selling real estate.

BOBBY: Well, exactly. It wouldn't work, would it?

GUY: Right.

BOBBY: If everybody sells real estate, the whole system falls apart. You see what I mean?

GUY: Right.

BOBBY: If you want to get ahead, you've got to understand how the financial system works.

GUY: All right!

Slight pause.

BOBBY: Right. (*another pause*) The only thing he doesn't tell you is how to raise the money to pay for the course in the first place.

GUY: (*exasperated*) Bobby, would you just for Christ's sake—

He stops abruptly as SUSAN enters. SUSAN is decidedly attractive, and wears rather tight jeans and a sweater—nothing overtly provocative, but the statement is made. She hesitates and looks around the cafe, clearly feeling out of place.

GUY: Hello. What's that?

BOBBY: What's what?

GUY: *That.* The little number that just came in.

BOBBY: (*vaguely*) Number?

He turns, and sees SUSAN. Stares at her, then stands up grinning.

BOBBY: (*to SUSAN*) Hey.

She sees him. Stares for a moment, then lights up in recognition.

SUSAN: Hey.

She hesitates fractionally, then goes to BOBBY and embraces him. BOBBY returns the embrace, awkward but pleased.

GUY: (*staring*) What do you know.

SUSAN: (*stepping back; to BOBBY*) Good God.

BOBBY: Jeez, eh?

SUSAN: It's got to be—

BOBBY: Two, three years.

SUSAN: Come on. Five or six.

BOBBY: Five or six? Jeez, eh?

SUSAN: Good God.

GUY: Hi.

SUSAN: Uh . . . hi.

BOBBY: Oh, this is Guy. Jeez. So how've you been?

SUSAN: Not bad. You?

BOBBY: Oh, you know. It goes. Pretty good. Jeez—

GUY: Hi. I'm Guy.

SUSAN: (*to GUY*) Susan. I went to high school with Bobby.

GUY: (*charming*) Good to meet you. Why don't you sit down?

SUSAN hesitates fractionally, then smiles and sits. BOBBY sits.

GUY: (*to BOBBY*) So why didn't you tell me?

BOBBY: Tell you what?

GUY: That you went to school with Susan?

BOBBY: (*baffled*) 'Cause you never met her.

GUY: (*to SUSAN charmingly*) Well, but that's exactly my point. All these years, and I've never met Susan. I could've spent my whole life, never—

BOBBY: (*interrupting*) So how's your parents?

SUSAN: (*rather coolly*) My parents?

She takes out a package of cigarettes and lights one— inexpertly.

BOBBY: Susan's dad's a doctor.

SUSAN: Walter Simpson, MD. Ears, noses and throats.

BOBBY: So how're they doing?

SUSAN: I wouldn't know. I've moved out.

BOBBY: What?

SUSAN: Told them if they want a nice and proper little girl, they can adopt one.

GUY: Hey, good for you. When did you do this?

SUSAN: This morning.

BOBBY: Wow. That's really heavy. That's— (*trails off as a thought occurs*) So where's your stuff?

SUSAN: What?

BOBBY: You know — clothes, suitcases.

SUSAN: At my parents'. I'll pick them up when I've found a place to stay.

Fractional pause, as the same thought occurs simultaneously to GUY and BOBBY.

BOBBY: Well, hey—

GUY: (*over him*) Listen. If you need a place to stay . . .

SUSAN: That's okay.

GUY: No, really.

BOBBY: (*echoing*) Really. We—

GUY: (*over him*) We've got lots of room. Big old house — me, Bobby and his twin brother.

SUSAN: Murray? He's living with you too?

GUY: Just the three of us. I mean, so far it's just the three of us. But if you'd . . . Look, this isn't any sort of come-on, or anything . . .

BOBBY: (*agreeing*) Oh, shit no.

GUY: But if you need a place for a couple of nights.

SUSAN: (*rather titillated*) Three guys in some old bachelor house?

GUY: Hey, it's wonderfully Bohemian. You'll love it. You'll—

GUY is interrupted by the flamboyant entrance of J.J., followed by GRIMSHAW.

J.J.:   The point, Wilf, the one essential point is— (*He trails off as he sees SUSAN.*) Oh my God who's that?

J.J. stares at SUSAN. SUSAN sees his stare, and averts her eyes uncomfortably.

GRIMSHAW: Who?

J.J.:   That . . . that vision.

GRIMSHAW: You mean the girl?

J.J.:   I mean . . . I mean Aurora, goddess of the dawn.

GRIMSHAW: Steady on.

GUY and BOBBY have been staring at J.J.

SUSAN: (*turning to* GUY) I mean, really. Thanks, but . . .

GUY: Hey, there's lots of room.

J.J.:   Wilf, you've got to introduce me.

SUSAN: It's a really nice offer, but . . .

GRIMSHAW: I've never seen her in my life.

J.J.:   Just introduce me. (*starts toward the table*)

GUY: (*to* SUSAN) Look, it's no trouble. I mean it. A couple of days. Three days. However long you—

J.J.:   (*arriving; winningly*) Hello.

They look at him. J.J. continues to smile winningly at SUSAN.

GUY: (*rather hostile*) Yeah?

GRIMSHAW: (*hurrying over*) I, ah . . . I believe my friend would like to be introduced to the young lady. (*to* SUSAN) Your name is—?

SUSAN: Susan.

GRIMSHAW: Susan. Lovely, black-eyed Susan . . . No, it won't do, will it? Susan, I would like you to meet J.J. Davenport.

J.J.:   It's an honour.

SUSAN: Uh . . . hi.

J.J.:   Susan, I don't believe you've met my companion. I'd like you to meet my very good friend, Wilfred Grimshaw.

GRIMSHAW: Charmed.

SUSAN: Hi.

J.J.:   (*to* GRIMSHAW) There. We've managed it.

GUY: Hey, did somebody invite you guys over?

GRIMSHAW: No. Could I trouble you for a cigarette? (*helping himself to one of* SUSAN's *cigarettes*) You're very kind.

J.J.:   (*fetching a chair*) You don't mind if we sit down, do you?

GUY: Yes.

BOBBY: Well . . .

J.J.:   Susan?

SUSAN: Uh . . . no.

J.J.:   (*sitting*) The nays have it.

GRIMSHAW fetches a chair and sits.

SUSAN: (*uncomfortably*) Ah, this is Bobby, and this is his friend . . .

GUY: Guy.

SUSAN: Guy.

J.J.:   It's a pleasure.

SUSAN: I've seen you somewhere.

J.J.:   Really?

SUSAN: I've seen you. Where was it?

J.J.:   Have you ever been to Monte Carlo?

SUSAN: No.

J.J.:   Neither have I. So it wasn't, alas, Monte Carlo.

SUSAN: It's J.J., is it?

J.J.:   It stands for James Jeffrey when I'm at home, and Jean-Jacques when I'm in Paris.

BOBBY: Oh, Paris. Right.

J.J.:   Have you been there?

BOBBY: No.

GUY: (*with some hostility*) Have you been there?

J.J.:   Not in this life. But I knew it well when I was a wine-waiter in a little bistro frequented by Georges Danton and his friends. Oh, those were great days. Danton, standing on a table and making speeches about the ideals of the Republic, while in the background you heard the swoosh-snock of the guillotine . . .

GUY: As a matter of fact, the three of us were having a conversation.

J.J.:   Wonderful. I love conversations. (*clears his throat; slight, dramatic pause*) Has it ever occurred to you that we are living on the verge of a New Renaissance?

BOBBY: A new what?

GRIMSHAW: I'll take this down. It may be memorable. (*takes out a tattered note-pad and pencil*)

J.J.:   (*resuming*) Have you ever, I say, considered that we are in fact living—

SUSAN: I know I've seen you somewhere. What do you do?

J.J.:   (*losing his rhetorical stride*) Ah . . . what?

SUSAN: What do you do?

J.J.:   (*recovering*) What do I do? I idle.

SUSAN: What?

GRIMSHAW: Idle. From Old High German *wital*, by way of the Anglo-Saxon *idel*, "to be useless."

J.J.:   Useless, yes—as society defines it. Of course, society defines utility in terms of the dogged pursuit of the meaningless. When we call a man "useful," we imply that he is futile, but very earnest about it. Some of us, on the other hand, dare to embrace the ultimate freedom. We dare to think, rather than to do. To confront leisure, rather than to shrink from it. We dare, in short, to be useless.

GRIMSHAW: Splendid! I'll put that in the Biography.

GUY: The what?

J.J.:   (*modestly*) Oh, Wilf is compiling a chronicle of our experiences together. We hope it will be a bitter-sweet treatise on our times . . .

GRIMSHAW: And perhaps the basis for a television mini-series. (*quoting approvingly*) "We dare, in short, to be useless."

J.J.:   Do you, Susan?

SUSAN: Do I what?

J.J.:   Dare to be useless?

Slight pause.

SUSAN: You guys are strange.

GUY: (*standing*) Come on. Let's go.

J.J.:   (*somewhat at a loss*) Are you going?

SUSAN, GUY and BOBBY move off.

BOBBY: See you around.

SUSAN: (*as they exit*) Those guys are bizarre.

GUY: Bozos.

And they're gone. Pause.

J.J.:   (*visibly deflated*) Wilf? I talk too much, don't I?

GRIMSHAW: Well . . . from time to time, perhaps.

J.J.:   No, you don't have to be kind. It's true. I talk too much. That's the difficulty with the art of conversation. There's a fine line between being an artist of conversation, and having a big mouth. Samuel Johnson managed to walk that line. I'm not always very good at it.

GRIMSHAW: Yes, but Samuel Johnson had years of practise. He spent much of his youth as a young man with a big mouth, and gradually matured into his genius.

J.J.:   I shouldn't have come right out and asked her if she dared to be useless. She wasn't quite ready for that kind of question.

GRIMSHAW: Your timing could have been better.

J.J.:   Wilf? She's beautiful.

Scene Two

The apartment. GRIMSHAW is seated, composing. The gin bottle is beside him, nearly depleted.

GRIMSHAW: It is often to be observed that men of genius do not make good first impressions, and this was sometimes the case with J.J. Davenport. And J.J. Davenport was undeniably a man of genius. (*He puts the pen down and continues, reflectively.*) For quite some time, I confess, I couldn't quite pin down what his genius was for. But gradually, it began to dawn upon me — J.J. Davenport's genius was for navigation. Let me explain.

He has a drink and continues, speaking more or less to himself.

J.J. Davenport was a man who lived for ideals—which was in itself a fine human accomplishment, even if the ideals themselves lacked a certain practicability, as ideals are wont to do. But the problem with living for ideals is that they are apt to run aground on the rocks of reality. And J.J. Davenport's genius lay precisely in his ability to avoid those rocks. Where countless others had sunk, J.J. Davenport sailed blithely on, secure in the conviction that he was getting somewhere. This was his genius although it was not a genius which was well understood by a society which prefers to build condominiums on the rocks.

J.J. enters hastily, slightly out of breath but delighted. He clutches a slip of paper.

J.J.:   Wilf!

GRIMSHAW: (*startled*) J.J.

J.J.:   I've got it!

GRIMSHAW: You've got what?

J.J.:   The address! Where those guys live — the ones who were with Susan. Got it from a waitress at the cafe. (*disappears into the bedroom*)

GRIMSHAW: (*looking straight ahead; to himself*) We have observed such signs before. The bloom in the cheeks, the bovine brightness of the eye . . .

J.J.:   (*from the bedroom*) Damn. I was sure I left it here.

GRIMSHAW: (*calling*) Left what where?

J.J.:   (*off*) A five-dollar bill. On the dresser.

GRIMSHAW: (*looking rather furtive*) What was the serial number?

J.J.:   (*off*) What?

GRIMSHAW: Nothing.

J.J.:   (*re-entering, only marginally discouraged*) Well, I guess I'll have to do this without money. I'll have to carry it off with . . . you know . . . charm. (*starts toward the door*)

GRIMSHAW: Ah . . . J.J. Do I take it that you're setting off to see this Susan person?

J.J.:   (*brightly*) Yep.

GRIMSHAW: Ah. And you think this is entirely wise?

J.J.:   (*faltering just slightly*) Well, we kind of got off on the wrong foot this morning. But I'll patch that up.

GRIMSHAW: J.J. As a friend. I wouldn't recommend this.

J.J.:   (*bridling*) What's it got to do with you?

GRIMSHAW: It has a great deal to do with me. As your biographer. How am I supposed to fit this into the biography? I mean, it's just not the image we're after. The man of the intellect, the philosophical spirit, pursuing young women whose blue jeans have shrunk in the wash? No, no . . .

J.J.:   See you, Wilf.

He exits. GRIMSHAW looks after him. Then he picks up the bottle, prepares to take a drink—and discovers that the bottle is empty. He looks at it gloomily.

GRIMSHAW: And all of his friends disappeared simultaneously.

Lights down on the apartment.

Lights up on the living room of the house. SUSAN and GUY on the chesterfield. Simultaneously, very loud, very obnoxious music begins. A voice— MURRAY's—is heard, shouting from off-stage. (If possible, it should sound as if MURRAY is shouting from upstairs.)

MURRAY: Would you turn that damn thing off?

SUSAN jumps up and turns off the stereo. Calls in the direction of MURRAY's voice.

SUSAN: Hi, Murray. It's Susan.

Slight pause.

MURRAY: (*off*) Susan who?

SUSAN: Susan, from high school. (*Waits for a reply. None is forthcoming.*) I guess I didn't make much of an impression on him.

GUY: Nothing makes much of an impression on Murray. Our industrious little graduate student, beavering away in the attic. (*calling off*) Say hello to Hegel for me, Murr. Ask him how his dialectic's doing.

SUSAN sits back down on the couch.

GUY: Yes, Murray certainly is hard working. It's all a waste of time, of course.

SUSAN: Is he still—?

GUY: Yep, he's still waiting for the Revolution to come. In the meantime, he's studying dead philosophers. If Murray had been in charge of storming the Winter Palace, the Czar would still be playing croquet on the lawn.

SUSAN: So what are you doing, while waiting for the Revolution to come?

GUY: (*scornfully*) There isn't going to be a Revolution. Sooner or later, this whole rat-bag system is just going to come crashing down.

BOBBY enters.

GUY: In the meantime, I'm collecting money from it. Bobby, why don't you get us a beer, or something?

BOBBY: I don't think there's any left.

GUY: Well, you don't know until you look, do you?

BOBBY: (*looking from GUY to SUSAN, he shrugs*) Okay. (*exits*)

GUY: (*shifting toward SUSAN, becoming "intimate"*) So. Whose bed do you want?

SUSAN: What?

GUY: I mean, you can have my room—I'll sleep on the floor in Bobby's.

SUSAN: I couldn't move you out of your room.

GUY: (*charmingly*) Well, if that's the way you feel, you don't need to.

SUSAN: I'll sleep on the couch.

GUY: Suit yourself. You can always change your mind, you know, if—

SUSAN: Look, I'm not moving in. It's just for a couple of days, until I find a place.

GUY: What sort of place?

SUSAN: (*vaguely*) Well . . . you know . . .

A sprightly knocking at the front door.

GUY: (*calling*) It's open.

J.J. enters, holding something large behind his back.

J.J.: Good evening!

GUY: Oh, God. I said "it's open." I didn't say "come in."

J.J.: I just happened to find myself in the neighbourhood, so I thought I'd drop by. Susan . . . I've brought a little gift.

He holds it out: a pink flamingo with a kerchief tied rakishly round its neck.

GUY: You're strange, man. You are really strange.

J.J.: Susan, I'd like you to have it, by way of apology for my rudeness this morning.

SUSAN: A pink flamingo?

J.J.: I was going to bring flowers, but as I was about to steal them from your neighbour's garden, I saw the flamingo. And I thought to myself: what a crime to uproot tulips, when the aesthetic tone of the entire neighbourhood could be improved by uprooting the bird instead.

GUY: You stole that from the neighbour?

J.J.: Heavens, no. I confiscated it, in the name of good taste. I'll slip back under cover of darkness to assassinate the plaster gnomes. Susan, will you accept this, and my apology?

SUSAN: (*warming to him*) I don't know about the apology. But I like the flamingo. (*takes the flamingo and holds it up admiringly*) My mother has two of them. And a Venus de Milo, beside the bird bath. (*hands the flamingo to GUY*)

GUY: What the hell am I supposed to do with it?

SUSAN: Put it in a vase.

GUY: We don't have a vase.

SUSAN: Then it's a good thing he didn't bring flowers, isn't it?

GUY glares rather venomously at the flamingo, then gets up to deposit it in a corner.

SUSAN: (*to J.J.*) Why don't you sit down? Now that you're here.

J.J.: (*a bit gushingly*) Thank you.

He sits beside SUSAN on the couch—in the spot GUY has vacated.

SUSAN: Where's your friend?

J.J.: Wilfred? Oh, Wilfred is at home, working.

SUSAN: On your biography?

J.J.:   (*modestly*) Well . . .

GUY: How did you know we lived here, anyway?

J.J.:   Oh, I simply asked round the Sunshine Cafe. I described two young gentlemen, accompanied by Aurora, goddess of the dawn.

SUSAN: Aurora?

J.J.:   (*quoting*) "As soon as Dawn with her rose-tinted hands had lit the east, Odysseus' son put on his clothes . . . ."

BOBBY enters with one beer.

BOBBY: There's one left, if . . . (*stops short as he sees J.J.*) you.

J.J.:   (*brightly*) Good evening.

BOBBY: (*to GUY*) But you and me should really get going.

GUY: (*checks his watch; a bit evasively*) Oh. Right.

SUSAN: Where are you going?

GUY: (*more evasively*) Oh, we've got to see a couple of people.

BOBBY: Actually, we've kind of got some business to—

GUY: (*over him; sharply*) We've got to see some people.

SUSAN: See you, then.

GUY: (*fractional hesitation; to SUSAN*) You going to stay here?

SUSAN: Isn't that okay with you?

GUY: Sure. Fine. Great. (*Looks narrowly at J.J., then back at SUSAN. Then scowls and goes to the door. To BOBBY*) Come on.

BOBBY starts to follow. Realizes he still has the beer in his hand. Looks at it vaguely for a moment, then hands it to J.J.

BOBBY: See you. (*exits.*)

J.J. stands, smiling (rather foolishly) at SUSAN. She glances back toward him. Pause.

J.J.:   Well!

He starts to take a sip of beer. Stops and offers the beer to SUSAN instead. She takes it and strolls across the room.

J.J.:   I was just wondering . . .

SUSAN: What?

J.J.:   I mean . . . here you are. Here *I* am. And I don't know anything about you. I mean . . . what do you do?

SUSAN: At the moment? I idle.

J.J.:   (*delighted*) You idle. Oh, God. I am alone in the living room with Aurora who idles.

SUSAN: From the Anglo-Saxon "whoosit" and the Old German "whatsit," "to be useless."

J.J.:   Yes! (*hastily*) Of course, not "useless" as in "useless." That's not what I meant. I mean, that's kind of the opposite of what I meant. I meant "useless"—

SUSAN: As in "unfettered."

J.J.:   (*delighted*) Exactly!

SUSAN: As opposed to "useless" as in "tits on a bull."

J.J.:   (*somewhat less delighted*) Uh . . . right.

SUSAN hands him back the beer. J.J. looks at the beer in his hand and takes a very small sip.

J.J.: So! Here we are.

SUSAN: Here we are.

J.J.: And you're a . . . an old friend of Bobby's, are you?

SUSAN: Yes.

J.J.: And you and he are . . . ? Well, I mean . . .

SUSAN: (*enjoying this*) The answer is no, if that's what you mean. We're just friends. I went to school with him—Grade Eleven. I didn't see much of him in Grade Twelve—that's the year he spent in his parents' basement, playing Mott the Hoople backwards.

J.J.: Ah, yes. Mott the Hoople. I never went in much for Mott the Hoople. I preferred the classics—The Turtles, that sort of thing.

SUSAN: The Turtles. Before my time.

J.J.: (*singing*) "Remember me and you—I do—I think about you day and night, it's only . . ." (*trails off, then resumes awkwardly*) And Guy is Bobby's friend, rather than . . . ?

SUSAN: Rather than mine, you mean? Yes.

J.J.: Ah.

SUSAN: (*sitting on the chesterfield*) Does that clear things up, to your satisfaction?

J.J.: I . . . get the feeling Guy doesn't like me very much.

SUSAN: I'd say he can't stand you.

J.J.: I wonder why that is.

SUSAN: I'd say it's obvious, wouldn't you?

J.J.: Would you?

SUSAN: Maybe it isn't so obvious, then. Never mind.

J.J. takes another small sip of beer, then goes to the couch and sits beside SUSAN.

J.J.: So! You're staying here now, are you?

SUSAN: Looks like it. (*stands and strolls across the room*) The result of a small disagreement with my father. My father insists that I won't get into law school if I don't buckle down and pull up my marks. I insist that I wouldn't be caught dead going to law school even if I did buckle down and pull up my marks—which I'm not keen on doing in the first place. There it stands. Mommy and Daddy perplexed and reproachful. "Where did we go wrong?" Tell me about the New Renaissance.

J.J.: (*struggling to keep up*) What?

SUSAN: At the cafe, this morning. You were about to tell us about the New Renaissance.

J.J.: Oh, right. (*stands and starts toward her eagerly*) The New Renaissance, you see, is—

SUSAN: It's redundant, of course.

J.J.: What is?

SUSAN: The phrase. "New Renaissance." It's redundant. But go ahead.

J.J.: Uh . . . right. Well . . . (*faltering a bit*) Well, the thing is that I am . . . well, I am someone who sees potential where others see devastation. I see an unemployed generation—us—and I see almost limitless possibilities. Time—the ultimate gift. Time to think, to converse, to create . . . (*hitting his stride*) All of us. The first literate generation in four hundred years that isn't tied down to menial labour, to uncreative drudgery. I see the seed-bed, in short, of a renaissance.

SUSAN: (*lighting up in recognition*) Of course.

J.J.: (*delighted*) Of course it's of course! And that's my dream, you see—to bring together a circle of people who think the way I do, who can—

SUSAN: No, no. I meant, of course—it's just clicked. Where I've seen you.

J.J.: What?

SUSAN: You're the Cookie Man—the one who was selling those cookies on the beach, last summer.

J.J.: That's right.

SUSAN: Those huge cookies with little slogans written on them in icing.

J.J.: (*rather sheepishly*) My one attempt to wed commerce and philosophy. Giant oatmeal cookies with metaphysical insights.

SUSAN: Food for thought?

J.J.: They didn't sell very well.

SUSAN: They were interesting, though.

J.J.: You've read my cookies?

SUSAN: Well, I saw one of them. I couldn't quite figure it out.

J.J.: The messages tended to be a bit cryptic.

SUSAN: It said "only reflect," or something.

J.J.: That was the problem. It's tough to fit a complex thought onto a cookie. Next summer, I'm thinking of branching out into submarine sandwiches.

SUSAN: Good idea.

J.J.: You can get a lot more onto a submarine sandwich.

SUSAN: A short paragraph, even.

J.J.: Well, exactly.

SUSAN: The Cookie Man from the beach. Wreck Beach. (*rather coyly*) Well, we *have* seen each other then, haven't we? You wild thing.

J.J. looks enormously embarrassed. Attempts a laugh. Takes a small sip of beer. Then takes a much larger gulp. SUSAN takes the beer from him, has a very small sip and sets it down.

J.J.: (*very awkwardly*) University, eh?

SUSAN: What's that?

J.J.: You've dropped out of university?

SUSAN: Looks like I have, doesn't it?

J.J.: (*half-turning away*) University. Yes, that's a good place to drop out of.

SUSAN: You've done it?

J.J.: (*mustering his flamboyance*) Oh, a number of times. The great mistake that students make, you see, is that they complete courses. This is a terrible waste of time. I, on the other hand, spent four years at university without ever turning in a paper. This is why I was able to cover so much ground in such a short time, and became so well rounded at such a tender age. In fact—

SUSAN: Why do you talk so much?

J.J.: What?

SUSAN: Is it because you're afraid there'll be nothing there if you shut up?

J.J emits a high-pitched and decidedly silly laugh. It trails off.

SUSAN: That's all right.

Slight pause. J.J. turns awkwardly toward her.

SUSAN: The New Renaissance, flamingoes and philosophical cookies. J.J. Davenport, you are an unusual man.

J.J.: I . . . guess I should go?

SUSAN: Guy said I could use his room tonight. I wonder if it's nice.

Blackout.

Scene Three

The living room, the following morning.

JASON is alone in the room, "inspecting" it—wiping furniture with his finger to check for dust, etc. He wears a trendy suit, and exudes a tangible air of possession. He notices the flamingo. Picks it up and stares at it.

J.J. is heard off-stage, singing as he approaches.

J.J.: *(off)* "I can't see me loving nobody but you, for all my life . . ." Dee-dee dum-dum . . .

He enters, barefoot and with his shirt unbuttoned. Stops short as he sees JASON.

J.J.: Uh . . . hi.

JASON: Good morning.

JASON puts the flamingo down, carefully.

J.J.: Can I help you?

JASON: I don't know. Who are you?

Fractional pause as J.J. tries to size JASON up.

J.J.: In what sense?

JASON: What are you doing here?

J.J.: Do you mean, as in—? *(a thought occurs)* Oh, I see. What is the meaning of my presence here.

JASON: Yes.

J.J.: Who, in an ultimate sense, am I, and what, in an ultimate sense, is my purpose. You're a Jehovah's Witness.

JASON: What?

J.J.: Well, look, you've caught me at a bad time. But if you'd like to drop off a magazine . . .

JASON: Mr. Wagner. The landlord.

J.J.: No, I don't know him.

JASON: *I'm* Mr. Wagner. I own the house.

J.J.: Good God. *(quickly)* I mean, there's no reason why you shouldn't own the house. No necessary contradiction between the ownership of property and your religious convictions . . .

JASON: *(losing patience)* I am not a Jehovah's Witness.

Slight pause.

J.J.: Could we start again?

JASON: *(as if to a dim child)* I own the house. The rent is overdue. I would like the rent. While I'm at it, I would like to know who you are and what you're doing here.

J.J.: Oh. I'm J.J. I'm . . . visiting Susan.

JASON: Who?

J.J.: Susan. She's . . . visiting Guy and Bobby.

JASON: And are Guy and Bobby here?

J.J.: I don't know. I don't think so.

JASON: Is Murray here?

J.J.: Who?

JASON: (arctic pause) I see. You claim to be visiting a visitor of my tenants . . .

J.J.: I'm not just claiming . . .

JASON: Who are somewhere else entirely. Which leaves you as an unauthorized person in my house.

J.J.: Hang on . . .

JASON: All of which leaves me wondering whether I should be talking to you at all, or whether I should be talking to the police. What do you have to say to that?

J.J.: (considering this for a moment) I think I liked it better when you were a Jehovah's Witness.

SUSAN: (off) J.J., are you—?

SUSAN enters, wearing a man's dressing gown — it is, as it happens, GUY's. Stops short when she sees JASON, and pulls the gown tighter. JASON gives her an appreciative once-over, and becomes "charming."

JASON: You must be Susan. Good morning.

SUSAN: Uh . . . hi.

He extends his hand, and they shake.

J.J.: (to SUSAN) This is Mr. Wagner. The landlord.

J.J.: He owns the house.

JASON: (simultaneously) I own the house.

SUSAN: Oh.

JASON: You're staying here, are you?

SUSAN: Just for a few days. Guy and Bobby said it was okay.

JASON: Of course it is. Perfectly all right. (glances toward J.J. but continues to address SUSAN) And J.J. here is—?

SUSAN: (quickly) No, no.

J.J.: No.

SUSAN: He isn't staying. He's just a friend.

JASON: Ah. Just a friend. (smiles at SUSAN)

SUSAN: (smiling back, but shifting a bit awkwardly) I guess I should put something on.

JASON: Oh, not on my account.

J.J.: He isn't staying. He just came for the rent.

JASON: (waving this off, magnanimously) No rush. Just ask the fellows to drop it off in the next few days, would you?

SUSAN: Sure.

JASON takes a long look round the room, still smiling.

J.J.: (affecting nonchalance) Yes, it's a nice old house, isn't it?

JASON: (affably) Not really. That's why I rent it for a song. I've been too busy with the other properties to give much thought to this one, but I have some ideas. Fix it up — redo the interior, put in two or three suites . . .

J.J.: Oh, you don't need to do that on our account.

JASON: Your account?

J.J.: I mean . . .

JASON: On the other hand, I've half a mind just to tear it down and rebuild. What do you think, Susan?

SUSAN: Let us know, before you bring in the bulldozers.

JASON: Oh, don't worry. It'll be a few months yet. (*checks his watch*) Well, have to run. Nice to meet you, Susan.

SUSAN: You too, Mr. Wagner.

JASON: Jason. (*Smiles brightly at her, then starts toward the door. Stops and turns back.*) Perhaps I'll drop by some evening, and we'll have a chance to chat. Take a spin in the Benz.

J.J.:   The Benz?

SUSAN: That might be nice.

JASON: See you soon, then.

SUSAN: Sure.

JASON exits. SUSAN continues to look toward the door. Pause.

J.J.:   Yes, but has he read Plato?

SUSAN: What?

J.J.:   He may own houses and Mercedes-Benzes, but has he read Plato? That's what I want to know.

SUSAN: What does Plato have to do with it?

J.J.:   Plato has everything to do with it. We live in a society of aerobic dancers and fitness-club members . . .

SUSAN: How do you know Jason belongs to a fitness club?

J.J.:   Do fish swim? Do yuppies yup? Three hours a day pumping iron, but how many hours pumping Plato?

SUSAN: How many hours do you spend pumping Plato?

J.J.:   (*slightly deflated*) Well, more than I spend at a fitness club.

He registers the fact that SUSAN is unexpectedly frosty, and redoubles his efforts to be cheerful.

J.J.:   So! What are we going to do?

SUSAN: When?

J.J.:   With the rest of our lives?

SUSAN: J.J. . . .

J.J.:   With the rest of the day, then.

SUSAN: Well, there are some things I should probably get done.

J.J.:   Of course there are! The potential is limitless. If you're feeling rugged and fearless, we can go down to the zoo and bark at the timber-wolves. If you're feeling literary, we can stroll down Fourth Avenue discussing Shakespeare. If you feel like making poignant comments on the human condition, we can go leave some footprints on the shore at low tide. On the other hand we could always go and renovate a house.

SUSAN: (*warming to him*) Anything but renovating the house.

J.J.:   Good. We'll start at the zoo, and end up at the beach. But first, I guess, we'd better go downtown and get you signed up.

SUSAN: For what?

J.J.:   Welfare.

SUSAN: What?

J.J.:   The Horn of Bare Subsistence, if not quite Plenty.

SUSAN: Welfare? Are you joking?

J.J.: Why should I be joking? I mean . . . everyone does it.

Slight pause. SUSAN smiles—tightly.

SUSAN: Everyone?

J.J.: Well . . .

SUSAN: I'd better get dressed. (*exits, rather quickly*)

J.J. looks after her, anxiously. Begins to follow, but stops as the front door opens and GUY enters.

J.J.: (*awkwardly*) Guy. How are you?

GUY: I've been worse.

J.J.: Good.

GUY: I've been better, too.

J.J.: Were you out for a walk, or something?

GUY: Yeah.

J.J.: Out and about pretty early, this morning.

GUY: Didn't get much sleep. On the floor. In Bobby's room.

J.J.: Oh. Right.

GUY: Yourself?

J.J.: What's that?

GUY: Get much sleep?

J.J.: Oh. Yes. Buckets of it.

GUY: Good to hear.

J.J.: Actually, I'm just heading off.

GUY: Without your shoes?

J.J.: What's that? (*realizes he is barefoot*) Oh. Right. Shoes. I . . . must have left them under your bed.

GUY: Well, I guess you should probably go get them, eh?

J.J.: Right. (*hurries off*)

GUY: What does that bimbo see in that bozo?

Scene Four

The apartment. GRIMSHAW, looking hung over, is composing.

GRIMSHAW: (*lugubriously*) "And friendship, Sir," he concluded, with his winning smile, "is man's noblest duty." "You speak well of friendship, Sir," I replied, "but I have observed that many men speak well of duties which they do not in fact discharge." "What, Sir, do you mean?" he asked. "Sir," I replied, summoning what little strength remained to me, "Does a friend desert boon companions when they are old and unwell?"

J.J. enters, cheerily.

J.J.: Good morning, Wilf.

GRIMSHAW: Is it?

J.J.: Is something wrong?

GRIMSHAW: Is something wrong? You disappear without a trace, you roll in here at noon—

J.J.: It's ten-thirty.

GRIMSHAW: It's almost noon when you roll in, and you haven't left a message, you haven't telephoned, I have no idea where you are. I have no idea if you're in jail, if you've been robbed and beaten and left in an alleyway—

J.J.:   I was with Susan. (*starts toward the bedroom*)

GRIMSHAW: All night?

J.J.:   (*unable to stifle a grin*) Yep. (*disappears into the bedroom*)

GRIMSHAW: Well. She doesn't waste time, does she? No flies on that girl.

J.J.:   (*reappearing in the doorway*) Don't be insulting, Wilf. I think I may be in love. (*goes back into the bedroom*)

GRIMSHAW: Oh, that's very nice. That's lovely. You run off to fall in love, you don't leave a message, you don't telephone—

J.J.:   (*off*) For God's sake, Wilf, I'm your *friend*. We're not married.

GRIMSHAW: Excuse me, Sir, but we *are* married—bonded together in the pursuit of Art and Truth as biographer and biographee.

J.J.:   (*off*) Damn, that five bucks *has* to be here somewhere. Five bucks doesn't just get up and walk away.

GRIMSHAW: True.

J.J.:   (*off*) What?

GRIMSHAW: (*resuming*) Bonded together as biographer and biographee. This is a sacred trust, Sir, and you have no right to betray it by spending the night with young women.

J.J.:   (*off*) Why not, for God's sake?

GRIMSHAW: Because I have made you a celibate.

J.J.:   (*re-emerging from the bedroom*) You've what?

GRIMSHAW: You have pledged eternal fidelity to Dame Philosophy, spurning forever the vain pleasures of the flesh.

J.J.:   I have not!

GRIMSHAW: Oh, yes you have. It's on page fourteen, and it's a profoundly moving declaration. Shall I read it to you?

J.J.:   (*earnestly*) You don't understand, Wilf. I actually think I'm in love.

GRIMSHAW: Don't be ridiculous. You've known her for twenty-four hours.

J.J.:   I've known her all my life, because she's exactly the person I've always wanted. She's so . . . so self-possessed, Wilf, so totally in control of herself, and yet she wants *me*. It's poetry, Wilf, it's—

GRIMSHAW: Ridiculous.

J.J.:   It is not! (*quietly*) Wilf? Take this down. For the Biography. (*declaiming*) I, J.J. Davenport, wish all the world to know the truth. And the truth is that my heart is in the clouds, my feet are six inches above the pavement, and—

SUSAN enters.

SUSAN: Your toilet's flooded.

J.J.:   What?

SUSAN: Your toilet. It's flooded.

GRIMSHAW: Oh, it's not our toilet, then. When it floods, it's Mr. Lombard's toilet.

SUSAN: Who?

J.J.:   Mr. Lombard. Down the hall. He's one of the people who shares the bathroom.

GRIMSHAW: He's not a bad fellow, really, so long as he takes his medication. He threatens to kill us, from time to time, but he only does it for affect.

SUSAN: I think I may have seen him. There was someone staring at me from the top of the stairs. Big fat man with a moustache?

GRIMSHAW: No, that's Mrs. Pivak. She's in 3B.

SUSAN: (looking slowly around the room) So this is where you live.

GRIMSHAW: I suppose it's not for everyone. But J.J. and I call it home.

J.J.:   (to SUSAN; gesturing vaguely toward the door) I guess we should . . .

SUSAN has picked up a battered old violin with no strings. She looks inquiringly at J.J.

J.J.:   (a bit embarrassed) Oh, my violin.

GRIMSHAW: (taking it from her) Yes, I gave it to him, for his birthday. I picked it up one day. I'm a sort of collector.

SUSAN: You collect musical instruments?

GRIMSHAW: No, I collect empty bottles and cans from Smithrite bins. The violin was in the bin.

SUSAN: Oh. (to J.J.) Why don't you buy some strings for it?

J.J.:   Well, that wouldn't make much difference—it's got a big hole in the back.

GRIMSHAW: You can still practise on it, though. (extends the violin to J.J.) Play something for us.

J.J.:   (embarrassed) Naw.

GRIMSHAW: Go on.

J.J. hesitates. Then—clearly feeling a bit foolish—takes the violin and tucks it under his chin.

GRIMSHAW: Elbow up. You're not a music-hall fiddler.

J.J. raises his "bow" elbow to the proper position. GRIMSHAW raps the desk, like a conductor signalling the beginning of a performance. J.J. mimes playing the violin; he and GRIMSHAW hum the melody in unison.

SUSAN: (to GRIMSHAW) What's he playing?

J.J. stops playing.

GRIMSHAW: Beethoven. "Für Elise."

GRIMSHAW motions to J.J. to resume. J.J. does so and GRIMSHAW resumes humming.

SUSAN: Yes, I thought I recognized it.

Rather hastily, J.J. abandons the "concert" and hands the violin back to GRIMSHAW.

J.J.:   (to SUSAN) I mean, it's hardly the real thing, but you can still work on your technique.

SUSAN: Absolutely. And who knows when you'll come across a real violin?

J.J. grins sheepishly, then motions SUSAN to precede him to the door.

J.J.:   Well . . . ?

GRIMSHAW: I don't suppose you remembered my cigarettes?

J.J.:   What?

GRIMSHAW: My cigarettes?

J.J.:   (wearily) Okay, we'll go and pick you up some cigarettes.

GRIMSHAW: Oh, there's no need for Susan to go too. We can have a bit of a chat.

J.J. hesitates. SUSAN shrugs.

SUSAN: Sure.

J.J.:   I'll just be a sec. (*exits*)

GRIMSHAW motions graciously for SUSAN to take a seat. He is about to speak to her as J.J. re-enters.

J.J.:   Wilf?

He makes a gesture indicating that he has no money. GRIMSHAW shrugs eloquently, then turns to SUSAN.

SUSAN: (*to J.J.*) I thought we were coming back here to pick up some money.

J.J.:   That was the initial plan, yes.

GRIMSHAW: (*philosophically*) They go oft astray. The best laid plans of mice and men. (*to SUSAN; by way of explanation*) Burns.

SUSAN: I know.

She fishes a five-dollar bill from her handbag and hands it to GRIMSHAW. He nods graciously and passes it on to J.J. who exits.

GRIMSHAW: (*calling after him*) No need to hurry. (*turns slowly toward SUSAN, and smiles*) Susan, could I—? Dear me, this is being terribly forward. Susan, could I ask you a personal question?

SUSAN: You can ask anything you like. You just might not get an answer.

GRIMSHAW: (*laughing—with studied affability*) That's good. Very good. Spunk. (*the laugh trails off*) Susan? What do you see in J.J.?

SUSAN: What?

GRIMSHAW: What do you see in him? I merely ask . . . out of interest.

SUSAN: (*shrugging*) I like him.

GRIMSHAW: You like him.

SUSAN: Sure. What do you see in him?

GRIMSHAW: (*another affable chuckle*) Well, but that's hardly the question, is it? We're men. Old comrades who have stuck together through thick and thin and a considerable amount of thinner. It's not a question of "seeing" anything in each other. We're simply . . .

SUSAN: "Soul-mates"?

GRIMSHAW: I met him in the bus depot, one Friday night. He was reciting "I Wandered Lonely as a Cloud" to a group of loggers who were in town for the weekend. His assumption, as I recall, was that they, as men of the land, would appreciate the Wordsworthian link between daffodils and stars.

SUSAN: That must have been interesting.

GRIMSHAW: Oh, it was. Fortunately, I've always been able to think on my feet. I managed to create a diversion, and whisked him away to the relative safety of a pub.

SUSAN: And you've been looking after him ever since.

GRIMSHAW: You could put it that way, yes.

SUSAN becomes absorbed in studying the contents of the room. GRIMSHAW watches her as she drifts toward the desk.

GRIMSHAW: Does it surprise you to discover that J.J. is someone who requires looking after?

SUSAN: Nope.

GRIMSHAW: Ah. So you have notions of looking after him yourself?

SUSAN: Nope. (*picks up a sheaf of papers from the desk and reads*) "Grimshaw's Life of Davenport." Good God — it actually exists.

GRIMSHAW: Of course it actually exists.

SUSAN: (*reading*) "An account of the life and times of two gentlemen of—"

GRIMSHAW: (*taking the papers from her*) Thank you.

SUSAN: You're actually writing his biography.

GRIMSHAW: Of course I'm actually writing his biography.

SUSAN: Why?

GRIMSHAW: (*floundering slightly*) Why not? I have things to say. Points I wish to make. Life presents the raw materials . . .

SUSAN: Have I made an appearance yet?

GRIMSHAW: Almost. I edited you out.

SUSAN: Thanks.

GRIMSHAW: Nothing personal, Susan, but you didn't fit.

SUSAN: Ah. Artistic license.

GRIMSHAW: Not at all. Merely careful management of the facts, to make sure they don't obscure the true portrait of J.J. as he ought to be seen.

SUSAN: Or as you would like to see him?

GRIMSHAW: One and the same. Which brings us back to my original question: what do you see in him?

SUSAN: He's different.

GRIMSHAW: Try again.

SUSAN: He makes me laugh.

GRIMSHAW: Marginally better.

SUSAN: (*defiantly*) Maybe he's great in bed.

GRIMSHAW: (*considering this, then shaking his head*) Not likely.

SUSAN: Look, what the hell is this?

GRIMSHAW: Susan. Susan, Susan, Susan. How shall I put this delicately?

SUSAN: Why don't you just spit it out?

GRIMSHAW: (*facing her*) You've picked him up. Now put him back down.

Slight pause.

SUSAN: Screw yourself.

GRIMSHAW: You don't know him. You don't have any idea who he is.

SUSAN: He's whoever he wants to be.

GRIMSHAW: You don't want him.

SUSAN: Don't tell me what I want.

GRIMSHAW: Susan—

SUSAN: (*angrily*) I'll want what I damn well want to want, okay?

GRIMSHAW: And you honestly want—?

J.J. enters.

J.J.: (*brightly*) Hi.

SUSAN and GRIMSHAW turn away, quickly.

J.J.: I'm back. (*tosses a cigarette package to GRIMSHAW*)

GRIMSHAW: Filters.

J.J.:   What?

GRIMSHAW: You've bought the ones with filters.

J.J.:   Oh.

GRIMSHAW: (*sulking*) No matter. I'll just break the filters off.

J.J.:   (*to SUSAN*) Shall we . . . ?

SUSAN: Look, I've got some stuff I really have to get done. I'll see you later. (*starts toward the door, rather quickly*)

J.J.:   But what about the timber-wolves?

GRIMSHAW: What timber-wolves?

J.J.:   (*to SUSAN*) I thought we were going to the zoo.

SUSAN: (*at the door*) I think I'm going to have to pass.

J.J.:   (*anxiously*) Tonight, then?

SUSAN: Tonight?

J.J.:   Are we still on? Eight o'clock? In front of the concession stand?

SUSAN: (*hesitating, then looking defiantly at GRIMSHAW*) Of course we're still on for tonight. See you then.

She exits. J.J. gazes after her, then turns to GRIMSHAW.

J.J.:   We're going down to the beach, tonight. Starlight. Sea air.

GRIMSHAW: You devil.

J.J.:   She's great, isn't she?

GRIMSHAW musters a grimace/smile.

J.J.:   I . . . guess I'd better take a look at that toilet. (*exits*)

GRIMSHAW: (*gloomily*) Art, you can edit. Life . . .

Scene Five

The beach. Night. Waves in the background, etc.

J.J. is alone. He has clearly been waiting for some time—fidgets anxiously, peers around, etc. At last he seems almost ready to give up . . . and SUSAN enters.

J.J.:   (*delighted*) Susan!

SUSAN: Sorry I'm late. I got . . . tied up.

J.J.:   That's okay. I'm always happy on a beach. Waves coming in, tide going out—lots of things to think about.

He smiles at her, brightly. SUSAN averts her eyes.

SUSAN: J.J. Um . . . listen.

J.J.:   Breathe, Susan.

SUSAN: I am breathing.

J.J.:   No, I mean breathe deeply. The salt air.

SUSAN: Right. J.J. . . .

J.J.:   I wrote a novel about the sea, once—well, part of a novel. "The Young Man and the Sea," in which wind-surfing became a metaphor for man's eternal struggle to find purpose and direction in a shifting universe. The hero gets eaten by a great white shark that turns up unexpectedly off Kits Beach.

SUSAN: You write novels, do you?

J.J.:   Oh, yes. Well, parts of novels. You know how it is — you get one idea, and then you get another idea . . . One of these days, though,

I'll go back and finish my wind–surfing novel. Wilf says it has potential. He said . . . how did he put it? . . . he said it shows a fine sensitivity to the confusion which is all round us.

SUSAN: Uh–huh.

J.J.: Maybe you'd like to read it, sometime.

SUSAN: J.J.? Can I ask you something?

J.J.: Sure.

SUSAN: What exactly do you do? I mean, from day to day.

J.J.: Well, I . . . I get up, I read, I think, I stroll . . .

SUSAN: And the next day?

J.J.: I stroll, I converse, I read . . .

SUSAN: Practise the violin and write cookies . . .

J.J.: And novels . . .

SUSAN: And the day after that?

J.J.: The day after that I devote to my stock portfolio and my stable of race–horses.

SUSAN: I was just asking.

J.J.: On alternate Tuesdays I make rezoning applications for shopping malls.

SUSAN: You don't need to be defensive.

J.J.: I wasn't being defensive. Why should I be defensive?

SUSAN: I don't know. Should you? (quickly) J.J., just listen for a moment. Look. I like you.

J.J.: (fervently) I really like you.

SUSAN: But I've been thinking that maybe we should just leave it at that.

J.J.: Leave it at what?

SUSAN: I think we should just . . . be friends.

Slight pause.

J.J.: (the ghost of a voice) Why?

SUSAN: I just think it's best. For both of us.

Another pause.

J.J.: Is there someone else?

SUSAN: No, of course there isn't. J.J. . . .

JASON enters.

JASON: (affably) Hi.

J.J. stares at JASON.

SUSAN: (to JASON; through her teeth) I told you to wait in the car.

JASON: (taking a deep breath and looking appreciatively skyward) What a view, eh?

J.J.: (looking at JASON, and then at SUSAN, and then gazing skyward) Yep, it's quite something.

SUSAN: (to J.J.) Jason said he'd give me a lift. Because I was running late.

J.J.: (still looking skyward) That's Sirius.

SUSAN: J.J., it was only a ride in a car.

J.J.: No, I mean up there — that's Sirius. The Dog Star.

SUSAN: Oh. Right.

J.J.: Brightest star in the northern sky, although it's almost nine million light-years away.

SUSAN: Really?

J.J.: Just off to the north is the Constellation of Orion, the Great Hunter. See the red star? That's Betelgeuse.

JASON: (*pointing*) See that, Susan?

SUSAN: See what?

JASON: Right there. That little light.

SUSAN: What is it?

JASON: That's my apartment. Twenty-first floor. It costs a bit, but you wouldn't believe the view.

J.J.: As you can see, Orion is looking upward over his left shoulder toward Taurus the bull.

SUSAN: What?

J.J.: Taurus, the bull. Right up there.

SUSAN: I don't think I can see it.

J.J.: Well, it's pretty faint. The stars get blocked out by the light from the city.

JASON: See that one, Susan? That's the Royal Bank Tower. Three blocks that way is 1055 West Hastings Street. Executive offices of the Jimmy Pattison Group. Jimmy Pattison. Just a kid from East Vancouver, and look where he is now. Hell of a nice guy, too.

SUSAN: You know him?

JASON: Sure — I know a lot of those guys. Pete Pocklington. Nel Skalbania. (*searching for another name*) Teddy Meridien.

SUSAN: Who?

JASON: Owns the Meridien Hotel.

J.J.: (*quiet desperation*) Susan? In classical myth, Taurus is associated with the god Jupiter.

JASON: And the thing about all those guys, Susan, is that they're independent men. They're rebels. They refused to conform — they did things their own way, and look at them now. They've got everything they want, and they can go to bed at night knowing that they've helped build up the country. Creating jobs for people — helping people who don't have the kind of ability that they have.

J.J.: Legend has it that Jupiter changed himself into a bull when he swam away from Phoenicia to Crete with the Princess Europa on his back.

JASON: See that light, Susan?

SUSAN: Which one?

JASON: The one that's moving.

J.J.: That's an airplane.

JASON: It's a bit tough to tell from this distance, but it looks like a Cessna 128. Oh, they're beautiful little machines. (*to SUSAN*) Would you like me to take you up, sometime?

SUSAN: Jason. Please. Would you just go wait in the car?

JASON: Oh. Sure. (*Begins to stroll off. Pauses and looks skyward.*) That's Betelgeuse, is it?

J.J.: Yep.

JASON: Son of a gun.

JASON exits. Pause. J.J. looks skyward again.

J.J.: Just north of Taurus are the Pleiades. According to myth . . .

SUSAN: J.J. I'm sorry.

J.J.: You'll get over it.

SUSAN turns and exits. J.J. continues to look skyward.

J.J.: According to myth, the Pleiades were daughters of Atlas, and nymphs of Diana. Orion saw them and pursued them. But Jupiter came to the rescue and changed them into doves. And then into stars.

Scene Six

The living room. GUY and BOBBY.

BOBBY: (*eagerly*) But listen, Guy. Like I was saying. This guy I met downtown, today. Eight thousand dollars!

GUY: Planting trees?

BOBBY: For seven weeks' work. For sure. He says, like you don't need any experience. You just tell them you want to go planting—seven weeks, and he made eight thousand dollars.

GUY: For sure, eh?

BOBBY: For sure. He said some guys make even more. Eight thousand dollars, and then you go down to Mexico for the winter. You just sleep on the beach, and pick fruit when you're hungry, and everybody down there is really together. I mean . . . you and me, Guy—if we both did it, we could make sixteen thousand dollars. And if Susan came, that's twenty-four thousand. We could, like, set up a recording studio, or something.

GUY: Planting trees?

BOBBY: That's what I'm telling you.

GUY: You want to know about tree-planting? I'll tell you about tree-planting. The contractors rip off the sub-contractors, and the sub-contractors rip off the planters, and you

work seven days a week for three months and come home with six hundred bucks after taxes.

BOBBY: God, you are such a . . . (*searching for the word*) cynic. (*exits through the hall door*)

GUY: (*calling after him, rather disgustedly*) Bobby . . .

SUSAN enters through the front door.

SUSAN: (*brightly*) Hi.

GUY: (*sourly*) Hello.

SUSAN: Grumpy bear. What's wrong with you?

GUY: I guess I didn't get much sleep last night.

SUSAN: (*coyly*) Neither did I. (*quickly*) Guy, you said I could use your bed.

GUY: I said *you* could use it. Singular.

SUSAN: J.J. is just a friend. That's all.

GUY: Oh, yeah?

SUSAN: Yeah. He's just a friend.

GUY: You've got lucky friends.

SUSAN: Don't be disgusting. And stop sulking—Jason'll be here in a minute.

GUY: Jason?

SUSAN: He's just parking the car.

GUY: The wank?

SUSAN: What?

GUY: Jumping Jason, the prince of the fern-bars?

SUSAN: What are you talking about? Jason Wagner, the landlord.

GUY: The landlord? What are *you* talking about?

SUSAN: Jason, who owns the house.

GUY: Are you kidding? His father owns it. It's Daddy's house, Daddy's Mercedes.

SUSAN: What?

GUY: Jason runs errands for Daddy, and pretends he's Conrad Black. The guy's pathetic.

JASON enters, breezily.

JASON: Hey, Susan, what do you say we— (*stops short as he sees GUY*) Oh. Hello, Guy.

GUY: Good to see you, Jason. Got the keys to the car tonight, eh?

JASON: (*to SUSAN*) Look, I, uh . . . really can't stay.

SUSAN: Why not?

GUY: Sure, come on in. Sit down. How's Pop these days?

JASON: My father is fine, Guy. Thank you for asking.

GUY: Good to hear. (*to SUSAN*) Yep, he's a fine man, Jason's father. Looks after his boy.

JASON: (*to SUSAN*) I'll give you a call. I've, ah . . . got some business to attend to.

He starts toward the door. A thought occurs, and he stops. Turns back toward GUY, trying to muster his most authoritative air.

JASON: By the way, my friend.

GUY: (*to SUSAN*) See? We're buddies.

JASON: Your rent's overdue.

GUY: No it isn't.

JASON: It's the sixth.

GUY: Right. And we don't have to pay till the seventh. Check the rental agreement. (*fractional pause*) Or ask your dad.

For a long moment, JASON tries to stare GUY down. It doesn't work. He turns abruptly to the door.

GUY: Straight home with the car, Jason. Don't stop at any fern-bars.

JASON: (*at the door*) Why don't you just drop dead, Guy? Why don't you just collect your Welfare cheque, and feel clever, and drop dead? Some of us have things to accomplish. (*exits, banging the door behind him*)

GUY: There he goes. The water-boy on the upwardly mobile team. God, I feel better now.

SUSAN: Do you have to feel so smug about everything?

GUY: (*cheerfully*) Probably not. Poor old Jason — the boy doesn't live in the real world. Did he tell you about the penthouse apartment and the pilot's license?

SUSAN: He mentioned something about that.

GUY: And you believed him? Oh, God. Did he tell you about the condominium in Corfu?

SUSAN: No.

GUY: Well, he usually saves that for the second date. Say, did he tell you—?

SUSAN: I don't want to talk about it. It's late.

GUY: You're right. It's late. Time for bed. (*smiles winningly at SUSAN*) Go ahead. You can have mine.

SUSAN: (*rather archly*) You're not planning to use it?

GUY: No, I don't think so. No, I'm pretty sure I'm not planning to climb into my good ol' bed tonight.

SUSAN: Be real sure.

GUY: I am. I am absolutely sure I won't be climbing into that bed.

He holds one hand up—and reacts in mock surprise as he discovers his fingers are crossed.

GUY: Whoops. Fingers were crossed.

SUSAN: Guy . . .

GUY: (*grinning and waving this off, to indicate that it was just a joke*) Sleep tight.

SUSAN eyes him narrowly for a moment, then exits. GUY watches her leave, then leans back on the couch.

GUY: She'll come round.

Scene Seven

The apartment. J.J. enters, clutching a bunch of flowers, and sinks despairingly down in the chair. Groans tragically. In a moment GRIMSHAW appears in the bedroom doorway wearing pyjamas and clutching a blanket around him.

GRIMSHAW: J.J. You're home.

J.J.: Oh, Wilf.

GRIMSHAW: What's wrong?

J.J.: She's thrown me over, Wilf. She's cast me aside. Like an old boot.

GRIMSHAW: An old boot?

J.J.: It's over.

GRIMSHAW: I . . . can't tell you how sorry I am.

J.J.: We were on the beach. I was telling her about my novel. She told me she wanted to be . . . just friends. And then she rode off into the night in the Mercedes of Wagner, Jason, landlord and youthful entrepreneur.

GRIMSHAW: The old story. The old, old story.

J.J.: I stood on the beach. I stared at the stars. They stared back. I thought, No, it's not possible, there must be some misunderstanding. So I went to her house. (*gets up and starts pacing agitatedly*) I ran down the sidewalk, flowers in my hand, flowers so fresh there was still dirt on the roots. But when I arrived, there *it* was. The Mercedes. My heart sank. I walked round the block. The Mercedes was still there. I realized . . . what's the point?

He tosses the flowers to the floor, and slumps back in the chair.

GRIMSHAW: J.J. At a time like this, I know this is cold comfort. But I speak as a friend. And as one who is older, and has seen more of life. J.J. . . . believe me . . . it's for the best.

J.J.: For the best?

GRIMSHAW: It wouldn't have worked.

J.J.: (*anguished*) Why wouldn't it have worked? How can you say that? Last night, it . . . it sang. I'm talking about love, about . . . children.

GRIMSHAW: Already?

J.J.: (*forlornly*) You could have been Uncle Wilf.

GRIMSHAW: Uncle Wilf?

J.J.:   You could have taken them on walks. To the petting zoo.

GRIMSHAW: To the pub. When they were a bit older. (*goes to the desk to pour himself a drink*) J.J., don't you think you're getting a bit ahead of yourself? I mean . . . one night together . . .

J.J.:   And that's all there's going to be. For one reason or another.

Slight pause. Then a thought strikes J.J. He leaps to his feet and advances upon GRIMSHAW.

J.J.:   What did you say to her?

GRIMSHAW: What?

J.J.:   This morning. What did you say to her?

GRIMSHAW: (*furtively*) Nothing.

J.J.:   You said something.

GRIMSHAW: (*very furtively*) I didn't.

J.J.:   You must have.

GRIMSHAW: How can you think that? Me, your best friend . . . (*floundering*) Well, we talked about you, yes. And perhaps . . . perhaps she realized that you and I are so close that it would be difficult . . . impossible . . . for someone else to—

J.J.:   What's that got to do with it? You're my best friend. Nothing's going to change that.

Slight pause. GRIMSHAW takes a large drink. It doesn't go down very well—he grimaces and holds his chest.

J.J.:   (*listlessly*) You okay?

GRIMSHAW: Just a small . . . pricking sensation.

J.J.:   (*giving up*) To hell with it. What's the point. What's the point in anything?

He shuffles back across the room, and slumps back down in the chair. GRIMSHAW stares at him. Then be bangs his glass down on the desk.

GRIMSHAW: That is not something that J.J. Davenport would say.

J.J.:   I just said it.

GRIMSHAW: (*indicating the sheaf of papers*) Not the J.J. Davenport whose life is recorded in these pages.

J.J.:   Wilf . . .

GRIMSHAW: This J.J. Davenport would say, Wait. He would say, Let me stop and reflect upon what she said.

J.J.:   She said she just wants to be friends.

GRIMSHAW: And have women not said this since time immemorial, to test the devotion of their suitors?

J.J.:   (*dully*) Have they?

GRIMSHAW: Precedents. Countless precedents. Bad literature is full of them.

J.J.:   And life imitates bad literature?

GRIMSHAW: It certainly doesn't imitate good literature. (*seizing upon an example*) Abelard and Heloise. Abelard, the greatest scholar of his age, is hired as a private tutor to young Heloise. Love blossoms. A passion scarcely comprehensible to mortal mind. A furious father finds out. Dispatches Heloise to a nunnery. Dispatches hired thugs to Abelard's lodgings, to perform the unkindest cut of all. (*makes a cutting motion in the direction of his groin*) In his agony, Abelard writes to Heloise: "Whatever shall we do?" And Heloise, cloistered in her tiny cell, writes back: "I think we should just be friends."

GRIMSHAW pauses briefly to consider this. J.J. groans.

GRIMSHAW: Bad example.

J.J.:   But what about him? And his car? How can I compete with that?

GRIMSHAW: Compete? Is this where twenty-five hundred years of Western culture have led us? To the point where a man of refinement surrenders to a car?

J.J.:   It's not just a car. It's a Mercedes.

GRIMSHAW: No. No, no, no. That is not what J.J. Davenport would say.

J.J.:   And there *he* is, oozing self-confidence and real-estate transactions. What do I have to offer?

GRIMSHAW: Is philosophy nothing to offer? Are literature and art nothing to offer?

J.J.:   He has a pilot's license.

GRIMSHAW: And so do you—a license to soar on the wings of imagination into the stratosphere of the soul. (*impressed with this turn of phrase, jots it down*) Not bad. (*resuming*) What is a real-estate transaction to the goddess of the dawn? What is an automobile to the soul of a woman? For you have led me to believe, Sir, that she has a soul.

J.J.:   Of course she has a soul. She has a very nice soul.

GRIMSHAW: Then how can she spurn what you have to offer?

J.J. considers this. Then, very slowly, stands. As he does, we hear the faint strains of eighteenth-century music—measured and orderly—in the background. J.J. begins to pace, hands behind his back, adopting "Johnsonian" cadences.

J.J.:   It does seem strange.

GRIMSHAW: 'Tis very strange.

J.J.:   'Tis passing strange.

GRIMSHAW: 'Tis strange.

The music becomes louder.

J.J.:   Sir, you have known women.

GRIMSHAW: I have met them.

J.J.:   And you have observed, Sir, that it is a habit of the sex to strew sharp stones along the primrose path to love?

GRIMSHAW: Sharp stones and rusty nails, Sir, to test the mettle and unhinge the unmanly.

J.J.:   Fie, fie upon the unhinged and unmanly.

GRIMSHAW: Stoutly said.

J.J.:   Then the path that lies ahead is clear. I banish despair from my heart.

GRIMSHAW: Banish it, Sir.

J.J.:   And tomorrow morning, at the crack of eleven, I go to her house.

GRIMSHAW: At the very crack of eleven.

J.J.:   I'll do it, Sir.

GRIMSHAW: Well done, Sir.

J.J.:   I am not, Sir, beaten, Sir, yet, Sir. (*with a flourish, exits into the bedroom*)

GRIMSHAW: Well said, Sir. Well said! You are not beaten yet.

Music fizzles out. Slight pause. GRIMSHAW turns away, his optimism visibly evaporating.

You are not beaten yet. It is a little-known historical fact that this is precisely what a well-meaning standard-bearer said to Napoleon on the morning they discovered there are winters in Russia.

Blackout.

ACT TWO

Scene One

The living room. J.J. is alone, having just entered.

J.J.:   Is anyone home? Susan?

MURRAY enters from the hall door. He wears round-rimmed glasses, a vest, and baggy cords.

J.J.:   Oh, hi.

MURRAY: What do you want?

J.J.:   Is Susan here?

MURRAY: Nope. (*begins to exit*)

J.J.:   Do you know where she went?

MURRAY: (*turning back to him*) Who are you?

J.J.:   What? (*Stares at him for a moment. Then, believing this must be a joke, he begins to laugh.*) Right. Right.

MURRAY: Do you have a problem?

J.J.:   What?

MURRAY: She's with Guy and Bobby. I think they got tired of sitting here doing nothing, so they went out to do nothing.

J.J.:   Bobby?

MURRAY: (*beginning to exit again*) You can wait here if you want. Just don't turn on the stereo.

J.J.:   (*his face lighting up as the penny drops*) Murray!

MURRAY: Yeah.

J.J.:   I thought you were Bobby.

MURRAY: I thought you were brain damaged.

J.J.:   You're the philosophy student. Hi! I'm J.J. Susan may have told you about me. I'm basically a philosopher too.

MURRAY: (*not very interested*) Yeah? What's your field?

J.J.:   Oh, philosophy in general, I suppose. Philosophy of life. The meaning of things. What's your, uh, field?

MURRAY: Nineteenth-Century German Idealism.

J.J.:   Oh, right. German Idealism. Like . . . the Romantics.

MURRAY: No, like Schopenhauer. The Romantics have nothing to do with it.

J.J.:   (*out of his depth*) Oh. Right. Of course. Schopenhauer. Like . . . the philosophy of idealism.

MURRAY: The dichotomy between the material and the subjective, with the only reality being the subjective consciousness.

J.J.:   Like . . . the imagination.

MURRAY: That's part of it.

J.J.:   (*heartened*) Yes, well that's pretty much my philosophy too, as a matter of fact.

MURRAY: Of course, to Schopenhauer the subjective consciousness isn't worth anything either, in which case the only goal in life is being dead.

J.J.: Right. Actually, I'm probably more familiar with the Classics. Plato. The ethical works, mainly. What's the one . . . long name, begins with *N* or *M* . . .

MURRAY: *Nichomachean Ethics?*

J.J.: That's the one.

MURRAY: That's Aristotle.

J.J.: Oh, right. Aristotle.

MURRAY: Just leave the stereo alone, okay? (*exits*)

J.J.: (*calling after him*) Listen, we should get together sometime, when you're not busy. Talk about ... about philosophy, or something.

SUSAN enters through the front door.

J.J.: Susan. Hi.

SUSAN: Oh. Hi.

J.J.: I was waiting for you.

SUSAN: I was out.

J.J.: I tried to call you a couple of times, earlier on . . .

SUSAN: I've been kind of in and out.

J.J.: I was just talking to Murray. Fascinating guy. We had a great talk — German Idealism, that sort of thing.

SUSAN: Oh, yes?

J.J.: Actually, I've been thinking that maybe I ought to go back to school myself. Get my M.A. After I get my B.A.

SUSAN: Why?

J.J.: What?

SUSAN: Why? What are you and Murray going to do when you're finished. Set up a small philosopher's shop and do contract work or something?

J.J.: But that's not the point. I mean, it doesn't have to be practical.

SUSAN: (*patronising*) You guys. All of you. Sooner or later, don't you think you should do something? (*begins to go to the hall door*)

J.J.: Well actually . . . Actually I kind of thought that maybe *we* could do something.

SUSAN: J.J.

J.J.: Like . . . maybe dinner. (*quickly*) Somewhere really classy. A French restaurant. Bottle of wine, candlelight, sparkling conversation . . .

SUSAN: And sneak out the bathroom window when the bill arrives?

J.J.: As a matter of fact, I had a cheque come in today.

SUSAN: From where? It's not Welfare Day.

J.J.: No, it's a . . . a private connection. Someone I've done a few favours for. She sends me a bit, each month. A sort of relative. In fact, uh . . . my mother.

SUSAN: I've got to run. See you.

She exits through the hall door. Long pause.

J.J.: Sure. See you.

Scene Two

The apartment. J.J. is sitting dejectedly.

GRIMSHAW, considerably drunk, enters from outside. He stops and stares at J.J. Then begins declaiming, as if quoting from the Biography.

GRIMSHAW: In its original conception, "Grimshaw's Life of Davenport" was to have been the study of a philosophical mind, unsullied by the vagaries of the world.

Gives J.J. a pointed look. Then takes a mickey bottle from his coat pocket, plunks it down on the desk, and shambles into the bedroom, taking off his coat.

GRIMSHAW: *(off)* But life, unlike art, lacks an instinct for consistency.

J.J. glares after GRIMSHAW. Gets up, grabs the mickey, and paces across the apartment.

GRIMSHAW: *(off)* Thus it was that I returned to our lodgings one evening to find J.J. Davenport — idler and philosopher — lapsed into melancholy. *(re-enters and makes his way to the desk)* And from this melancholy he passed into a brown study, marked by the loss of his characteristic bonhommie. By the absence of his celebrated wit.

J.J.: Would you just for Christ's sake shut up?

GRIMSHAW: And ultimately by the collapse of his syntax. *(Sits at the desk. Picks up his glass, and extends it toward J.J.)*

J.J.: *(muttering)* You've had enough.

GRIMSHAW continues to extend the glass. J.J. relents, and pours him a small drink.

GRIMSHAW: Don't be rude.

J.J. pours another few drops into the glass.

GRIMSHAW: You're very kind. Your health. *(Takes a large drink as J.J. moves away.)* J.J., look. I blame myself. I should never have encouraged you. Listen—

J.J.: *(sharply)* I'm trying to think. *(Crosses the room, banging the mickey back down on the desk as he does.)* Ask yourself, Wilf. Ask yourself the question. What does she want?

GRIMSHAW: I have no idea. And I'll lay you odds that she doesn't, either.

J.J.: Of course she knows what she wants. We just have to work through this logically. So let's start with what she doesn't want. And what she doesn't want . . . is me.

GRIMSHAW: This, unfortunately, is the point.

J.J.: No, wait. That isn't true. What she doesn't want is the me I happen to be at the moment.

GRIMSHAW: What?

J.J.: She just doesn't take me seriously. In fact, I think she thinks I'm a bit . . . a bit of a bozo.

GRIMSHAW: Fie!

J.J.: Well, what if she's right? Wilf, I'm thirty years old. I have to face facts. Maybe I've overestimated the speed at which the new Renaissance is approaching. These things take time, after all. And perhaps . . . perhaps I'm not the sort of person who should be trying to lead the way. Perhaps I'm the sort of person who should be doing . . . something else.

GRIMSHAW: Like what?

J.J.: Well, perhaps she'd see me differently if I . . . if I had a job.

GRIMSHAW: *(staring at him and slowly draining his glass)* A job?

J.J.: I could still read books, in the evenings and on weekends. I could even write the odd one. But if I had a job . . .

GRIMSHAW: You don't want a job. You don't. Want a job.

J.J. looks at him steadily.

GRIMSHAW: I mean . . . if you got a job . . . what about me?

J.J.: You could get one too.

GRIMSHAW stares at him. Then begins to laugh—a drunken giggle that swells to an incredulous guffaw and finally ends in a coughing fit. GRIM-SHAW takes a drink from the bottle to compose himself.

GRIMSHAW: *(now very drunk)* J.J. Listen to me. I am going to make a speech.

J.J.: Wilf . . .

GRIMSHAW: It is not often that I make speeches. But when I do, they are of profound significance.

GRIMSHAW makes his way round to the front of the desk. Positions a footstool there and climbs onto it, as if mounting a platform to address an audience.

GRIMSHAW: I serve notice that my voice is going to ring. Like a mighty pipe-organ. I am going to speak of fidelity. To companions. To ideals. And ultimately to the self. *(voice rising)* Oh, yes. Fidelity to the self. And when I have finished this speech, I shall . . . *(begins to teeter precariously)* I shall . . . *(Another precarious teeter. He plops down so that he is sitting on the edge of the desk.)* When I have finished . . .

For a long moment, he stares straight ahead. Then he flops backward, lying across the desk, passed out.

J.J.: *(muttering)* Wilf.

J.J. goes into the bedroom, returns with a blanket, and drapes it over GRIMSHAW. Then exits back into the bedroom.

An abrupt lighting-shift signals the shift into "GRIMSHAW'S dream." Simultaneously, dark music begins. (If possible, some dry ice.) GRIM-SHAW sits bolt upright, eyes wide. From opposite sides of the stage, the two tempters enter, wearing black cloaks. (TEMPTER ONE is played by the actor playing JASON, TEMPTER TWO by the actor playing GUY.) GRIMSHAW stares from one to the other.

TEMPTER ONE: Where is he?

GRIMSHAW: Who are you?

TEMPTER TWO: *(calling)* J.J. Davenport.

GRIMSHAW: *(demanding)* Who are you?

J.J. enters, slowly, dreamlike. Dark music begins to swell.

TEMPTER ONE: I am the Spirit of Career Counselling.

TEMPTER TWO: And I, of Upward Mobility.

TEMPTER ONE: Summoned hither this night . . .

TEMPTER TWO: By the bleat of a soul in torment.

J.J.: Me?

GRIMSHAW: Get away.

TEMPTER ONE: *(to J.J.)* Come.

TEMPTER TWO: Speak with us.

J.J.: *(beginning to back away)* Uh . . . Jeez . . . Look . . .

SUSAN enters wearing a diaphanous gown. Stands on the side of the stage opposite J.J.

J.J.: Susan!

He begins to run toward her—and is stopped short, as if by an invisible wall.

TEMPTER ONE: *(chuckling)* No, no.

TEMPTER TWO: *(chuckling)* Dear me.

TEMPTER ONE: No. First, we must show you the paths.

J.J.: Show me!

GRIMSHAW: Don't!

TEMPTER TWO: Look.

TEMPTER ONE: One path is the Narrow Road that leads to the Professions.

THE TEMPTERS point out an imaginary path.

J.J.: (*anxiously*) It's a bit rocky, isn't it?

TEMPTER TWO: It is rocky and long, but look what lies at the end. There — what do you see?

J.J.: I see . . . a door. And on the door I see a sign.

TEMPTER ONE: And what does the sign say?

J.J.: It says . . . (*becoming excited*) It says "Abernathy, Abernathy and Davenport, Attorneys at Law." That's my name!

J.J. starts toward the "door," but TEMPTER ONE checks him.

TEMPTER ONE: But to get there, you must pass through the Law Library.

J.J.: (*peering ahead*) It's a . . . bit dark, isn't it?

TEMPTER ONE: Light does not pass through the pages of those mighty textbooks.

J.J. puts his hands to his ears, as if trying to block out a painful sound.

J.J.: That sound—that whine. What is it?

TEMPTER ONE: That is the droning of the great Conformity Generators in the basement. But come . . .

J.J.: No, wait. Just a sec . . . (*begins to pull away*)

SUSAN: J.J.?

J.J.: Susan!

TEMPTER TWO: There is another road.

GRIMSHAW: Don't listen to him.

TEMPTER TWO: See? It is paved with gold, and it leads to the shining City of Commerce.

J.J.: Oh, yes.

GRIMSHAW: No.

TEMPTER ONE: But first! What would you be willing to do to win the girl?

J.J.: I'd do anything.

TEMPTER TWO: Will you forswear philosophy and turn your thoughts to worldly things?

J.J.: I will.

TEMPTER ONE: Will you abandon idle comrades and idle books, and read the autobiography of Lee Iacocca?

J.J.: Yes.

GRIMSHAW: No!

TEMPTER TWO: Then look. Can you see that trendy-but-informal restaurant?

J.J.: That one there?

TEMPTER TWO: Where upwardly mobile young men and women gather to do lunch. Can you see yourself there?

J.J.: Yes. Yes I can! There I am—I'm saying, "Damn the risk, let's do the deal."

GRIMSHAW: No, that's not you! You're the other one. You're saying . . .

J.J.:   (*as if mesmerized*) Hi. My name's J.J., and I'm your waiter. The specials today are—

GRIMSHAW: Worse than death!

SUSAN exits.

J.J.:   Susan!

He starts after her. As he does, the TEMPTERS descend upon him, wrapping him in their cloaks and dragging him offstage.

GRIMSHAW: Get thee behind him!

Music builds to a terrible crescendo. GRIMSHAW stares in helpless horror. Then the music cuts out, and as it does GRIMSHAW slumps backward again across the desk, clutching his blanket.

Blackout.

Lights up quickly: Morning. Birds chirping. GRIM- SHAW lies sprawled across the desk as we had left him. He stirs, beginning to awaken. Sits up slowly.

J.J. enters. He is short haired and wears a cheap and ill-fitting jacket.

J.J.:   'Morning, Wilf.

GRIMSHAW stares at him, then shrieks in horror.

Blackout.

Scene Three

The living room. GUY is slouched on the chester- field, arms folded, staring straight ahead. SUSAN enters.

SUSAN: Morning.

GUY: Yeah.

SUSAN: You're up early.

GUY: Yeah. What time is it?

SUSAN: Noon.

GUY: God. Up with the bankers.

SUSAN: Where's Bobby?

GUY: What?

SUSAN: Bobby. Your friend. Our housemate.

GUY: He's not back yet.

SUSAN: Where did he go?

GUY: He's, uh . . . visiting people. He should be back soon. If all goes well.

SUSAN: What do you mean, if all goes well?

GUY: Well, I don't much care for the peo- ple he's visiting.

SUSAN: What are you talking about? Who are they?

GUY: Some people we met last night. Downtown. On the mall. They wanted Bobby to spend the night with them, so he did.

SUSAN: With some people you met on the mall? That's crazy.

GUY: Yeah, they were real scum-buckets.

SUSAN: Then why in God's name did he go with them? Why did you let him?

GUY: Didn't have much choice.

SUSAN: Why not?

GUY: 'Cause they were cops.

SUSAN: Bobby's in jail?

GUY: I figured you'd catch on.

SUSAN: Oh, for God's sake. Why?

GUY: Because there was some stuff in my knapsack.

SUSAN: Stuff?

GUY: Substances, okay? Drugs. We were trying to sell some dope. We got busted.

SUSAN: Oh, Christ.

GUY: Right. Nobody supports the small businessman.

SUSAN: Hang on. You said it was in your knapsack.

GUY: Yeah.

SUSAN: If it was in your knapsack, then how come Bobby got busted?

GUY: Because we told the cops it was his.

SUSAN: What?

GUY: A conviction might have dashed my hopes to go into the priesthood. Bobby insisted. Let me bear this cross alone, he said. Go forward. Save souls.

SUSAN: You let Bobby go to jail for your dope?

GUY: That's what I said.

SUSAN: How could you?

GUY: Because I've been busted before, okay? I get busted again, and I'm doing three months. This is Bobby's first offence, so he'll get off with a fine. Hundred bucks. Couple of hundred, tops.

SUSAN: Oh, my God.

GUY: We're buddies. We stick together. Look, it's no problem. I'll pay his fine. It's no sweat.

SUSAN: No problem? Bobby winds up with a criminal record.

GUY: True. His chances of becoming Minister of Justice are now slim.

SUSAN: Your friend is in jail for something that you did—

GUY: That *we* did.

SUSAN: And you sit here making jokes.

GUY: Well, what am I supposed to do? Sure, I feel bad. I'm sorry. I wish it hadn't happened, but it did. Look, they're not going to keep him in there. They'll haul him up before a judge this morning, set a trial date, and let him go. He'll get off with a fine. Honest. I have experience with these things.

SUSAN: (*sitting down wearily*) Why were you selling dope in the first place?

GUY: Because we have to eat.

SUSAN: The nice people at the Ministry of Human Resources send you a cheque each month.

GUY: Sure. For three hundred and seventy-nine bucks. You want to try to live on three-hundred-seventy-nine a month?

SUSAN: Then get a job.

GUY: Sure.

SUSAN: You could find something if you looked hard enough.

GUY: Maybe. For four bucks an hour. No thanks.

SUSAN: I see. It's all someone else's fault.

GUY: Tell me. How long have you known Bobby?

SUSAN: A few years.

GUY: You know him pretty well?

SUSAN: What's this got to do with it?

GUY: Would you hire him? To do anything? You just don't understand, do you? You just don't understand anything at all.

SUSAN: Don't try to patronize me.

GUY: You march out of Daddy's house, carrying the little savings account you managed to put together because Daddy's been paying all the bills. And you set up shop here—where, incidentally, you don't pay any of the bills either.

SUSAN: You invited me to stay here for a few days. As a guest.

GUY: That's what we did, all right. Because we're a couple of guys who just plain love to look after other folks.

SUSAN: (standing) Fine. I'm going. You can have your bed back.

GUY: No, no. What's mine is yours. We'll share it.

SUSAN: What?

GUY: It's big enough for two, as long as you snuggle up a bit. You know that already, of course.

SUSAN: That's very amusing.

GUY: I'm not being amusing. I'm being perfectly serious. I mean, all this free rent you've been getting—it would be downright unneighbourly not to make a friendly gesture in return.

SUSAN: Don't be repulsive.

GUY: (standing to face her) Really? You find me repulsive? You don't find I have a certain boyish charm?

SUSAN: Drop dead.

GUY: I've always thought I was kind of appealing, in a rascally sort of way. Don't you think so?

She begins to turn away: he grabs her wrist.

SUSAN: Let go of me.

GUY: Why?

SUSAN: Because I said to.

GUY: Let's go to bed.

SUSAN: What?

She tries to pull away; GUY holds on.

GUY: I think that's a swell idea. Don't you?

SUSAN: Let me go.

GUY: We could do it right here, if you like.

SUSAN: Murray!

MURRAY: (off; irritably) What is it?

Slight pause. GUY releases SUSAN and steps back.

GUY: Another sinner called back from the brink by the Voice of the Man Upstairs.

SUSAN runs out of the room through the hall door.

GUY: Hey, I was just joking. Can't you take a joke? (goes to the door and calls after her) Come on. For God's sake, I wasn't going to rape you or anything. Jesus!

Pause. GUY goes to the stereo and turns it on, angrily.

MURRAY: *(off)* Would you turn that damn thing down?

GUY glares in the direction of MURRAY's voice. Then turns the stereo on full blast and exits.

Scene Four

The downstage area is set for the bar of the Blackwater Hotel. A pub table and two chairs. Two or three empty beer glasses, and one half-full.

GRIMSHAW is at the table, alone. The sheaf of papers which constitutes the Biography is on the table in front of him. GRIMSHAW has a pen in hand but is "thinking aloud" rather than actually writing.

GRIMSHAW: A biographer's first allegiance, of course, is to the truth. And my sacred aim in compiling "The Life of Davenport" has been to record faithfully the facts as they have presented themselves. Allowing for a certain poetic license. But we are frail creatures, and too much truth is a thing we cannot bear. Thus it is that I draw a curtain across J.J. Davenport's quest for employment. Suffice it to say that he has tried, with a determination that does him credit. Suffice it to say . . . that there's not much point in saying anything.

J.J., still short haired and wearing the cheap jacket, enters and slumps down at the table, thoroughly defeated. Pause.

GRIMSHAW: Say, I heard a rather good one the other day. A piece of string goes into a bar, and he—

J.J.: How do they do it, Wilf?

GRIMSHAW: How does who do what?

J.J.: All those people, working in the shops and the restaurants. How do they get there? What's the trick to it?

GRIMSHAW: I believe it's something genetic, passed down in the blood. In any case, this piece of string—

J.J.: They all have nice apartments, Wilf, and ten-speed bicycles. People smile at them when they walk into a bank. When I walk into a bank, the tellers go all shifty and the customers fidget.

GRIMSHAW: And what do you think happened when Samuel Johnson walked into a bank, with his clothes unwashed and his wig on crooked?

J.J.: Yes, but Sam wrote a dictionary. That makes all the difference. What am I supposed to do in an age when all the dictionaries have been written?

GRIMSHAW: You need a drink. That's what you need. *(calling)* Waitress? Nurse? *(resuming)* In any case, the piece of string orders a drink. But the bartender says, "You aren't a piece of string, are you?" "Yes," says the piece of string, "I'm afraid I am." "Get out," says the bartender. "We don't serve string here." And so he—

J.J.: I'd forgotten one crucial thing, Wilf. I'd forgotten why I'd never tried to do anything in the first place. It was because I had the sneaking suspicion I'd find out I couldn't do it.

GRIMSHAW: What are you talking about? You've done all sorts of things.

J.J.: No I haven't. I mean, what have I *done*? What have I actually *done*?

GRIMSHAW: But the trick isn't to *do*, for heaven's sake—the trick is to *be*. Look over there, for instance. Look at The Belle.

J.J.: The what?

GRIMSHAW: Rose. The Belle of the Blackwater Hotel. Over there. Against the wall. Underneath the golden galleon on black velvet.

J.J.:   Oh.

GRIMSHAW: The Belle of the Blackwater has been sitting under that dreadful painting every day for twenty years. She likes that painting because the gold sets off the colour of her hair, and the black velvet sets off the colour of her mascara. Every year, her dress fades another little bit, but her hair just gets more and more golden, and she is still as radiant as the spring.

J.J.:   No she isn't.

GRIMSHAW: That's because you haven't been drinking. You aren't seeing her as she ought to be seen. And in forty years, J.J., the Belle of the Blackwater will still be under that painting, and she will still be radiant.

J.J.:   In forty years she'll be about eighty-seven.

GRIMSHAW: And in forty years I'll be a hundred and one, and thus she will still be a blossom of youth in my eyes. (calling) Hello, Rosie my love. Smile at us, Rosie, and let the flowers bloom again. (to J.J.) There. Did you see? She smiled.

J.J.:   She smiled.

GRIMSHAW: And what a smile it is. A tiny tilting of the head, a tiny upturning of the little lips. Oh, she's a lady, J.J. She never opens her mouth when she smiles.

J.J.:   That's probably because she doesn't have teeth.

GRIMSHAW: Don't be offensive, Sir. Don't be absurd. Of course she has teeth. She just may not have them with her, at the moment. (calling) Nurse? Another round. (to J.J.) In any case, the piece of string goes to a second bar, and the same thing happens. "Are you a piece of string?" says the bartender. "Yes, I'm afraid I am," says the piece of string. "Get out," says the bartender. "We don't serve string here."

And the same thing happens at every bar he goes to. At last, falling into despair, the piece of string goes back to his room—

While he has been speaking, GRIMSHAW has pulled three or four twenty-dollar bills from his pocket.

J.J.:   Where did you get that?

GRIMSHAW: (instantly furtive) What?

J.J.:   The money.

GRIMSHAW: Oh, I . . . I, ah, came into it, so to speak.

J.J.:   Okay, don't tell me. I probably don't want to know.

GRIMSHAW: Here. You take half of it.

J.J.:   No, no. It's your money.

GRIMSHAW: Yes, but ownership is . . . well, it's such a relative concept, isn't it? Here.

J.J.:   Keep it.

GRIMSHAW: What's mine is yours, and what's yours is mine, sir.

J.J.:   Forget it. For God's sake, just don't wave it around in a place like this.

GRIMSHAW: Why not, for heaven's sake? We're among friends here.

J.J.:   Sure we are.

GRIMSHAW: Of course we are. There is Rose, the Belle of the Blackwater Hotel. And there is Frank, who may have seen better days, but who can still swallow a whole pickled egg to win a wager. There is old Wally, who was a prospector in his youth. Or at least, he's read enough Robert Service to be able to tell stories about having been a prospector in his youth, which comes out to more or less the same thing.

J.J.:   Is this where it all leads, Wilf?

GRIMSHAW: Is what where what all leads?

J.J.:   Is this. Where it all leads.

GRIMSHAW: Well, I suppose it's one destination. Among others.

J.J.:   Do you ever look at people like that, and suddenly realize that they must have been children, once? What did they look like, when they were children? There must be old yellow photographs of them somewhere, their faces washed and their cow-licks on end. Standing with older brothers and sisters on the porch. Wearing caps and short trousers. Waiting for the photographer to leave so they could go play ball. Are you in an old yellow photograph like that, Wilf?

GRIMSHAW: Good God, how would I remember a thing like that? I don't know. Maybe. Probably.

J.J.:   So how did those children wind up here? Was it a series of slightly wrong turns? Was it one major miscalculation? Or did someone just build the Blackwater Hotel on the spot where they happened to find themselves standing at the time?

GRIMSHAW: Ah, there you have it, sir. There you have it. You are a philosopher.

J.J.:   (flaring) I am not a philosopher. I'm unemployed.

GRIMSHAW: You are an unemployed philosopher. All true philosophers are unemployed. It's an occupational hazard.

Slight pause. J.J. turns away.

GRIMSHAW: In any case, plunged into despair, the piece of string goes to his room. He hurls himself against the walls, he batters himself, he rolls on the floor tying himself into horrible contortions . . .

J.J.:   (looking round) Self-delusion, Wilf. That's what got them here. That's what did it. And what do you know . . . here we are.

Another slight pause.

GRIMSHAW: Having battered and contorted himself, the piece of string goes back to the first bar and orders a drink. "Hey," says the bartender. "Aren't you that piece of string I threw out a couple of hours ago?" And the piece of string looks him straight in the eye and says: "I'm afraid not."

GRIMSHAW laughs. No response from J.J. The laugh trails off.

GRIMSHAW: A frayed knot?

J.J.:   Look at us, Wilf. Who are we? Who are you?

GRIMSHAW: Me? (considers this for a moment) I am a man of refinement, now faded and occasionally misplaced, who is slightly battered and slightly bowed but largely unbroken by the vicissitudes of the world.

J.J.:   You're an old drunk.

GRIMSHAW: (staring, rather shocked; tries to collect himself) I may be old, and I may be drunk. But this does not in itself make me an old drunk.

J.J.:   Look at yourself, Wilf.

GRIMSHAW: (voice rising) I am Wilfred Grimshaw. What Wilfred Grimshaw is may not be much, but in all this wide world there is only one of him, and that in itself makes him worthy of notice.

J.J.:   (bitterly) Sure. The whole world should notice Wilfred Grimshaw. Just like it should notice me. Bullshit. We don't do a goddamn thing worth noticing.

GRIMSHAW: (*attempting* gravitas) Those who wish to know me better need only read my writing. (*picks up the sheaf of papers, dramatically*) As you are aware, I am writing a biography.

J.J.: And I wish to God you'd stop writing it.

GRIMSHAW: It is, perhaps, a personal statement as much as it is a biography, reflecting as it does my belief that there are ideals which are worth admiring, if only from afar, and a mode of life which is worth aspiring to, even if one cannot live it.

J.J.: Why don't you just burn that thing?

GRIMSHAW: My task as a biographer, I must confess, has not been made easy by my subject, who shows an increasing penchant for betraying the better part of himself, and running off down dead-end alleys, and abandoning the very ideals which—

J.J.: Stop trying to invent me!

J.J. seizes the papers and throws them across the room. GRIMSHAW lurches to his feet.

GRIMSHAW: Someone has to. You've made a total cock-up of inventing yourself.

Silence. GRIMSHAW wilts.

GRIMSHAW: I'm sorry. I had no right.

J.J.: (*quietly*) Don't be sorry. Just leave me alone. Now. And for good. (*exits swiftly*)

GRIMSHAW: (*starting after him*) Wait. J.J. . . .

GRIMSHAW shambles to a stop. Pause. Looks round at the scattered papers and begins, slowly, to collect them. Clutching the papers, he looks around the bar, then focusses on Rosie.

GRIMSHAW: (*attempting to rally*) Rosie. Rosie, my love. Would you do me a tremendous favour? Would you permit me to purchase

you a drink, and gaze lovingly at you across the table? (*musters a smile, in response to a presumably favourable reply*) Ah, Rosie. Whatever, whatever, whatever would I do without you?

Fade to black.

Scene Five

The living room. J.J. is alone, having just entered.

J.J.: Susan? (*slightly louder*) Susan?

Slight pause. GUY enters from the hall door.

GUY: Good God — what happened to your hair?

J.J.: I had it cut. Where's Susan?

GUY: Looks like she's gone.

J.J.: Gone where?

GUY: Where else? You look ridiculous—are you joining the army or something?

J.J.: Gone where?

GUY: Home. Mom and Dad.

J.J.: (*stunned*) What? Why?

GUY: Oh, I think maybe the game started to get real. That's Susan for you, takes a shine to things, then runs off when she finds out what they're really like. Course, I don't need to tell you about that, do I?

J.J.: When did she leave? I mean, she didn't call me, leave a message . . .

GUY: Why would she call you? You were Tuesday night. I was Friday night. Bobby was Saturday morning.

J.J.: That's not true.

GUY: If Murray had been willing to leave the books for five minutes, he could have been Sunday brunch.

J.J.:   That's not true!

MURRAY: (*off; irritably*) Keep it down, would you—I'm trying to work.

GUY strolls to the couch and sits down, preparing to enjoy himself enormously.

GUY: Susan's a butterfly, old son. She thought she'd flutter around for a bit, and now she's gone back to the glass case. Right about now, she'll be watching television in the rec room. By fall she'll be safely back in university, and by next Christmas she'll be engaged to a Business Major. That's the situation, old son — although it's kind of a shame. She wasn't bad, was she?

J.J.:   Take that back.

GUY: Not as experienced as she'd like you to believe, but she makes up for it in enthusiasm, eh?

J.J.:   (*voice shaking*) I'm warning you. Take back every word you've just said.

GUY: (*bursting into laughter*) Oh, God it's the Scarlet Pimpernel.

J.J.:   Apologize for what you've just said about Susan.

GUY stops laughing. Stands and approaches J.J. as if greatly concerned.

GUY: Oh, no. Oh, dear. This isn't . . . love, is it? You poor son of a bitch.

J.J.:   Take it back!

MURRAY: (*off*) Shut up, would you?

GUY: It's love, isn't it? My God. I've insulted the woman you love, and now . . . now you're going to Give Me A Thrashing.

J.J.:   That's it. You've had your chance.

Furiously, J.J. begins to pull his jacket off—and gets his arms temporarily entangled in the sleeves.

GUY: Don't you understand? She spent the night with you because it wasn't the done thing. Here was Susan, the little girl in rebellion, and there were you, a refugee from another galaxy altogether.

J.J. gets the jacket off and flings it to the floor.

GUY: Of course she had to sleep with you—and all the while she was thinking to herself, "Oh gosh, oh gosh, if only Dad could see me now."

J.J. lurches at GUY who pushes him to the floor and stands over him.

GUY: The problem was, she couldn't get rid of you afterwards. Every time she turned around, here were you, spanielling after her. You poor, pathetic son of a bitch.

MURRAY enters, quietly furious.

MURRAY: Will you shut up so that some of us can get some work done?

GUY: (*stepping back and becoming instantly "innocent"*) Oh, sorry Murr. We were just trying to make enough noise to raise the dead philosophers.

MURRAY: You useless prick.

GUY: (*to J.J.*) It's for you.

MURRAY: You make me sick—sitting here collecting your Welfare cheque . . .

GUY: (*mock astonishment*) I don't believe this. I'm going to get a lecture on the work ethic from our tame Marxist?

MURRAY: I'm a socialist, yes. And that's precisely why you make me sick.

GUY: But you'll put in a good word for us, won't you, Murr, when the Revolution comes? You won't let them send us to re-education camps in Regina?

MURRAY: (*calmly*) Sitting here, collecting your Welfare cheques and feeling clever. You like to think you're making some kind of political statement, don't you? Well, you're not. You're not wasting your life to make a point—you're wasting it because you can't be bothered to give a shit. You do nothing, you care about nothing, you're committed to nothing, and all of that adds up to being worth nothing. A few people out there are trying to change things. You sit in the living room feeling clever, and your friend here discusses the Philosophy of Life, while understanding very little about life and almost nothing about philosophy. (*to J.J.*) On a political level, I have no objection to parasites and bargain-basement bourgeois pseudo-intellectuals. They help destabilize the system. It's just on the personal level that they make me sick. (*exits*)

Long pause. At last, GUY turns to J.J. and musters a sort of comrades-at-arms grin.

GUY: That's Murray.

J.J.: Yeh.

GUY: He's a committed man, Murray. He tells us he's a democratic socialist.

J.J.: Yeh.

GUY: You can see why people vote Conservative.

GUY helps J.J. to his feet, and helps readjust his jacket. Slight pause.

GUY: Feel like a beer or something?

J.J.: No thanks. Another time, maybe.

GUY: Sure.

J.J. starts toward the door.

GUY: Hey, listen. That stuff I was saying about Susan. That was kind of . . . well, I kind of made it up. I'm, uh . . . sorry.

J.J. nods. Moves again to the door, but just as he reaches it BOBBY enters, looking thoroughly downcast.

BOBBY: Hi.

GUY: (*to J.J.*) Look. If you feel like dropping round sometime . . .

J.J.: Sure. (*exits*)

Pause. BOBBY has not moved.

GUY: So what's the matter with you?

BOBBY: I got busted again.

GUY: Oh you dumb shit.

Scene Six

In the background, a soft, slightly stylized soundscape—wind, sea birds. We are on a cliff overlooking the ocean. J.J. enters and walks slowly toward the front of the stage until he stands near the edge of the apron. Looks down—a long way down— and takes a half step backward. Summons his resolve, and takes a half step forward again.

J.J.: Dear Susan. Do not worry about replying to this letter, because by the time you read it I will be dead. I hope this will not upset you unduly. Dear Susan. Here, in the final moments of my life, I stand upon sea cliffs. Cliffs upon which, in happier days, I was wont to walk with my friend . . . my former friend . . .

Wilfred Grimshaw. But Grimshaw is gone, now. As you are gone. As all is gone. As I . . . am gone.

J.J. looks down again. Inches forward so that his toes are at the very edge of the apron. Spreads his arms to a T *position. like a diver poised for the plunge. Slight pause. Lowers his arms and inches back again.*

J.J.:   Dear Susan . . .

GRIMSHAW enters, carrying a mickey bottle. He is limping and his face is dirt stained. Stops short as he sees J.J. who does not as yet notice him.

J.J.:   Dear Susan . . .

GRIMSHAW clears his throat. J.J. turns, startled, turns quickly away again and faces front. GRIM-SHAW shuffles to the front of the apron so that he is standing parallel to J.J., on the opposite side of the stage. GRIMSHAW looks down—a long way down—and takes a drink.

J.J.:   (*stiffly*) If you don't mind. I'm using this cliff.

GRIMSHAW: Pay no attention to me. I'll just be a second.

GRIMSHAW looks down again. Then takes four or five steps back and braces himself, leaning forward, like a geriatric sprinter poised to burst out of the blocks. Slight pause. GRIMSHAW takes another drink and gives J.J. a sidelong look.

GRIMSHAW: Ah . . . what do you mean, you're "using this cliff"?

J.J.:   Should be pretty obvious, shouldn't it?

GRIMSHAW: Oh. You mean . . . ? (*makes a vague circling motion with his hand, to indicate a body tumbling through space*) Oh.

J.J.:   Exactly. (*slight pause*) What do you mean, you'll "just be a second"? (*glances at GRIMSHAW—and for the first time notices his condition*) Good God. What happened to you?

GRIMSHAW: Could it possibly matter now?

He laughs, briefly and mirthlessly. J.J. joins in—briefly and mirthlessly. They stop laughing, and look down. Dramatically, J.J. raises his arms once more.

GRIMSHAW: Rose.

J.J.:   (*lowering his arms slightly*) What?

GRIMSHAW: The Belle of the Blackwater. She discovered that I had a bit of the ready cash. She invited a friend to join us. Frank, as it happens.

J.J.:   The one who swallows pickled eggs.

GRIMSHAW: The same. They had a brief tête-à-tête, and then Frank said he had something he wanted to show me. Out back. In the parking lot. At my age, you'd think I wouldn't be so keen to trust in human nature.

J.J.:   No, human nature is not something you want to trust in.

GRIMSHAW edges forward again, looks down, and takes a drink.

GRIMSHAW: (*rather furtively*) Unfortunately, that's not the worst of it. The money.

J.J.:   Who could care less about the money?

GRIMSHAW: You might.

J.J.:   Why?

GRIMSHAW: Because it was your money.

J.J.:   At a time like this, what interest could I possibly have in money?

GRIMSHAW: None. True. None at all.

J.J. raises his arms to a full T *position. GRIMSHAW does the same—still holding the bottle in one hand.*

Slight pause. J.J. lowers his arms and looks sidelong at GRIMSHAW.

J.J.:   What do you mean it was my money?

GRIMSHAW: That little cheque you received in the mail. You cashed it, and left the money in your drawer, under the socks. I just happened to . . . stumble across it . . . by accident.

Slight pause.

J.J.:   What the hell. What's my money might as well be your money, since it's all my mother's money anyway.

GRIMSHAW: (*dropping his arms and turning to J.J., moved*) Oh, Sir. Spoken like a true—

J.J. snaps his arms back into a T *position, effectively cutting GRIMSHAW off. GRIMSHAW raises his arms again. Then he lowers them.*

GRIMSHAW: (*haltingly*) J.J. I know I have no more right to speak to you . . . as a friend. But as a friend . . . are you sure you should do this?

J.J.:   My mind's made up, Wilf. There's no turning back. I have to do it. But just before I do, I just want you to know that . . . I'm sorry. I had no right.

GRIMSHAW: Of course you did.

J.J.:   No, no.

GRIMSHAW: Yes. It was I who had no right.

J.J.:   Of course you did.

GRIMSHAW: None at all.

J.J.:   Every right.

GRIMSHAW: None!

GRIMSHAW takes another drink.

J.J.:   Wilf? As a friend. I think you should go home, now.

GRIMSHAW: (*lugubriously*) I am going home. (*gazes downward*)

J.J.:   Wilf . . .

GRIMSHAW extends the bottle to J.J. who hesitates, then nods. They sidle sideways toward one another, across the front of the stage. J.J. takes the bottle.

J.J.:   Thanks.

GRIMSHAW: What's mine is yours, sir.

J.J. takes a drink. Looks down, then makes as if to hurl the bottle dramatically over the cliff.

GRIMSHAW: (*horrified*) No! (*seizes the bottle and holds it protectively*) For Christ's sake, I haven't jumped yet.

They both look down. Pause.

GRIMSHAW: Well.

J.J.:   Well.

GRIMSHAW: You first?

J.J.:   (*blanching somewhat*) If you like.

GRIMSHAW: Or I could go first, if you like.

J.J.:   Let's . . . go together.

GRIMSHAW: That's it. Yes. We'll go together.

J.J. raises his arms to the T *position. GRIMSHAW takes a "last drink," puts the bottle in his pocket and raises his arms. They both stare straight ahead.*

J.J.:   Wilf? We had some times, didn't we?

GRIMSHAW: Oh, yes. We had some—

J.J.: (*over him*) Twilight is settling over the western hills as his body floats to shore. His face is hauntingly serene. Is it possible . . . is he just sleeping? But no: for telltale tendrils of seaweed are draped over his weary eyes. Green tendrils, and blue eyes closed forever.

GRIMSHAW: And what is that on the rocks, by the shore? A tattered coat upon a stick? Or is it . . . Grimshaw. Aye, 'tis only Grimshaw.

J.J.:   And had he eyes to see and breath to give utterance to his soul, what would he say to them, blighted youth? He would say: I blame you not, though you are right to blame yourselves. (*hastily*) All except Grimshaw, for Grimshaw bears no blame. Grimshaw, alone, was a true friend.

GRIMSHAW: (*touched*) Oh, Sir.

J.J.:   (*resuming; his voice now ringing*) He would say: As I stood upon the cliffs . . .

GRIMSHAW: Upon that sad height . . .

J.J.:   With the sun above me and the wheeling gulls below, I saw that this world cannot contain those whose nature is to soar.

GRIMSHAW: And so saw Grimshaw, who sleeps upon the rocks.

J.J.:   Yes, all this would he say, had he breath — but he has not breath.

GRIMSHAW: A dog, a horse, a rat hath breath . . .

J.J.:   And now there is no noise at all, save for the lapping of the sea, and the keening of his aged mother . . .

GRIMSHAW: Who loved him, and sent him cheques . . .

J.J.:   His mother, who points out across the bay and cries: "Look! There is his little scarf, still floating on the waves."

GRIMSHAW: "His scarf."

J.J.:   "It is floating."

GRIMSHAW: "It is sinking."

J.J.:   "It has sunk."

They follow the scarf with their eyes as it "sinks" into the audience. Pause. They lower their arms and step back.

J.J.:   You know . . . that wasn't bad.

GRIMSHAW: It sang.

Eighteenth-century music, grand and orderly, forms a bridge into the next scene.

Scene Seven

A tableau: J.J. and GRIMSHAW in the apartment. GRIMSHAW is at the desk, writing. J.J. stands beside him, reading the Biography. BOBBY and GUY in the Sunshine Cafe, seated. JASON on the beach, seated.

As the music fades out, BOBBY and GUY "unfreeze."

GUY: Bobby, you can't just not show up in court.

BOBBY: If I show up, they'll give me three months.

GUY: They'll still give you three months.

BOBBY: They haven't got me yet. So I've still got time. To think.

GUY: (*wearily*) Bobby . . .

BOBBY: (*sharply*) I'm thinking! (*gets up and paces in agitation*) The way I figure it, we've got to stop doing this kind of stuff. I mean, you get busted and fined. And then you get busted for trying to raise the money to pay the fine. I mean, this is no way to get ahead, is it?

GUY: (*wearily*) Right.

BOBBY: So that's why I was thinking. Maybe we should just do the big one.

GUY: What big one?

BOBBY: Malaysia.

GUY: Malaysia?

BOBBY: All you need is a couple of suitcases with false bottoms.

GUY: (*wearily*) Right.

BOBBY: So all we've got to do is raise the money to get to Malaysia.

GUY: Right.

BOBBY: Fast.

GUY: So how are we going to raise it?

BOBBY: Well . . .

GUY: Bobby, if they catch you in Malaysia, they hang you.

BOBBY: Well, so you make sure they don't catch you, right?

GUY: Sure.

BOBBY: Guy, we're not talking nickles and dimes, here we're talking hundreds of thousands. A million, maybe. And then you just buy yourself an island, and you sleep on the beach, and pick fruit when you're hungry. And you invite some friends you know, some people who are really together. Damn, those would be good times, Guy.

GUY and BOBBY freeze. Lights down on them.

Lights up on JASON. He has presumably been sitting on the beach for some while, and is just starting to stand as SUSAN enters. SUSAN stops short as she sees him. JASON scrambles to his feet.

JASON: Susan.

SUSAN: (*startled*) Hi.

JASON: What are you doing here?

SUSAN: It's a public beach.

JASON: No, I didn't mean it that way.

SUSAN: (*softening*) I know. (*shrugs, moves a pace or two away, and sits down*) I'm not sure what I'm doing here. I just kind of like it.

JASON: So do I.

SUSAN: Oh, yeah?

JASON: Yes, I, uh . . . come down here a lot. To, uh, think.

SUSAN: About what?

JASON: Oh, things. Things in general. I've been . . . quite into thinking, lately.

SUSAN: Uh-huh.

JASON: Guy tells me you've moved back in with your parents.

SUSAN: (*a bit sharply*) No I haven't. (*softer*) I'm just staying there, for a while. Until I find a job. Or go to Europe. Whatever.

JASON: Ah.

SUSAN: And you? Still beavering away at the business?

JASON: Actually, I've taken a few days off. I've always done that, from time to time. Take some time off to think, get in touch with yourself. Figure out . . . you know. That's just the kind of guy I am.

SUSAN looks at him. A bit awkwardly, JASON sits beside her. Looks skyward, and points.

JASON: You know . . . if it was night . . . Betelgeuse would be right up about there.

JASON and SUSAN freeze. Lights dim on them.

Lights up on J.J. and GRIMSHAW. J.J. reads eagerly.

J.J.:   Wilf? Have you ever considered the possibility . . . I mean, seriously considered the possibility . . . that this just might be a really good book?

GRIMSHAW: Yes.

J.J. stares at him. Then his face lights up in delight.

J.J.:   We were right, Wilf. Weren't we? We've been right all along.

Eighteenth-century music begins, softly, in the background.

Thanks to the marvels of modern unemployment, we are free. Free to live the life of Leonardo, of Botticelli. The New Renaissance, and here we stand upon its threshold. Oh, the potential, Wilf. The potential. The grand, the sweeping, the all–but–limitless potential!

Music swells. All freeze.

Fade to black.

THE WOLF WITHIN
ALEX BROWN

Alex Brown is the pen name of G. W. Bartram, a writer whose personal struggles with his faith and his sexuality are reflected in his first play. Alex Brown is also a casebook example of the New Play Centre's success in new play(wright) development. Born in Toronto in 1944, he got his B.A. and M.A. in English from the University of Toronto, and a Ph.D. at the University of London. A convert to Catholicism, Brown moved to Vancouver on his return from England, working for the Church for seven years as editor of the weekly diocesan newspaper. In 1980 he joined the federal civil service, and since 1989 has lived in Ottawa.

Between writing novels (*Brother Sebastian's Little Holiday* was published in 1987 under the name G. W. Bartram), Brown wrote a play in 1985. He sent it to John Murrell, who suggested Brown show it to the New Play Centre's Pamela Hawthorn. She liked it enough to give it a workshop. In 1986 Brown took a summer playwriting course with Tom Cone. The next year he was invited to join the New Play Centre Writers' Unit, led by John Lazarus. Out of that process emerged *The Wolf Within*, Brown's powerful study of a dedicated priest in torment, wrestling with his temptations.

"Even though the play is not autobiographical or based on an actual incident," Brown says, "it draws on all my experience with the Church, and it does certainly reflect my own struggle with my sexuality. I began it as a novel in 1980, and originally made the priest heterosexual. At some point I felt, 'This would be better as a play.' By that time I had begun writing more honestly, closer to the substance of my life. One of Tom Cone's great sayings is, 'Write what you fear.' So I bit the bullet and made the priest gay."

The New Play Centre production won the Jessie Richardson Award as Vancouver's best new play in 1989, and was followed in 1990 by a highly praised production at Phoenix Theatre, Edmonton. Liz Nicholls in the *Edmonton Journal* described the priest's dilemma as "a visceral and wrenching experience for the audience," and lauded *The Wolf Within* for embracing "large and complex theological questions in a literate, vivid way."

The script Brown prepared for the second production differs from the original New Play Centre production draft in two key respects. Act Two, Scene Seven has been rewritten to give Father Pine's assistant, Eileen, much fuller knowledge of his relationship with the boy, Matt. More significantly, the ending has changed, perhaps reflecting Brown/Bartram's willingness to come out from under his pseudonym once again. The two endings, so very different in tone and direction, are indicative of the way a living play may evolve from one production to another, in part as a result of the writer's own evolving attitude towards his dramatic material. For interest, both endings have been provided here. Otherwise, the text is that of the 1990 Phoenix production.

The Wolf Within was first presented by the New Play Centre at the Waterfront Theatre on March 17, 1989, with Brian Torpe as Father Pine, Scott Bellis as Matt, Lee Taylor as Archbishop Hodge, Kim Kondrashoff as Len, Barbara E. Russell as Eileen, and Barney O'Sullivan as Father Michael. Kathryn Shaw directed, with set and lighting design by Ross Nichol, and costumes by Elizabeth Raap-Wolski.

Brian Torpe as Father Pine, and Scott Bellis as Matt in the New Play Centre production of *The Wolf Within*. Photo by Martin Keeley.

THE WOLF WITHIN

CHARACTERS

FATHER GORDON PINE, 38

MATTHEW STEPHENS, 19

ARCHBISHOP HODGE, 62

LEN, 33

EILEEN McPHEE, 36

FATHER MICHAEL, 68

SET

Wooden reredos at rear, which dominates the set, with an agonized crucifix, angled so that it hangs slightly over the action, its face visible to the audience. The stage may have various acting areas, which serve different purposes: the altar, centre rear, directly below the cross; the Archbishop's office, where Archbishop Hodge may remain throughout the play, a brooding, ever-present, all-seeing force; Pine's study; the sacristy/Father Michael's room; and the parish kitchen or dining room. The central portion of the stage serves as the nave of the church, from which Pine gives his two sermons. Scenes flow into one another without blackouts or pauses, with light changes and perhaps music for transitions. In the Phoenix Theatre version of the play, actors remained on stage throughout.

ACT ONE

Scene One

PINE, fully vested in purple, is preaching. Sound of rain.

PINE: By His wounds we are healed. Christ's wounds heal my wounds. That's what St. Paul is saying. You don't see my wounds, do you? You look up here, and see the familiar face of Father Pine. You know me well. I've been jawing away up here for two years now. You're so used to the sound of my voice that you hardly hear it. You don't know about the secret wound I conceal beneath the façade of the ordinary parish priest. But it's there. It's like your secret wound. The one that pricks you from time to time, that festers like an unknown cancer. The wound you never like to acknowledge, that compels you — perhaps — to drink too much, and too often; that makes you want to hit your kids, or your wife. The wound that, again and again, makes you prefer the getting of money to the emotional needs of your family; that drives you downtown at night to leer at the girls, probably no older than the daughters you leave at home. The wound, as old as Adam, that makes you want to do dark and shameful things.

MATT approaches behind, listening.

That's the wound I'm talking about. No one likes to admit it — but all of us have one. I have one. No — don't worry. I'm not going to tell you what it is. But it's there. All of us turn this brave face to the world, we dress up, we look good, we act confident: and we pretend it does not exist. We all lead double lives.

Light remains on MATT; begins to dim on PINE.

But His wounds heal our wounds, if we let them. That's the marvelous thing. If we let them. His wounds heal our wounds. Think about that, those who are paying attention. Think about it. What does it really mean? Because I'm not going to lay it all out for you, now. I'll talk more about it next week, as our experience of Lent deepens. But I want you to do your homework, I want you to do your own exploration. I can't do it for you. I want you to decide what the Apostle means.

Light remains on MATT. PINE turns. Freeze to indicate time change. PINE moves to the sacristy, starts to unvest. He is exhausted.

Scene Two

The Sacristy.

MATT: I know the answer.

PINE: (*turns, assumes his cheerful, public face*) Yes?

MATT: I'm not disturbing you, am I? Eileen said you wouldn't mind —

PINE: (*approaches*) Of course not. What can I do for you?

MATT: What you were saying. In your sermon. I know how He heals those wounds. Those inner wounds.

PINE: Good for you!

MATT: It was really good to hear you talk about them so — openly. Though I don't think most people understood.

PINE: Oh — (*forced laugh*) No. Most people don't *want* to understand.

MATT: No.

PINE: Don't even want to admit they're wounded!

MATT: No.

PINE: But that admission is the beginning. (*same laugh*) Of something!

MATT: Of being close to Him. His door into our lives.

PINE: Yeah. That's right. At least, in theory.

MATT: Oh, but it's real, isn't it?

PINE: (*looks at him with interest*) I've seen you at Mass the last few days — but I don't know your name.

MATT: Oh. It's Matthew Stephens.

PINE: (*offers hand*) Glad to meet you, Matt. (*They shake hands.*) Just moved here?

MATT: Oh no. I'm in Dominic Savio Parish. But I've been coming here.

PINE: More convenient, is it?

MATT: Not really. But I wondered —

PINE: Yes?

MATT: Could I — come to confession? Sometime.

PINE: Sure. No problem. Come Saturday between four and five, if you like. Those are the regular hours. Or any other time. Just give me a call.

MATT: Sometimes I drop by. To visit the Sacrament. I'll knock at the rectory —

PINE: Best to call first. I may not be here.

MATT: I've gotta go. My mother's waiting. But I'll — see you tomorrow. At daily Mass.

PINE: Sure. See you, Matt. I'll — look forward to it.

MATT leaves. PINE looks after him for a moment; drops social smile; turns away, removes vestment, checks mirror, adjusts hair.

PINE: (*to mirror*) What a fool I am.

Scene Three

Dining room, same day; PINE and EILEEN are eating lunch.

EILEEN: So what did you think of Matthew Stephens?

PINE: Nice kid.

EILEEN: He was keen to meet you, so I sent him in. I was talking to his mother — *and* to Nora Gardner.

PINE: Uh-oh.

EILEEN: You know what she said?

PINE: Nora? Let me guess.

EILEEN: President of the Catholic Women's League. Head of the Parish Council. Her husband heads the Knights of Columbus. And she looked at me and said, "I never can see why we give so much money to the Third World. I think it's bad for them." She actually said that. "They should stand on their own two feet, the way we do. And they never will, if we keep throwing money at them."

PINE: You know Nora.

EILEEN: Honestly. Sometimes I don't know what to say to people like that.

PINE: But you answered her —

EILEEN: Of course. She's heard it a thousand times, though, hasn't she? She just glazes over and stops listening. She resents me.

PINE: Nora? No way.

EILEEN: She does. She's always reminding me that I'm only the parish secretary. Asking me to type envelopes and run errands for her.

PINE: She knows perfectly well you're the secretary in name only. You're my assistant. It's been discussed in council and everyone agrees.

EILEEN: Well, she wouldn't say anything in front of you.

PINE: Well, she better not. (*pause*) What did you think of the sermon?

EILEEN: It was all right.

PINE: You didn't like it.

EILEEN: Well, you know me, Father. I prefer it when you talk about *active* things. Things we can do something about.

PINE: Central America?

EILEEN: Yes! And the native people here. You're their conscience, Father. If you don't speak out —

PINE: But I do.

EILEEN: Oh, I know you do. More than any of the others.

PINE: All the time.

EILEEN: Yes.

PINE: And if Nora doesn't hear, it's because she doesn't want to hear.

EILEEN: Yes.

PINE: That's why I'm talking about inner things right now. During Lent. But you think they want to hear that?

EILEEN: Well —

PINE: I could see how restless they were. I could feel them wondering what the hell was wrong with Father? Does he have a drinking problem?

EILEEN: I wish you hadn't done it. You know all those news stories, Father. People may misunderstand you.

PINE: Oh, come on, Eileen! They're not going to think something like that. No. I just happen to think it's the heart of our message, that's all. By His wounds we are healed. And if we don't admit we need healing — well. There it is. I won't do it again. I won't embarrass them — or you next week.

EILEEN: You can talk about spirituality. You know that. We all need that. But it was so inward, Father. They have to understand that our whole society is wounded — and they can do something about it. Something practical.

PINE: Don't worry. I'll go back to nice, safe things. Nothing weird. Nothing introverted. (*gets up, goes to window*) Ah well. Sometimes I wish I could say something about the spiritual life that doesn't end with a question, you know? Be like Father Michael, or someone like that. (*looks at her*) I've got all the answers. I know them all. In theory.

EILEEN: Come to Nicaragua with us in September! See something different. When I went to the Philippines, my whole idea of the Church changed. Why don't you, Father? You could. And you need to get away.

PINE: Yeah, you're right.

EILEEN: Oh — I'm always right. When it comes to other people! But think about it. We'd love to have you.

PINE: I'll think about it.

EILEEN: You need a change, Father. That's what we both need. All this rain. And this diocese —

PINE: (*pause*) Yeah! Well, thanks for doing lunch, Eileen. You shouldn't, you know. I can manage, when Mrs. Reid isn't here.

EILEEN: (*joking*) Oh, sure!

PINE: (*smiles*) You never give me a chance! (*starts to clear*)

EILEEN: (*rises*) Don't spend the whole afternoon here.

PINE: Oh — I have lots to do. The paperwork's piling up — as usual. But I'll try.

EILEEN: Oh, Father! (*leaves*)

PINE looks out the window.

Scene Four

Before reredos, several days later, sunshine. PINE is praying in his office. MATT hovers behind, watching. PINE is distracted. He looks up, turns page restlessly, looks at his watch. Then he rises. Sees MATT.

PINE: Oh, hi. It's Matthew, isn't it? How's it going?

MATT: Fine.

PINE: Good. Just doing my Office. With even less success than usual, I'm afraid. All I can think about is the sunshine, after all that rain. Like everyone else, eh? Did you want to see me?

MATT: I wondered if you could hear my confession.

PINE: Sure could.

MATT: I could come back, if you —

PINE: No, I'm free now. (*closes book*) And nothing's more important than the Sacrament of Reconciliation. Come on —

PINE moves to chair, vests; MATT sits facing him.

MATT: You're sure.

PINE: Of course. Is there a piece of Scripture you'd like to start with?

MATT: Whatever you choose, Father.

PINE: Nothing you'd prefer?

MATT: Actually, there is one.

PINE: Yeah?

MATT: "By His wounds, we are healed."

PINE: (*smiles*) Hey, that's a good one. OK. (*pause*)

MATT: Well, I've been distracted at prayer.

PINE: Mmm.

MATT: And I've tried to meditate, but done a lousy job. And I've borne grudges. Against — you know — someone in my family. Many times. My dad. And my sister. They get on my nerves.

PINE: Sometimes it's hard not to resent the people you're close to. Especially family.

MATT: But it's wrong.

PINE: Oh, but not very wrong. Do something extra for them. Help your dad out with some project, maybe. Show him you love him. Anything else?

MATT: Well — (*looks away*) I've had dirty thoughts.

PINE: Well, that's been known to happen.

MATT: But I haven't fought against them. I — uh — fell into the sin of impurity.

PINE: (*looks away*) Anything else?

MATT: And — I've looked — at other men, Father.

PINE: (*draws away*) Oh. I see. (*pause*) Well — that's a serious problem, Matt. You know that.

MATT: Yes.

PINE: It's not your fault. But you have to struggle against it. It's a cross. A big one.

MATT: I know.

PINE: And you may be mistaken. Just because you have certain feelings about other men doesn't mean —

MATT: No.

PINE: You have to consecrate yourself to God. We're all called to do that, of course. That's what Christian sexuality is, a consecration to God. But in your case, you do it through abstinence.

MATT: (*looks at PINE*) Like you.

PINE: Well, yes.

MATT: That's what I want to do. It's just that — I keep failing.

PINE: We all fail, Matt. That's what it's all about.

MATT: I don't mean I go chasing after — you know.

PINE: That's why you come to confession. To give you the grace to go on.

MATT: And it works, doesn't it? It really works.

PINE: Of course.

MATT: I mean, one day you stop failing.

PINE: Well, maybe. You stop failing so often.

MATT: I've read the saints. I know how important purity was to them. You see, Father — I think it's a gift. My affliction, I mean. It's the wound you spoke about on Sunday, isn't it. It's my path to holiness.

PINE: That's right, Matt. That's a very important insight. Very important. But you still have to be very careful. You understand that, don't you?

MATT: Oh, yes. I know.

PINE: Good. Well — is there anything else?

MATT: No.

PINE: I'll give you absolution, then.

MATT: Thank you, Father.

PINE: (holds up his hand) By the authority vested in me —

MATT: Oh, my God, I am truly sorry for all my sins —

PINE: I absolve you from all your sins —

MATT: And by the help of your grace —

PINE: (makes sign of the cross) In the name of the Father —

MATT: I will not sin again.

PINE: The Son, and the Holy Spirit, Amen. (rises; removes stool) So —

MATT: I've never told anyone before.

PINE: Uh — if you'd like to talk to someone about that problem — a professional, I mean — I could give you a name. I could arrange it for you. Might be a good idea.

MATT: I feel so free!

PINE: Dr. McGuire is a Catholic psychiatrist. Don't be scared off by the word: he's been very helpful to several men I've sent to him. I'll get you the number, OK? (starts to leave) Wait here: I'll only be a minute. (turns away)

MATT: Father —

PINE: Yeah?

MATT: I don't think I need his number. Not now. I don't think I want a psychiatrist.

PINE: It's a good idea, Matt.

MATT: No. I'm not ashamed of who I am. Not now. Not after this. You know. Opening it up, in confession, to you. And to God. I don't have to be afraid. I have to be vigilant, I know that, I have to be wary. But I don't have to be ashamed, do I?

PINE: (still turned away) No. Although it's normal to be ashamed of your imperfections.
MATT: Not if God loves us. Not if our wounds are the way He draws us into His embrace.

PINE: (turns, reluctantly) Well, yes — you're right. You don't have to be ashamed. That's good. But Doctor McGuire could still help you. On the natural level, you know.

MATT: I don't want the natural level. I want God. He can do anything. He can heal me, if He chooses. Can't He? I mean, you're a priest. You know what He can do. He can do anything. The way He filled the church with grain for St. John Vianney. It must be so great for you to have a parish named after him. The ideal priest!

PINE: Well, it gives me something to live up to, eh? (looks at his watch) Matt — I've got to go downtown. Think about it. Pray about it. Because I'm telling you —

MATT: What's it like? Being a priest, I mean. Lots of people must ask you that. But I wonder, sometimes, whether God might be calling me.

PINE: Oh, be careful of that, Matt. With your — predeliction. Oh — you won't understand it right now. You're full of enthusiasm. You think you can do anything. And I'm not saying you can't. But enthusiasm doesn't last. It's like a drug. There's a big high — that's what you're riding now, because you've just admitted this secret in confession, and you feel that God accepts you and loves you. But feelings don't last. They change. Moods swing. So vocations can't be based on feelings. Vocations are based on the day-in, day-out ability to go on doing holy things — which you believe in, don't get me wrong, which you really believe in, which you give your life for — without any feelings at all.

MATT: Come on, Father. That can't be true.

PINE: Ask any priest. Any priest who's honest.

MATT: You're telling me you sit there reading your Breviary — or that you offer Mass, or preach a sermon — like that great sermon you did on Sunday — without any feeling?

PINE: Well — yes. That's what I'm saying. Yes.

MATT: Just like some boring old teacher. Like somebody taking a piss or something? (*PINE laughs.*) Without anything? Without some little touch of God? You know — the way He kind of breathes into your heart, sometimes. Lightly. Quietly. So you hardly notice He's there. Without even that?

PINE: (*laughs uneasily; grasps MATT's shoulder briefly*) I've really got to go, Matt. The Archbishop's expecting me.

MATT: But really, Father — *is* that what you're telling me?

PINE: Yes.

MATT: That you go through all this — without Him?

PINE: (*annoyed*) I said *yes*. Now, leave it alone.

MATT: Sorry.

PINE: There are things you don't understand.

MATT: Sorry. I was bugging you.

PINE: That's OK. I didn't mean to bite your head off.

MATT: It's just that — you know — I've been wanting to talk to you for such a long time. There are things I can't say to anyone else. I don't mean my homosexuality. I don't mean that. I mean spiritual things. And I thought —

PINE: You thought I'd be another John Vianney. On a perpetual high.

MATT: Yeah.

PINE: I'm a pretty ordinary guy, Matt. Insofar as you can be ordinary — and be a priest. (*smiles*) Sorry to disappoint you.

MATT: I just don't understand how you can do that. I mean, it's really heroic, when you think about it. Doing all the things you do, helping people all the time, without —

PINE: Well, not *without* God.

MATT: Without feeling Him.

PINE: Yeah. That's right.

MATT: Is that what they mean by spiritual dryness? I've read about that. I've read that everybody goes through it. That it's a stage. Some writers call it a desert. Others call it darkness. Is that what they mean?

PINE: Maybe. I suspect it's not as exalted as that. You do a lot of reading, do you?

MATT: Oh, yeah. But I don't understand a lot of it. John of the Cross. St. Teresa. The Cloud of Unknowing.

PINE: You go to school?

MATT: Faculty of Music. It's my first year.

PINE: Good for you! What do you play?

MATT: The cello.

PINE: I love the cello. The instrument closest to the human voice.

MATT: Do you play?

PINE: No. No. I just listen. When I have time. Which isn't often. (*glances at his watch*)

MATT: Who do you like?

PINE: Oh, I'm eclectic. You could call my tastes Catholic.

MATT: I like Mozart, Scarlatti, and Bach. Especially Mozart.

PINE: Actually, I'm a country-western guy.

MATT: Country-western!

PINE: Yeah. You should listen to it. It's poetry.

MATT: (*laughs*) You're putting me on.

PINE: No, I'm serious. But I don't mind the big *M*. Except he always writes about love and death. I prefer optimistic music. I really like Beethoven and Wagner. And Strauss. Especially Strauss. The music of man's defiance! Do you like him?

MATT: I don't know. I tried to listen to *Salome* once — and I couldn't stand it. It seemed so weird and perverse.

PINE: It is perverse. It's very perverse.

MATT: I don't call it optimistic! I mean — why not have a story that shows her being converted?

PINE: And going to heaven?

MATT: Yeah.

PINE: Well — because she didn't, I guess. And people don't find heaven all that interesting. Look, Matt, I'm late. Can I drive you somewhere? I'm heading down to the Chancery.

MATT: No — I'll stay here and do my meditation.

PINE: Good for you. Make that your penance. Think about what I've told you. And take care, eh? (*leaves*)

MATT: Thanks, Father. (*Looks after him. Sits, opens devotional book, looks up at crucifix.*)

Scene Five

Archbishop HODGE's office, same day. HODGE sits behind his desk; PINE enters in haste.

HODGE: Good to see you, Father.

PINE: Thank you, Your Grace. Good to see you. You're looking well.

HODGE: I don't feel well.

PINE: Oh?

HODGE: I'm exhausted.

PINE: Been working too hard.

HODGE: Oh, that's not it. True, of course, but not the point. No. I don't sleep, that's the problem. I don't sleep, Father.

PINE: I'm sorry to hear that, Your Grace.

HODGE: Nothing you can do about it. A cross, that's all. So. (*motions for PINE to sit*) I have something to say to you.

PINE: Yes, Your Grace? (*sits*)

HODGE: I've always had confidence in you.

PINE: Thank you, Your Grace. I'll try to deserve —

HODGE: (*waves hand*) When I first saw you, I knew that you were solid. You had short hair. Still have. Not always running around espousing causes. Nicaragua. Women in the church. Homosexual rights. Nuclear disarmament. Intercommunion. I've never had to worry about St. John Vianney as long as you've been there.

PINE: Thank you, Your Grace.

HODGE: And you've turned the parish around. Paid off the debt. Built up the school. Father Ruffs almost gave it away to the union, but you brought it back.

PINE: I didn't do much, Your Grace.

HODGE: It's a good parish. My old parish. You knew that, didn't you? I built that school. And that church. I used to have nine baseball teams. Nine! You don't have that any more. But you've done well. Collections are up, too: that's always a sign of a parish that's on the right track, Father.

PINE: You think so, Your Grace?

HODGE: Don't you?

PINE: Oh, yes, I — uh — do, Your Grace.

HODGE: I wouldn't talk too much about social justice. You don't want to confuse the people.

PINE: I only teach what the Church teaches, Your Grace.

HODGE: It does no harm, if it's only talk. But if you let people like Eileen have their way —

PINE: She helps me a lot.

HODGE: So I understand.

PINE: She's a great woman. We should let her do more.

HODGE: (*laughs*) I wouldn't have her do too much, Father. (*pause*) But you provide a steadying influence in the diocese. I like that. The other priests seem to respect you.

PINE: They're good men, Your Grace.

HODGE: Do you think so?

PINE: Well — of course.

HODGE: I don't think so.

PINE: They're a tremendous resource.

HODGE: You don't know them as well as I do.

PINE: I know them pretty well.

HODGE: I went to the seminary with most of them. Known them all my life. Monsignor Powell. Father Ruffs. Father Chute. They can't put anything over on me. Can't trust them.

PINE: I think you're misjudging —

HODGE: So I want you to know this. The Nuncio called the other day. I talk to him quite often. Every ten days or so. He respects me, I think. Knows that this is one diocese where the Church is faithful to the Holy Father. He listens to me.

PINE: I'm sure he does, Your Grace.

HODGE: There's listening and there's listening, Father. The Nuncio listens to everyone, but for some of my colleagues (*laughs without opening his mouth*) it would be better if he didn't! (*laughs again, covers his mouth with his hand*) Oh, it would be much better for Archbishop Kennedy if the Nuncio didn't listen half so much. (*laughs again, same gesture*)

PINE: Ah.

HODGE: So he asked me whether there were any men in my diocese who had the capacity to take on episcopal responsibilities. (*pause*) To become bishops.

PINE: (*uncertain*) Are — uh — any sees vacant, Your Grace?

HODGE: No.

PINE: I didn't think so.

HODGE: But Bishop McNally's been a long time dying, hasn't he?

PINE: I knew he was sick.

HODGE: Just so. Very sick. Lingering, but very sick. East Kootenay could be a good diocese. But it needs a strong bishop.

PINE: I see.

HODGE: I told him that no one could be more reliable than you in keeping a diocese faithful to the Holy Father. The Church needs strong bishops, Father. Even more than it needs strong priests.

PINE: Well, thank you, Your Grace. I'll think about it. Pray about it. And — see what happens.

HODGE: You won't tell anyone.

PINE: Of — of course not, Your Grace.

HODGE: No one at all. Not Eileen.

PINE: I won't tell anyone.

HODGE: Priests talk to their secretaries. They shouldn't, but they do. Tell them everything. Oh, I know. (*laughs*) But we don't want anyone to know this, do we?

PINE: I guess not, Your Grace.

HODGE: Good. (*rises; Father PINE rises, too*) Keep me in your prayers, Father. And if I need anything — I'll call. (*offers hand*)

PINE: (*takes hand*) Thank you, Your Grace. (*leaves*) I hope you sleep better —

HODGE: Oh, no hope of that.

HODGE remains sitting, hands clasped in front of his mouth, as the room darkens.

Enter LEN.

LEN: You're still here.

HODGE: Of course I'm here. Where have you been?

LEN: Oh, I had some things to fix. And I paid a visit over at Maria Goretti Parish.

HODGE: Monsignor was looking for you.

LEN: Saw Father Chute.

HODGE: You're supposed to be here. Not cruising around the diocese. (*pause*) So — what's Father Chute up to?

LEN: Oh, I dunno. Had a word with Maureen.

HODGE: Yes?

LEN: Couldn't get anything out of her.

HODGE: He still drinking?

LEN: Dunno.

HODGE: But you saw him?

LEN: Only for a minute.

HODGE: And?

LEN: Looked like he always does. (*imitates nervous tick*) Ticking away, you know. (*HODGE*

laughs, covers mouth. LEN does it again.) More
than ever.

HODGE: *(laughs)* Monsignor wants to fire
you. You know that. And I'm not sure he isn't
right.

LEN: He better try it. This isn't the only job
in town. The wife is always clipping ads out
of the paper.

HODGE: I've heard that before.

LEN: Well — I tell you — if he says one
word to me — one word —

HODGE: How's Monsignor doing?

LEN: What do you mean?

HODGE: You know.

LEN: I haven't noticed anything.

HODGE: Nothing?

LEN: Nothing.

HODGE: Good. Men like Monsignor are
loyal. That's why I picked him. For loyalty. So
he hasn't been up to anything.

LEN: Well, not that I can tell — but what do
I know, Your Grace? I can't judge anything
around here. All I know is the mechanical
systems. And Sister Joanna's — *(gestures to
indicate breasts)* you know. That's the whole
extent of my knowledge.

HODGE: You know me, Lenny.

LEN: I dunno —

HODGE: You know me very well. What I
want.

LEN: Oh, I'm just the court jester, sir. But
he sure spends a lot of time on the phone.

HODGE: Well, that's his job.

LEN: What's a Nuncio?

HODGE: Has Monsignor been talking to
the Nuncio?

LEN: I dunno.

HODGE: You heard the word.

LEN: Yeah, well, that's right, I heard the
word. Could have heard it anywhere. Could
have heard you use it.

HODGE: Don't fool with me, Lenny. Don't
ever fool with me.

LEN: I wouldn't do that.

HODGE: Monsignor's been talking to the
Nuncio? *(LEN nods.)* What about?

LEN: Well, he was talking real low, sir; I
couldn't hear. But I think it was about you.

HODGE: Me.

LEN: I heard your name.

*HODGE rises, goes to window, stands with his back
to LEN, clenching and unclenching his hands.*

HODGE: Thank you, Lenny.

LEN: You finished with me now?

HODGE: I want you to watch.

LEN: Monsignor?

HODGE: Someone else.

LEN: Who?

HODGE: You don't need to know why.

LEN: No.

HODGE: Father Pine.

LEN: Never see him. He doesn't work down here.

HODGE: Watch him too.

LEN: Well, I can't, if I never see him.

HODGE: I want you to watch him, too.

LEN: OK, OK. But it won't be easy. You know that. I'll need time away from the job.

HODGE: That's nothing new.

LEN: And you'll have to talk to Monsignor.

HODGE: I'll talk to Monsignor.

LEN: What do you want to know?

HODGE: Just watch.

LEN: OK. But you'll talk to Monsignor —

HODGE gestures impatiently. LEN goes. HODGE watches him disappear, returns to the window, where he stands, clenching and unclenching his hands behind his back as the light dies on that part of the set. Lights up on EILEEN and Father PINE in the kitchen of the rectory, and for a while it's as though the Archbishop is looking in.

Scene Six

PINE and EILEEN in the kitchen, at table.

EILEEN: Well, I'm glad someone's got a lot to say.

PINE: Mmm.

EILEEN: That's what I like about life in this house. Chatter, chatter, chatter all the time.

PINE: Yeah.

EILEEN: You see the Archbishop. Before you go we wonder what's up. You come straight back — and tell me all about it.

PINE: He told me not to tell.

EILEEN: You're being sent to Nicaragua to give spiritual support to the Contras. That's about his style.

PINE: *(smiles)* No, it's not that.

EILEEN: But it's good news.

PINE: Well —

EILEEN: Are you being moved?

PINE: No. I don't know. Look, don't grill me. It's a secret. And the more I think about it, the more unlikely it seems. You know Hodge. You can't trust him.

EILEEN: He's dangling something in front of you. He told six different priests he'd make them Chancellor — and then he chose Monsignor. Is that it? He's offering you Monsignor's job?

PINE: *(laughs)* No, that's not it. Who'd want that?

EILEEN: But you do want whatever he's offering. I can see that.

PINE: Oh, yes. I want it. If —

EILEEN: Badly.

PINE: Oh, come on, Eileen — cut it out.

EILEEN: I know. He's offering you a free passage from the diocese! You can get off and lead a normal, happy life someplace else, and never look back! No wonder you want it.

PINE: *(laughs)* No. That's not it. *(pause)* All right, I give in. I'll tell you. But you musn't tell anyone.

EILEEN: Oh, I never talk to anyone. You know that.

PINE: Really. You won't tell.

EILEEN: Well — that depends what it is.

PINE: You're teasing me.

EILEEN: I never tease you. You're too serious. I never tease serious people.

PINE: He's given my name to the Nuncio as a possible successor to Bishop McNally. I could be Bishop of East Kootenay, Eileen.

EILEEN: Oh, Gordon.

PINE: That's what he said.

EILEEN: That's the best news we could have. The best news the Church could have. That's wonderful. (*hugs him*) How could you possibly keep news like that to yourself?

PINE: It may not happen. Probably won't happen.

EILEEN: Oh, it will. I can feel it. It's a nice diocese, too. I've been there. It's just the right size to really build an active community.

PINE: You know the first thing I'd do? I'd visit every priest in the place, and spend a few days with each one. Get to know him. Understand his problems, his strengths, his needs. And I don't mean visiting the parish. I don't mean the big welcome and the kids lined up for photos and all that. That could come later. I mean visit the priests. Make sure they matter. Not like here, eh!

EILEEN: You're not leaving me behind. You know that, don't you? You'll have an office of social action — and I'd like to work in it, Gordon.

PINE: You'll head it up.

EILEEN: Oh, I couldn't do that.

PINE: Sure you could. You'll do a great job.

EILEEN: Oh, Gordon, we could do so much, couldn't we? We could make that diocese a light for the whole country.

PINE: We will. But you know — I wish I knew what he wants. Hodge. I never thought he liked me. I still don't. So what game is he playing here?

EILEEN: I wouldn't waste one minute wondering why he does anything. What does it matter? Once you have a diocese of your own, Hodge can't touch you. You won't owe him anything.

PINE: I guess not.

EILEEN: You won't. He'll be senior, but you won't report to him. You'll report to the Pope. You'll have your own priorities. You certainly won't be his man.

PINE: I don't think it's quite that simple, Eileen. He's very influential. He'll expect East Kootenay to be another reactionary bastion —

EILEEN: Well, that depends on you. Whether you're willing to be influenced.

PINE: Yeah.

EILEEN: Come to Nicaragua with us.

PINE: Oh — I don't think I can.

EILEEN: You should. It would give you so much inspiration, Gordon.

PINE: I'm sure it would.

EILEEN: You'd see a different kind of Church there — a Church that's poor, a Church that's open to the Gospel.

PINE: Maybe.

EILEEN: You would. Oh, it won't be perfect. I know that. Nothing's perfect. But if I were a bishop, taking on a new diocese, that's what I'd do. Come on. Take the chance, Father.

PINE: Well, I'd like to. I'll try.

EILEEN: Don't just try!

PINE: All right. I'll come. You arrange it, and I'll come.

EILEEN: (hugs him) Everyone will be so happy. Just wait till I tell them the news. (starts to exit)

PINE: But — you won't say anything about the other thing.

EILEEN: Of course not. (exits)

PINE: (to himself) Bishop —

Scene Seven

FATHER MICHAEL's bedroom. The old Franciscan wears a brown robe; he sits sideways to PINE, listening, as PINE makes his confession. PINE faces audience.

MICHAEL: I'm very pleased, dear boy. Very pleased. That is good news.

PINE: It may not happen.

MICHAEL: It will. When the Lord wills something —

PINE: But — is it the will of God? Just because something's offered doesn't make it the will of God. I should stay.

MICHAEL: Why?

PINE: I'm not worthy. I can't be bishop.

MICHAEL: No one is worthy. That's no reason to refuse the will of God.

PINE: I want it too much. For all the wrong reasons. Out of ambition. Spiritual pride. And — I don't pray, Father. I read the words, but they're empty. I read them, and think of other things. I keep on reading them, and keep on thinking of other things. Sinful things. Sexual things. After all these years. It's as if the sinful thoughts are encouraged by the holy words, you know? (silence) Does that happen to you, Father? (FATHER MICHAEL looks at him, but says nothing.) And so I give up and do something, anything, just so long as it's active. And the result is, I don't pray. I feel like a man who's been told to water a field — and he has no water, you know? Because something's dried up in my soul. And now maybe the field's going to be even bigger. And I'll have even less, you know? (FATHER MICHAEL nods.) It didn't use to be like this. Prayer used to be such a rich experience. So emotional. (gets up, walks around) You'll tell me I shouldn't trust the emotions, and I know that. And you're right — because look where I've ended up. No emotion, no prayer. But it used to be so great. I felt that He was right there, so close to me, that He was with me, not just in the room with me, but in my heart. It felt so light — you know? — as long as He touched you that way. And now He's gone.

MICHAEL: (quietly) Tell me about the sinful thoughts, Gordon.

PINE: (looks away) Well — you know. The usual thing. Temptations. Against purity.

MICHAEL: Is there some particular association? Some person?

PINE: (looks away, then back at him) Oh — I wouldn't say that. No. No particular person. Thoughts like that — just happen. Don't they?

MICHAEL: They can. (pause)

PINE: Well, there is this young person in my parish, who I try to help.

MICHAEL: And you think of her.

PINE: Well, yes. A bit. Well, quite a bit. And in fact — it isn't a girl.

MICHAEL: Oh.

PINE: It's a young man.

MICHAEL: It had to be male, Gordon, if it wasn't female. I didn't suppose it was an angel. (*pause*) You've never told me you had this problem.

PINE: No.

MICHAEL: You've never breathed a word about it.

PINE: (*annoyed*) I know.

MICHAEL: You should have.

PINE: I just didn't think it was important.

MICHAEL: It was. If you were going to be honest, it was important.

PINE: It wasn't causing me any trouble. Well, nothing serious. I know how to handle it. I know the warning signs.

MICHAEL: So there have been problems before?

PINE: Yes.

MICHAEL: Often?

PINE: Well, yes. But not as a priest. Never as a priest. And I'm not talking about *abuse* or anything like that. You realize that, Father.

MICHAEL: Before the seminary?

PINE: Yes. And I left it all behind me, Father, when I decided to follow my vocation. And I've been successful. It doesn't bother me. It's a twist in the soul. A wound. An addiction. I'm like an alcoholic — that's all. So I keep it under control. And when the temptation gets real — here I am.

MICHAEL: And you want me to congratulate you for that. You always have to be in the right, don't you dear boy. Always have to do the right thing. Why is that, do you think?

PINE: I don't know! That's what a priest's life is. Doing the right things. Following the rules. That's what you do. That's what we all do. Our lives have structure.

MICHAEL: But what's the structure for?

PINE: Well — to keep things together. To keep us on track. To prevent us from —

MICHAEL: Does the structure emerge *from* our lives, as a flower emerges from a seed? Or do we seek refuge in a structure — like hoops around a barrel?

PINE: Well, both, I suppose.

MICHAEL: You're talking about hoops.

PINE: I'm not.

MICHAEL: Yes you are. You're saying that if the structure weren't there, you'd run amok.

PINE: I wouldn't. There's no way. Absolutely not. I resent that suggestion. Father — I'm sorry — this isn't going the way it should. Maybe we should call it quits and talk again some other day.

MICHAEL: We can talk another day, Gordon. We can talk any time you want. But — if you want my advice, you won't take that post.

PINE: But you just said —

MICHAEL: That was before you told me your secret.

PINE: That's ridiculous. You think I can't control this? You think I'm going to do something stupid? Throw away my whole life? My identity?

MICHAEL: My dear boy, there's never any knowing what anyone will do. Look at those men in Newfoundland —

PINE: That's different, and you know it! Completely different. That's an abuse. An abuse of power.

MICHAEL: And this isn't?

PINE: Look, Father, I'm only telling you this because it's my duty. Out of thoroughness. Not out of need. I'll deal with it. I never even gave him a hint. And if he comes back, I'll refer him to someone else. You think I haven't handled this a hundred times?

MICHAEL: You're a victim of pride, Gordon. You're trying to stand on your own, without God. You can't do it. And believe me, you won't be ready for larger responsibilities until the structure blossoms from the seed — in your own life.

PINE: What is this — some kind of Zen puzzle? There's not a Catholic priest in this country — not a bishop in the country — who'd have any idea what you're talking about, Father! Not one! And I bet half of them wrestle with exactly the same demon!

MICHAEL: That isn't the point, Gordon. You're not responsible for them. The question is, what are you going to do?

Pause. PINE masters his frustration.

PINE: Pray more. Refer the boy to someone else.

MICHAEL: And East Kootenay?

PINE: It won't come, anyway.

Pause. PINE fidgits. MICHAEL is still.

MICHAEL: Think about what I said, in tranquility of spirit. There's no use building up a wall of little rules if there's nothing inside, and that's what I think you've been doing. That wall won't defend you. And the Master won't be served. Think about it. Pray about it. And come and see me again — next week. And now I'll give you absolution.

PINE: Oh my God —

MICHAEL: By the power vested in me, I do absolve you —

PINE: I am heartily sorry for all my sins —

MICHAEL: In the name of the Father, the Son —

PINE: And with the help of your grace —

MICHAEL: And the Holy Spirit.

PINE: I will not sin again.

Scene Eight

PINE's study, evening, a couple of days later. PINE is reading evening prayer. He paces as he reads.

PINE: (*reads*) "Brethren: Be sober, be watchful! For your adversary the Devil, as a roaring lion, goes about seeking someone to devour. Resist him, steadfast in the faith. But you, O Lord, have mercy on us."

EILEEN: (*knocks; then enters*) What a day! I made the arrangements for Nicaragua, so you're committed now, Father. (*throws herself into a chair; PINE puts book down*) What a day! It's September 14th to 25th. Let's put the dates in your diary. Where is it? (*rises, searches desk for his diary*) There! You can't back out.

PINE: I won't.

EILEEN: (*sits again*) I'll see to that. So. How are you?

PINE: Fine.

EILEEN: What's the matter?

PINE: You haven't heard about Bishop McNally?

EILEEN: No.

PINE: Passed away peacefully in his sleep, yesterday.

EILEEN: Such a gentle man. So that's why you're up here, doing your prayers. You're waiting by the phone.

PINE: Hah! Not likely. It won't come my way. Father Michael tells me I shouldn't take it.

EILEEN: What?

PINE: Doesn't think I'm ready.

EILEEN: He wants you to wait till you're sixty-five and so trampled down you can't even choose a new hymn without Hodge's say so.

PINE: (*laughs*) He has his reasons.

EILEEN: Well, they're lousy reasons. They'll offer it to you, I'm sure of that. And if you dilly-dally around with scruples because of some ancient Franciscan — well, you and I are through. Oh, by the way. Your little disciple called.

PINE: Who?

EILEEN: Matt. He wanted to see you. I said you had an hour between eight and nine.

PINE: Oh, hell —

EILEEN: Well, you have a slot.

PINE: No, no, it's OK. I can see him. But if that happens again — let me know before giving him a time, eh?

EILEEN: (*looks at him; he has never given such instructions before*) OK. I have to go. There's a Development and Peace meeting tonight.

PINE: I'll drop by.

EILEEN: (*looks at him*) You're tired. Another time.

PINE: No, I'd like to come.

EILEEN: You've been going since six o'clock this morning. Why don't you put on one of your tapes or something? You've got half an hour. Or — I'll call Matthew and tell him not to come.

PINE: No, no, that's OK. I'll see him.

EILEEN: You relax now. Don't take any calls. I'll put the machine on.

PINE: Dear Eileen! (*puts an arm around her shoulder*)

EILEEN: So — play something. Go on. Father! You're so stubborn. You have to be bullied into everything. (*picks out a tape at random*) Here.

PINE: No. Not that.

EILEEN: Choose something else, then.

PINE: (*chooses a tape; rejects it*) Oh — I don't know. I'm not in the mood for music. (*chooses another*) Salome. I was thinking about this the other day. Ever heard it?

EILEEN: Of course not.

PINE: Well, you know the story. Herod's step-daughter. In love with John the Baptist, who rejects her. So she demands his head on a dish. (*puts on tape*) Listen to this. Here's the part. When they bring her the severed head, she holds it up and kisses him.

EILEEN: Ugh!

PINE: There it is. Hear that? (*MATT appears in the doorway, unnoticed.*) "Now I have kissed your mouth." That's what she's saying. (*listens*) She sounds almost innocent, doesn't she, in her triumph.

EILEEN: That's sick.

PINE: I suppose. But listen to it — how beautiful it is. And scary. In a few seconds, Herod will put her to death. Oscar Wilde wrote the play — (*sees MATT*) Oh — you're early.

EILEEN: I'm on my way. Don't come to our meeting, Father. You take it easy, OK?

PINE: I'll be there.

EILEEN: Don't you dare. (*to MATT*) Don't stay long, Matthew. He's tired. (*She leaves.*)

Pause. They listen to the music.

PINE: So — what do think of it? Perverse?

MATT: Well, you summed it up. Human — and scary. You don't have to turn it off.

PINE: That's OK. That was the best part. (*shuts off music*) How are you doing?

MATT: Oh, fine. Great, really. So this is your room.

PINE: Yeah. We could move downstairs.

MATT: You sure have a lot of books. (*looks at them*) Are they all theology?

PINE: Mostly.

MATT: I buy a lot of books — but nothing like this. You've got a whole set of Aquinas. I'd like to try him.

PINE: (*laughs*) You'd be bored. Not with his ideas. With the way they're laid out. (*takes out a book*) See? It's very dry. A series of propositions, and he argues for and against each one. No — (*MATT takes book.*) What you want is a book about Aquinas. You'd find that interesting. Let's see if I've got anything — (*searches shelves*)

MATT: (*looking at book*) What's usury?

PINE: Loaning money for interest. That's an interesting debate. Because Aquinas — and the whole Church — thought it was seriously wrong to charge interest. At the time, it was one of the most serious sins against nature you could commit. Although medieval economies — even the popes — depended on it. They blamed the Jews for it — and persecuted them accordingly. Hypocritical, eh?

MATT: But it's not wrong now.

PINE: No, of course not.

MATT: So the Church changed her mind.

PINE: Well, we don't say that. We say that there were developments. That we understand the issues better.

MATT: So at one time, charging interest was a sin against nature, and now it's not.

PINE: Yes.

MATT: Like — homosexuality.

PINE: Well, no. That's different. Although you're quite right, the Church has always considered it a sin against nature, too.

MATT: Do you think it's a sin against nature?

PINE: Well — yes. Of course.

MATT: Because it's found in nature, isn't it? I mean, some animals are gay. I heard a show on the radio about (*laughs*) "sweet ass bulls."

PINE: Maybe. OK. So there's gender confusion in animals. Sometimes. But that doesn't make it right for humans to follow their sexual impulses. Any more than you'd want to go down the street raping every girl you see.

MATT: I wasn't talking about rape.

PINE: No. Well, neither was I. We were talking about controlling animal impulses.

MATT: So the Church controls straight impulses by marriage. Why not control gay impulses the same way?

PINE: (*annoyed*) Because it's different, that's why. Look, Matt. Do you want to deal with your problem within the Church — or do you want to just take a walk, go with the crowd, live by the latest poll? Which is it?

MATT: Sorry. I didn't mean to —

PINE: Because that's the way it is. You love holiness. You love the Church. You feel close to God. So you give up the other thing. You can't have both. You take your choice.

MATT: Yeah. I see. (*replaces book*)

PINE: I made that choice. It wasn't easy. Everyone makes that choice. Aquinas made that choice. Every priest and mystic in history has made that choice.

MATT: Well, I want to make it, too.

PINE: I'm sure you do.

MATT: I was just asking questions.

PINE: Well, don't ask too many. Because you can ask yourself right out of the Church, if you aren't careful.

MATT: Don't get mad.

PINE: I'm not mad.

MATT: You sound mad.

PINE: Well, I'm not. (*Pause. Hesitates, then put his arm around MATT's shoulders. MATT is very still.*) It's a difficult subject, Matt. You're in a no-win position, in a way. In fact — maybe you need more help than I can offer. You know. Expert help. Remember what I was saying? I think you should see someone else. I'll arrange it, OK? I think it would be a good idea — (*removes arm, turns away*)

MATT says nothing. Looks at PINE. MATT has realized the truth.

PINE: Anyhow, I have another appointment. Sorry to chase you out, but —

MATT: I understand.

PINE: I haven't upset you.

MATT: No.

PINE: I probably have. I'm not very good at this. (*turns*) Just remember. We have to make a choice, eh? We always have to make a choice.

MATT: Don't worry, I understand.

PINE: Good. Now I've got some things to do. And the parish accountant's coming. (*Puts his arm around MATT again, and pilots him toward the door. MATT responds by looking at him. PINE instantly draws away, standing back so that MATT can leave.*) See you — OK?

MATT: I'll be at Mass —

PINE: See you there, then.

MATT: Yeah. I'll see you there. (*exits*)

Pause.

PINE: (*returns to his book*) "Brethren, be sober, be watchful, for your adversary the Devil, as a roaring lion, goes about seeking someone to devour. Resist him, steadfast in the faith. But you, Oh Lord, have mercy on us.''

Scene Nine

A couple of days later. Sunshine. The church, early in the morning, before Mass. LEN enters, whistling or singing. Looks around. PINE enters, carrying altar things.

PINE: You're bright and early, Len. What brings you here?

LEN: Morning, Father. Just looking around. Archbishop wants a kind of inventory. You know. Report on the state of the buildings. The heating systems. So I gotta go to every parish in the whole diocese.

PINE: Why's he want that?

LEN: I dunno. You know him. Always wants to know things. I just do as I'm told, eh?

PINE: Well — I'll let you into the basement, if you like. (*Puts down altar things. MATT enters with book.*) We have to go outside — (*Leads way out of church. Meets MATT.*) Hi, Matt. Back in a minute.

Pause. MATT kneels. PINE re-enters, approaches.

PINE: How's it going?

MATT: Fine. Great. I've been thinking about what you said about making choices — and I've made mine.

PINE: Good. And I've been thinking about you. I've talked to a priest who could really help you.

MATT: Oh?

PINE: Yeah. Father Chute. Great guy. He could help you better than I.

MATT: How come?

PINE: Well — he knows more about these things. More than I do. It's kind of an apostolate with him. He's got this group called "Courage" —

MATT: You mean he works with — gays.

PINE: Yeah.

MATT: But I told you. I don't want someone like that.

PINE: He might help. He'd be better than me, Matt. Way better.

MATT: You don't want me hanging around—

PINE: I didn't say that. I just think you should see him. He's a nice guy. You'd like him.

MATT: I don't want that. I want —

PINE: I've spoken to him. Told him what a special person you are. He's expecting your call. I'll give you his number, OK? Wait right here — I'll just get it. I'll be right back, OK? (*leaves*)

MATT hesitates, then follows PINE into the sacristy area. PINE is writing.

MATT: Father —

PINE: Just a sec.

MATT: Father, listen. You don't have to send me away. I mean, I want to do what you say, even if you're rejecting me, or running away from me, or something. But you don't have to play this game, because I know. I understood the other night, in your room, remember? I realized you were just hiding your feelings.

PINE: Don't be silly, Matt.

MATT: You're scared, that's all. (*moves forward; laughs; moves forward*) But there's nothing to be scared of. Nothing. We won't do anything. We won't sin. (*moves forward; takes his arm*) Because — I love you. We can be pure. We don't have to be afraid of sin. We can be like brothers. Like David and Jonathan. Or John and Jesus. Can't we? I've been watching you for so long. I know every gesture. Every expression. Sometimes I've asked myself, do I love him too much, Jesus? Do I love him instead of You? But I don't. That's not possible. As long as I love you in Him and through Him and for Him —

PINE: Stop.

MATT: I'll stop talking. But I'll never stop loving —

PINE: Stop it! (*Pause. PINE does not look at him.*) I want you to go now. And you musn't come back.

MATT: No.

PINE: (*looks at him*) Matt. The kind of love you're talking about doesn't exist. Whatever you may think. It's a fantasy. There's no way on this earth that I can have you hanging around here, telling me how much you love me, without us falling into sin. (*pulls away, stands*) No way. Absolutely no way. You know something about me that you shouldn't. And now — I can't see you again. Understand? I can't trust myself near you. And I'm not going to destroy you. Or myself. Or my vocation. You see? So — go. (*pause*) Please, Matt — I'm asking you. (*MATT does not move. PINE shouts.*) Go, damn you!

PINE grabs him by the shoulders, shakes him. Pause. MATT is passive. Suddenly PINE kisses him hungrily on the mouth. Cut to black.

ACT TWO

Scene One

A short time later. PINE and MATT have made love; PINE is standing, straightening his clothes.

PINE: Anyone could have seen us.

MATT: Who cares?

PINE: Get up. Come on. Of all the stupid things to do —

MATT: Stupid! (*catches at his legs*)

PINE: (*pushes him away*) It's almost time for Mass. People will start showing up any minute.

MATT: They won't come in here.

PINE: They could. What a *fool* I am. Come on, Matt: get up, and get dressed. Anyone could come in.

MATT: (*stands; hugs him*) It's not wrong.

PINE: Don't say that.

MATT: It can't be. I feel closer to God than I've ever felt before. I feel so happy. I feel like flying. Gordon — it's not wrong.

PINE: Shh. Be quiet. There are people out there. I have to —

A knock. Both PINE and MATT start. EILEEN opens the door.

EILEEN: Everyone's here, Father. They're waiting. (*sees MATT*)

PINE: Thanks, Eileen. I'll be ready. I was just — hearing a confession. (*EILEEN goes. PINE turns to MATT, who is laughing.*) She knows.

MATT: Confession!

PINE: She saw it all. She knows everything. Stop laughing, will you? This is serious. I have to go out there — and offer Mass in front of Eileen and the others —

MATT: Don't do it. Say you're sick.

PINE: I can't do that.

MATT: Sure you can. Gordon — (*touches him*)

PINE: Don't! (*MATT draws back.*) I'm sorry, Matt. You've got to go. I can't do it with you here. OK? We'll talk later. I'll see you later. OK? Matt — don't worry, I'm OK. I'll do — what I have to do — and see you later.

MATT hugs him. PINE holds him, caresses him, they kiss, briefly. PINE draws away.

PINE: Now — go.

MATT: I love you.

PINE: I — We'll talk later.

MATT leaves. PINE watches him go, turns, vests slowly, as if he were preparing for his own crucifixion.

Scene Two

PINE, fully vested in purple, preaching.

PINE: In a few moments, I will go to the altar, as I do every morning, and take a large, perfectly round, and perfectly white wafer of unleavened bread — as I do every morning — and say some words. And I'll do the same thing with a few drops of wine and water in a gold-lined chalice. And after I've said those words, I'll genuflect deeply and hold up each in turn, so that all of you can behold and adore, as you do every morning, most of you; so you can behold and adore the body and blood of Jesus Christ, our God. These hands — these sinful hands — my hands — will — as they do every morning — bring God into existence. And

after adoring Him, we will, all of us — whatever our various spiritual states — consume Him. We will eat God. How do we dare do that? How do we dare even hold Him in our two hands — as Salome held the severed head of the Baptist — how do we dare even look at Him, even kiss Him — knowing ourselves to be what we are? Let alone eat Him. We are not worthy. We are never worthy. If we thought too much about the enormous gulf between His Divinity and our unworthiness, we would go crazy — or we'd run out of the church. We would. So — (*loses track; pause*) — we just soldier on, don't we? We just have to trust in His mercy, to throw ourselves on His mercy, that's all. Knowing ourselves to be hypocrites, knowing ourselves to be all sorts of evil things: complacent, lying fools, destroyers of innocence, people who are so accustomed to the feel and taste of sin that we don't even notice it. (*a hopeless shrug*) We just have to trust that this crazy, impossible abyss between our sin and His grace can be crossed — that this gulf can be crossed.

He turns abruptly; goes to altar, facing audience; begins to unveil the chalice. Dim to black.

Scene Three

Kitchen. LEN, EILEEN.

LEN: Is he always like that?

EILEEN: I don't know what you mean.

LEN: You know. Weird. Stressed out. Looked like he was having a breakdown. And then, when he just stood there, staring at that bit of bread, just holding it. He always like that?

EILEEN: No.

LEN: So — what's up?

EILEEN: Nothing.

LEN: I mean, it's not normal. You gotta admit that.

EILEEN: What kind of report are you doing, Len?

LEN: Just curious.

EILEEN: Well, don't be. People have their ups and downs, that's all. There's nothing wrong.

LEN: I wasn't saying there was something wrong.

EILEEN: Well, there isn't.

LEN: No. (pause) So — how are you? You OK?

EILEEN: Well, of course I'm OK. I'm always OK. That's my job, isn't it? Being OK.

LEN: You look kinda — well, down —

EILEEN: Me? That'll be the day.

LEN: So you're happy up here.

EILEEN: Oh yes. Very happy.

LEN: Busy as ever, eh? Always running around.

EILEEN: Yeah.

LEN: And you like it.

EILEEN: I told you.

LEN: We sure miss you down at the Chancery.

EILEEN: Hah!

LEN: It's true. Place seems dead, ever since you came up here to wait on Father Pine. You should come down for a visit.

EILEEN: You'll never get me down there.

LEN: Why not? Nice bunch of people.

EILEEN: I talk too much. I'd be sure to say something he wouldn't like — and he'd hear all about it, wouldn't he?

LEN: (pause) Well — just thought I'd say hello. See how you're getting along.

EILEEN: Thanks.

LEN: Good to see you. Glad things are working out. Glad you're so happy.

EILEEN: Yeah!

LEN: Guess I should be going. (does not move) Say — who was the — uh — young guy with the blond hair?

EILEEN: I don't know.

LEN: Saw him hanging around before Mass.

EILEEN: I don't know.

LEN: Went into the sacristy and didn't come out.

EILEEN: I don't keep track of everyone in the parish, Len.

LEN: Sure you do! Bet he's here all the time. People think he's Father Pine's little boyfriend.

EILEEN: They don't!

LEN: You know what people are like.

EILEEN: They'd never think that. Don't you ever say something like that again.

LEN: I wasn't saying it was true.

EILEEN: You shouldn't be saying it at all. If you know anything — anything at all about parishes — you'd know there's always one or two like that hanging around. Always.

LEN: (*gets up*) Yeah, well, I'd better get back.

EILEEN: He'll hear his confession, he'll give him some guidance, he'll talk to him — but there's no way, absolutely no way, he'll ever do anything else. Not with Matthew Stephens. Not with anyone.

LEN: Matthew Stephens?

EILEEN: It's not true!

Scene Four

Same day. HODGE's office. HODGE at desk. LEN enters.

LEN: Hey, I've got some news, Your Grace.

HODGE: It's cold in here.

LEN: It's not cold. It's 70 degrees. At least 70. Maybe more.

HODGE: I feel cold.

LEN: That's just your heart. Froze up years ago. But listen, Your Grace, I've got news.

HODGE: Can't you do anything about it?

LEN: You're at the end of the line. And you've got all those big windows. If I crank it up for you, the others'll fry. It's already about 85 up on the third floor. Worth my life to go up there. That Sister Joanna'd be out like a flash, laying into me —

HODGE: (*laughs*) You'd like that.

LEN: I like her tits but I don't like her temper. (*HODGE laughs.*) And all I ever get's her temper. Not like you, eh? (*HODGE laughs.*) So hot up there I wonder they wear clothes.

Course they don't when you pay them a visit, do they, sir?

HODGE: (*laughs*) That's enough, Len.

LEN: I figure it's a real party when you're there, eh? You've got your little secrets —

HODGE: (*no longer smiling*) That's enough, Len.

LEN: All those naked nuns —

HODGE: That's enough!

Pause.

LEN: I guess I better get back to work.

HODGE: You meant no harm.

LEN: I'll see what I can do about the heating system.

HODGE: You were trying to cheer me up, I know that. You don't understand, that's all.

LEN: Oh, you're right there, Your Grace. I don't understand, I don't understand nothing around this place. You're hot, you're cold, you joke around, you don't joke around, you want news, you don't want news —

HODGE: Sit down, Lenny. I'm sorry if I spoke sharply. We can chat for a few minutes. (*LEN sits. HODGE removes his glasses, rubs his face.*) I just finished with Father Clancy. He sat there for a full hour, telling me on and on how wrong I was. About the school. The union. Church discipline. Everything. A full hour.

LEN: Oh, I don't feel sorry for you, sir. You're a real bastard, that's all.

HODGE: (*laughs*) They're all like that, Lenny. Misdirected. Weak. Useless. Completely useless. Always want the wrong things. Yet these are the men God has chosen. These are the men who call Him into being, and hold Him in their hands.

LEN: Oh, you lose me there, sir.

HODGE: I'm sure I do, Lenny. You don't worry about wanting the wrong things. You just let the wolf run free. Ravening and devouring as it likes.

LEN: You're in a funny mood today, sir.

HODGE: I'm tired. I don't sleep, Lenny —

LEN: I got some news you'd be interested in.

HODGE: Not now. I don't want news. Let's just chat. Tell me about your little girl.

LEN: It's a little boy, sir.

HODGE: How's he doing?

LEN: Oh, he's doing great. Real little fighter. But — it's about Father Pine, Your Grace.

HODGE: Father Pine.

LEN: Yeah.

HODGE: So. (*pause*) So. You have some information about Father Pine.

LEN: Yup.

HODGE: (*pause*) What?

LEN: He's queer.

HODGE: Queer.

LEN: As a three dollar bill. Got a little boyfriend.

HODGE: A boy?

LEN: No, no. Older.

HODGE: Not a child.

LEN: A young guy.

HODGE: Who told you?

LEN: Nobody told me. I saw it myself. Saw them together.

HODGE: Not Father Pine.

LEN: You don't have to believe me.

HODGE: The one man in the diocese I thought I could trust, I could recommend — how long's it been going on?

LEN: I dunno.

HODGE: Who else knows?

LEN: I dunno. Maybe Eileen. She gave me the kid's name. She might know. She knows something. And doesn't like it.

HODGE: She won't say anything. A woman like Eileen will talk and complain about all kinds of things, but when it really matters — when it's a question of the Church's reputation — she won't say anything. She's the only one?

LEN: I said I don't know.

HODGE: I don't want you talking. Understand?

LEN: Oh, you can trust me, sir.

HODGE: (*snorts*) Not a word. To anyone.

LEN: Course not. Don't want someone like Monsignor calling up the Nuncio over something like this, do we?

Pause.

HODGE: What's the young man's name?

LEN: You know, speaking of Monsignor — you probably don't even know this, Your

Grace. I mean, it's certainly not *your* fault. But Monsignor's idea of a living wage is not what you'd call "living."

HODGE: No. I'm sure it isn't. (*pause*) What's the young man's name?

LEN: Matthew Stephens.

HODGE: Stephens. There's a Stephens in Dominic Savio Parish. Monica Stephens. Good Catholic family.

LEN: Might be the one.

HODGE: I've probably met him.

LEN: Medium height. Blond hair.

HODGE: (*shakes his head*) I don't know. (*gets out the telephone book*) You'd better get back to your work.

LEN: Hope you're pleased. You had to know, didn't you? I mean, I had to tell you. Can't have a priest pretending to be so good, and all the while he's fucking other guys. (*pause*) What you going to do?

HODGE: I'll deal with it. You get back to work. And not a word —

LEN: Oh, don't worry about me, Your Grace. But you won't forget to speak to Monsignor —

HODGE: I won't forget. (*LEN leaves. HODGE dials.*) Is Matthew Stephens there?

Scene Five

Same day. FATHER MICHAEL's room. Confession is in progress as the scene begins. Sound of rain. Corpus lit above. FATHER MICHAEL sits sideways; PINE, also seated, faces audience.

MICHAEL: And so you fell into sin with your young man.

PINE: Yes. I was referring him to Father Chute when —

MICHAEL: I don't want the details, Gordon. Or the self-justifications.

PINE: No.

MICHAEL: And then you offered Mass.

PINE: Yes.

MICHAEL: Why did you do that?

PINE: I don't know. I didn't have any alternative. The people were waiting. I had no excuse.

MICHAEL: Did you need an excuse?

PINE: Well — what would they think if I suddenly cancelled Mass, for no reason? What would they think?

MICHAEL: So human fear was more important than profaning the sacrament?

PINE: (*pause*) Yes. I suppose so. Yes.

MICHAEL: And lust was more important than your vocation.

PINE: Yes.

MICHAEL: You've sinned grievously. You don't even realize that — for all your posturing. You're just upset because you can't pretend to be perfect anymore. You're a victim of vanity, my boy. And self-pity. I don't have much time for you. You haven't even mentioned the boy.

PINE: No.

MICHAEL: He came to you for help and guidance — and what did you do? You toyed with him, you encouraged him, and then — you took him into your arms.

PINE: I don't know what more I could have done to send him away.

MICHAEL: (*puts his hand on PINE's arm*) My poor friend. It isn't easy, is it?

PINE: (*rises*) You see, Father — I couldn't control it. I wasn't myself. I'd have done anything to have him in that moment. I'd have thrown anything away. Virtue, honour, the priesthood, my parish, being a bishop — none of it meant a thing. And it wasn't love. I can't even claim it was love. It was nothing but animal lust. And you know, I hate myself, I disgust myself — but inside, I'm laughing. I'm not really sorry it happened. Not really. I hate myself — but I'm glad. (*pause*) So what do I do now? Are you going to tell me to go home and pray? Or take cold showers? Are you going to tell me to let the flower bloom from the seed?

MICHAEL: I'm going to tell you to let go. Remember the hoops on the barrel? Drop them. Let the barrel cave in. Maybe you should possess the desire of your heart. Maybe that's the best thing you can do. Maybe that's your choice —

PINE: I can't do that! I have no choice!

MICHAEL: I want you to look at your choice, without fear. Maybe you don't really belong in the priesthood. Maybe that's what this means. You have to consider that. And you have to think about the young man.

PINE: I won't see him again.

MICHAEL: You have to see him again.

PINE: I can't. If I see him again, you know what will happen.

MICHAEL: Not if there's something you want more. You chose lust because you didn't want your vocation.

PINE: That's ridiculous. You're saying all the wrong things. You don't know what you're talking about. I come in here with a problem — and all you do is make it worse. Of course I want my vocation. Of course I worry about Matt. Of course I want to do the right thing. That's why I'm here, isn't it? I can't leave the Church. I can't conceive of life without a collar round my neck.

MICHAEL: Sometimes, my dear Gordon, well-intentioned men enter the Church for the wrong reasons. They take refuge in it, because of problems they don't want to deal with in some other way. And those are precisely the men who, very often, reach power in the Church. You know one of them well. You know him very well.

PINE: Hodge.

MICHAEL: (*nods*) If, on reflection, you find that you've become a priest for the wrong reason — don't be afraid to admit it. I'm not suggesting that you may leave. I'm only suggesting that you must look at your heart honestly — whatever the consequences.

PINE: Thank you, Father. I know you mean well — but you're mistaken. I think my course is clear. I mustn't see him; I must pray more; I must do penance; I must guard against falling into sin again. That's the way of salvation; and that's the way I shall go.

MICHAEL: And that's the way to East Kootenay?

PINE: (*angry*) Forget East Kootenay! I'm not thinking of that. I'm not going there! I don't even want it! (*masters himself*) And now — if you're not prepared to give me absolution —

MICHAEL: I shouldn't, should I? Because you haven't repented.

PINE: I have. I do. And I won't sin again.

MICHAEL: Oh, don't worry, I'll give you absolution, Gordon, although your repentance is doubtful. I'll give you absolution.

PINE: Good. (*sits; bows head*)

MICHAEL: But — I beg you to consider what I have said. Think about it as your penance — before you do further harm. Because you can do harm. Grievous harm. You understand that, don't you?

PINE: I'll be OK.

MICHAEL: By the authority vested in me, I absolve you from all your sins —

PINE: Oh, my God, I am heartily sorry for all my sins —

MICHAEL: In the name of the Father, the Son —

PINE: And by the help of your grace —

MICHAEL: And the Holy Spirit.

PINE: I will not sin again.

Scene Six

Same day. Archbishop's office; HODGE at his desk. MATT enters, approaches timidly. LEN is hanging around.

MATT: Excuse me?
LEN: Yeah?

MATT: Is this the Archbishop's office?

LEN: He expecting you?

HODGE: Who's out there, Len?

LEN: (*approaches; quietly*) The Stephens kid.

HODGE: Send him in.

LEN: (*to MATT*) In you go. But don't look at his mouth. Rotten teeth. Every one of them.

MATT enters.

HODGE: (*rises*) You're Matthew Stephens.

MATT: (*uncertain*) Yeah.

HODGE: (*warm; approaches*) I've met your mother. You look like her. (*pause*) How is she?

MATT: OK, I guess.

HODGE: Good. Wonderful woman. Father O'Brien would be lost without her, eh?

MATT: I guess so. I'm not sure.

HODGE: Sit down, Matthew. We'll have a chat. (*Indicates chair. MATT hesitates, then sits. HODGE remains standing.*) So. Go ahead. Make yourself comfortable. I'll sit down in a minute. Don't worry about me. We'll have a chat. (*turns away*) You probably know why I've asked you to come down here.

MATT: You said it was about Father Pine.

HODGE: (*turns back to him*) I've come to you, rather than him. That may seem odd. But I've handled things like this before. I can trust you, I think. You're still young enough to have ideals. You look sensible. You have short hair. So I'm appealing to you. Leave him alone. Oh — I'm not blaming you. Not at all. You're not to blame. You're the victim. That's why I think you will respond to my appeal. So — I want you to leave Father Pine alone. For your sake. And his. And for the Church. Will you do that for me? (*MATT says nothing.*) I think you will. You're troubled about what's happened, aren't you, Matthew? Confused. I've seen it before. You'd give anything to change it. To make things as they were. As if it never happened. You feel guilty. But you were the innocent one, the naive one, the one who —

MATT: I don't feel guilty.

HODGE: Good boy. Just as I said —

MATT: It wasn't wrong.

HODGE: Oh, but of course it was. You know it was wrong.

MATT: It didn't feel wrong.

HODGE: Feel! Nothing ever feels wrong. You're old enough to know that, Matthew.

MATT: Some things feel wrong. Lots of things feel wrong.

HODGE: Feelings are nothing, Matthew, as you'll find, in time. Never trust feelings. (*pause; sits*) I'll take you into my confidence. Father Pine isn't just *any* priest. Not that all priests aren't good and holy men, they are, you know that and so do I. But Father Pine is special. He's a man who might be picked for bigger things. Not now — but some day. Do you know what I mean by bigger things?

MATT: Promotion, or something.

HODGE: What kind of promotion?

MATT: I don't know. A monsignor or bishop or something like that.

HODGE: You see, Matthew, the Church expects more of people like Father Pine. Much more. And the damage — not only to him, but to the Church —

MATT: Oh — you're afraid I'll tell.

HODGE: I don't mean scandal, although of course we have to be aware of scandal, especially these days. I mean that this must not continue. You must promise to leave him alone. I'm appealing to you. To your good sense. To your love of the Church. To your love of God. (*pause*) I think you agree.

MATT: I — I won't leave him. I'm sorry, but I won't do that. Well, I'm not sorry, not at all. I just won't. He's mine. And I'm his. As long as I live. And I don't care what you say. Or what the Church says. Or what anyone says.

HODGE: (*rises; changing tack*) Tell me, Matthew, do you have any brothers or sisters?

MATT: I have a sister.

HODGE: No brothers.

MATT: No.

HODGE: And you're going to inflict this on your parents. Especially your poor mother. That wonderful woman. Have you thought about that?

MATT: (*looks down*) Yes.

HODGE: That will be a very heavy cross for her, won't it? Perhaps the heaviest of all. Not just the disgrace of it — what her friends will say, and what they won't say. More than that. Because she'll know the truth, even if you blind yourself to it, won't she? A son destined for hell. Think how she'll feel about that.

MATT: Yeah, but that's the thing. I'm not going to hell.

HODGE: You know what the Church says—

MATT: I'm not against God, you see. I'm with God. That's the thing I've understood. So she'll be OK, because He'll take care of her, He'll give her His light, He'll help her understand. Just as He gives me light. Of course I've thought of that. Of course. You see, you're missing the whole point. And I think you're missing it on purpose. You're forgetting about love.

HODGE: You're the one who's forgetting that. Love for your mother.

MATT: Not for my mother. Love. You left out the only thing that matters. Don't you see? Because it's God himself who's calling us. Father Pine and me. Through our love. He's the one who's calling us out. Like those guys in the Bible. Peter. And Paul. Or St. Francis. People like that. It's the same thing.

HODGE: It's not the same thing! Listen. Forget hell. Forget your family. Forget the other things. Let me tell you something. You think Father Pine returns your love. Of course you do. But he doesn't. He can't. He's a man of the Church. He may make a mistake. He may fall. But it's an accident. If you imagine he's going to abandon every value on which he's based his life — throw it all away — is that what you think? You think he's going to run away with you?

MATT: (*uncertain*) No.

HODGE: Well, what's he going to do?

MATT: I dunno. We'll work it out. Maybe he'll leave, you know, leave the Church. Maybe we'll go someplace else. Start a new life. I dunno.

HODGE: You believe that.

MATT: Yes.

HODGE: Well, you're wrong. Dead wrong. He may have faltered on his path — but he'll never leave the Church. And to do what you want, he'd have to leave. You're young. You don't know how long life is. You don't know how men go on, year after year, dragging a decaying body through a desert in the dark. How they'll clutch at anything — alcohol, women, boys — anything for relief. You know nothing of that. Not yet. Life's all glory to you. All hope. All splendor. You know nothing —

MATT: I don't believe that! It's not like that! You're the one who's wrong! You're saying we have to leave the Church. Well, OK, so maybe we will. I don't know. I don't care. Maybe that's the best thing! Because you're trying to shut love out of your church — that's what you're trying to do. Like shutting out life. You try, and you can't do it. It's like shutting out the sun. It's like reversing a river or something. It's not natural —

HODGE: Natural! (*changes tone*) Well, Matthew. I've tried to warn you.

MATT: I won't give up. I won't do what you want. And you're wrong about him, too. Totally. You'll see. (*leaves*)

LEN enters.

LEN: Boy, he really stood up to you, eh? Really gave it to you. I had to admire him. I mean, you didn't have a thing to say, did you? You gotta admire the kid: he's really got guts, for a queer.

HODGE: Don't ever do that again! Not to me.

LEN: I was just doing my work. My real work, I mean.

HODGE: No spying on me. Understand?

LEN: Oh, I wasn't spying. I wouldn't do that. Not to you. (*Lights cigarette. HODGE looks at him.*) But listen. Thanks for speaking to Monsignor. It's much better now. I really appreciate that, Your Grace. I really do. (*looks at HODGE*) So — I'd better get back to work, eh? Got lots to do. But you know where to find me — (*eases his way out*)

Lights down; up on PINE in his study. Lights up on reredos.

Scene Seven

PINE's study, the same afternoon. Phone is ringing. He stands at window, ignoring it. Eventually it stops. EILEEN enters.

EILEEN: What did you tell him?

PINE: Who?

EILEEN: The Nuncio. (*pause*) Didn't you call him?

PINE: No.

EILEEN: You got the message. I put it right on top. Where you'd see it.

PINE: The Nuncio called here? In person?

EILEEN: What did you do with your messages? There was one from him and about six from Matthew Stephens. (*pause*) He said he'd be there until six-thirty his time. That's three-thirty here.

PINE: He called me? There's only one reason he'd call me —

EILEEN: Here they are. You threw them away. Why'd you do that?

Phone rings. PINE turns away. Pause. EILEEN answers.

EILEEN: Saint John Viannen. Yes, Your Grace. No, he's not here. I'll tell him. No, I don't know where he is, but I'm sure he won't be long. I'll tell him. Yes, Your Grace. Goodbye. (*hangs up*) That was Hodge. He wants to see you. You're a popular man, Gordon.

PINE: Did he say what he wanted?

EILEEN: Isn't it obvious?

PINE: Not to me.

EILEEN: Well, I'd say that the Nuncio is offering you that diocese; and that Hodge has something else on his mind.

PINE: Oh?

EILEEN: Don't pretend with me, Gordon. I know what I saw. Right in the sacristy. With all those people waiting for Mass. I don't know how you — thought you'd get away with that.

PINE: I wasn't thinking about getting away with anything.

EILEEN: Len was here, snooping around; and you can be sure that Hodge knows all about it by now. So — if I were you, I'd call the Nuncio right away, while the offer's still good. That's what I'd do. Though I suppose there's no way it'll happen now. Not after what you've done. (*pause*) Would you take it?

PINE: I don't know. Father Michael —

EILEEN: Father Michael! You throw a diocese away, you betray the trust of a whole parish, you wreck a young man's life — and all you can do is talk about Father Michael! What does he have to do with it? It's not his business.

PINE: He just happens to be my confessor. So it is his business. And it's not yours.

EILEEN: Not mine!

PINE: That's right.

EILEEN: After what I've given you. What I've done for you. And for this parish. After — Gordon, we've been partners here —

PINE: You just want another job. You want to get out of this diocese. You're frustrated. And you're using me to get ahead.

EILEEN: Using you!

PINE: Yes! That's what you're doing. You can't get anywhere here, no woman can, so you want me to have a diocese of my own where you'd have influence, you'd have power, be able to run your own show, drive everyone crazy with justice, justice, justice every minute of the day. Of course you're using me —

EILEEN: I can't believe you'd say —

PINE: Of course, everybody uses me, don't they? You. Hodge. Matt.

EILEEN: Matt! You say that about Matt!

PINE: Yes! I didn't want it. I didn't go looking for it. He forced himself on me.

EILEEN: I thought more of you than this,
Gordon Pine. I thought you were a bigger
man.

PINE: Well, now you know, don't you. You
like to know everything. I hope you're happy.

EILEEN: Stop this!

PINE: And now you want me to phone the
Nuncio. Tell him how much I want to be
Bishop of East Kootenay. As long as it's the
will of God, and we can all conspire together
about that, can't we? Everyone but Father
Michael. Oh, we all have our reasons for wanting it, so it's the will of God, if —

EILEEN: (*pause*) You're very bitter, Gordon.

PINE: Who wouldn't be bitter?

EILEEN: I didn't realize —

PINE: Oh — I'm just talking.

EILEEN: Gordon —

PINE: What?

EILEEN: Maybe you shouldn't push
yourself to take that diocese. Maybe it's not
right for you, just now —

PINE: I'm not pushing.

EILEEN: And — you're right, I know that,
I've been selfish in wanting you to do it. It's
true. I want to get out of this diocese. I want
to do something people respect, something
that's recognized. And it would have been
good for you, too. You're bored, you're
in a rut, you're not being challenged, you're
wasted here — and that's why you've done
this, that's the whole reason, don't you see? But
Gordon —

PINE: Look, Eileen, you don't have to tell
me this.

EILEEN: I wasn't using you.

PINE: No. Of course not.

EILEEN: Ever.

PINE: (*pause*) I'll go see the Archbishop. Find
out what he's going to do. And I'll take the job,
if they still want me. It's as simple as that. I'll
let the Church decide.

They look at each other; he looks away; leaves.

Scene Eight

*Archbishop's Office. HODGE is in shadows, as
before, at the window. PINE enters quietly. It's late
in the day. Everyone has gone home.*

PINE: Excuse me, Your Grace.

HODGE: Congratulations, Father.

PINE: He called you?

HODGE: Of course. And you've accepted.

PINE: I haven't talked to him yet.

HODGE: No?

PINE: I wanted to see you first.

HODGE: (*pleased*) I understand.

PINE: I want to let the Church decide.

HODGE: Good. You're thinking about the
young man.

PINE: Yes.

HODGE: I didn't tell the Nuncio about that.
He'll never know. Nobody will. As long as
you've learned your lesson.

PINE: Oh, I've done that.

HODGE: What lesson?

PINE: Well — you know. Self-control. Avoiding occasions of sin. Praying more. Carrying my cross.

HODGE: That's not what I meant.

PINE: Oh?

HODGE: Only one thing matters, Father. That the Church survive. You and I both know that.

PINE: Yes.

HODGE: The age is against us. People want things. Success. Happiness. Freedom. Fulfillment. Oh, they've always wanted those things, in every age, but it's different now. Once, they felt guilty. Now they feel proud. Unashamed. They don't need us anymore, Father. That's why we're only talking about survival. Not growth. Survival.

PINE: I don't accept that, Your Grace. We're not just trying —

HODGE: The Church needs bishops who can look at the truth without flinching. Bishops who have understood the futility of human ties. The illusory nature of love. We have to be immune to love, Father. That's the lesson. (pause) The Church needs bishops who can realize these things and still go on with the charade, just as if it were true.

PINE: But it is true. It may be a charade for me, but it's true.

HODGE: I saw your friend.

PINE: Matt was here?

HODGE: I called him in, I wanted to see him, I wanted to — warn him. And he said something that caught my attention, when he

was preaching his bright new adolescent gospel.

PINE: Why go after him? Why didn't you come to me?

HODGE: Maybe he's said the same thing to you. I don't know. (pause) He suggested that the love that called him to abandon his family and the Church was exactly the same as the love that called Saint Francis or Saint Paul or the Apostles to embrace God. And you know something, Father? He's right. The enemy against whom I have struggled all my adult life — to which I've dedicated my priesthood — the wolf within — is the voice of God. Of course it's true. The force — which he calls "love" — the force that animated the saints and the heretics — all those dangerous people, those extremists — that force is the God that you and I shut out. That's what a bishop must understand, Father.

PINE: You can't shut God out of the Church, Your Grace. Or your life. You can't do that.

HODGE: Let's not pretend, Father. He's not here. And we don't want Him here.

PINE: I believe He's here.

HODGE: In your life, Father?

PINE: Not now. But one day.

HODGE: When?

PINE: (annoyed) I don't know. Look, Your Grace — maybe you've lost all hope, that's what it sounds like. But I can still hope. I can still try to be — well — a different kind of bishop. Close to people. Human. (pause) Just because I've masked naked ambition — called it the will of God — just because I'm a hollow man who talks about God all the time but can't find Him. That makes me a hypocrite, I know that. I'm a hypocrite. But I still hope that through it all, somehow, His will will prevail.

That I'll do the right thing. That I'll do what He wants — and find Him. Find God.

HODGE: Find God. And what kind of God will you find, Father?

PINE: I don't know. A loving God.

HODGE: You're homosexual.

PINE: Yes.

HODGE: You seek the God whose "love" created you, condemned you to that condition—

PINE: Not condemned.

HODGE: Was that love, Father? To make you that way. An outcast? Tell you that your condition was no sin, no sin at all — but send you straight to hell if you express it? Is that your God?

PINE: No. That's not my God.

HODGE: Who is He, then? The God who causes sickness and starvation? Whose love creates little children and lets them starve in Sudan or Bangladesh? Who loved His own people so much that He nailed down the tracks that led to Auschwitz? Is that the God you long to find, Father?

PINE: No!

HODGE: Then which God is it? (*pause*) It makes no sense, Father. Abandon your illusions. You of all men should know that. You share the curse of Cain. Unless, like the Jews, you imagine your condition is the mark of special favour! (*laughs*) Nothing makes sense, Father, does it? Except the Church. Because what we've done — what we've achieved — is a kind of Noah's ark. We've made a selection from the nature that confronts us, with all its obvious chaos and contradiction. We've chosen what we need, and shut the doors on all the rest. That's what any religion does. And we've done it better than most. And once we've

shut the doors — we'd better keep them shut, Father. That — or sink. I wouldn't say these things to everyone. I didn't say them to your young friend. But you'll understand, won't you? You do understand. Because we want the same things, you and I. We have the solution to the human tragedy. We are the voice raised on the hilltops, to which no one listens. This is our cross. And we go on bearing it, as if there were a God who cared, one way or another.

PINE: No. No. I reject all that. You're showing me hell — my place in hell.

HODGE: As you like. You'll see. But — you want to let the Church decide. Here you are. (*Holds out his hand. PINE hesitates.*) Congratulations, Father.

PINE takes his hand.

Scene Nine
(Phoenix Theatre version, 1990)

PINE's room. MATT is waiting. PINE enters, removing his coat.

MATT: Gordon! (*pause*) Where have you been? I've been calling and calling.

PINE: Look, Matt — you shouldn't be here. I have something to do. Something important.

MATT: Gordon —

PINE: You'll have to go.

MATT: I saw Hodge.

PINE: Yes, I know. And you want to talk to me, I can see that. But I don't want to talk to you right now. I have a call to make —

MATT: He wanted me to leave you alone. I told him I wouldn't. I told him there was no way —

PINE: Matt, I said I have to make a call. It's important. You have to go.

MATT: He told me you'd dump me. He was wrong, wasn't he? (*laughs*) Totally wrong!

PINE: Will you let me make my call!

Pause.

MATT: What call?

PINE: It wouldn't mean anything to you.

MATT: Tell me.

PINE: I have to call the Nuncio. They want to make me a bishop.

MATT: A bishop! You want to be a bishop?

PINE: I don't know what I want. I mean, it's important. Big. And I have something to offer. I can move things. Change things. Do what I like. Make a difference. But —

MATT: What about me?

PINE: Matt, I don't want to talk about this right now. I've got to make my call. He won't be there for long, I'm already late, I want to —

MATT: Hodge was right. You don't want me.

PINE: It was a mistake.

MATT: A mistake!

PINE: Yes!

MATT: I love you.

PINE: You don't! You've imagined me. You don't even know me. Matt — what happened in the sacristy — it wasn't your fault. It was mine. I should have known better. I encouraged you. I liked talking to you. I liked — well, I liked you. But it was a mistake.

MATT: What are you telling me?

PINE: The truth.

MATT: No! It's not the truth. It's not the truth at all. He's sucked you in. He's got you so convinced that being a bishop is — that you've got to do it or else go to hell or something. And it's not true. It's dumb. You don't want that.

PINE: You don't know what I want! Oh — I admit — it is a kind of violation. There's something in me that cries out against it, that tells me it won't work. But —

MATT: So don't do it.

PINE: Easy to say. For you.

MATT: Gordon — (*tries to hug him*)

PINE: (*pulls away*) But Matt. Whatever I do. Please, understand. And this is the truth. There's no future for us. I have my path. And it doesn't include anyone else. I have to find God — alone. It's what I have to do. Even if —

MATT: Gordon.

PINE: Yeah.

MATT: You don't find God alone. You don't have to. That's what I've understood. (*pause*) When you and I — made love. When we were together. He was there, too. You felt Him. You can't deny it. You can't say it wasn't Him. (*PINE moves away.*) We were one, Gordon. We weren't just close. We were one. And it wasn't a mistake! You have to admit that. And it wasn't a fantasy. It was all the things those mystics talk about: you know, losing ourselves to find ourselves. I was you and you were me and we were both transfigured. That's what it was. We'll never be the same again. You can't say it wasn't God. You can't say it wasn't love—

PINE: (*near tears*) Yes! You're right! I can't.

They look at one another: a long look.

MATT: (*touches him*) You want to make your call.

Slowly, PINE picks up the paper bearing the Nuncio's number, takes the phone and dials, as light dies on the set and goes up on the crucifix.

PINE: His Excellency, the Apostolic Pro-Nuncio, please. Oh. Perhaps I could leave a message. It's Father Pine, Father Gordon Pine, returning his call. He was trying to reach me earlier. Tell him I called back; and that — I don't want the job. OK? No. That's all. He'll know what I mean. But he can call me back if he wants an explanation. Thank you. Goodnight.

Hangs up. Then, slowly, he removes his collar and drops it on the desk, with immense relief. MATT appears, behind, as in Scene One. PINE looks up at corpus for the first time. Lights bright on PINE and the Crucified. Slow fade to black.

Scene Nine
(New Play Centre version, 1989)

PINE's room. MATT is waiting. PINE enters, removing his coat.

MATT: Gordon.

PINE: Matt! What are you doing here?

MATT: I want to see you. I've been calling and calling. (*approaches, hugs him*) I saw Hodge.

PINE: I know. (*detaches himself*) Look, Matt, we have to talk, I realize that. We have to talk. But later, OK? I'm in the middle of something now — I have to make a call.

MATT: Gordon — he wanted me to leave you alone. And he tried to make me think you'd dump me. But he's wrong, isn't he? I told him there was no way —

PINE: (*puts arm around his shoulder*) Matt, we have to talk. Hodge is sick. Don't listen to him. But there are other things I've got to explain, OK? (*MATT caresses PINE's face. PINE pulls away gently.*) And there's something I have to do, Matt. I'm going to call the Nuncio, and I'm going to accept that job. Despite Hodge. I think it's the right thing to do. I think —

MATT: What job?

PINE: Oh — they want to make me a bishop. And I told Hodge I'd do it. But I shook his hand. I don't know why. Well, I *do* know. I did it because — whatever he says — whatever he shows me — it's still the best thing, the only thing for me. I don't have a choice, Matt. It's all I have.

MATT: You have me. Always. You can do what you want. You can leave the Church. You can do anything. With me.

PINE: Oh Matt! Matt! I'm sorry. But that's a fantasy. You have to understand that. You imagine — I don't know — that love conquers everything. But it's not true. You've imagined me. You hardly know me. And I think you're a great guy, I think you're wonderful, I admire you. But what happened in the sacristy was a mistake, Matt.

MATT: What are you telling me?

PINE: I'm telling you the truth.

MATT: No. It's *not* the truth. It's not true at all. It can't be. He's sucked you in, he's got you so convinced that being a *bishop* is — that you've got to do it or else go to hell or something. And it's not *true*. It's dumb. You don't want that. You don't want to be a jerk. Like Hodge.

PINE: No. I don't want to be a jerk, like Hodge.

MATT: So don't do it.

PINE: Easy to say. For you.

MATT: Gordon — (*Tries to hug him again. PINE pulls away.*)

PINE: No, Matt. I mean it. I don't know what to do about East Kootenay. You're right. I shouldn't do it. There's something in me that cries out against it, that tells me it's wrong, that it won't work, that doing that — or even staying here, even staying here — is a kind of violation. You know? But — Matt. Whatever *I* do. Please. Understand. And this is the truth. There's no future for us. You want someone else.

MATT: I don't.

PINE: I don't love you, Matt. Not the way you want. (*puts arm on his shoulder, in characteristic gesture*) I'm sorry.

MATT: (*throws off his hand*) Keep away from me, you bastard. I don't want your — professional comfort! I don't even want your love anymore. You don't have any. You're not worth *anything*! You're not worth *me*. I thought we had something wonderful, something great. I offered you something beautiful. Like David and Jonathan or — I don't know. I thought we could really make it together. I was so wrong —

PINE: Yes, you were wrong! That's what I'm saying! Now you know!

MATT: (*looks at him*) You make me sick. I offer you everything. And all you can *think* about is being a stupid bishop. (*leaves*)

PINE: That's not what I said! Matt!

Feet on stairs; front door slams. PINE goes to the window, watches MATT go down the sidewalk. Pause. Then, slowly, he picks up the paper bearing the Nuncio's number, takes the phone and dials, as light dies on set and goes up on crucifix.

PINE: His Excellency the Apostolic Pro-Nuncio, please. Oh. Perhaps I could leave a message. It's Father Pine, Father Gordon Pine, returning his call. He was trying to reach me earlier. Tell him I called back, and that — I don't want the job. OK? No. That's all. He'll know what I mean. But he can call me back if he wants an explanation. Thank you. Goodnight.

Hangs up. Looks up at crucifix. He pulls off his collar, drops it on the desk. Lights further down on stage, up on PINE and crucifix, as he looks it in the face; freeze; slow dim to black.

1976 New Play Centre workshop. Clockwise from left: Jerry Wasserman; Pamela Hawthorn, Sheldon Rosen; Otto Lowy; Brian Torpe. Photo by Glen Erikson.

Twenty Years at Play
A New Play Centre Production List

All plays included in this list received at least two fully staged performances. Staged readings are not included. Plays are notated as full length (fl), one act (oa), or short take (st). Short takes are not always easily distinguishable from one acts, but generally a short take lasts less than a half hour and is presented in a program with at least two other pieces. One acts usually appear in a double-bill.

1972
Sharon Pollock, *A Compulsory Option* (fl) — dir. Pamela Hawthorn
Tom Grainger, *The Helper* (oa) — dir. Jon Bankson
Cherie Stewart, *Dandelion* (oa) — dir. Bill Millerd

1973
George Povey, *The Gook* (oa) — dir. Pamela Hawthorn
Margaret Hollingsworth, *Bushed* (oa) — dir. Jane Heyman and David Latham

Leon Rooke, *Swordplay* (oa) — dir. Jon Bankson
Elizabeth Gourlay, *Andrea del Sarto* (fl) — dir. Pamela Hawthorn
Bette Speers, "Solitaire" (st) — dir. Jane Heyman
Don Stanley, "The Car and the Skeptic" (st) — dir. Jane Heyman
Cherie Stewart, "Sometimes It Doesn't Take Much to Kill a Man" (st) — dir. Jane Heyman
Cherie Stewart, "Follow the Leader" (st) — dir. Jace van der Veen
Anne Hungerford, "Treatment" (st) — dir. Jace van der Veen
Michael Bullock, "Look It's Floating" (st) — dir. Jane Heyman
Sheldon Rosen, *The Box* (oa) — dir. Jace van der Veen
Russell Fitzgerald, "Tom, Dick and Harry" (st) — dir. Jace van der Veen with Jane Heyman

Sharon Pollock, "In the Dark" (st) — dir. Jane Heyman
Leonard Angel, *Forthcoming Wedding* (oa) — dir. Jace van der Veen
Jake Zilber, "Family Circle" (st) — dir. Pamela Hawthorn
Anne Hungerford, "Metamorphoses" (st) — dir. Jane Heyman
Betty Lambert, "Sqrieux-de-Dieu" (st) — dir. Jane Heyman
Marjorie Morris, "Mamma" (st) — dir. Pamela Hawthorn
Marjorie Morris, "Verandah" (st) — dir. Pamela Hawthorn
Thomas Cone, *The Organizer* (oa) — dir. Jace van der Veen

1974
Thomas Cone, *The Organizer* (oa) — dir. Jace van der Veen
Sheldon Rosen, *The Box* (oa) — dir. Jace van der Veen
Thomas Cone, *Cubistique* (oa) — dir. Jace van der Veen
Tom Grainger, *The Great Grunbaum* (oa) — dir. Jim McQueen
Margaret Hollingsworth, *Operators* (oa) — dir. Pamela Hawthorn
Sheldon Rosen, *Frugal Repast* (oa) — dir. Jace van der Veen

1975

Thomas Cone, *Herringbone* (oa)   dir. John Gray
John Lazarus, *How We Killed the Moose* (oa)   dir. Jane Heyman
Tom Walmsley, *The Working Man* (oa)   dir. Pamela Hawthorn
Sheldon Rosen, *Like Father, Like Son* (oa)   dir. Jace van der Veen
Cam Hubert, *Rites of Passage* (fl)   dir. Pamela Hawthorn
Lois Atkinson, *Waiting* (oa)   dir. Svetlana (Zylin) Smith
Sheila Stowell, *The Gathering* (oa)   dir. Kathryn Shaw
Betty Lambert, *Sqrieux-de-Dieu* (fl)   dir. Richard Ouzounian
Thomas Cone, *Whisper to Mendelsohn* (fl)   dir. Jace van der Veen

1976

Leonard Angel, *Incident after Antietam* (oa)   dir. Kathryn Shaw
Dennis Foon, *Peach* (oa)   dir. Jim McQueen
Sherman Snukal, *The Whispering Time* (oa)   dir. Jace van der Veen
Thomas Cone, *Beautiful Tigers* (oa)   dir. Pamela Hawthorn
Tom Grainger, *Roundabout* (fl)   dir. Robert Graham

1977

Margaret Hollingsworth, *Alli-Alli-Oh* (oa)   dir. Jane Heyman
Thomas Cone, *Shotglass* (oa)   dir. Pamela Hawthorn
Leonard Angel, *Isadora and G.B.* (oa)   dir. Kathryn Shaw
Christopher Dafoe, *The Frog Galliard* (oa)   dir. Jace van der Veen
Richard Ouzounian, *British Properties* (fl)   dir. Robert Graham
Sheldon Rosen, *Ned and Jack* (fl)   dir. Pamela Hawthorn

1978

John Lazarus, *Midas* (fl)   dir. Jackie Crossland
Christian Bruyere, *Walls* (fl)   dir. Jace van der Veen
Tom Walmsley, *Something Red* (fl)   dir. Kathryn Shaw

1979

Charles Tidler, *Blind Dancers* (oa)   dir. Bob Baker
Ted Galay, *After Baba's Funeral* (oa)   dir. Jane Heyman and
                                                         Kathleen Weiss
Ian Slater, *The Far Garden* (oa)   dir. Pamela Hawthorn and
                                                         Christopher James
Richard Ouzounian, *The City Show* (fl)   dir. Stephen Katz
Betty Lambert, *Clouds of Glory* (fl)   dir. Richard Ouzounian
Eric Nicol, *Free at Last* (fl)   dir. Pamela Hawthorn

1980

Ted Galay, *Sweet and Sour Pickles* (oa)   dir. Jace van der Veen
Alex MacMillan, *The Agreeable Moment* (oa)   dir. Kathleen Weiss
Sherman Snukal, *Perfect Plastic* (oa)   dir. Bob Baker
Jo Ledingham, *Ask at the Nearest Gas Station* (oa)   dir. Jace van der Veen
John and Joa Lazarus, *Dreaming and Duelling* (fl)   dir. Bob Baker

1981

Charles Tidler, *Straight Ahead* (oa)	dir. Kathleen Weiss
Helen Hodgman, *Oh Mother, Is It Worth It?* (oa)	dir. Bob Baker
John Selkirk, *Ruthie Doesn't Mother* (oa)	dir. Larry Lillo
Roger Mitton, *La Segunda* (oa)	dir. Jace van der Veen
Gwen Ringwood, *Garage Sale* (oa)	dir. Jace van der Veen
Eric Nicol, *Ma! A Celebration of Margaret Murray* (fl)	dir. Pamela Hawthorn
Betty Lambert, *Jennie's Story* (fl)	dir. Jace van der Veen

1982

Leonard Angel, *The Unveiling* (fl)	dir. Pamela Hawthorn
Joe Martin, *The Dust Conspiracy* (oa)	dir. Jace van der Veen
Joan Egilson, *Shadowplay* (oa)	dir. Kathleen Weiss
John Abbott, "Joey Lying Low" (st)	dir. Michael McLaughlin
Daniel Conrad, "The Great Wall of China" (st)	dir. Jace van der Veen
Stanley Rogal, "Sleepwalk" (st)	dir. Ines Buchli
Ken Salmond, "Drama with Balls" (st)	dir. Charles Siegel
Ann St. James, "Not Quite Right" (st)	dir. Ines Buchli
Peggy Thompson, "Street" (st)	dir. Michael McLaughlin

1983

Margaret Hollingsworth, *Islands* (oa)	dir. Kathleen Weiss
Ted Galay, *The Grabowski Girls* (oa)	dir. Larry Lillo
David Berner, *T.E.* (oa)	dir. David Berner
Leslie Mildiner, *Bonny's Confession* (oa)	dir. Leslie Mildiner
Campbell Smith, *Timestep* (fl)	dir. Campbell Smith
Patricia Ludwick, *Alone* (fl)	dir. Kathleen Weiss
Jesse Glenn Bodyan, *The Store Detective* (fl)	dir. Pamela Hawthorn

1984

Margaret Hollingsworth, *War Baby* (fl)	dir. James Roy
Tom Wayman, *Parts Yard* (oa)	dir. Kathryn Shaw
Glenda Leznoff, *Rings* (oa)	dir. Kate Weiss
Peter Eliot Weiss, *St Mar* (oa)	dir. Paul Mears
Peter Williams, *Owners* (oa)	dir. Kathryn Shaw
Elizabeth Gourlay, *No Recourse* (oa)	dir. Paul Mears
Peggy Thompson, *Bad Brains* (oa)	dir. Kate Weiss
Leonard Angel, ed., *The Senior Stage* (fl)	dir. Kathryn Shaw

1985

Ted Galay, *Tsymbaly* (fl)	dir. Jane Heyman
John Lazarus and Ralph Cole, *Napoleons with Cream* (oa)	dir. Paul Mears
Peter Eliot Weiss and EDAM, *Knitequest* (oa)	dir. Kathleen Weiss
Leonard Angel and Gisa Cole, *Six of One* (oa)	dir. Jane Heyman
David John Smith, *Some Starless Night* (fl)	dir. Paul Mears
Betty Lambert, *Under the Skin* (fl)	dir. Pamela Hawthorn
L.A. Hunt, "Backing Away" (st)	dir. John Cooper
Melissa Bell, "Countertypes" (st)	dir. Paul Mears
C.M. Pinvidic, "Waist Deep" (st)	dir. Paul Mears

Patricia Robertson, "Twilight Factor" (st)   dir. John Cooper
Patricia Ludwick, "Trip the Light Fantastic" (st) dir. Susan Astley

1986

Ann St. James, *Waves of White* (fl)   dir. Paul Mears
Athena George, ed., *Signs in the Air* (fl) dir. Jane Heyman and
              Pamela Hawthorn

Colleen Curran, "El Clavadista" (st)   dir. Pamela Hawthorn
Richard Whelan, "Chat" (st)   dir. Paul Mears
Steve Petch, "Midnight" (st)   dir. Pamela Hawthorn
Campbell Smith, "Secs" (st)   dir. Paul Mears
Marco Micone, "Deja l'agonie" (st)   dir. Maureen Labonte
Michel Tremblay, "L'impromptu des deux 'presses' " (st) dir. Maureen Labonte

1987

David King, *Backyard Beguine* (fl)   dir. Kathryn Shaw
Ian Weir, *The Idler* (fl)   dir. Paul Mears
Dennis Foon, *Zaydok* (fl)   dir. Roy Surette

1988

Steve Petch, *Service* (fl)   dir. Pamela Hawthorn
W.P. Kinsella, *The Thrill of the Grass* (fl) dir. Pamela Hawthorn
Ian Weir, *The Delphic Orioles* (fl)   dir. Paul Mears
Bryan Wade, *Dinosaurs* (fl)   dir. Ray Michal

1989

Alex Brown, *The Wolf Within* (fl)   dir. Kathryn Shaw
Gordon Armstrong, *The Mona Lisa Toodle-oo* (fl) dir. Paul Mears
Tom Cone, *Love at Last Sight* (fl)   dir. Henry Tarvainen
David King, *Harbour House* (fl)   dir. Paul Mears

1990

Terry Jordan, *Reunion* (oa)   dir. Jane Heyman
Jaan Kolk, *Chew the Blade* (oa)   dir. Robin Nichol
David Widdicombe, *The River Lady* (oa) dir. Robin Nichol
Maureen Robinson, *Nitebooth* (oa)   dir. Jane Heyman
Ian Weir, *Bloody Business* (fl)   dir. Paul Mears
Deirdre C. Dore, *Inside Waters* (fl)   dir. Paul Mears